D0364565

The Multicultural Dimension
of the
National Curriculum

For
Sophia King
and
Julia Reiss

The Multicultural Dimension of the National Curriculum

Edited by

Anna S. King and Michael J. Reiss

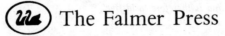

The Falmer Press

(A member of the Taylor & Francis Group)
London • Washington, D.C.

UK   The Falmer Press, 4 John St, London WC1N 2ET
USA   The Falmer Press, Taylor & Francis Inc., 1900 Frost Road, Suite 101, Bristol, PA 19007

First published 1993

A catalogue record of this publication is available from the British Library

ISBN 0 75070 068 8 cased
ISBN 0 75070 069 6 paperback

Library of Congress Cataloging-in-Publication Data are available on request

Jacket design by Caroline Archer

Typeset in 9.5/11 pt Bembo by
Graphicraft Typesetters Ltd., Hong Kong

Printed in Great Britain by Burgess Science Press, Basingstoke on paper which has a specified pH value on final paper manufacture of not less than 7.5 and is therefore 'acid free'.

Contents

Preface   vii
David H. Hargreaves

Part One — The Context

1   Introduction   2
    Anna S. King
2   The Multicultural Task Group: The Group That Never Was   21
    Sally Tomlinson

Part Two — The Curriculum

The Core Subjects
3   Culturalizing Mathematics Teaching   32
    Alan J. Bishop
4   English   49
    Anthony Adams
5   Science   63
    Michael J. Reiss

The Foundation Subjects
6   History   78
    Martin Booth
7   Geography   91
    Rex Walford
8   The Design and Technology Curriculum in a Multiethnic Society   109
    John Eggleston
9   The Cultural Dimension of Information Technology   118
    Brent Robinson
10 Music: Respect for Persons, Respect for Cultures   128
    Marjorie Glynne-Jones
11 The Visual Arts   145
    Sudha Daniel and Rachel Mason
12 Physical Education and Dance   162
    Maggie Semple

Contents

13 Foreign Language Teaching and Multicultural Teaching   173
    Michael S. Byram
14 Religious Education and the Multicultural Perspective   187
    Peter Mitchell

Part Three — The School

15 Whole School Issues   202
    Daphne Gould
16 A Primary Case Study   212
    Marie-France Faulkner and Rachel Willans
17 A Secondary Case Study   223
    Carlton Duncan

Part Four — Policy and Practice

18 The European Dimension and The National Curriculum   240
    Witold Tulasiewicz
19 Black and Anti-Racist Perspectives on the National Curriculum
    and Government Educational Policy   259
    Maud Blair and Madeleine Arnot
20 Assessment: Social Processes   275
    Bruce A.G. Gill

Notes on Contributors   286

Index   290

Preface

As I write, in October 1992, it is clear that the National Curriculum is in trouble. Most of the faults were predictable, indeed predicted, from the early stage of the ill-considered consultative document issued in July 1987. Hastily produced and subject to inadequate discussion, this became the flawed framework for the subject working groups. Since they were established and asked to report in sequence, rather than concurrently, the opportunity for cross-subject co-ordination and collaboration in depth was lost. In short, a major educational reform that could and should have created a holistic model of the curriculum as an entitlement of all our children has become the victim of those who insist on a political timetable — every change must be devised and then irreversibly implemented before the following general election. As a result, the National Curriculum quart does not fit into the timetable pint; the orders and guidance, on which the ink is barely dry, are already being re-written; curriculum fragmentation and confusion persists. The National Curriculum is neither coherent nor manageable.

Given this approach to the production of a National Curriculum, the issues with which this book is concerned could never have been handled in a satisfactory way. This is partly because there was (indeed still is) a lack of political will in the sphere of equal opportunity; it is also partly because the pace and programme of reform did not permit the careful and intensive work necessary in an area of curriculum development that is both delicate and intricate. It will take time to work out how multicultural and anti-racist issues should permeate the foundation subjects, as they surely must. The National Curriculum has marginalized social studies, a part of the curriculum where issues of equal opportunity might receive the most systematic treatment. In consequence multicultural education could easily find itself decanted into cross-curricular provision, if indeed any timetable space can be found for this. Even here the National Curriculum Council lost its nerve and failed to provide the much needed advice on the multicultural dimension.

Since the mid-1970s Labour and Conservative governments have rightly seen the need to reform the education system to help to meet changing national needs and to create a different kind of society. This, as on many previous occasions, required an intervention by no means always welcomed by professional educators. The imagination of earlier reformers has, however, frequently been noticeably lacking. For example, recent ministers apparently believe that moral education, a central concern in any system of cultural transmission designed to promote social cohesion, is best provided — or in their terms 'delivered' — through a (largely Christian) religious education. This neither recognizes the need for a broader base for moral education in the late twentieth century nor seizes the opportunity to promote a related political education within the compulsory curriculum.

The 1944 Act looked forward with optimism and determination to a better post-war Britain offering secondary education for all. It reflected the need for a moral base to education in schools as well as for a more open system to give a better match between educational provision and the abilities and aptitudes of individuals. In the following years, the debate on the meaning of equality of opportunity and equity and the implications for the organization of the education service continued. More recently, all the political parties in Britain, as in many other countries, have put the need to educate a larger proportion of the nation for a longer period and to higher standards at the top of their agenda, though leaving unresolved the relationship between equity and quality.

The 1988 Act, in seeking — rightly in my view — to provide the curriculum reform essential to the achievement of new and more ambitious educational goals, should have looked forward with confidence and determination to a better multi-cultural, multi-lingual and multi-faith Britain entering into a new relationship with itself and with the rest of world as the year 2000 approaches. But it did not.

Now all this may be a good thing for those interested in or committed to multicultural and anti-racist education within the National Curriculum. For in the present climate it is arguably better not really to have attempted to address the issue than to have done so very badly and then, when everybody is thoroughly confused and dejected, to set about a fundamental revision. In any event I believe the best work in this field has almost always been 'bottom-up' rather than 'top-down'. Whilst there is a huge literature on the National Curriculum and a huge literature on multicultural and anti-racist education, there is very little indeed that offers sustained coverage of the two together.

I offer this book a warm welcome, because it thus meets a real need. But it does so in a pleasingly anarchic way. It is an intensely practical book, deeply concerned with what happens and what is to be done in schools and classrooms. As always, practice reflects some theory, much of it implicit. There is little agree-ment among the contributors about a definition of the basic concepts, such as multicultural or anti-racist, let alone about any more sophisticated theory of the field. But for me that makes the book the more interesting. If there were some agreed theoretical base, each chapter would simply apply it to a particular area, such as each subject on the curriculum. In reality, we are all still working at the theory, just as we work at the practice: each must influence the other. So readers can enjoy and profit from all the chapters, not just those relevant to one's subject specialism or phase. What the contributors share is a belief in the importance of the topic; a commitment to clarifying the issues at stake; and a passion for seeking out practical answers.

This is, of course, the kind of base on which the National Curriculum itself should have been constructed. The 1988 Education Reform Act has led to a whole range of paradoxical outcomes, and it would be a delightful irony if the work represented in this collection — which of course also reflects the concerns and activities of many people in many places — were to exemplify the enrichment of thought and action on which true curriculum improvement rests. But then that would be no surprise, for multicultural and anit-racist education has always been a critique of process as well as of content.

David H. Hargreaves,
Cambridge,
October, 1992.

Part One

The Context

Chapter 1

Introduction

Anna S. King

The Education Reform Act of 1988 is a landmark in the history of English and Welsh education — a landmark quite as significant as the legislation of 1870 and 1944. For the first time a British government took direct responsibility for the school curriculum and its assessment. The long term consequences of this legislation for multicultural education are not clear, although its general implications, potentialities and shortcomings have been fiercely debated. Yet, whatever the political future of the Education Reform Act (ERA), it seems certain that a national curriculum is here to stay. Issues of racial equality and justice must be addressed and redressed through this statutorily imposed curriculum.

There are therefore very urgent reasons why there should be informed debate of what the National Curriculum Council (NCC) calls 'the multicultural dimension'. The first is that in our preoccupation with new legislative developments, we should not lose sight of the fact that education for the late twentieth century is necessarily pluralist, and that multicultural perspectives and practices are integral to all good teaching and learning. Secondly, the National Curriculum has created an entirely new situation for teachers and schools committed to pluralist approaches to education. Yet the fact that the National Curriculum Council has decided not to issue formal guidance on the multicultural cross-curricular dimension means that at present there are no unifying guidelines to support its implementation. References to issues of cultural diversity and racial justice, where they exist, are dispersed in statutory Orders and in non-statutory guidance documents. Thirdly, the formative literature on multicultural and anti-racist education refers to the situation prior to the advent of a mandatory national curriculum and is becoming increasingly outdated. Thus, educators, teachers and management now have a very real practical need for advice on issues of cultural diversity and racial justice within schools.[1]

This need is all the more pressing since it is the response of school management, governors, teachers and parents that has become critical. The regulations governing the National Curriculum do not prescribe its manner of delivery and the National Curriculum Council's guidance on the whole curriculum and on the cross-curricular elements is not statutory. Thus individual schools now have the responsibility for developing and interpreting the National Curriculum for multicultural purposes. Without their active support and enthusiasm, there must be a real fear that the multicultural dimension will be diminished, marginalized or even lost.

We therefore decided to invite contributors with a variety of responsibilities — subject specialists, practising teachers and heads, teacher educators, advisers and inspectors — to respond to the emerging documents and assessment procedures of the National Curriculum. This has proved a challenging task, not only because the issues themselves are innately controversial and complex, but also because information is constantly changing. Although the Orders for all subjects of the National Curriculum are in place and being implemented by schools, they remain subject to reappraisal and revision. Moreover, a few contributors have had the formidable task of evaluating interim Working Reports or consultation documents while they waited for the publication of the final Orders. Meanwhile, there is a continuing flow of legislation and official advice on assessment and testing procedures, the role of Local Education Authorities (LEAs), Her Majesty's Inspectorate (HMI) and the new Registered Inspectors and on possible harmonization with Europe. The 1992 Education White Paper promises even more radical changes (DFE, 1992a).

We are writing at a time of great educational change and uncertainty; a time when the role, funding and centrality of multicultural education is open to intense debate. For some writers the very emphasis on a *National* Curriculum and a *national* system of testing has implications which are incompatible with the *internationalist* curriculum that is one of the objectives of the multicultural approach. For others there is scope within the subject areas and the cross-curricular elements for ensuring that the curriculum becomes more relevant to our modern multiethnic, multifaith and multilingual society.

However inadequate, muddled or attenuated NCC references to multicultural education may be, the documents can be used collectively to justify and assert the importance of the pluralist approach, and it can be argued that those working for anti-racist, multicultural and global approaches to the curriculum now have considerable statutory and non-statutory support. The multicultural cross-curricular dimension is an accepted entitlement for all pupils in all maintained schools, and multicultural education is defined as the professional responsibility of all teachers. Within many documents it is possible to find an emphasis not only on cultural pluralism but also on equal opportunities, and both these strands are given a clear non-racist perspective. All schools are to engage directly with issues of racism, racial discrimination and disadvantage, and to eradicate racism and prejudice within their own structures and policies. Similarly, the general advice on the whole curriculum requires the specific needs of ethnic minority pupils to be met. Their cultures, languages and religions are to be treated with dignity and respect and are regarded as an educational enrichment for all pupils. Lastly, we can find within much of the advice a moral base. Pupils themselves are to be encouraged to consider fundamental issues of social justice and equality and to develop an appreciation of, and commitment to, the principles of equality and justice.

The major question which this book addresses is how these educational ideals are to be given significance, within each separate subject area and the curriculum as a whole. It investigates how these general principles can be translated into practical action. Indeed, it is only through the detail of practice that these precepts can be properly understood. Theory and practice illuminate each other.

It has been argued that the National Curriculum, by providing a single system of attainment targets and programmes of study, actually enables primary and secondary teachers to create links between and within schools and to share multicultural resources and expertise across the curriculum. In this book we hope to substantiate this claim by giving practical examples of resources which can be precisely focused, and by suggesting activities and strategies which have been found to be valuable at different key stages.

In trying to explore issues of cultural identity and racial justice throughout the curriculum, we are aware that we are writing for a wide and diverse audience. We want to support those teachers and professionals who are already committed and who will interpret any curriculum in ways that challenge racism and empower pupils. We want also to persuade those managers and governors who remain unconvinced or even frankly sceptical.

Our assertion is that *multicultural* education is simply good education, which will result not only in a happier school environment for all children but in higher standards and achievement — quality as well as equality. By developing in pupils the principles of justice and equality and enriching the educational experiences of all, it raises standards and ultimately benefits both the pupils themselves and society in general.[2]

We are writing for both primary and secondary teachers, and have sought to reflect both primary and secondary perspectives. The fact that primary teachers are, to a great extent, responsible for teaching the whole curriculum creates all kinds of opportunities for multicultural teaching which are not often shared by their secondary colleagues. This holistic understanding is enhanced, despite the subject-based nature of the National Curriculum, by the thematic and cross-curricular teaching which is still practised in most primary schools.

Finally, we should like to contribute to an educational debate that is rapidly intensifying in political importance. Issues of diversity and cohesion, of personal and national identities, of 'belonging' and of openness to a variety of perspectives are becoming increasingly sensitive and challenging as Britain enters Europe and as the need to educate pupils for responsible citizenship as members of a global community becomes inescapable. The National Curriculum cannot ignore such concerns. If it does, it will offer pupils an education 'fettered by the past and fearful of the future'.

The Education Reform Act 1988

As long ago as 1977, the Green Paper, *Education in Schools: A Consultative Document*, called for a core curriculum reflecting the cultural and ethnic diversity of Britain and its interdependence with the wider world. The Swann Report of 1985 argued that multicultural education should be the basis of every child's schooling, not only those in minority groups. It accepted the reality of racial prejudice and discrimination, advocated a global perspective and sought 'a good and relevant education for life in the modern world'.

The Education Act of 1988 itself contains little or no direct reference to multicultural education, although it could be said to be implied in the principles and objectives set out in Section 1. This places a statutory responsibility upon schools to provide for every pupil a curriculum which is balanced and broadly based and which:

(a) promotes the spiritual, moral, cultural, mental and physical development of pupils at the school and of society; and

(b) prepares such pupils for the opportunities, responsibilities and experiences of adult life.

Later documents suggest that these aims offer support for pluralism. For example, DES Circular 5, 1989, paragraph 17, declares:

It is intended that the curriculum should reflect the culturally diverse society to which pupils belong and of which they will become adult members. (DES, 1989)

The Education Act set out the curriculum for pupils of compulsory school age, and the new legal requirements for that curriculum. It also created the National Curriculum Council and the School Examinations and Assessment Council to advise the Secretary of State for Education and Science on the development of subjects in the curriculum and the assessment arrangements. The membership of NCC and SEAC was determined by the Secretary of State, and he also made the final decisions guided by their recommendations. (This strong political context to the National Curriculum is highlighted by several contributors.)

In NCC's initial account of their remit and responsibilities, it is specifically stated (NCC, 1988, p. 4) that NCC 'will be taking account of ethnic and cultural diversity and ensuring that the curriculum provides equal opportunity for all pupils, regardless of ethnic origin or gender'. Similarly SEAC, which became responsible for developing the assessment system at ages 7, 11, 14 and 16 for the National Curriculum, claimed that the development agencies would be

making every effort to ensure that the SATs [standard assessment tasks] avoid race, culture or gender bias; that they should be amenable to translation into a language other than English or Welsh; and that they do not contain material that would put pupils from the ethnic minorities at a disadvantage. (SEAC, 1989)

The GCSE, which has been designated the main means of assessing pupils' attainments in Key Stage 4 of the National Curriculum, is governed by national criteria, both general and specific. The new general criteria for GCSE establish that

Syllabuses and examination papers must. . .reflect the linguistic and cultural diversity of society. They must be designed to be as free as possible from ethnic, sex, religious, political or other forms of bias and Examining Groups must be able to demonstrate how they have sought to achieve this objective. (SEAC, 1990, p. 5)

Despite these reassurances, great anxiety is expressed by contributors about national assessment procedures which in practice discriminate against bilingual or bicultural pupils. Such pupils are not given the equal opportunity to demonstrate their knowledge and skills by tests which are culturally and linguistically appropriate. Contributors acknowledge that there are complex problems which would result from assessing and testing in a number of languages; nevertheless, they fear that the new direction towards written tests that are formal and time-constrained will mean that there will be fewer opportunities for substantial teacher modification, and that this can only further disadvantage black and ethnic minority children.

The Multicultural Debate

Kenneth Baker (1987a, p. 8), when Secretary of State for Education, claimed that the Education Reform Act would 'open the doors of opportunity' for our children. He declared in Parliament that it would create a new framework which would 'raise standards, extend choice and produce a better-educated Britain' (Baker, 1987b, p. 771). The National Curriculum was above all an 'entitlement curriculum'.

Generally speaking, those committed to multicultural and anti-racist education who supported the new legislation did so because they hoped that the Education Reform Act would provide pupils with equal access to a common curriculum, and create a system of public evaluation that would ensure equality of treatment. They accepted that many pupils at this time were not receiving a 'balanced and broadly based' curriculum, and that some ethnic minority pupils were being denied equal educational opportunities by the system of assessment used in schools, in particular by the low expectations of some teachers.

This was, however, not a majority view. Few educationalists working in this area gave an unambiguously optimistic response to the provisions of the Education Reform Act and the emerging documents of the National Curriculum.

Beverly Anderson was one of those who understood the Education Reform Act as requiring every school to take multicultural issues very seriously:

> . . .I do not see the National Curriculum as a device for diluting multicultural, anti-racist education in the 1990s and beyond. On the contrary, it can offer a means of spreading good multicultural practice to all schools in a systematic way. (Anderson, 1989, p. 7)

Yet in the same journal Robin Grinter wrote:

> The situation and prospects for anti-racist education — and for the whole range of equal opportunities education — have been radically altered by the Education Reform Act and the emerging National Curriculum. This alteration is in almost every respect for the worse, and all the curriculum developments of the last fifteen or twenty years are under threat. (Grinter, 1989, p. 34)

Jan Hardy and Chris Vieler Porter (1990, p. 177) claimed that: 'The Education Reform Act aims to provide a "popular" education within an ideological framework which is individualistic, competitive and racist'. Barry Troyna and Bruce Carrington (1990, p. 11) contend that 'The pursuit of egalitarian reforms. . .ended, in our view, with the introduction of the Great Education Reform Bill (GERBIL) into the House of Commons in November 1987'.

Others maintained that the whole thrust of the Education Reform Act in introducing a 'market' into education, was antipathetic to the kind of multicultural and anti-racist education developed in the 1980s. Their arguments were as follows:

Firstly, the legislation greatly undermined the influence of local educational authorities by transferring power both to central Government and to parents and school governors. This movement towards greater centralization and greater school autonomy at the expense of the local educational authorities created a vacuum as far as multicultural education was concerned. It had been the local educational authorities who had been able to offer the most practical support to multicultural policies and practices in the previous decade and whose advisory teams had built up considerable expertise in the area of equal opportunities. Now the battle for multicultural education would have to be won in each school separately and at a time when the new atomized school governing bodies would have very little to gain by supporting multicultural issues. Public accountability, interpreted in competitive terms, would make examination results and high assessment scores all-important. The main priority of governors would be to attract parent consumers.

Secondly, it was predicted that local management of schools, greater freedom of parental choice and opting out would create greater inequalities between schools, increase racial and cultural segregation and lead to diverse educational outcomes. National testing would further penalize pupils from ethnic minorities. They would be victimized by standardized tests which take as normative the language and culture of the majority.

Thirdly, it was feared that the National Curriculum would become a strait-jacket. Not only was it divided into traditionally defined subject areas, but these subject areas were ordered hierarchically with greater weight being given to the core subjects. Many educators believed multicultural education to be necessarily associated with inter-disciplinary, collaborative work, and the individualistic and competitive element within the National Curriculum was seen to be at odds with more democratic and participatory teaching and learning styles. A growing worry was the fear that teachers would teach towards the new standard assessment tasks, thus marginalizing still further the inter-curricular elements of the whole curriculum.

Fourthly, it was noted that the social science disciplines (Sociology, Politics, Economics, Law) were not included within the National Curriculum which would consume the bulk of the timetable provision. Yet many educationalists took the view that, in the absence of such subjects, schools would be unable to give pupils a moral and political education that was in any way adequate. Pupils would lack the conceptual framework and skills needed to analyze issues of social injustice and inequality. The question of timetabling was also recognized as crucial. Competition for classroom time would be intense, and it was anticipated that non-statutory subjects and cross-curricular elements would struggle for survival.

Perhaps above all, it was felt that the Act seriously overloaded schools. It created numerous new initiatives and directions within the Curriculum (for example, a movement towards vocationalism, as exemplified in the Technical and Vocational Educational Initiative, and a stress on science and information technology). At the same time staff had to cope with the introduction of the National

Curriculum itself, with assessment procedures, with local management of schools and with open enrolment. As a result, many teachers and teacher educators found that multicultural education (and its funding) was becoming a very low priority. Later this neglect was extended to initial teacher training. In a consultative document on their new plans for school-based secondary teacher training, the Conservative Government abandoned any requirement that student teachers should consider the principles of multicultural education (DFE, 1992b).

The Emergence of the National Curriculum

As the details of the National Curriculum became known, some of these anxieties were allayed. All the statutory Orders for foundation subjects can be said to offer 'windows of opportunity' for global and pluralist perspectives. However, subject documents and NCC non-statutory guidance (closely associated with the statutory Orders) vary greatly as to how far they explicitly present opportunities for incorporating the multicultural dimension into teaching foundation subjects. They also transmit very different understandings of the national heritage, culture and identity.

Some documents aroused considerable public controversy, particularly those relating to history, mathematics and modern languages. Religious education, which was already a statutory requirement for pupils in county and voluntary schools, also presented problems for the multicultural educator. Religious education remained primarily a local responsibility, but it was required to be of a 'broadly Christian character' and the collective worship was to be 'wholly or mainly Christian'. Criticism (see Chapter 14) centred on how far these requirements conflict with multicultural ideals, and how far they would alienate ethnic minority parents and possibly strengthen the desire for separate Muslim and other similar religious schools.

History proved to be one of the most contentious of all National Curriculum subjects, arousing 'the fiercest controversies and the widest debate' (Chapter 6, p. 78). There was great discussion of many aspects of the consultative documents and the statutory Order but among the most important issues was the debate over the balance between British, European and world history. This debate became heavily politicized as the educational New Right argued that the study of history was bound up with questions of national identity and the central place of British culture and values.

Mathematics came in for the strongest criticism from multicultural educationalists for its rejection of the multicultural approach, and its unimaginative and arid treatment of the multicultural dimension.

The Modern Languages documents were on the whole cautiously received. However, the original appointment of two schedules for languages — the working languages of the European Community and non-EC countries — was fiercely attacked as implying that the languages of ethnic minority pupils were of lower status. Moreover, little thought seemed to have been given to ensuring that the community or mother-tongue languages were developed as part of Britain's heritage of languages.

The response of contributors to other curriculum documents is equally varied. Anthony Adams reports (Chapter 4) that most teachers have welcomed the English Curriculum proposals as enabling rather than prescriptive. He suggests that an acceptance of the spirit of the Cox Report allows Statements of Attainment to be interpreted in ways 'that make multicultural education central to the work of the English classroom. . . .' (pp. 50–51). This, however, is not inevitable. The future of the English curriculum remains uncertain, and there is a more pessimistic prognosis if a narrower, more exclusive, view of English teaching were to become dominant. John Eggleston affirms (p. 111) that National Curriculum Technology is 'particularly sensitive to the way issues of culture and race can be incorporated into a rigorous curriculum and also be firmly based within the educational objectives of the subject'. Brent Robinson in Chapter 9 shows how information technology can not only support multicultural initiatives across the curriculum but provide teachers with the means to create the global classroom. Rex Walford is more cautious. He accepts that the final Orders in Geography which return the curriculum to a clear base of knowledge, neither preclude not affirm multicultural perspectives. Nevertheless, in Chapter 7 he describes in sympathetic detail the revolution in consciousness that occurred in school geography in the 1980s and concludes that the multicultural dimension remains an integral aspect of school geography. Maggie Semple acknowledges that the Order for Physical Education makes 'rather stark' reading, but advises teachers to turn to the working party's final report to see how equality of opportunity can be assured and cultural diversity celebrated in the Physical Education curriculum. In the visual arts and music, assessment of the initial documentation was also optimistic. Sudha Daniel and Rachel Mason praise (p. 146) the National Curriculum Final Report for Art as a 'welcome glimmer of light in a bleak official scene', and add the further comment that it contains 'a comprehensive policy statement demonstrating commitment to cultural pluralism'. However, they criticize the Order that followed for retreating to a more 'conservationist', Eurocentric position. Similarly Marjorie Glynne-Jones praises the release of creative energy and imagination that the Music Order promotes but points out that pupils' introduction to 'our' cultural heritage is interpreted predominantly in terms of the Western classical tradition and in a way which belies the dynamic of musical influence and inspiration and the global mobility of contemporary music cultures. Moreover, even where the original subject documents are progressive and benign, retrogressive alterations have been made. For example, Michael Reiss indicates (p. 70) that the multicultural content of the science curriculum has been gradually eroded and that pupils may now learn more of the international and human nature of science *outside* their science lessons.

The Multicultural Dimension of the Whole Curriculum

The prescriptions of the subject curricula may in some cases project conservative and traditional understandings of Britain and the world. They are, however, transcended by the (non-statutory) requirement that the entire curriculum incorporate multicultural perspectives. The NCC News Issue 5 (1991, p. 3) carries the following key statement which tries to institutionalize multicultural education within the formal curriculum and within the structures and organizations of schools:

> The National Curriculum Council does not see multicultural education as a 'subject', but as a dimension which permeates the entire curriculum. As such, it should be at the heart of curriculum planning, development and implementation.

The reference to cross-curricular elements is first found in NCC Circular No. 6 (1989a, p. 8) which says:

> The term 'cross-curricular' is used in various contexts and it may be helpful for review and organization of the curriculum and the planning of its content, to distinguish three aspects of cross-curricular provision: dimensions, skills and themes.

Major cross-curricular dimensions are said to promote personal and social development through the curriculum as a whole and to include 'equal opportunities, and education for life in a multicultural society'.

Curriculum Guidance 3: The Whole Curriculum (NCC, 1990a) expands these statements on the cross-curricular dimensions. The NCC comments first on issues of equality, claiming (p. 2) that the National Curriculum itself represents a major step in ensuring that all pupils have access to the curriculum. It removes the opportunity for premature choice and specialization which disadvantages some children. However, the Guidance also acknowledges that identical treatment does not ensure that all pupils receive equal educational opportunities. There are 'more subtle barriers' that stand in the way of access. Schools must therefore recognize that pupils of ethnic minority background may need language support in the classroom. They must also take account of the fact that learning is likely to be influenced by pupils' different cultural backgrounds and different experiences:

> In their choice of materials and illustrations teachers might make assumptions about pupils' previous experience and knowledge of the subject matter which could prove an obstacle to understanding.

NCC then argues (p. 3) that the introduction of multicultural perspectives into the curriculum is a way of enriching the education of all pupils:

> It gives pupils the opportunity to view the world from different standpoints, helping them to question prejudice and develop open-mindedness. (NCC, 1990a)

If we carefully examine NCC advice on the multicultural dimension we find several distinct strands which are characteristically interwoven through many official documents, and brought together under the umbrella term of multicultural education. These strands or themes stress the importance of education which helps to develop:

- intercultural understanding and harmony;
- global awareness and knowledge;
- equality of opportunity and access for all;
- freedom from racism and discrimination.

Conversely, NCC recognizes that an education lacking these concerns will be in danger of inculcating in pupils insular and narrowly nationalistic attitudes, and of turning out citizens inappropriately prepared for the contemporary world and unable to contribute to it.

These are undoubtedly worthy statements, but we have to ask what kind of practical guidance is given in the subject documents to translate policy into action. How much of the advice is rhetorical and exhortatory rather than substantive? How far does it seek to bring about real change, how far does it maintain the *status quo*? Are they guiding principles or empty platitudes?

The concept of an interdisciplinary 'dimension' is, on the one hand, extremely attractive. Firstly, and perhaps most important of all, it gives those interested in issues of pluralism and equality ammunition and legitimacy. They can brandish documents stating that a multicultural education is an entitlement for all pupils. Secondly, it sets multicultural education 'at the heart' of curriculum development and offers a framework for curriculum debate. The notion of a dimension acknowledges that multicultural education is a process rather than simply a product; multicultural ideas and perspectives cannot be simply added on or injected into a topic or programme of study. They have to be part of the ethos and atmosphere of the classroom and school and must inform the attitudes of the teachers and pupils. Thirdly, a cross-cultural dimension is open-ended; to define its content might be to limit its capacity to develop and respond to a changing world. Fourthly, it enables the specificity of each school community to be respected — official national policies can be interpreted in terms of the perceived needs of the school's local community. Lastly, it avoids the charges of political bias and ideological commitment to which a more closely defined subject approach might become vulnerable.[3]

However, there are also dangers. The most obvious is that the objectives may seem so broad and global that they offer no clear guidance. The concept of a dimension and the principle of 'permeation' remain woefully vague until given practical life. Everything is left to the teacher or school for whom the multicultural dimension may continue to be ill-defined and certainly underfunded. The dimension may also lack status by comparison with core and foundation subjects. It may become lost within the curriculum, and its organization and development may be overlooked. Finally, there are no built-in forms of evaluation to ensure that the multicultural dimension has any real impact on pupils' attitudes. The lack of formal assessment of the cross-curricular elements is in sharp contrast with that of the subjects of the National Curriculum.

The NCC tried to deal with some of these problems by setting up a Task Group to 'consider ways in which the National Curriculum can broaden the horizons of *all* pupils as well as the particular needs of pupils from ethnic minority backgrounds' (NCC, 1989b, p. 17). This finished its work in April 1990, but a guidance document on the multicultural dimension was not published. In Chapter 2 Sally Tomlinson shows that this failure to give a government imprimatur to multicultural education has grave consequences. It is likely to give the impression to schools that multicultural education is of relatively low priority. This is particularly calamitous in view of the fact that multicultural education is already under-resourced, with the Section 11 funds provided under the Local Government Act of 1966 (see Chapter 19) cut back stringently and focused narrowly on bilingual support and home-school liaison. As Blair and Arnot (p. 262) state: 'Funding arrangements signify the government's underlying intentions and can shape teachers' work just as effectively as curriculum policy'.

Education for Citizenship

Those seeking information about the multicultural dimension were referred by NCC to their *Curriculum Guidance 8: Education for Citizenship* (NCC, 1990b). 'Citizenship', which had become an important concept in the philosophy of all three political parties since 1988, was later identified by the NCC as one of the five cross-curricular themes.[4] At first sight this looks like a further attempt to render innocuous the challenges of multicultural approaches by placing them within the context of citizenship. However, close examination shows that *Curriculum Guidance 8* does indeed include much material that is of significance and importance for the multicultural dimension; probing beneath the surface the astute reader is able to see the centrality of the ideas with which multicultural education has sought to grapple.

Curriculum Guidance 8 is presented as a pragmatic document to be used flexibly by all schools. Its emphases are on the whole, as Porter (1991) suggests, on citizenship as legal status and volition rather than political competence. Controversial issues are avoided and the activities recommended for pupils seem to fall very much into categories such as community service, fund-raising for charities, etc. It is for many critics a muddled document which does not clearly set out ways in which schools could prepare pupils for active political participation. Used unimaginatively, the guidance document could become an instrument of social control.

However, the importance of this document for multicultural education lies in the fact that it endeavours to put political and social education into the formal curriculum for all pupils. They are to be taught not only about the common or shared values by which a 'civilized' society is identified — 'justice, democracy and respect for the rule of law', but also about 'various forms of injustice, inequality and discrimination, including sexism and racism'. The Guidance also recommends (p. 7) that pupils study 'the major conventions on human rights — *The Universal Declaration of Human Rights* (1948), *The European Convention on Human Rights* (1950) and *The United Nations Convention on the Rights of the Child* (1989)' (NCC, 1990b). Moreover, this document is one of the very few to consider empowering pupils by offering them an opportunity to be involved in decisions about aspects of their life at school and by allowing them (p. 10) some control over the use of their time. Whether these recommendations will be implemented is, of course, another matter.

This book shows that the citizenship strand and the multicultural dimension of the National Curriculum are necessarily symbiotic. A realistic curriculum must accept that the identities, loyalties and obligations of future citizens will be multiple and multi-layered rather than simply those of the nation-state. It is absolutely right that any adequate education today must extend and develop pupils' knowledge and understanding of the pluralist nature of these different communities. Yet, as Jonathan Sacks (1991) has pointed out, pluralism can lead to a 'contemporary tribalism'.\It is therefore vitally important for pupils not only to be aware of different cultural traditions, but to understand the values, rights and entitlements they share as citizens./This interdependence of political and multicultural education is summed up excellently by Heater (1990, p. 344):

> If the citizenship ideal is to remain strong, then multicultural education
> for both the host and minority populations is imperative. Multicultural

education may well, indeed, be the key to achieving further progress in consolidating citizenship in both its cosmopolitan and national democratic senses. It can strengthen world citizenship by showing that, if people of diverse ethnic and religious backgrounds can live in harmony in a state, then the division of the world into separate states on those same ethnic and religious criteria is not immutable.

Consensus and Controversy

NCC advice on the multicultural dimension and on equal opportunities necessarily expresses a consensus view of this area. It does not, and perhaps cannot, consider the many controversial issues upon which there is no clear agreement but which inspire passion and commitment. The documents are, after all, not philosophical works, but guidance to be used practically by all schools whatever their ethnic composition or local context. We should not be surprised therefore if such guidance is very general, often ambiguous and sometimes bland.

Thus the advice maintains a middle path. It is distanced both from the complete integrationist view that all pupils should be initiated into a common British culture and from a perspective that would endorse cultural separatism and possible fragmentation. It advocates a sharing of cultures within a common structural framework and a common set of core values. These values are assumed to be at the heart of all educational processes and practices and to underlie the way schools are run. They imply that pupils should have an appreciation of, and commitment to, ideals of justice, tolerance, equality and care and concern for others. It is assumed that to inculcate these ideals and values is not indoctrinatory: they are, as Heater proclaims, 'inseparable from the human good life' (1990, p. 340).

The careful terminology of NCC guidance documents reflects the fact that the present Conservative Government regards anti-racist interventionism with actual hostility and multicultural education itself with a degree of suspicion. The area is therefore one of great political and ideological sensitivity. Multicultural education has not only been under continual assault from the New Right (see Chapter 2), it has also been attacked by the Left, which claims that it legitimates the present order by its cultural rather than structural emphasis. Anti-racist critics claim that the focus on cultural pluralism masks the very real issues of racism and racial discrimination and exploitation based on ethnicity or race. Some have also argued (for example, Sarup, 1986, p. 111) that multicultural education models are in reality power models constructed by dominant white groups for the protection of their interests. Multicultural education is therefore seen as an instrument of control and stability rather than of change, and one which fosters the cultural subordination and political neutralization of black people.

Contributors to this book recognize that inequalities in the distribution of power within society as a whole institutionalize racism and systematically disadvantage some pupils. However, many take the pragmatic view that, for the practising teacher, multicultural and anti-racist approaches are complementary rather than opposed, and that multicultural knowledge is itself a vehicle for combatting racism and injustice.

What are the other kinds of problems that arise from the very general advice of the NCC? The puzzles and perplexities which underlie multicultural education are not explored. It is assumed that cultural pluralism can exist within a frame-work of democracy based on shared values. Yet it is very problematic for schools to inculcate uniform moral values in a society characterized by moral diversity and pluralism (cf. Parekh, 1991). Several writers have drawn attention to the possibility that minority cultures or faith communities may have values that are in conflict with the educational objectives of the school. Halstead (1988), for example, argues that the Western liberal values of the school may themselves be perceived as undermining particular religious traditions and as a form of cultural dominance or imperialism. What are seen by Western educationalists as liberal, universalistic values may be seen by others as secular, technological and reductionist. It is therefore important that multicultural education should not be superficially con-structed in terms of a liberal, white, Western consensus.

Moreover, NCC advice on cultural pluralism does not, and cannot, consider the heterogeneity within and between ethnic minority groups. Advice is targeted to such groups in general rather than to specific groups, and class and gender differences are given little prominence. The desire to celebrate the richness of ethnic diversity is uneasily juxtaposed with the concern for the educational achievement of minorities. The focus on raising the educational performance of ethnic minority pupils tends to stereotype all minority groups by associating them with educational underachievement. Many contributors in this book (for example, Duncan, Chapter 17; Eggleston, Chapter 8; Blair and Arnot, Chapter 19) show just how complex the factors are that create and institutionalize ethnic disadvantage in all aspects of education. However, recent research shows that in Britain, as in Australia, Canada and the USA, some ethnic minority pupils are achieving better results than their majority culture peers. Bullivant (1989, p. 95) writes that:

> if multiculturalism means anything, it is that the contributions of all ethnic groups within a pluralist society should be equally valued, includ-ing their high academic aspirations and upward social mobility, regard-less of whether this risks usurping a fairer share of economic and social rewards from the dominant groups.

Finally, we must beware that the language of multiculturalism used in these documents does not become over-familiar and tired. We may weary of the apparent impotency of the rhetoric. Yet important and central principles such as 'respect for diversity', 'tolerance' and 'care for others' regain their vitality and power in an educational context when we remember that we are dealing with children and young people who are very real and who have a deep emotional need to belong and to feel valued.

The Way Forward

This book is characterized by a rich variety of approaches presented under the umbrella term of multicultural education. Some contributors approach the subject primarily from a cultural diversity, or even anthropological, viewpoint, others from a more explicitly political stance. This diversity reflects the fact that multicultural education is not a closed subject with boundaries and known content, but involves an open and dynamic debate within an ever-changing social and political context.

The school curriculum necessarily both reflects and shapes attitudes to national and personal identity, and so its construction and monitoring will always be contested issues of great political sensitivity. The National Curriculum is not immutable and documents which at one time seemed final can now be seen to be provisional. The debate continues and a multicultural anti-racist curriculum remains to be fought for. In this book contributors argue that a curriculum fostering a narrowly traditional and exclusive sense of national identity is a limiting and anti-educational curriculum. There are also powerful economic and instrumental reasons for a wider, fairer and more inclusive curriculum.

Contributors suggest that all the National Curriculum subject proposals *can* be interpreted by teachers in ways that incorporate multicultural, anti-racist perspectives. In other words, whether the subject documents are strong or weak in multicultural terms they can be interpreted in ways that make issues of justice and culture central to the classroom. Even where an author (Chapter 3) judges a subject curriculum to be reactionary — 'a disaster' in fact — he is able to show how it can be humanized, given multicultural content and made relevant to a pluralistic society.

Having said this, it is also clear that the transition from policy to practice is often left to class teachers. Yet overburdened with the demands of the National Curriculum, they may have very little time to create resources and materials or possibly even to reflect upon how they might develop new strategies. It is for this reason that contributors feel that it is quite inadequate to assume that multicultural guidance (where it exists) is somehow enough. They therefore suggest a whole variety of strategies, tasks, activities and styles that enlarge the repertoire of teachers and which can be used to break down popular but culturally narrow perceptions of school subjects.

All contributors note the vigour and intellectual excitement that multicultural perspectives can give to their particular subject. At the same time they emphasize the very distinctive contributions that their own curriculum areas can make to the pupils' knowledge and understanding and the different skills that they promote. For example, history, according to Martin Booth, is above all 'a subject which can focus on issues of diversity within British society and help pupils to understand the interdependence of individuals, groups and nations' (Chapter 6). While for Michael Byram, of all the subjects in the National Curriculum, the study of a foreign language most directly addresses the existence of other cultures. He stresses the transforming power of foreign language learning in opening up new cultural perspectives. By introducing pupils to 'otherness' in a direct way, it can contribute to an education which is 'looking beyond and within national boundaries, at the cultures of other minorities and majorities' (Chapter 13, p. 182).

Contributors also accept that the individual subject curriculum is a necessary but not sufficient condition for effective multicultural education. The cross-curricular dimension must help to integrate and make sense of the whole curriculum. Yet, here too, there is concern (Chapter 19) that teachers are being asked to put ' "flesh on the bones" of the curriculum skeleton, to design for themselves the cross-curricular dimensions and to find ways to raise the performance of all children within their schools'.

The issues stressed by contributors can be categorized very roughly into four areas of concern. Firstly, there is a concern with *issues of entitlement and access*. How can the entitlement to a 'broad and balanced curriculum' become a reality for all pupils?

For those contributors who are practising teachers or involved in school management, the first and essential priority for each school is to create, implement and monitor a whole school policy which affirms unequivocally positive attitudes to race and gender equality, cultural diversity and special needs of all kinds. The policy should be developed and agreed by all staff and should address existing inequalities and obstacles in educational provision not only at the level of the formal curriculum but also in the structures of school organization and in assessment procedures.

Contributors emphasize that individual teachers' attitudes, practices and procedures are equally decisive in ensuring equal opportunities. Do they have high expectations of all pupils and assess each pupil's interests and skills fairly — without any assumption that their abilities will be determined by ethnic background? How unbiased are their criteria for grouping, setting and examination entry? Do they manage the classroom in such a way that they inspire all pupils to want to contribute? Do they ensure that all pupils benefit equally from their time and attention? Do they clearly model respect and empathy for different faiths and cultures, and employ a variety of teaching strategies that draw upon the experience and knowledge that all pupils bring to the classroom? In particular, do they treat biculturalism and bilingualism as a very positive achievement and resource?

Contributors show that equal entitlement also depends upon the sensitivity of teachers in identifying bias and stereotyping within the curriculum and within resources, and either eliminating them or using them to develop in pupils an informed and responsible scepticism. They further suggest strategies that help teachers to reflect upon and guard against their own political and ideological biases.

Assessment procedures are considered to be potentially the most damaging barriers to pupils' achievement and confidence. Bruce Gill, for example, argues in Chapter 20 that unless these are carefully thought out and implemented, black children and children from ethnic minorities will continue to suffer.

Ultimately, equality can only be assured by a strong national commitment to policies which seek to create a just social order. Maud Blair and Madeleine Arnot argue in Chapter 19 that real, as opposed to formal, equal opportunity and entitlement depends upon national policy and funding and the political will to challenge racism in education.

Next, contributors stress the importance in a multicultural society of *education for democracy and social justice*. They suggest ways in which pupils can be enabled to better understand and challenge racism and injustice. There is agreement that this can best be achieved where the school itself has a democratic ethos with freedom of expression for pupils and teachers alike.

Contributors are concerned with why, how and when issues of inequality and injustice should be addressed through the subject curricula. In many foundation subjects, statements of attainment can be so interpreted that such questions can be relevantly and properly explored. Alan Bishop argues passionately in Chapter 3 that mathematics educators and teachers cannot step aside from the real world — they have a responsibility to address social and cultural issues through the mathematics curriculum. The myth that subject teaching is 'culturally neutral' is exploded not only by the chapters on the humanities, religious studies and the creative arts, but by those on science, technology and mathematics. Indeed, since values pervade the entire curriculum, it is essential that concepts of justice and fairness should inform all teaching. Racism, which directly threatens these central values, must be viewed as an implacable enemy of the educational process, whether it be found in the individual or institution.

A major and recurring theme of the book is therefore the fundamental importance of teaching and learning which is informed by attitudes of open-mindedness, political and social awareness, mutual respect, impartiality and a critical spirit.

A third theme is the need to *educate for a multicultural society and world*, and this involves exploring complex ideas of diversity and unity, similarity and difference. The Swann Report (DES, 1985) held out the ideal of a pluralist democracy 'both socially cohesive and culturally diverse'. Throughout this book it is argued that the intercultural or multicultural approach can move society closer to this goal by helping pupils to understand themselves as well as others by:

- enabling them to prize and reflect upon their own cultural identity and traditions while valuing the languages, religions and cultures of others;
- clarifying the values they share with others;
- recognizing the interdependence of cultures;
- preparing them for the responsibilities and duties of active citizenship while acknowledging the great diversity of cultures;
- exploring their own cultural identity in a society and a world which are rapidly changing;
- enabling them to view the world and understand it from multiple perspectives;
- helping them to co-operate with others and understand and appreciate other people's situation and points of view;
- fostering in them a willingness to challenge injustice.

As Tariq Modood (1991, p. 2) has said, 'multiculturalism must rest on an affirmation of shared moral certainties: it cannot just be about differences.'

A fourth theme concerns the kind of education which is appropriate for pupils in the late twentieth century. Our deeper understanding of different world cultures, faiths and histories has had a transforming effect upon the way in which we view our own traditions whether scientific, mathematical, technological, musical, artistic, religious, ethical or cultural. This understanding in turn is *changing the knowledge base of the curriculum.*

Each of the contributors in turn supports teaching and learning which is cross-cultural and global in approach and which respects and values the different contributions of the world's peoples. The curriculum that they promote is inclusive and self-critical. In mathematics, for example, Alan Bishop shows how anthropological and historical research is transforming our understanding of mathematics as cultural knowledge. In the creative arts, the change is equally fundamental. Sudha Daniel and Rachel Mason argue in Chapter 11 that a genuinely pluralistic art curriculum would involve a real revolution of thought and perception which would embrace alternative conceptions of art, art history and aesthetic value. Maggie Semple's sensitive 'fusion' model of traditions and styles in dance and physical activity (Chapter 12) is globally creative in its implications, while Marjorie Glynne-Jones takes for granted music teaching and learning which encompasses European, African, Asian and Afro-Caribbean traditions. She observes in Chapter 10 that (p. 141):

The world phenomenon at the end of the twentieth century is not only that children and young people are, to differing degrees, surrounded by music, but that music is surrounded by other music in a similar way. As a result of international communication and travel systems music cultures now have a mobility across the world.

In this book contributors show how exposure to, and enjoyment of, different musical cultures, art traditions, dance genres, literatures, languages, technologies, histories and religions can develop a more sensitive and cognitively complex understanding of the world. Such experiences can challenge ideas of cultural superiority and inferiority and help pupils question taken-for-granted views of social reality and personal identity.

Thus multicultural education need not be a superficial white middle-class 'liberal' concern with cultural externals. It can imply a fundamental questioning and continuing critique of the whole education process and what it means to be educated today. Is to be educated today to be inducted into a particular national history and culture, or is it to be informed about, and appreciate, different cultural or religious traditions and to be able to take a global perspective of a particular issue? Does multicultural experience lead to a relativization of values and a loss of national identity and pride, or is it a means by which pupils are enabled to develop their intelligence and to function as humane persons?

This book as a whole sounds a warning and offers a hope. The warning is that the advent of the National Curriculum and its associated programmes of study and assessment procedures could direct teachers away from concern with issues of racial justice and equal opportunities. In this case the lives and life-chances of pupils will continue to be damaged.

There is also however a message of hope. There are opportunities within the structure of the National Curriculum for those who retain a vision of pluralism. It therefore depends upon the choice of teachers, schools and communities as to whether multicultural education is affirmed or pushed to the periphery. The will to look forward is particularly essential as Britain moves into the new Europe, where the resurgence of public racism, both ethnic and cultural, has come to be seen as so complex and intractable. As the Council for Europe (1991) affirms, at the wider level education for a pluralist society is a tool for combatting racism and xenophobia and for promoting respect for human rights and dignity.

Notes

NB In a book which has twenty contributors, there can be no absolute consensus on the meanings of key terms and phrases. 'Racism', 'race' and 'racial' are problematic terms which have been used by contributors (some with reservations) to draw attention to the social realities of racial discrimination, prejudice and harassment and to inequalities of power and status between and within societies and cultures. For further discussion of terminology, see *Equality Assurance* Runnymede Trust.

1   It became very clear during the course of the Cambridge University Department of Education's UFC INSET Project, *Multicultural Education in a Pluralist Society 1989–1990*, that teachers and teacher educators needed formal guidance urgently.

As a consequence of a national conference (*Entitlement for All*) which took place in April 1991 at the University of Warwick, the Runnymede Trust, under its

Director, Robin Richardson, was requested to set up a working group to compile a document to provide authoritative guidance and advice on multicultural education. This document, *Equality Assurance*, is now in press.

2 There is considerable research evidence to indicate that schools do matter. See particularly *The School Effect: A Study of Multi-racial Comprehensives* (1989) by David J. Smith and Sally Tomlinson; *Young Children at School in the Inner City* (1988) by Barbara Tizard, Peter Blatchford, Jessica Burke, Clare Farquhar and Ian Plewis; *School Matters: The Junior Years* (1987) by Peter Mortimore, Pamela Sammons, Louise Stoll, David Lewis and Russell Ecob; *Towards the Effective School: The Problems and Some Solutions* (1987) by Ken Reid, David Hopkins and Peter Holly.

3 The Education (No 2) Act (1986) places duties on LEAs, governing bodies and headteachers to forbid partisan political activities in primary schools and to avoid the one-sided promotion of partisan political views in the teaching of any subject in all schools.

4 The Speaker's cross-party Commission on Citizenship, established in December 1988, published its findings in *Encouraging Citizenship*, HMSO, 1990.

References

ANDERSON, B. (1989) 'Anti-racism and education — Strategies for the 1990s', in *Multicultural Teaching*, **7**(3), pp. 5–8.

BAKER, K. (1987a) *Speech to Annual Conservative Party Conference*, Blackpool, 7 October.

BAKER, K. (1987b) *Parliamentary Debates* (Hansard), Sixth Series-Vol. 123, Session 1987–1988, 1 December, London, HMSO.

BULLIVANT, B.M. (1989) 'The pluralist dilemma revisited' in VERMA, G.K. (Ed.) *Education for All: A Landmark in Pluralist*, London, Falmer Press.

COUNCIL OF EUROPE (1991) Seminar held in Klagenfurt, Carinthia, Austria, October.

DEPARTMENT OF EDUCATION AND SCIENCE (1977) *Education in Schools: A Consultative Document* (Green Paper), Cmnd 6869, London, HMSO.

DEPARTMENT OF EDUCATION AND SCIENCE (1985) *Education for All: Report of the Committee of Enquiry into the Education of Children from Ethnic Minority Groups* (The Swann Report), Cmnd 9543, London, HMSO.

DEPARTMENT OF EDUCATION AND SCIENCE (1989) *Circular No. 5/89, The Education Reform Act 1988: The School Curriculum and Assessment*, London, HMSO.

DEPARTMENT FOR EDUCATION (1992a) White Paper on Education, *Choice and Diversity: A New Framework for Schools*, London, HMSO.

DEPARTMENT FOR EDUCATION (1992b) *Reform of Initial Teacher Training*. A Consultation Document, 28 January, London, HMSO.

EDUCATION REFORM ACT (1988) London, HMSO.

GRINTER, R. (1989) 'Anti-racist strategies in the National Curriculum', in *Multicultural Teaching*, **7**(3), pp. 34–8.

HALSTEAD, J.M. (1988) *Education, Justice and Cultural Diversity*, London, Falmer Press.

HARDY, J. and VIELER PORTER, C. (1990) 'Race, schooling and the 1988 Education Reform Act', in FLUDE, M. and HAMMER, M. (Eds) *The Education Reform Act 1988: Its Origins and Implications*, London, Falmer Press.

HEATER, D. (1990) *Citizenship: The Civic Ideal in World History, Politics and Education*, London, Longman.

MODOOD, T. (1991) *Ethnicity, Common Values and Citizenship*, Paper presented at Conference on Education for Citizenship, University of London Institute of Education, London, 30 November, pp. 1–5.

MORTIMORE, P., SAMMONS, P., STOLL, L., LEWIS, D. and ECOB, R. (1987) *School Matters: The Junior Years*, Wells, Open Books.

NATIONAL CURRICULUM COUNCIL (1988) *Introducing the National Curriculum Council*, London, National Curriculum Council.

NATIONAL CURRICULUM COUNCIL (1989a) *Circular No. 6, The National Curriculum and Whole Curriculum Planning: Preliminary Guidance*, October, York, National Curriculum Council.

NATIONAL CURRICULUM COUNCIL (1989b) *Annual Report of NCC 1988–1989*, York, National Curriculum Council.

NATIONAL CURRICULUM COUNCIL (1990a) *Curriculum Guidance 3: The Whole Curriculum*, York, National Curriculum Council.

NATIONAL CURRICULUM COUNCIL (1990b) *Curriculum Guidance 8: Education for Citizenship*, York, National Curriculum Council.

NATIONAL CURRICULUM COUNCIL (1991) *News Issue*, No. 5, February, York, National Curriculum Council.

PAREKH, B. (1991) *Education and the Good Life*, Lecture given at the University of London Institute of Education, London, 6 November.

PORTER, A. (1991) *Three Elements of Citizenship*, Paper presented at Conference on Education for Citizenship, University of London Institute of Education, London, 30 November.

REID, K., HOPKINS, D. and HOLLY, P. (1987) *Towards the Effective School: The Problems and Some Solutions*, Oxford, Basil Blackwell.

RUNNYMEDE TRUST (in press) *Equality Assurance in Schools*, London, The Runnymede Trust.

SACKS, J. (1991) quoted in Bonham-Carter, M. 'The making of a cultural mosaic', *The Guardian*, 30 December, p. 19.

SARUP, M. (1986) *The Politics of Multiracial Education*, London, Routledge.

SCHOOL EXAMINATIONS AND ASSESSMENT COUNCIL (1989) *An Introduction to SEAC*, London, HMSO.

SCHOOL EXAMINATIONS AND ASSESSMENT COUNCIL (1990) *General Criteria for the GCSE*, London, HMSO.

SMITH, D.J. and TOMLINSON, S. (1989) *The School Effect: A Study of Multi-racial Comprehensives*, London, Policy Studies Institute.

TIZARD, B., BLATCHFORD, P., BURKE, J., FARQUHAR, C. and PLEWIS, I. (1988) *Young Children at School in the Inner City*, London, Erlbaum.

TROYNA, B. and CARRINGTON, B. (1990) *Education, Racism and Reform*, London, Routledge.

Chapter 2

The Multicultural Task Group: The Group That Never Was

Sally Tomlinson

In her seminal book on *The Social Origins of Education Systems*, Margaret Archer set out the simple proposition that an education system has the characteristics it does because of the goals pursued by those who control it, and changes occur because new educational goals are pursued by those with the power to change previous practice. She contended that 'most of the time the forms education takes are the political product of power struggles' (Archer, 1979, p. 3). What actually goes into the curriculum is seldom the realization of some ideal form of instruction, because those with the power to do so can eliminate certain forms of knowledge and modes of instruction. The crucial question, as Denis Lawton pointed out in 1980, is who actually selects the knowledge which becomes 'the curriculum' (Lawton, 1980). To understand a curriculum we need to know who won the struggle for control of form and content and who lost!

This chapter documents the story of a group who lost in an attempt to influence the National Curriculum in a multicultural direction. The group was the Task Group set up by the National Curriculum Council in July 1989 as one response to a letter to the Council from the Secretary of State for Education in August 1988. This letter instructed the National Curriculum Council to 'take account of ethnic and cultural diversity, and the importance of the curriculum in promoting equal opportunity for all pupils regardless of ethnic origin or gender' (Department of Education and Science, 1988). What follows describes the proceedings of the Task Group which worked over a nine-month period to produce what it believed would be a published report providing non-statutory guidelines for schools on multicultural education. The chapter also describes the subsequent rejection of this report and concludes with a brief discussion as to the possible reasons for non-publication of a report which was intended to help teachers to develop principles, policies and practices appropriate for a multicultural society, within the framework of the National Curriculum.

Setting up the Task Group

In May 1989 the Council approved the establishment of a multicultural Task Group and asked a member of the Council, the Head of a large multiracial secondary school, to chair the group. Individuals were invited to join the group over the summer of 1989, on the basis of known interests, not as representatives of other groups. Eventually the group included nine people: two Headteachers, four local education authority inspectors or advisors (one of whom was also a language specialist), two lecturers (one a member of Council), and a Professor of Educational Research. In addition there were observers from HMI, the DES and SEAC (see Appendix 1). Six of the group members were of Afro-Caribbean or Asian origin, possibly the largest number of minority group educationalists on any committee concerned with the National Curriculum.

The Group met for the first time in September 1989 and on six subsequent occasions, either at York, the home of the NCC, or in London. The members were given leave to attend meetings by their various employers; this eventually made it more difficult for them to explain that there was no obvious outcome to their work.

At the first meeting the group was presented with their remit (see Appendix 2) which was essentially to consider ways in which the National Curriculum could broaden the horizons of all pupils in a multicultural society and address the curriculum needs of ethnic minority pupils, especially bilingual pupils. The remit included 'preparing by Easter 1990 — guidelines on multicultural education in the National Curriculum', and at the first meeting a document written by the Chair was circulated as a first step towards preparing a report. Naively, the group assumed that they were writing guidelines for schools along the lines of the subsequent eight curriculum Guidance booklets which deal with 'aspects of the curriculum not subject to statutory orders' (National Curriculum Council, 1990a).

The Work of the Task Group

A document produced by an NCC officer for the Task Group noted that 'NCC recognises that multicultural education is a controversial area and the subject of considerable debate which should be central to the thinking of all those throughout the country with a responsibility for curriculum planning'. To some extent, this was a coded acknowledgment that, despite vigorous conceptual debates about the nature of multicultural education and the need for anti-racist education, many in government, and probably the majority of the general public, were not moved by those who suggested that education had a part to play in preparing all young people for a multicultural society. The Task Group was well aware that any debate prefaced by 'multi' or 'anti' had become anathema to influential people with access to the ear of government (see Palmer, 1986; Lewis, 1988) and that, politically, multicultural and anti-racist policies and practices were proving to be a potent weapon in attacks on Labour-controlled local education authorities. The Group was also aware that many teachers, particularly those in 'white' schools and areas, still regarded issues of ethnic and cultural diversity, race and racism, multicultural and global education, as irrelevant to the curriculum. The Group, therefore, set out to write guidelines that would concentrate on good educational principles and practice which would apply to all schools. By the second meeting the Group had agreed that a publication should set out a rationale for guidelines on multicultural education, discuss effective schooling in a multicultural society, focus on curriculum issues, (including the way in which multicultural aspects could be included in core, foundation and other subjects), contain a section on bilingualism and a section on policy implementation, and include studies of good practice.

Between meetings group members worked on their own or together to produce draft sections and collect examples of good practice — many of which were derived from the government's own Education Support Grant projects in multicultural education, which were then in operation around the country (see Tomlinson, 1990a). The officers serving the group produced five drafts over nine months, members receiving the fifth draft by the end of May 1990. Below is the preliminary section of the fifth draft which sets out what the report was all about:

NCC offers this document as preliminary guidance on using the framework of the National Curriculum to promote multicultural education. This is a discussion document intended for use in all schools. It is meant to initiate debate and to provide professional support.

Schools need to be clear about the reasons for multicultural education and the issues which need to be addressed before considering how to set about the task of implementing it.

Chapter 1, therefore, proposes a rationale for multicultural education and a set of aims which should form the basis for a school's policy. It attempts to set multicultural education in its historical context and to tackle the difficult question of terminology.

The next chapter of the booklet deals with planning a whole school policy which covers every aspect of school life, and which involves all those with an interest in the school, including governors and parents.

Chapter 3 deals with the heart of the matter — planning a curriculum which addresses the needs of all pupils, including pupils of ethnic minority origin and bilingual pupils. The main vehicle for this will be the National Curriculum, which is a statutory entitlement for all pupils.

Chapter 3 also considers the implementation of the school's policy and curriculum planning in terms of school and classroom organisation and management. It offers some examples of effective practice which schools could consider adapting to their own needs.

Chapter 4 provides case study examples of ways schools have approached the task of incorporating multicultural perspectives in the curriculum.

Chapter 5 sets out the implications for action by local education authorities, governors and parents. (Source: Fifth draft of Task Group Multicultural report)

The final report was to be presented to a management meeting at NCC and then to the full National Curriculum Council, but the Task Group remained under the impression that it would be published as non-statutory guidance for all schools by the autumn of 1990.

Non-publication

By September 1990 none of the Task Group members had received a copy of the completed report with case-studies of good practice, and had heard nothing further from NCC. Teachers and other interested groups and individuals were beginning to enquire when guidelines would be published. The National Anti-Racist Movement in Education noted in its September newsletter that:

> It is now September 1990. Local authorities are well underway with their national curriculum training, and schools are implementing the content of curriculum documentation in the core subjects; but what has happened to the Multicultural Working Party? It may be that you did not expect much useful support from the National Curriculum Council working group on multicultural education. Nevertheless it is interesting to speculate on reasons for non-publication. (Arena, 1990)

The Task Group members were also speculating on reasons for non-publication, especially as £49,000 had been set aside in the Council's 1990 Corporate Plan to publish multicultural guidance.

In the autumn of 1990 three members of the group wrote to the Chief Executive of NCC asking when the guidelines would be published. Tomlinson wrote in September noting the interest expressed by schools, LEAs and a conference of Race Equality Advisors held at Warwick University. The Chief Executive replied that 'the working group — to whose members we are very grateful — was set the task of better informing the work of Council and its committees. . .clearly Council will have to decide in due course how best to do this'. Turner wrote in October explaining why the publication of guidelines was essential and asking for a publication date, and Deshpande wrote in early December suggesting that NCC publish examples to illustrate the multicultural dimensions in the curriculum.

However, on 28 November, the Chief Executive wrote to an inquirer at Warwick University that 'there seems to be some misunderstanding of NCC's position, it is not our intention to publish guidelines on multicultural education because that runs the risk of this vital work being seen as a separate and perhaps side issue'. This decision appeared to have been taken before the full Council discussed the work of the Task Group. This discussion did not occur until December 1990. When the meeting was convened the Council did not have before them a full copy of the report, but a version of it produced by an NCC officer.

In November 1990, the NCC Chief Executive had published an article in the Times Educational Supplement suggesting that NCC had 'emphasised the importance of cross-curricular elements, dimensions such as equal opportunities and education for a multicultural society' (Graham, 1990). A Task Group member subsequently wrote to the Times Educational Supplement that 'until Mr Graham can offer some explanation as to why the report produced by his Task Group has not appeared, I will remain sceptical of his claim that the Council does value the multicultural dimension' (Tomlinson, 1990b).

The Chief Executive found the tone of this and other letters 'unfortunate' and wrote in December that the Council had now considered how best to use the materials provided (private correspondence). The decision of the Council was not to publish any curricular guidance on multicultural education, apart from an article in the NCC Newsletter and a short circular on linguistic diversity. A one-page article appeared in the February NCC Newsletter, containing extracts from the Task Group report (NCC Newsletter, 1991); interested inquirers have been referred to this and to extracts in *Curricular Guidance* number 3 and number 8, which briefly refer to the importance of a multicultural dimension and educating for a plural society (NCC, 1990a and 1990b).

Speculation on Non-publication

In his book describing the creation of a national curriculum in English, the Chair of the National Curriculum English working group wrote that 'during the period when I was preparing my report, three groups of people were involved in man-oeuvres to control the National Curriculum in English — journalists, politicians and professional teachers' (Cox, 1991, p. 13). In the case of the multicultural dimension in the National Curriculum, it appeared that three groups had influence — executive officers at the National Curriculum Council, officials at the Department of Education and Science, and politicians. However, as there was no publication and no open debate about multicultural education and the National Curriculum, professional educators and journalists never had the chance to present their views. Any decisions taken over the publication of multicultural guidelines were secret and unattributable. Non-publication of even draft guidelines precluded the vigorous debate which followed publication of the English working party proposals. The Task Group heard rumours that some NCC officials and some Council members opposed publication, as did a high-placed official at DES. During the summer of 1990 a junior Education Minister with noted traditional views was appointed and may have been against publication. There were hints of political interference but no actual information.

In retrospect, the members of the Task Group were perhaps over-optimistic that any report or guidelines on multicultural education in the National Curriculum would be published. Despite a twenty-year debate on suitable curriculum policies for a multicultural society and official policies after the publication of the Swann Report (DES, 1985) that endorsed the development of a curriculum for an ethnically diverse society, the 1980s had also seen a sustained and determined attack on multicultural education.

Opposition to a Multicultural Curriculum

Opposition to multicultural and anti-racist curriculum developments was relatively low-key until the 1980s. This may have been because up to the late 1970s such development was confined to urban multi-racial schools, was associated with the demands of ethnic minority parents, and had produced divisions among supporters. Such development was regarded as relatively unthreatening and unimportant. When it became apparent that changes in all schools for all pupils were advocated, and that white areas would be affected, opposition became more vocal. A major source of organized opposition came from New Right groups such as the Centre for Policy Studies, the Hillgate Group and the Salisbury Group, plus a number of smaller organizations claiming parental support (see Hempel, 1988; Tomlinson, 1990a). These pressure groups published literature arguing against any form of multicultural education, influenced parliamentary legislation and received con-siderable sympathetic press coverage. Although opposition was claimed to be educational, it was in the main political. Multicultural education was accused of being associated with, at best, left-of-centre egalitarianism, and at worst, with hard-left political subversion. Opposition groups also insisted that multicultural education posed a threat to traditional British values, culture and heritage, and any curriculum change was regarded as a particular threat to conservative political values dominant in Britain in the 1980s. At the 1987 Conservative Party Conference, Margaret Thatcher, then prime minister, commenting on the 1988 Education Act, specifically linked left-wing extremism and lowered educational standards to supposed anti-racist curriculum development.

> In the inner cities where youngsters must have a decent education if they are to have a better future, the opportunity is all too often snatched away from them by hard-left education authorities and extremist teachers. Children who need to be able to count and multiply are learning anti-racist mathematics, whatever that is. (Margaret Thatcher, reported in Hughill, 1987)

Political critiques of multicultural anti-racist education have persistently linked any kind of education activity perceived as likely to challenge existing political value systems with political indoctrination. Thus, the Hillgate Group has attacked world studies, peace studies, sociology, political education, life skills, social awareness courses and 'alien multiculturalism', claiming that they are propaganda and social engineering (Hillgate Group, 1986, 1987). A member of the right-wing political Monday Club, attacked Lord Swann's report *Education For All* — a report elsewhere widely acclaimed as a just and liberal document — as 'a profoundly dangerous document aimed at re-shaping British Society' (Pearce, 1986, p. 136). Pearce articulated a fear expressed by many of those who have attacked multicultural education — that it would lead to a 'loss of identity for the native British, who have a right to preserve their way of life, and this means that their culture must predominate in our schools' (*ibid*, p. 141).

Ray Honeyford, the Bradford Headteacher who became a *cause célèbre* during the 1980s over his views on the education of ethnic minorities, has expressed fear that the National Curriculum, which he hoped would lead the state education system to 'rediscover that true sense of purpose which has systematically been undermined by the ravages of the social engineer and the ideologue' has now been taken over by 'progressive zealots'. Writing in the *Salisbury Review* he stated his beliefs that continued references in the National Curriculum to cultural diversity, equality for women and the handicapped, and to personal and social education, are all evidence that the curriculum is still dominated by left-wing extremists (Honeyford, 1990).

Opposition to multicultural and anti-racist curriculum development thus became, during the 1980s, a right-wing political tool for encouraging a populist belief that such development threatens the nation's heritage and culture and erodes educational standards. With this kind of opposition it should not be surprising that those who believe that multicultural developments are in fact intended to produce a just, decent, humane education system, have found difficulty in making their views prevail. An editorial in the *Times Educational Supplement* in June 1990 suggested that:

> unspoken anxieties about ethnic differences underlie several bits of educational policy, all of which are beginning to show a pattern. There

seems to be a definite, though unformulated intent to starve multicultural education of resources and let it wither on the vine. (*Times Educational Supplement*, 1990, p. 23)

Conclusion

This short chapter has described the work of the multicultural Task Group set up by the National Curriculum Council in July 1989 and officially disbanded in January 1991, the production of multicultural guidelines, and the subsequent non-publication of any such guidance for schools. In Margaret Archer's terms, this was a group that lost out in any attempt to influence the National Curriculum and could perhaps be described as 'the group that never was'.

However, Archer has also pointed to the 'structural relations of contradiction' when attempts are made to influence education (Archer, 1979, pp. 3–4). There may be conservative forces which seek maintenance and tradition in education, but there are also liberal forces which lead to innovation and change. No one group, however powerful, can design or influence a National Curriculum in a democracy without being influenced by alternative conceptions, values, interests and ideologies. It is thus possible for a multicultural dimension to be incorporated into the National Curriculum even though official action has sought to exclude or minimize such a dimension.

Note

The views expressed in the above chapter are entirely my own and must not be attributed to any other member of the Multicultural Task Group.

References

ARCHER, M.S. (1979) *The Social Origins of Education Systems*, London, Sage.

ARENA (1990) *Newsletter of the Anti-Racist Movement in Education*, No. 23.

COX, B. (1991) *Cox on Cox — An English Curriculum for the 1990s*, London, Hodder & Stoughton.

DEPARTMENT OF EDUCATION AND SCIENCE (1985) *Education For All*, London, HMSO.

DEPARTMENT OF EDUCATION AND SCIENCE (1988) *Letter to the National Curriculum Council*, London, HMSO.

GRAHAM, D. (1990) 'The wealth of nations', *Times Educational Supplement*, 10 November 1990.

HEMPEL, S. (1988) 'The real consumer backlash', *Times Educational Supplement*, 29 July 1988.

HILLGATE GROUP (1986) *Whose Schools? A Radical Manifesto*, London, Hillgate Place.

HILLGATE GROUP (1987) *The Reform of British Education*, London, Claridge Press.

HONEYFORD, R. (1990) 'The National Curriculum and its official distortion', *Salisbury Review*, **8**(4), pp. 6–9.

HUGHILL, B. (1987) 'Dramatic steps that will carry Britain forward', *Times Educational Supplement*, 16 October 1987.

LAWTON, D. (1980) *The Politics of the School Curriculum*, London, Routledge.

LEWIS, R. (1988) *Anti-Racism — A Mania Exposed*, London, Quartet Books.

NATIONAL CURRICULUM COUNCIL (1990a) *Curriculum Guidance 3, The Whole Curriculum*, York, National Curriculum Council.

NATIONAL CURRICULUM COUNCIL (1990b) *Curriculum Guidance 8, Education for Citizenship*, York, National Curriculum Council.

NATIONAL CURRICULUM COUNCIL (1991) *Newsletter No. 2*, February, York, National Curriculum Council.

PALMER, F. (Ed.) (1986) *Anti-Racism: An Assault on Education and Values*, Wiltshire, The Sherwood Press.

PEARCE, S. (1986) 'Swann and the spirit of the age', in PALMER, F. (Ed.) *Anti-Racism: An Assault on Education and Value*, London, Sherwood Press.

TIMES EDUCATIONAL SUPPLEMENT (1990) 'Editorial', June 1990.

TOMLINSON, S. (1990a) *Multicultural Education in White Schools*, London, Batsford.

TOMLINSON, S. (1990b) 'Letter' *Times Educational Supplement*, 30 November 1990.

Appendix 1

Multicultural Task Group Members

Mrs Daphne Gould (Chair), Headteacher and Member of Council
Ms Beverly Anderson, Educational Consultant and Member of Council
Ms Shirley Chase, Headteacher
Mr Pratap Deshpande, Curriculum Advisor
Mr Alec Fyfe, Advisor
Mrs Gulzar Kanji, Inspector
Ms Shahwar Sadeque, Lecturer
Ms Farzana Turner, Inspector
Professor Sally Tomlinson, Professor of Educational Research

Observers

HMI — Mr Geoff Robson
DES — Mrs Pat Masters
SEAC — Mrs Kate Seager

Appendix 2

Multicultural Task Group

Remit

1 The Secretary of State's remit letter of August 1988 requires Council to 'take account of the ethnic and cultural diversity of British society, and of the importance of the curriculum in promoting equal opportunity for all pupils regardless of ethnic origin and gender.' In May 1989, Council approved the establishment of a Multicultural Task Group.

2 The role of the Task Group will be to consider:
   a. ways in which the National Curriculum can broaden the horizons of all pupils so that they can understand and respect, learn from and contribute to the multicultural society around them and realise that they do share a national identity and common citizenship.

    b.   the particular curriculum needs of pupils from ethnic minority backgrounds. Here issues relating to bilingual pupils will be an urgent priority.

3 The Task Group is to prepare for Council by Easter 1990:
    a.   guidance on multicultural education in the National Curriculum;
    b.   suggestions for the incorporation of multicultural issues into subject-specific Non-statutory Guidance;
    c.   advice on multicultural matters to the Secretary of State's subject working groups;
    d.   advice on a strategy to deal with multicultural issues arising in future consultations.

4 The Task Group will report to the [Curriculum Committee] and liaise with Council's other committees as appropriate. The Task Group will be reviewed at Easter 1990.

5 Members of the Task Group will work in close partnership with NCC's professional officers for National Curriculum subjects. The officers will attend meetings of the Task Group and play a full part in discussion as appropriate.

Part Two

The Curriculum

Chapter 3

Culturalizing Mathematics Teaching

Alan J. Bishop

Introduction

Mathematics is a paradoxical subject. On the one hand it is about universal truths — three threes are nine everywhere in the world, all triangles contain 180° wherever you are on the earth's surface (and would be if you could draw a triangle in space!), and $(a + b)^2 = a^2 + 2ab + b^2$ in whichever country you live. It is universally applicable, and it is universally applied, whether in the shops, on the street, in the farm, factory or business. It belongs to everyone.

On the other hand it seems to transcend the real world, and its objects, its symbols, rules and processes seem not to be visible parts of the world. It seems to be invented by no one and it seems to belong to no one. It is common knowledge, but yet it is an unknown quantity. It doesn't exist in many people's minds as a cultural object, and yet it is arguably one of the most multicultural school subjects. But you won't find the word 'culture' in the national mathematics curriculum (NMC).

So what are the aims of this chapter? First, to demystify this rather mysterious cultural subject; second, to offer examples of how its cultural nature can be revealed; and third, to develop some principles whereby the universal and multicultural mathematics curriculum can contribute to all children's education in a pluralistic and modern technological society.

Background to the NMC

Before proceeding further, however, it is necessary to share some perspectives on the situation which led up to the introduction of the NMC. Before the Mathematics Working Party was established in 1987, the situation regarding mathematics teaching in the UK was extremely fluid. Post-Cockcroft (1982) there had been a great deal of national development. Investigations were becoming a well-established component of the mathematics classroom, although they and coursework projects were rather ritualized and shackled versions of what many educators would like to have seen, due largely to their slow acceptance by the Examining Groups. Calculators and computers were being integrated into classrooms, again at a slow pace in some schools. Small-group seating arrangements were appearing more and more, although the learning activities used were not necessarily created for group working.

Multicultural developments during the 1980s were very patchy and were confined to certain areas of the country and to groups of enthusiasts. The Cockcroft Committee (1982) had not referred at all to this aspect, even though its terms were 'to consider the teaching of mathematics with particular regard to the mathematics required in further and higher education, employment and adult life generally'. The fact that 'adult life' happened in a pluralistic society was never mentioned, neither were there any statistical data presented on the relative numbers of second-language learners, nor on the underachievement of many of the minority pupils in the schools. The only such underachievement which was recognized was that of girls, and this 'problem' was accorded not a chapter, but an appendix!

Interest in matters cultural post-Cockcroft was largely confined to urban areas such as London, Leeds and Birmingham, and most of the standard textbooks in use contained little reference to anything of a cultural nature in mathematics. Multicultural mathematics teaching during the 1980s was mainly associated with schools having large numbers of ethnic minority pupils, and those schools which 'didn't have that problem' rarely considered mathematics teaching from that perspective. Ignorance was widespread — the Prime Minister at that time, Margaret Thatcher, was widely quoted expressing her total lack of understanding and awareness of 'anti-racist mathematics teaching' — although one suspects that large sections of the populace were equally dumbfounded by that juxtaposition of words.

It was a time when few people realized that mathematics teaching had anything to do with values. In another famous episode of that period (at least, for mathematics education) candidates in a GCSE examination in 1986 were presented with some information on military spending in the world, which was compared with a statement from a journal (*New Internationalist*) that 'The money required to provide adequate food, water, education, health and housing for everyone in the world has been estimated at $17 billion a year.' The candidates were asked 'How many weeks of NATO and Warsaw Pact military spending would be enough to pay for this?' The outcry from the nation's press and from society's establishment was remarkable, with one headline asking 'What has arms spending to do with a maths exam?' (Daily Mail, 14 June, 1986). The public correspondence and discussion on this issue continued for a surprising length of time.

In this largely ignorant and reactionary atmosphere, towards the end of the 1980s, mathematics was the first National Curriculum subject to be put 'on stream', and it should therefore come as no surprise to find that the cultural nature of mathematics would not just be played down, but would be almost totally denied. The mathematical content offered in their report by the Mathematics Working Party (DES, 1988) contained no cultural, or value, references, and the whole rationale was revealed in the extremely telling section headed 'Ethnic and Cultural Diversity'. That this was the only section of the report to mention cultural aspects, reflected the aforementioned belief that multicultural matters were for consideration *only* in schools where there were large numbers of ethnic minority pupils, who thereby created 'a problem'. Another important aspect of this presentation of the cultural issue is that it appeared solely in the area of the report concerned with *implementation* of the National Curriculum. The *intended* curriculum was to contain no mention of cultural aspects. It is important to quote fairly extensive passages from this section in order to represent adequately the enormous obstacles created by the Working Party, with which present educators concerned with cultural developments are having to grapple.

Paragraph 10.18 refers to children whose mother tongue is not English, and who may be 'disoriented by differences between their home culture and the culture of the school. A further problem may be overt or covert racial prejudice: some teachers may unconsciously have lower expectations of pupils from certain ethnic minority backgrounds' (p. 87). Having made this point, however, paragraph 10.19 then denies any responsibility. 'It is outside our remit to address the language problems of children for whom English is a second language. . .' (p. 87). No mention is made of how an intended curriculum *could* address overt or covert racial prejudice — the report itself is guilty of prejudice by omission.

Paragraph 10.20 continues the excuses, and is quoted here in full, to reveal the centrality of this thinking:

> It is sometimes suggested that the multi-cultural complexion of society demands a 'multi-cultural' approach to mathematics, with children being introduced to different number systems, foreign currencies and non-European measuring and counting devices. We are concerned that undue emphasis on multi-cultural mathematics, in those terms, could confuse young children. Whilst it is right to make clear to children that mathematics is the product of a diversity of cultures, priority must be given to ensuring that they have the knowledge, understanding and skills which they will need for adult life and employment in Britain in the twenty-first century. We believe that most ethnic minority parents would share this view. We have not therefore included any 'multi-cultural' aspects in any of our attainment targets. (p. 87)

Paragraph 10.21 proposes the following strategy, hinting by example that it is recommended *only* in relation to children of ethnic minority parents:

> However, it will be important for teachers, within the broad framework of National Curriculum attainment targets and programmes of study, to select examples and materials which relate to the cultural backgrounds of their pupils. It may help if teachers, in planning lessons, can use contexts or material drawn from the backgrounds of their pupils. Some attention to the history of mathematics could show the contribution to the development of mathematical thinking of non-European cultures: for example, it would be right to point out that the number system is of Hindu-Arabic origin. (p. 87)

Paragraph 10.22 contains a confused mix of assumptions and arguments:

> Many of those who argue for a multi-cultural approach to the mathematics curriculum do so on the basis that such an approach is necessary to raise the self-esteem of ethnic minority cultures and to improve mutual understanding and respect between races. We believe that this attitude is misconceived and patronising. Pupils with language problems will certainly need extra help. It is also important that knowledge and understanding of mathematics is not held back by any teaching methods or

forms of school organisation which inadvertently discriminate against minority groups. (p. 87)

Finally, Paragraph 10.23 says a little about the assessment issues, again from the cultural and linguistic stance of the English speaking majority, but offers nothing about the role of the intended curriculum in creating situations of disadvantage.

Even if these kinds of views represented the majority views in the teaching profession, and that was never tested, of course, it has to be said that they are reactionary views. The Mathematics Working Party failed to represent the more progressive and informed view that the multicultural nature of the subject is critical to emphasize in the *intended* curriculum for a pluralistic society.

The Current National Mathematics Curriculum

From a cultural perspective, the current NMC is a disaster, but with the previous section as a brief backdrop, it is not hard to see why it happened. The same ideological stance illustrated in the Working Party's report is evident by omission in both the statutory documents and in the non-statutory guidance (DES, 1989). The statutory documents list the Attainment Targets (ATs) which are topic oriented, such as Number or Algebra, with one other Target 'Using and Applying Mathematics'. In the non-statutory guidance, not only is there no mention of anything cultural in the curriculum, there is no mention at all of the situation of ethnic minority children.

In particular, the following points about the current NMC all seem significant if we are to redress its cultural imbalance:

- *There is no attention given to the history of the mathematical content.* There is no reference to where the concepts, symbols and processes come from, why they are important, and how many cultures have contributed to the global store of mathematical knowledge. There is no awareness of the different kinds of mathematical knowledge developed and developing in different periods and in different countries. The words 'imperial' and 'metric' appear merely as adjectives for the word 'units'.
- *There is no attention given to people.* Only two mathematicians' names appear in the ATs, again as adjectives — Pythagoras' Theorem, and Cartesian coordinates, while two others occur in a similar way as examples: Fibonnacci sequences and Carroll diagrams. There are tens or even hundreds of names which could be mentioned — women as well as men, non-European as well as European. People are zero-rated in this curriculum.
- *There is no attention given to values.* There are no descriptions of aims, and there are few words of any evaluative nature. We find terms like 'precise', 'critically', 'clearly', 'appropriately' and even 'mathematically' used without explanation or encouragement to analyze. We also find 'justification', 'initiative', 'spotting inconsistencies', 'right order'. As before they are mainly adjectives, or adverbs, and not foci for attention. Political or moral issues are never mentioned.

- *There is no attention given to aesthetic aspects.* The emphasis is entirely on conceptual understanding, algorithmic performance and problem-solving processes. Affective and attitudinal aspects are ignored and the aesthetic appeal of, for example, geometrical design is never mentioned. Motivationally there is no appeal to imagination, feeling, stimulating interest, fascination, awe or wonder. The mathematics curriculum is culturally cold, barren and dead.
- *There is no attention given to issues in society.* Society is an unproblematic context to be drawn on as a source for examples on which to practise mathematical procedures. There is no reflection on the role of mathematics in helping to create that society — the good aspects, the bad, and the ugly. There is no focus on the relationship between democratic citizenship and mathematized society. Society is assumed to be acceptable as it is, and mathematics is likewise assumed to have a benign influence.
- *There is no attention given to the pluralistic society.* References to the ubiquitous 'child', and use of lowest common denominator examples from society like 'objects', 'real life problems' and 'opinion', conceal the differences which reflect the challenges for education in a pluralistic society. This minimalist approach fails to convey the power of mathematics to reveal inequalities, differences, discriminations and orders in society which ought to be addressed.

What we now have in England and Wales is an NMC which is culture-blind. The impression it conveys is of a subject totally divorced from any connection with culture and in which any cultural perspective is considered irrelevant. It is a curriculum which, for example, allows teachers, schools and parents the *choice* of whether or not to inform and educate their children about the multicultural nature of the knowledge which has helped to shape the pluralistic society into which they have been born. It is not an entitlement curriculum for this society.

In practice, it is likely that this is not even a choice for many teachers. Because of the omission of any cultural references in the intended curriculum, there is little incentive for any publishers to develop appropriately culturalized teaching materials. Because of the shortage of appropriate teaching materials, those teachers who wish to encourage a cultural perspective have to create their own teaching materials. Because of all the paraphernalia of assessment, restructuring, and record keeping associated with the introduction of the National Curriculum, few teachers have any time or any energy left to create additional teaching materials. Someone with a cynical mind could read an obstructive and reactionary objective into this situation.

One might therefore be forgiven for thinking that within this bleak scenario there is little scope for optimism or positive ways forward. This is far from the case, however, as I hope to now be able to demonstrate. Fortunately, before the NMC took over much of the thinking about the mathematics curriculum, there was a variety of relevant activity occurring in the mathematics education field, and this activity was indeed increasing in both range and intensity at all levels. We will, therefore, look at some of this activity in the next three sections of this chapter, which will consider in turn, mathematics as cultural knowledge, humanizing the mathematics curriculum, and mathematics teaching in a pluralistic society.

Mathematics as Cultural Knowledge

Central to any development of serious multicultural mathematics teaching is the idea that mathematical knowledge is part of culture. Culture is not being used here to refer to grand culture or high culture (as in a cultured person) but merely to reflect the fact that like language, religion or morals, mathematics is part of a culture's store of knowledge, developed by previous (and present) generations and made accessible to succeeding generations. Anthropological and historical research is supporting this view and is revealing more and more of the rich tapestry of mathematical knowledge existing in the world.

Perhaps the most interesting development in this light is what is called 'ethnomathematics', variously defined, but essentially referring to mathematical ideas and processes created by people who have not been a part of the Western cultural tradition (see, for example, Ascher, 1991). We can find literally hundreds of different counting systems, using different objects and materials to help, and varying with the cycles, or bases, used to deal with large numbers. We can find very different conceptions of space from our own Euclidean notions of points, lines and regions. The Navajos, for example, assume that objects are always in motion (some more slowly than others) and that space cannot be subdivided. The symbolic and religious properties of geometric figures are of more interest in some societies than in ours, as are the predictive powers of certain numerological practices. However, if we want to try to find mathematics in different cultures then we have to broaden our thinking — mathematics isn't just about sums, fractions and equations. Mathematical ideas develop everywhere because people may live in different cultures, but they do very similar things, like arguing, worrying about how to find food, enjoying themselves or fighting each other. Some activities which all people do are very important in developing mathematical ideas, and there are six key activities which are important to recognize (more data on these activities are in Bishop, 1991).

Counting. This is to do with answering the question 'How many?', with inventing ways to describe numbers, recording them and calculating with them. Fingers, parts of the body, stones, sticks and string are just some of the objects which are used as counters. One researcher in Papua New Guinea has analyzed more than 800 different counting systems found there!

Locating. This concerns finding your way around, navigating, orienting yourself and describing where things are in relation to one another. Compass direction, stars, the sun, wind, maps, are used by people all over the world to find their ways and position themselves. Many geometrical ideas come from this activity.

Measuring. 'How much?' is a question asked and answered everywhere. Whether it is amounts of cloth, food, land or money which you value, measuring is a skill you need to develop. Parts of the body, pots, baskets, string, beads, coins have all been used as units, as have written and drawn amounts on paper or cloth.

Designing. Shapes are very important in geometry, and these come from designing objects to serve different purposes. The objects can be small and mundane, like a spoon, or symbolically important like a church. Mathematically we are

37

Alan J. Bishop

Figure 3.1 Universal mathematical activities and the Attainment Targets

	NAT1 Using and Applying	NAT2 Number	NAT3 Algebra	NAT4 Shape and Space	NAT5 Handling Data
Counting	✔	✔	✔	—	✔
Locating	✔	—	✔	✔	—
Measuring	✔	✔	—	✔	—
Designing	✔	—	—	✔	—
Playing	✔	—	✔	—	✔
Explaining	✔	✔	✔	✔	✔

interested in the shapes and the designs which are used, together with their different properties.

Playing. Everyone plays and everyone takes playing very seriously! Not all play is important from a mathematical viewpoint, but you only have to think of puzzles, logical paradoxes, rules of games, strategies for winning, guessing, chance and gambling to realize how playing contributes to the development of mathematical thinking.

Explaining. Understanding why things happen the way they do is a universal human quest. In mathematics we are interested in why number patterns happen, why geometric shapes go together, why one result leads to another, why some of the natural world seems to follow mathematical laws, and in the process of trying to symbolize answers to these kinds of 'why' questions. A proof is one kind of symbolic answer, but there are many others, depending on what else you believe to be true.

We can see how these universal activities relate to the NMC by referring to figure 3.1. It shows which activities relate to which Attainment Targets, and therefore how mathematical ideas from other cultures can be introduced into the NMC.

This means, for example, that counting activities from other cultures can be used in NAT1, 2, 3 and 5. In NAT2 it would be appropriate to explore different cycles of finger counting, or different number symbols, to show how numbers are recorded (see, for example, Flegg, 1989, or Crump, 1990). In NAT3 number pattern work with different multiplication algorithms could be carried out (see, for example, Joseph, 1991). In NAT5 the quipu's knotted string system for recording categories of numerical data could be demonstrated (see Ascher and Ascher, 1981).

Similarly, designing activities from different cultures can easily be incorporated into NAT1 and 4 (see Lawlor, 1982). Playing and games from different cultures can be built into NAT1, 3, 5 with magic squares, number combination games, games of chance and strategy (see, for example, Zaslavsky, 1973; Bell and Cornelius, 1988).

At present there are few teaching materials which have been published (for example, City of Birmingham, 1988; Wiltshire Education Authority, 1988; Dodd, 1990, and materials in the SMILE project), so it is largely a matter of teachers introducing different cultural ideas themselves into the classroom work. For example, Gerdes (1988) reports that in Mozambique certain rural house builders use four pieces of rope tied together to lay a rectangle, which is the shape of the house.

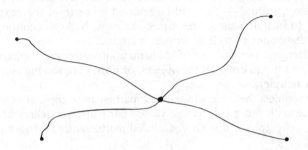

The four pieces of rope are the same length and tied together as shown.

This situation can be used as an introduction to some geometrical features of rectangles, squares and other quadrilaterals:

• Give the pupils some string tied as shown. How do you make a rectangle? Can you make different rectangles?
• How do you know when you have a rectangle?
• What angles are the same?
• What other shapes can you make with these strings?
• What other angles are important?

The situation can be investigated further:

• Suppose the strings are not all equal, what shapes can you now make?
• Suppose you have five strings all the same length. What shapes can you now make?
• What other polygons could be made this way?

Investigations can very easily be stimulated by mathematical activities from different cultures. Here are some stimulating starting points:

Body-counting and finger-counting methods
Circular calendars
Rug-weaving patterns
Basket weaving methods
The quipu
The abacus and the soroban
Gnomons and sun-dials
String games
Body measures (cubits, etc.)
Numerological and astrological prediction
Board game analyses
Magic squares.

There are several principles which are important in using the ideas in this section:

1 Keep as much as possible of the cultural *context* involved with the activity. Usually the meaning and significance of a particular activity is given by its context.
2 Don't just contrast 'old' ideas from other cultures with 'new' ideas from Western culture — this will be referred to again in the next section.
3 Try to include material resources like rugs, baskets, counting frames, in the classroom as well as written material.
4 Collect, and use, pictures of mathematically interesting objects from other cultures if you can't get the objects, or if they are too big (such as a house or a temple).
5 Try to inject these ideas into every mathematical topic as you teach them.
6 Liaise with other subject specialists, particularly teachers of art, design, RE, geography and science. Cultural mathematics is cross curricular too!

Humanizing the Mathematics Curriculum

The second area of development concerns putting 'people' back into the mathematics curriculum. This area reflects a slightly different concern in multicultural awareness for us in mathematics — so often our interest is so concerned with the mathematical ideas themselves that we lose sight of the fact that these ideas are developed by people. Another point is that children are not merely recipients of cultural knowledge, they are recreators and reconstructors of it. Each generation must in some way relive earlier experiences to ensure that the ideas are live ideas contextualized within today's society rather than dead knowledge merely passively received and quickly forgotten.

One important aspect, then, is to put social history into the mathematics curriculum context, particularly to signal the fact that many people from different cultures have made significant contributions to the mathematical knowledge that we now have. Perhaps the first thing to do is to recognize the contributions of different peoples. For example, Joseph's (1991) book on non-European roots of mathematics gives us an excellent set of entries into African, Egyptian, Babylonian, Chinese, Indian and Arabic contributions to the global store of mathematical knowledge. Other useful historical references are Critchlow (1979), Dilke (1987), Ross (1984).

Perhaps these texts don't emphasize the social history quite enough. One book which does this is Swetz (1987), which documents the social and economic conditions prevailing in Italy when the first printed arithmetic book was printed in Treviso in 1478. It also includes the original text, which is a rich source for discussing the development of mathematical knowledge.

Turning now to individual people who have contributed to mathematical knowledge, one should first of all refer readers to John Fauvel's excellent resource guide '*Mathematics through History*' (1990) which contains a wide range of accessible materials, including Coolidge (1990), Mitchell (1987) and Perl (1978).

All of these books contain biographical, social and human aspects, all of which can humanize the process of doing and inventing mathematics. By reading extracts and discussing them children can become aware of why people did what they did, and they themselves can perhaps imagine being a mathematician in that situation. Consider, for example, the issues which can be provoked by reading the following extract concerning the mathematical applications of Archimedes:

> Archimedes in writing to Hiero, who was both a relative and a friend of his, asserted that with any given force it was possible to move any given weight. . .Archimedes chose for his demonstration a three-masted merchantman of the royal fleet, which had been hauled ashore with immense labour by a large gang of men, and he proceeded to have the ship loaded with her usual freight and embarked a large number of passengers. He then seated himself at some distance away and without using any noticeable force, but merely exerting traction with his hand through a complex system of pulleys, he drew the vessel towards him with as smooth and even a motion as if she were gliding through the water. The king was deeply impressed, and recognizing the potential of his skill, he persuaded Archimedes to construct for him a number of engines designed both for attack and defence, which could be employed in any kind of siege warfare.

This Archimedes did, for example:

> At the same time huge beams were run out from the walls so as to project over the Roman ships: some of them were then sunk by great weights dropped from above, while others were seized at the bows by iron claws or by beaks like those of cranes, hauled into the air by means of counter-weights until they stood upright upon their sterns, and then allowed to plunge to the bottom, or else they were spun round by means of wind-lasses situated inside the city and dashed against the steep cliffs and rocks which jutted out under the walls, with great loss of life to the crews.

However:

> . . .for Archimedes, he was a man who possessed such exalted ideals, such profound spiritual vision, and such a wealth of scientific knowledge that, although his inventions had earned him a reputation for almost superhuman intellectual power, he would not deign to leave behind him any writings on his mechanical discoveries. He regarded the business of engineering, and indeed of every art which ministers to the material needs of life, as an ignoble and sordid activity, and he concentrated his ambition exclusively upon those speculations whose beauty and subtlety are untainted by the claims of necessity.

> (From Plutarch's description of the siege of Syracuse in 214 BC, reprinted in Fauvel and Gray, 1987)

One could touch on the status of mathematicians, the applicability of the so-called 'pure' knowledge which they develop, the role of the mathematician in warfare, and generally the personal versus societal tensions felt by those doing fundamental research.

Another vehicle for exploring this area are group projects based on ideas from the histories of mathematicians. As coursework, investigations and projects are becoming more accepted within mathematics teaching at all levels (despite recent Government protestations), it would seem appropriate to include historical topics in the agenda as well, and doing these in small groups can be an involving, engaging and thoroughly worthwhile activity.

Projects have particular merits which are worth emphasizing here:

1   A project allows for group involvement to whatever depth is wanted in a particular situation, and it therefore offers a social personalizing aspect of teaching so often missing from the usual mathematics curriculum.

2   A project encourages the use of a variety of resource materials which stimulate thinking about the importance of the mathematical approach to interpreting and explaining reality. Just to come into contact with the many books, films and video material available can enable mathematical ideas and values to be connected with other aspects of the school curriculum.

3   Involvement with projects encourages activity at a reflective level. Through researching and documenting a societal situation and with the teacher's encouragement to analyze the relationship between the mathematical ideas and the particular societal situation, the learners can begin the process of critical analysis, which is so necessary if the values which mathematics brings to society are not merely to be taken for granted.

Moreover, when producing the report on the project, individual pupils are legitimately allowed to express their personal views and feelings about the mathematical situation they have been researching. This context also gives an opportunity for pupils to evaluate their deeper feelings about mathematical ideas — whether they experience wonder, surprise, awe, beauty, fascination, or boredom. It is rare for such personal views to be allowed to enter the mathematics classroom, yet we know just how strongly held some of those views are.

Several principles are important if the task of humanizing the mathematics curriculum is to be successfully achieved:

• Keep as much as possible of the personal and social aspects of the mathematician's work included in the activity.
• Legitimize pupils' personal views, judgments, feelings about the mathematician's work included in the activity.
• Make the pupils aware of the subjectivity of the biographical accounts, and question the historical record, such as Plutarch's story (see p. 41).
• Liaise with other teachers, particularly history and geography specialists.
• Build up the resources of appropriate books, and videos.

Finally, although there is scope within all the NATs for focusing these projects, perhaps more could be done within NAT1 — 'Using and Applying Mathematics'. That is the area which needs to be more 'peopled' and personalized, if only because that is where decisions are made, and should be analyzed, about the goals and values of applying and using mathematical ideas. At present the NMC in NAT1 gives the impression that no person is involved with the application and use of mathematics. This view needs challenging.

Mathematics Teaching in a Pluralist and Technological Society

The third area of multicultural development in the mathematics curriculum is concerned with the pluralistic nature of the society in Britain today. Our society is extremely diverse, with many kinds of traditions, social structures, living arrangements, economic situations, expectations and values. We can recognize similarities, and we can recognize differences, particularly when there are disparities and inequalities resulting in disadvantage, in discrimination and in disincentive. Does mathematics teaching have any role in this sphere? Does it contribute, by omission or ignorance, to the negative aspects of difference? Can it contribute anything positive to the situation?

Recall that in the early sections of this chapter it was pointed out how, and perhaps why, the NMC completely ignores any of these issues. Indeed there are many mathematicians and mathematics teachers who firmly believe that mathematics has *nothing* to do with society, and that mathematics education *should* have nothing to do with societal issues. It should be clear to the reader where I stand on these points — all the evidence points to the fact that mathematicians are as much a part of their society as anyone else, that mathematics has structured so much of our present technologically-based society that it can be criticized just as much as it can be applauded, and that mathematics is likely to have an increasing influence on society in the future. From that perspective it is irresponsible for a mathematics educator *not* to address the relevant issues in society, particularly in a technological and pluralistic society which also claims to be a democracy.

To a certain extent then, this section builds on the ideas contained in the previous two sections. Culturalizing the mathematics will enable pupils to see mathematics as a certain kind of knowledge, while humanizing it helps to clarify the role people play in its development, that they are individual people living and working in a relationship with their society. In this section then we need to focus more on the issues of the pluralistic society.

The first and most obvious area to consider is how mathematics education can make pupils more aware about the society in which they live, and NAT5 'Handling data' is a good focus for this aspect of mathematics education. Data from different sources can be collected, analyzed and displayed in various ways to help reveal features of society — there is a wealth of statistical data available from a variety of sources. NAT5 also encourages pupils to carry out surveys, which can be done on any topic which interests them; here again is an ideal opportunity to collect data, to sample views and opinions both within their peer-groups and within the wider society. Statistical analyses can reveal similarities and differences which are then open to further analysis.

This kind of activity also lends itself easily to group projects; the points made in the previous section become relevant here also. Many kinds of topics could be suggested for such 'societal' projects, and here are some suggestions:

Home ownership and living conditions	Immigration quotas
The weekly food bill	Opinion polls
Holidays	World food availability
Life insurance	Land ownership
Borrowing money	How far is it to the hospital?
Town planning	

The value of such projects can often be limited by the lack of 'surrounding' and interpretative data. For example, a recent study found that more students from ethnic minority communities went to the former polytechnics than to the more traditional universities. Without a range of surrounding data, such 'findings' become open to wild misinterpretations. It will not of course be possible for pupils to collect huge amounts of data, but by analyzing data which exist already and by collecting a small sample of similar data (if possible), some very interesting similarities and differences can often be revealed. Pupils should not be restricted only to specified projects — they can easily create interesting statistical projects on their own.

The other way in which mathematics education can be a positive force in a pluralistic society draws on its hypothetical nature. Statistical analysis can reveal features of the present situation, but also makes it possible to survey preferences and ideas for future activity. Moreover the data obtained from a present situation can provoke discussion and debate about what future data one would wish to see revealed. For example, comparative data on money borrowing rates could be used, altered, and a simulated exchange situation explored. Simulation techniques can be used in many societal situations; a useful reference is Ruthven (1989). This is an excellent collection of activities on aspects of society such as routes and connections, locations of community facilities, and decisions on business and industrial projects. There are also several simulations involved, and the whole book is loose-leafed and photocopiable.

Another kind of simulation is the Development Game available from agencies such as OXFAM and Christian Aid. Having analyzed data from an economic situation such as coffee production, through the international chain, to coffee buying by a customer, one can then create a simulation, or game, using those data or altered data to enable the pupils to experience the problems of inequality, exploitation and profiteering which emerge. The 'anti-racist mathematics teaching' which Margaret Thatcher claimed she couldn't understand, can use techniques and materials like this to reveal potentially racist practices amongst employers, landlords, etc. It is extraordinary that in a pluralist society which assumes that it is a democracy, such educational aims should be derided and trivialized.

Finally in this section we need to consider how mathematics teaching in the classroom should be accommodated to the diversity of the pupils there. In terms of the focus of this particular book we particularly need to address the issues of cultural, ethnic and linguistic pluralism, although social and economic pluralism should also be recognized. Perhaps the book which contains teaching ideas focusing most on our pluralistic society, with all its conflicts and inequalities, is by Sharan-Jeet Shan and Peter Bailey (1991).

To a large extent, if the advice and suggestions contained in the two previous sections and in the earlier parts of this section are followed, the mathematics classroom will become a social context in which pluralism can be recognized, valued and explored. However there are some specific principles which are important to describe here:

- Even when *content* is specified by the curriculum, the *context* is open to decision and choice. Teachers have the power to select appropriate societal and environmental contexts within which the particular content can be developed. It does not have to be the meaningless nonsense of taps filling baths with the plugs out, but the same mathematical content can be dealt with in bank accounts, market stall economics, small businesses or giant multinationals. There is rich scope here for development in meaningful and relevant contexts.

- Try to localize some situations being mathematically investigated. Even if the context is a meaningful and imaginable one, it can be made more open and effective by using relevant local information. Instead of an imaginary school outing, the pupils can plan one of their own, instead of finding their way on a map of a town or city they don't know, they can use a local map. Instead of artificial store prices they can use real, local prices, and instead of artificial timetables, loan information, house and flat costs, they can use real, local data. Realia from the local environment will tend to be more meaningful, relevant and interesting than either imaginary data or generalized data from a textbook.

- Encourage more small group work in whatever language the pupils wish to use. There is a vast difference between working in one's first or in one's second (third, fourth) language, and the development of language work in mathematics should not just be in English. The 'problems' of being a bilingual learner are now recognized as being seen from the mono-lingual (teacher's) perspective. To be bi- or multi-lingual is of positive value and should be welcomed in the classroom. Multilingual pupils tend to be more sensitive to, and aware of, language issues in mathematics lessons, particularly when their languages are far apart in structure and in vocabulary.

  However, they should also be encouraged to use English in their pres-entations of solutions and conclusions to the class or to the teacher — all pupils need opportunities to do this in our society, and teachers should encourage a range of presentation methods. Single talks to the class, group presentations, posters, pictures, displays, reports, summary sheets, should all be exploited because of their different demands on communication skills.

- Find opportunities to internationalize the situations and data being explored. Statistical projects and simulations can be based in a more global context, rather than just preparing children 'for adult life and employment in Britain in the twenty-first century', as the Working Party report jingoistically stated. We should be preparing them for life in pluralistic Europe and the world. This is important for all children, but it is particularly important in classes containing children from different cultural and ethnic groups, because it is likely that they will already have contact with other countries, and thus have different experiences and knowledge to bring to the class-room situation. As well as being bilingual they may well be bi-cultural and even bi-national. Such situations are also likely to increase rather than decrease in the future as world travel becomes more necessary, easier and cheaper. There may also exist the opportunity for exchanges and other connections with schools in a variety of countries, which can therefore offer different sources for realia, information and perspectives.

Remaining Issues

- The first point to reinforce is that, as there is no statutory requirement for culturalizing the mathematics curriculum, the decision to do this rests with the teachers and the schools themselves. This chapter has demonstrated some of the significant possibilities which exist, but the matter is still one of educated choice, not mandatory requirement. Much will depend on teacher development, on school development and on community development. Communities, parents and others in the wider society can perhaps be better informed as a result of reading this chapter and can exert their influence on schools to represent thoroughly the multicultural dimension in the school's mathematics teaching.

- Tokenism remains as an issue — referring to a minimalist nod in the direction of other cultural references. Tokenism refers both to the limited attention being paid to cultural reference and also to the spirit in which it is done. If the recommendations in this chapter are accepted and practised in the spirit in which they are offered, they will be neither minimalist, patronizing nor tokenist. They will be seen in the wider context of offering equal opportunity to all pupils to engage in mathematical activities which will introduce them to the wider pluralistic and multicultural society in which we all live.

- As another difficulty we can recognize the 'optional extra' syndrome — the argument that the mathematics curriculum is so crowded and there is so much pressure to improve the pupils' skills in the narrowly tested terms of the NMC, that there is no time to do multicultural mathematics *as well*. This chapter is predicated on the assumption that the multicultural dimension is not an optional extra, but should permeate and affect the total mathematics curriculum and its assessment. That, once again, will be a matter for choice by the teachers, the schools and the communities.

- It has been admitted, and it clearly is a problem, that there is a shortage of good teaching resources in this area at present, but there are several reference books from which useful teaching ideas can be drawn; these have been referred to in this chapter. The situation will, however, only change when there is a general awareness of the importance of this provision at all levels, and when publishers begin to recognize that a need is waiting to be met.

- The last point links well with the previous one. Much depends on the political will of those in positions of influence in the wider educational community. The ignorant and reactionary backdrop painted in the early part of this chapter is still there. There is still the feeling and belief among many schools that 'we don't have that problem here'. It was a tragedy that the opportunity offered by the advent of a National Curriculum was not seized, to require mandatorily all subjects to demonstrate the multicultural dimension in all their teaching. The possibilities exist to do this in mathematics, the expertize and the resources are growing, the awareness has been raised, and the curriculum framework makes it feasible. What is needed is the *will* to do this, for the benefit of society at large as well as for the benefits due to all the pupils in schools.

References

ASCHER, M. and ASCHER, R. (1981) *Code of the Quipu*, Ann Arbor, Michigan, University of Michigan Press.

ASCHER, M. (1991) *Ethnomathematics — A Multicultural View of Mathematical Ideas*, Pacific Grove, California: Brooks/Cole.

BELL, R. and CORNELIUS, M. (1988) *Board Games Round the World: A Resource Book for Mathematical Investigations*, Cambridge, Cambridge University Press.

BISHOP, A.J. (1991) *Mathematical Enculturation — A Cultural Perspective on Mathematics Education*, Dordrecht, Holland: Kluwer.

CITY OF BIRMINGHAM (1988) *Mathematics in a Multi-cultural Environment 1*, Birmingham, City of Birmingham Support Services.

COCKCROFT COMMITTEE (1982) *Mathematics Counts*, London, HMSO.

COOLIDGE, J.L. (1990) *The Mathematics of Great Amateurs*, Oxford, Oxford University Press.

CRITCHLOW, K. (1979) *Time Stands Still*, London, Gordon Fraser.

CRUMP, T. (1990) *The Anthropology of Numbers*, Cambridge, Cambridge University Press.

DES AND WELSH OFFICE (1988) *Mathematics for Ages 5–16*, London, HMSO.

DES AND WELSH OFFICE (1989) *Mathematics in The National Curriculum*, London, HMSO.

DILKE, O.A.W. (1987) *Mathematics and Measurement*, London, The British Museum.

DODD, P. (1990) *Mathematics from Around the World: A Multi-cultural Resource Book*, Newcastle-upon-Tyne, Rutherford School.

FAUVEL, J. and GRAY, J. (Eds) (1987) *The History of Mathematics: A Reader*, London, Macmillan.

FAUVEL, J. (1990) *Mathematics Through History: A Resource Guide*, QED Books, York.

FLEGG, G. (1989) *Numbers Through the Ages*, Milton Keynes, Open University Press.

GERDES, P. (1988) 'On culture, geometrical thinking and mathematics education', *Educational Studies in Mathematics*, **12**(2), pp. 137–62.

JOSEPH, G.G. (1991) *The Crest of the Peacock: Non-European Roots of Mathematics*, London, I.B. Taurus.

LAWLOR, R. (1982) *Sacred Geometry*, London, Thames and Hudson.

THE MATHEMATICAL ASSOCIATION (1988) *Mathematics in a Multi-cultural Society*, Leicester, The Mathematical Association.

MITCHELL, M. (1987) *Mathematical History: Activities, Puzzles, Stories and Games*, Reston, Virginia: NCTM.

PERL, T. (1978) *Math Equals: Biographies of Women Mathematicians and Related Activities*, New York, Addison-Wesley.

ROSS, A. (1984) *The Story of Mathematics*, London, Black.

RUTHVEN, K. (1989) *The Maths Factory*, Cambridge, Cambridge University Press.

SHAN, S.J. and BAILEY, P. (1991) *Multiple Factors: Classroom Mathematics for Equality and Justice*, Chester, Trentham Books.

SWETZ, F.J. (1987) *Capitalism and Arithmetic: The New Math of the 15th Century*, La Salle, IL., Open Court Press.

WILTSHIRE EDUCATION AUTHORITY (1988) *Mathematics for All*, County Hall, Bythesea Road, Trowbridge, Wiltshire.

ZASLAVSKY, C. (1973) *Africa Counts*, New York, Lawrence Hill Books.

Additional Bibliography

Other books which contain several examples of mathematical ideas from different cultures are:

BAIN, G. (1977) *Celtic Art: The Methods of Construction*, London, Constable.
Contains many examples of knot-work patterns on borders and panels, spiral designs, key patterns and lettering, together with instructional diagrams.

BOURGOIN, J. (1973) *Arabic Geometrical Pattern and Design*, New York, Dover.
Sheets of examples of patterns found in Islamic art and design work.

CRITCHLOW, K. (1976) *Islamic Patterns, An Analytical and Cosmological Approach*, London, Thames and Hudson.
This text is one of the most thorough analyses of geometric and numerical patterns developed by Islamic mathematicians. Contains an extensive range of diagrams and figures.

FALKENER, E. (1961) *Games Ancient and Oriental and How to Play Them*, New York, Dover.
This is a reprint of the 1892 original which presents Egyptian games, many versions of chess from different countries, draughts and backgammon, together with a very detailed analysis of magic squares.

VON FRANZ, M-L. (1978) *Time*, London, Thames and Hudson.
Multicultural and cross-curricular ideas about time, and its representation.

KOZMINSKY, I. (1985) *Numbers: Their Meaning and Magic*, London, Rider and Co.
First published in 1912, it is a good introduction to numerology and the notions of prophesying by numbers.

PENNICK, N. (1979) *The Ancient Science of Geomancy*.
A readable introduction to this complex area, which relates to geometry, measures and design, but is close to geography as well.

PURCE, J. (1974) *The Mystic Spiral*, London, Thames and Hudson.
Another excellent example of the kinds of materials which should be more available. Inexpensive and impressive in presentation, it shows just how important the spiral is to many cultures.

RESNIKOFF, H.L. and WELLS, R.O. (1984) *Mathematics in Civilization*, New York, Dover.
This is an historical approach to mathematics and culture. Rather traditional and narrow, it does have some good mathematical activities for sixth formers and college students.

RONAN, C.A. (1981) *The Shorter Science and Civilisation in China* **2**, Cambridge, Cambridge University Press.
Part of Needham's classic work in Chinese science and mathematics. This volume presents the mathematical ideas.

SYDENHAM, P.H. (1979) *Measuring Instruments; Tools of Knowledge and Control*, London, Peregrinus.
A beautiful book with many photographs and descriptions of measuring instruments.

WALSHE, J. (1989) *Dates and Meanings of Religious and Other Festivals*, London, Foulsham.
This book is all about calendars in different cultures, with significant dates picked out.

WILLIAMS, K.R. (1984) *Discover Vedic Mathematics*, London, Dinah Grice.
A transcription and excellent reworking of the systems of Vedic mathematics, showing how their mental solutions to simple problems can be generalized to more complex problems.

Chapter 4

English

Anthony Adams

The Cox Report and the English National Curriculum

As a core subject in the National Curriculum in England and Wales, English differs from the other core subjects in a number of respects. Chronologically, it is a year behind the other two core subjects of Mathematics and Science, as the Orders in Council establishing it had not been laid before Parliament until March 1990. This resulted from the necessity of allowing the Kingman Inquiry into the Teaching of English Language to complete its work in 1988 and to report before setting up the English Working Party, under the Chairmanship of Professor Brian Cox, who had himself been a member of the Kingman Committee. Both the Kingman Report (DES, 1988) and The Cox Report (DES, 1989) have consider-able importance for the subject-matter of this chapter and will be referred to frequently in what follows.

However, by the time that Cox came to report, the model for the National Curriculum documents had already been well established along the lines of the TGAT model, and Cox was constrained to produce the now familiar Statements of Attainment with their Ten Levels 'ladder' in relation to each of the Attainment Targets. There is much internal evidence in the Cox Report itself that the Work-ing Group was less than happy about the use of this model. A key phrase is that contained in paragraph 17.25:

> Children do not learn particular written features of language once and for all at a particular stage. Development is recursive. (DES, 1989)

If this position is accepted, then the scaffolding of the TGAT model collapses.

Therefore, on the whole, the Cox Report and the associated Profile Com-ponents and Levels of Attainment, which were accepted by the Secretary of State with few modifications, aimed at as much simplicity as possible. They are much more vague than their counterparts in Mathematics and Science and the Profile Components have been reduced to a bare minimum. Consequently most teachers of English have welcomed the National Curriculum proposals as being essentially enabling rather than prescriptive. So far as it involves multicultural education, therefore, much will depend upon how an individual English teacher and English Departments interpret the wide ranging remit that they have been given by the curriculum. In this chapter I shall argue, however, that, if due weight is given to

the Programmes of Study (which are, of course, no less statutory than the Statements of Attainment), and these are interpreted in the light of the theoretical
concerns of the Cox Report as a whole, attention to multicultural education is
inescapable from the work of the English classroom.

Brian Cox himself frequently reminds us that his Working Group intended
the Report to be read as a whole; those elements which have attained statutory
force make no sense when divorced from the rest of the document. It was a matter
of regret that, because of a political decision, Chapters 15, 16 and 17 (which contain the Statements of Attainment) were published at the beginning of the Report
on tinted paper and, therefore, given a primacy of importance that the Working
Party had not intended. In the first chapter of his own book (Cox, 1991), entitled
'The Political Context', Brian Cox provides a number of important revelations:

> Mr Baker very much disliked the Report. He had wanted a short Report,
> with strong emphasis on grammar, spelling and punctuation, which would
> have been easy for parents to read. In contrast. . .I was most anxious to
> persuade the teaching profession to implement our recommendations with
> good will. . .I understand that Mrs Rumbold also found our Report
> distasteful. . .it seemed that she found repugnant our insistence that a
> child's dialect is not inaccurate in its use of grammar and should be
> respected. (Cox, 1991, p. 11)

This reference to dialect is obviously central to the concerns of multicultural
education, since language and dialect are at the very heart of cultural identity. One
of the areas of the Report around which battle has raged amongst linguists, if not
teachers, has been the issue of Standard English. Again Cox's own comment is
revealing:

> Mrs Thatcher agreed to allow the Report to be sent out for consultation,
> but asked for one alteration. In the attainment targets for Writing we had
> put: 'Use Standard English, where appropriate.' The Prime Minister asked
> for 'where appropriate' to be deleted. I presume she feared — rightly, I
> suspect — that in some schools where children spoke in dialect the teach-
> ers might decide it was never appropriate. (Cox, 1991, p. 12)

These instances emphasize that the foundations of the National Curriculum in
English were fraught with political discord from the beginning, and the controversy surrounding the teaching of English in our schools has shown no sign
of going away in the year subsequent to its promulgation, especially in the field
of the teaching of reading and what 'methods' are best adopted, a matter on which
the National Curriculum, quite properly, gives no real guidance.

Multicultural and Multi-ethnic Education

An acceptance of the spirit of the Cox Report will, therefore, allow us to interpret
the essentially permissive Statements of Attainment in ways that make multicultural
education central to the work of the English classroom. Many would feel that the
concern to introduce multicultural elements should be greatest of all within the
monocultural classroom, whatever the ethnic origins of the pupils.

We ought not to confuse the terms 'multicultural' and 'multi-ethnic'. It is quite possible in a comprehensive school to have a highly multicultural community in terms of social class and economic background in spite of the fact that all the pupils are of the same ethnic origin. It is perhaps unfortunate that the two terms have often come to be used interchangeably. In what follows the major concern is with the multi-ethnic class and school, where there may, of course, be special needs associated with pupils for whom English is not their mother tongue. Many would feel that the National Curriculum is deficient in its recognition of the needs of such pupils, not only in English itself but also in the development of the national assessment tests in other subjects.

The 1991 first unreported run of testing at Key Stage 1 (age 7) has led to many misgivings in this respect, as children from ethnic minorities may well seem to be performing at less than their real level because of language difficulties. The National Curriculum as a whole does not appear to have adequately addressed the needs of bilingual, or multilingual pupils, and this issue is the subject of a critical chapter by Savva (1990) in Harris and Wilkinson, '*A Guide to English in the National Curriculum*', upon which I draw in what follows.

The Cox Report addresses the issue directly in less than three pages (Chapter 10). These suggest that they were the result of compromise within the Committee, and they may be sound enough so far as they go, but their apparent insistence upon the cultural hegemony of Standard English may be seen as in some senses objectionable. Contrast, for example, the following paragraphs which may reveal something of the dilemma at the heart of the Committee's argument:

> We believe that all children should be enabled to attain a full command of the English language, both spoken and written. Otherwise they will be disadvantaged, not only in their study of other subjects, but also in their working life. We note that in this respect we are following the path already trodden by the Swann Committee. They stated firmly: '. . .the key to equality of opportunity, to academic success and, more broadly, to participation on equal terms as a full member of society, is good command of English and the emphasis must therefore we feel be on the learning of English'. The Swann Committee had also noted: '. . .the views expressed very clearly to us at our various meetings with parents from the whole range of ethnic minority groups that they want and indeed expect the education system to give their children above all a good command of English as rapidly as possible'. (DES, 1989, para. 10.5)

> . . .where bilingual pupils need extra help, this should be given in the classroom as part of normal lessons and. . .there may be a need for bilingual teaching support and books and other written material to be available in the pupils' mother tongues until such time as they are competent in English. (DES, 1989, para. 10.10)

Cox further contrasts minority languages in England with the position of Welsh in Wales:

> The positions are not comparable. In Wales, Welsh is an official language and a core subject of the National Curriculum for pupils in Welsh medium schools or classes. . .(DES, 1989, para. 10.9)

In this Cox again follows the lead provided by Swann, which stresses, somewhat dubiously, that Welsh is the national language of the country and, quite rightly, that it is at the heart of its culture and traditions. Yet, an article in *The Independent* (1 August 1991) written by Frank Barrett, himself a Welshman, cogently puts an alternative view:

> The 1967 Welsh Language Act gave Welsh equality with English, thus road signs had to be in Welsh as well as English. There was worse to come. Under the Educational Reform Act of 1988, Welsh was made a compulsory subject in the National Curriculum for every schoolchild in Wales up to the age of 14.

> When there is so much wrong with the Welsh economy, it is curious that so much energy and expense is devoted to the revival of an almost extinct language. A misplaced romanticism is to blame. (Barrett, 1991)

This raises two problems. First, the Swann Report (DES, 1985), whose recommendations are taken over here, was at the time of its publication widely criticized as being too limited in its understanding of the need for recognizing the importance of the child's home language. Second, the contrast with Welsh does not hold totally when we recall that, even within thirty miles of Cambridge, where I am writing this chapter, it is quite possible to find schools where 90 per cent of the 7-year-olds are mother-tongue speakers of Punjabi or Urdu and live in what is predominantly an Asian culture to whom the English language and culture is at least as alien as it would be to Welsh children of their age. (Such a school is not, of course, correctly described as multicultural. Rather it is mono-cultural, though its culture is not that of the dominant white majority.)

It would be folly to deny the need for such children, like their Welsh contemporaries, to have access to English, and ultimately to Standard English, for the reasons well rehearsed by Cox, but their own sense of their cultural identity is not helped by the way in which these reasons are formulated. Rather we may prefer the much more positive affirmation of the Bullock Report of 1975 in its para. 20.5:

> No child should be expected to cast off the language and culture of the home as he crosses the threshold of the school. (DES, 1975)

Most of the theoretical work and practical experience of the past two decades confirms the view that the educational progress of such pupils is likely to be enhanced if there is, alongside increased access to English, continued maintenance and respect for the mother-tongue, which many believe, in spite of Swann, should continue to be used as a language of instruction, particularly in the early years. (For this, see the report of the Linguistic Minorities Project, 1985, and the very helpful practical advice in Harris and Wilkinson, 1990.)

Multicultural Education for All

Apart from the need to provide language support throughout the whole curriculum for those whose mother-tongues are other than English, the question that arises, therefore, is how to implement the National Curriculum in English in essentially monocultural schools, whether their culture be working-class or middle-class, whether it be English, Asian, or Welsh, so as to extend the pupils' range of understanding of, and sympathy with, cultures other than their own.

Here the National Curriculum gives us two important starting points: the approach to the teaching of literature within the Profile Component of Reading, and the concern with the need for knowledge about Language.

We may contrast Cox here with a much earlier, and in its time, very influential report on the teaching of English. This is the Newbolt Report of 1938, significantly entitled, *The Teaching of English in England* (Board of Education, 1938). This report unequivocally took as its starting point the value of English literature as an index of the nature of 'Englishness':

> For English children no form of knowledge can take precedence of a knowledge of English, no form of literature can take precedence of English literature: and. . .*the two are so inextricably connected as to form the only basis possible for a national education.* (Board of Education, 1938, para. 9 — my emphasis)

In spelling out precisely what this means, the Newbolt Report has many objectives in common with Cox, though one feels that Margaret Thatcher, Prime Minister at the time of the Cox Report, and her Secretary of State would have been happier with the Newbolt Report than that produced by Cox and his colleagues. It is, in any case, startling to see how little things have changed so far as the 'orthodox' view is concerned during the intervening years.

Newbolt goes on to say:

> English, we are convinced, must form the essential basis of a liberal education for all English people, and in the earlier stages of education it should be the principal function of all schools of whatever type to provide this basis.
>
> Of this provision the component parts will be, first, systematic training in the sounded speech of standard English, to secure correct pronunciation and clear articulation; second, systematic training in the use of standard English, to secure clearness and correctness both in oral expression and in writing: third, training in reading. Under this last head will be included reading aloud with feeling and expression, the use of books as sources of information and study, and finally, the use of literature as we have already described it, that is, as a possession and a source of delight, a personal intimacy and the gaining of a personal experience, an end in itself and, at the same time, an equipment for the understanding of life. (Board of Education, 1938, para. 13)

Cox, in presenting his Report, was consciously aware that he was setting out, amongst other things, to redefine the nature of the English tradition and to widen this to a concern for a culture that extends far beyond the shores of the British Isles. The Report is a direct counterblast, in this respect, to Newbolt:

> We have taken within our remit literature from all parts of the English speaking world. Children whose families come, for example, from the Caribbean, from countries in Africa or from the Indian sub-continent can greatly enrich discussion about English as a world language and about literature and drama as world concepts. (DES, 1989, para. 10.15)

This is a theme that occurs throughout the Report and it is also encapsulated in Attainment Target 2: Reading from Level 7 onwards, where the example cited in the Orders in Council explicitly calls for reading 'works from a range of cultures, and in translation' in respect of fiction, literary non-fiction and drama, including pre-twentieth century literature.

This is also supported by the Programmes of Study where the point is explicitly made, amongst the statutory provision, that pupils should read 'a variety of genres. . .<which> should include literature from different countries written in English'.

Thus, if teachers are to fulfil the statutory requirements of the National Curriculum, there is no escaping this widening tange of cultural materials that must be subsumed within the English programme. There is, of course, no reason why this should wait until Level 7, and, indeed, every reason why it should not. Most infant and junior schools nowadays make a good deal of use of picture books, folk-tale and fairy stories, especially in the form of oral story-telling. Increasingly teachers are drawing upon a wealth of different cultures to inform this work, and one of the great publishing achievements of recent years has been the explosion of high quality picture books drawn from an ever-widening range of cultures.

A later chapter in this book (Chapter 16) provides an excellent case-study of the kind of imaginative teaching which can bring together teachers and pupils working collaboratively across cultures, ethnic backgrounds and age phase. Such collaborative teaching may provide one of the best means of ensuring continuity within the demands of the National Curriculum. (For this see also: *Collaboration and Writing*, Styles, 1989).

There remains, however, still more to be done of a positive nature. Modern post-structuralist approaches to the analysis of text enables well-established texts to be subjected to critical scrutiny from a variety of perspectives, be they Marxist, feminist, anti-racist, or whatever. Griffiths has shown in *Literary Theory and English Teaching* (Griffiths, 1987) how such a seemingly simple work as *The Adventures of Tom Sawyer*, by Mark Twain, can be explored through such analysis and, in so doing, opens up ways in which teachers can introduce multicultural concerns within their teaching of classic texts. Similarly, Sarland, in a recent book, *Young People Reading: Culture and Response* (Sarland, 1991), shows how working-class pupils can be engaged with books by widening the 'canon' of what is used in the classroom to include such texts as James Herbert's *The Rats* and popular videos.

In a pluralist society, in order to achieve the lofty and laudable aims of the Newbolt Report to ensure through reading 'a possession and a source of delight, a personal intimacy and the gaining of a personal experience, an end in itself and, at the same time, an equipment for the understanding of life', the canon of established work needs to be extended in this way to ensure the inclusion of material drawn from a wider range of cultures of different ethnic origins. (Some useful practical advice for teachers in respect to both the selection and treatment of such material will be found in Dabydeen, 1988 and Gunner, 1984.)

In the section on Literature in his own commentary on the Cox Report, Brian Cox points to some of the criticisms that he has received for seemingly arguing for a pluralist rather than a purely 'English' culture and asks pertinently:

> Only so much time is available in the classroom. Should we insist that children spend all their time with a literature whose main non-white

representatives are Othello, Man Friday in *Robinson Crusoe* and the savages in Conrad's *Heart of Darkness*? (Cox, 1991, p. 71)

He also quotes Robert Scholes as arguing in *Salmagundi* that:

> . . .in England the desire for an 'English' tradition is said to hide a deep fear of our present multi-cultural society, a determination to maintain our present class structure, the hierarchies of power which give Oxbridge dons their privileged and cushioned existence. (Cox, 1991, p. 71)

To this Oxbridge don, at least, it seems that there is much truth in this position and that the need to replace the tradition of 'English literature' by that of 'literature in English' is of paramount importance to encourage the growth of readers in a pluralist society.

The references above to Defoe and Conrad are also illuminating. For historical reasons much of the literature of the past will appear to be racist in its attitudes. Even Shakespeare is not totally to be exempted from this. Apart from Othello, there is also Caliban in *The Tempest*, and the character of Shylock is ambivalent to say the least. It is often suggested that the inclusion of Shakespeare as the one named compulsory author in the National Curriculum can be attributed to the evidence given by Rex Gibson, Director of the 'Shakespeare in Schools' Project. The pioneering methods of teaching Shakespeare in the classroom devised by Gibson and his colleagues show, amongst other things, how Shakespeare can be taught so as to raise issues of racism and also be taught from a non-racist standpoint. We are still only at the beginning of discovering how much of the canon, the pre-twentieth century literature called for by the National Curriculum, can be taught and reinterpreted in such ways. (For an up-to-date discussion of the application of these ideas to the practical teaching of Shakespeare in both primary and secondary classrooms see Leach, 1992.)

An earlier phase of thinking about anti-racist approaches to reading in the classroom tended to place the emphasis upon the negative aspects of anti-racism. Thus we have seen the throwing out of the classroom cupboards of *Little Black Sambo* by Helen Bannerman and grave doubts about the presentation of the Oompa-Loompas in Roald Dahl's *Charlie and the Chocolate Factory*. I doubt whether much is achieved by this or whether such books really fall within the category of 'racist'. We must beware in matters of race and gender issues alike of a concentration on the surface features only, paying far too much attention to the superficialities of the texts we puritanically attack. At its worst this leads to an intolerance which results in the defacing, then the rewriting, and, finally, the burning of the books to which we object. There is enough recent history that demonstrates where, ultimately, this leads. The cause of cultural pluralism is not best served by a self-righteous intolerance.

A more valuable approach is to seek ways in which we can use books to establish positive attitudes to other races and cultures. In his recently published book, *Reading Against Racism*, Emrys Evans (1992) draws upon a wide range of cultural traditions to show how this can be achieved and in so doing, provides a useful focus for ways in which the intentions of the Attainment Targets in Reading can step off the pages of the National Curriculum and into the practical activity of the classroom. It should be appreciated that, if this is done, something revolutionary will have happened to the English curriculum in our schools. Certainly the group of academics, teachers of university English, who got together on 22 February 1991 at Birkbeck College, London, to affirm traditional values in English teaching, did so because they were fearful that English studies, both in terms of the canon and the traditional nature of texts and their analysis, were under threat from the radical approaches of English in the National Curriculum.

Knowledge about Language

Earlier the links between the Report of the Kingman Inquiry (DES, 1988) and that of the Cox Working Group (DES, 1989) have been mentioned. Kingman, it has been alleged, was set up at the direct intervention of the Prime Minister, Margaret Thatcher 'to undo the harm done by the Bullock Committee', itself set up when she was Secretary of State at the Department of Education and Science in response to a now largely repudiated scare report on *The Trend of Reading Standards* (Start and Wells, 1972). Bullock produced what many feel to be one of the most progressive reports on the teaching of English this century; amongst its many recommendations was a carefully researched argument against any return to the teaching of traditional grammar in school. Since the 1960s teachers of English, in the wake of considerable evidence from research (for a summary of the research findings on this issue see Sawyer, Watson and Adams, 1989, pp. 72, 73 and Watson, 1987, pp. 157, 158), have resisted any notion of the return to formal grammar teaching. The position was clouded for a while by the publication of the HMI Report, *English 5–16*, No. 1 in the *Curriculum Matters* series (DES, 1984). This, for the first time in many years, revived the idea of Language as a separate component of the English curriculum, proposing areas of linguistic knowledge in which pupils should receive instruction. All manner of alarm bells were set ringing amongst English teachers who feared this might mark a return to formal grammar teaching. In consequence, the response to this publication was almost entirely negative; and HMI produced a second edition entitled, *Curriculum Matters 1: English 5–16* (DES, 1986), which was virtually a repudiation of the original statement. However, Language had now been very firmly placed upon the agenda and the Kingman Inquiry was set with the following terms of reference:

1 To recommend a model of the English language, whether spoken or written, which would:
   i.   serve as a basis of how teachers are trained to understand how the English language works;
   ii. inform professional discussion of all aspects of English teaching.
2 To recommend the principles which should guide teachers on how far and in what ways the model should be made explicit to pupils, to make them conscious of how language is used in a range of contexts.
3 To recommend what, in general terms, pupils need to know about how the English language works and in consequence what they should have been taught, and be expected to understand, on this score, at ages 7, 11 and 16. (DES, 1988, p. 73)

Somewhat to the dismay of then Prime Minister (Margaret Thatcher) the Kingman Committee, which contained a large number of eminent linguisticians, refused to recommend any return to formal grammar teaching in schools. (For an insider's view of this see Cox (1991) p. 3.)

It is against this background that the National Curriculum has been produced. In the light of the experience of Kingman, one of the most significant elements in Cox has been the inclusion of an element, Knowledge About Language (KAL), as an integral part of the National Curriculum in English.

With characteristic sensitivity to the feelings of teachers, Cox avoided including Knowledge About Language as a separate Profile Component, but Chapter 6 of the Report brings together those elements of Knowledge About Language which inform the Attainment Targets elsewhere. They now have statutory force. This is of the greatest importance. It places Language and its study, based upon the latest linguistic principles and knowledge (as evidenced in Kingman), firmly upon the English teaching agenda. Also, subsequent to Kingman, there was a heavily subsidized programme, Language in the National Curriculum (LINC) intended to disseminate modern linguistic theory to teachers across the whole curriculum. Unfortunately, it now appears that the excellent work done by the LINC co-ordinators under their Director, Dr Ronald Carter of the University of Nottingham, was suppressed by the Department of Education and Science because LINC did not say what the Government wished. The report was, however, subsequently published in an amended form by Hodder and Stoughton (LINC, 1992).

This brings us back to Knowledge About Language. There are, for example, two ways of looking at Standard English. One is the view quite rightly taken by the Cox Working Group that anyone in our society without access to this particular dialect of English is likely to be at a social and employment disadvantage (DES, 1989, para. 4.36); the other, equally true, and certainly espoused by one of the most distinguished linguists on the Working Group, is that to teach Knowledge About Language is also teach about the class-based nature of British society. This would entail teaching, for example, that Standard English is not only the standard of English as an international language. . . . powerful ruling elite. It would also entail teaching the generally accepted view of linguists that no one language or dialect is any 'better' than another though there may be occasions when a particular dialect (say Standard English) may be more appropriate than another, which is, of course, the whole basis of the Cox Committee's recommendations.

If we now place all this within the context of multicultural education, we can see that Knowledge About Language is potentially one of the most radical elements within the National Curriculum in English. It is also one of the areas where, because of their degree background (which in most cases will have been wholly in English literature, often with a narrowly defined canon of texts), many teachers of English feel least confident.

There is all too little time to do much about this in initial teacher training and this is one reason why, in my own in-service work with teachers, I have found the area of Knowledge About Language one of the most fruitful starting points. To tackle such issues as the role of Standard English and the nature of accents and dialects (as well as the differences between them) is an excellent way to begin to open up awarenesses about a variety of issues, not least that of multi-cultural education. To begin to raise these linguistic matters with teachers is inevitably to reveal the passions with which linguistic views are held and to expose a whole variety of prejudices and assumptions that underlie them. At the same time teachers find discussion and argument about language fascinatingly interesting and it provides them with material they can readily take into their classrooms and use with children of virtually any age.

In this work one area that may prove especially fruitful is to bring together teachers of English and other languages to work together on common elements of interest in the languages curriculum. Kingman explicitly proposed the need for some joint work in English and other languages in initial teacher education. This view is also supported in Cox (DES, 1989) and in Harris (Harris and Wilkinson, 1990), the advice given to the government by the Modern Languages Working Group. In one school in which I have worked recently we prepared for a whole day's work on language issues with the Year 7 classes by working as a group of lecturers and teachers drawn from English, Modern Languages and Special Needs. Normally locked into the compartmentalized world of subject specialisms of most secondary schools, this was the first time this group had got together for extended professional discussion of this kind.

The day began with the whole of Year 7 playing a well-known language game, 'Our Word House' (for a description of this see Fisher and Hicks, 1985, pp. 42–47), which enabled active exploration of the etymology of the English language and introduced the notion of how all languages 'borrow' words from other languages and cultures. This immediately led into a discussion of the link between language and culture — the fact that we have a number of words of Scandinavian origin in our language because of the Viking Conquests and also words of Indian origin because of our conquest of India, for example. It also became possible to explore the range of new words brought into the language with the coming of immigrants from the new Commonwealth and as a result of new technological development.

The point here, explicitly linked in our planning with several of the English Attainment Targets in the National Curriculum, was to establish some awareness of the history of the language and the intricate connection between language and culture.

After playing the game on this occasion and others, we have found it rewarding to teach the pupils languages with which most of them are unlikely to be acquainted, preferably involving a different writing system. We have, for example, used Bengali, Urdu and Russian in this way. Again, knowledge about language is being gained and, if one is fortunate enough to be working in a school where there are mother-tongue users of a language like Bengali, these pupils can be pressed into service as helpers in the classroom. On one occasion, when I was working in this way, the status of such pupils immediately rose, as the members of the class with English as their mother-tongue found that their classmates produced fluent Bengali script, whilst they found the necessary motor skills very difficult to acquire.

Of course these are only 'tasters'. Although some users of English as a first language may go on take GCSE in Bengali or Urdu, these will remain a small minority. But it is valuable for all to realize that there are many different writing systems, and that all languages have their own rules and complexities, whilst sharing also in the commonality of language itself. (An invaluable source of reference for teachers here is *The Cambridge Encyclopedia of Language*, Crystal, 1987.)

From work of this kind we have frequently gone on to explore the language of gesture and come to a recognition that the same gesture may mean different things in different cultures. It comes as something of a shock to realize, for example, that even sign language (as used by the deaf) is by no means universal but also has different dialects of its own. This leads again naturally enough to work on accent and dialect and this can, in turn, lead into discussion of Standard English and its unique role as a particular dialect form.

This is only one illustration of the way in which a course of Knowledge About Language can be built into a whole programme of work extending over the period of schooling (ideally it should begin long before Year 7, of course) providing an opportunity for exploring cultural diversity through that of linguistic diversity. One hopes that in meeting the Attainment Targets of both the English and the Modern Languages curricula schools will be able to devise their own work programmes which will enrich pupils' learning in this way. Certainly, in the wake of the National Curriculum, a number of books are beginning to appear on the market to help them. (In addition to the books cited in the text of this article the following will be found especially useful: Raleigh, 1981; Garson, *et al.*, 1989, and, as a textbook, Seely, 1991.)

The Way Forward

Finally, in the English curriculum, much stress is placed upon the value of providing real purposes and audiences for pupils' work. If these audiences can be drawn from widely diverse cultures, the narrowness of much of what we do in school can be ameliorated. The case study in Chapter 16, already referred to above, is one example of what can be undertaken. I have been struck, too, by a description of some pioneering work carried out over a period of time in the Bradford and Humberside LEAs in terms of what they call 'cross-cultural, inter-class "twinning"'. Over a sustained period they built up relationships between very different schools in the two LEAs between both pupils and staff involving exchanges of work and visits so as to provide an enriched immersion into different cultures and experiences. Subsequently the two Authorities produced a report based upon their experience. This is probably no longer available since it was in no way intended as a formal publication but it is worth quoting at some length what the report had to say about their aims.

It will be seen that many of the Attainment Targets in the English National Curriculum can be effectively delivered through such work:

Aims

The advantages of a sustained cross-cultural link between two classes of children are many and various. The aims of such a project may be summarised under three main headings:- Language/Communication, Multi-cultural and Social.

Language/Communication

1 To provide a wider, more meaningful audience for children's communications;
2 To provide a variety of language models and to encourage a variety of forms of communication i.e. oral, written and visual, and an appreciation of, and skill in, using modern technology through media work and the use of computers;

3   To encourage an awareness of, and response in, language modes appropriate to differing purposes and contexts, e.g. necessity for drafting, development of letter-writing, scripting and compiling a programme;

4   To involve children in co-operative group work which offers opportunities for taking control of planning, for decision making and for exploratory talk;

5   To high-light the need to use language clearly and with appropriate detail, by providing an audience at a distance so that assumptions and experiences cannot be presumed to be held in common;

6   To generate enthusiasm for writing by ensuring the reward of receiving a reply and maintaining this over a substantial period of time.

Multi-cultural

7   To establish the exchanges as being between children who are equal partners in the sharing of information, ideas and experiences;

8   To be fully aware of the strong possibility of encountering prejudiced, stereo-typed and racist attitudes in both children and adults and to be committed and prepared to address these issues;

9   To help to develop the children's awareness and understanding both of the diversity of cultures within British society and of the similarities which exist between them;

10   To help children to develop an openness and responsiveness to cultural diversity by positively promoting bi-lingualism and language awareness;

11   To facilitate and encourage inter-ethnic friendships between individuals and groups.

Social

12   To help children to undertake the roles of both host and guest to other children, taking responsibility for the social and emotional well-being of others;

13   To help to develop the ability to empathise;

14   By means of visits and shared expeditions to broaden the children's experience of, and confidence in, new places and situations;

15   To encourage and widen parental participation in, and awareness of, school activities and thereby increase community involvement;

16   To raise perceptions of the status and value of one's own culture and environment by sharing positive aspects of it with others.

(Bradford-Humberside Link Project 1982–1988)

There is a brief reference here to the use of media work and computers. We have found that our own experiments in getting pupils to work with tape and slide photographs or to communicate using electronic mail have proved very fruitful. These approaches can again be directly related to the demands of the National Curriculum.

One thing that has been found especially effective in working with two monocultural schools, one all white, the other all Asian, has been to get the pupils to exchange letters, followed by slides of themselves and their local environment.

It comes as something of a shock for them to realize that, until they see the photographs, they may not even be aware whether it is a boy or a girl to whom they are writing, a realization which can lead, of course, to further work on different naming systems in different cultures and different parts of the world.

The coming of Information Technology into the schools has enabled these links to be ever more widely established. I have come across work linking pupils in a school in Sydney, Australia, and Dublin, Ireland; work of this kind is continually being developed. It should become increasingly possible for a global culture to become the context for talking and listening, reading and writing in our classrooms.

What is needed to move schools and teachers further in the directions explored in this chapter is the development of a series of strategies which will enable them to take the initial steps in such work with reasonable confidence. The particular examples described in the latter part of this chapter offer illustrations of such strategies in action.

However all this has to be done against a continuing background of uncertainty about the future of English in the National Curriculum. The tensions between the 'professional' view of English teaching and the 'common-sense' view of government ministers which has been the background to much of the argument advanced in this chapter continues even as the material is finally being prepared for publication. As recently as 17 July 1992 the *Times Educational Supplement* reported that the National Curriculum Council had advised the Education Secretary that 'the English curriculum should be revised to define the kind of books, plays and poetry all pupils should study and to emphasise the importance of spelling, grammar and handwriting'. The same article cites the reservations felt by such professional bodies as the National Association for the Teaching of English (NATE) and the National Association of Advisers in English (NAAE) about the need to introduce revisions to the English National Curriculum just as it appears to be working well in the schools.

English has proved to be one of the most politically sensitive areas in the National Curriculum as a whole and it is likely to continue to be so. Just as a person's sense of identity is linked with his or her use of language so a sense of national identity is linked with the attitude that prevails towards national language and cultural inheritance and transmission through literature. Within the past three years we have seen the political importance ascribed to minority national languages in many parts of Europe. In the same way the debate that Cox opened up about both language and the definition of the literary canon is a debate that has important political dimensions for the way in which we construct the notion of 'Englishness'. Whether this is to be seen in narrowly exclusive or widely inclusive terms is also central to the debate about multi-cultural education making 'English' of fundamental importance to the overall topic of this book.

References and Further Reading

BARRETT, F. (1991) 'Let's Not Waste our Energy Talking Welsh', in *The Independent*, London, 2 August 1991.

BOARD OF EDUCATION (1938) *The Teaching of English in England* (The Newbolt Report), London, HMSO.

BRADFORD-HUMBERSIDE LINK PROJECT 1982–1988 (1988) *Inter-School Cross-Cultural Links*, Bradford, City of Bradford Metropolitan Council.

CARTER, R. (1990) *Knowledge about Language and the Curriculum*, London, Hodder & Stoughton.

COX, B. (1991) *Cox on Cox: An English Curriculum for the 1990s*, London, Hodder & Stoughton.

CRYSTAL, D. (1987) *The Cambridge Encyclopedia of Language*, Cambridge, University Press.

DEPARTMENT OF EDUCATION AND SCIENCE (1975) *A Language for Life* (The Bullock Report), London, HMSO.

DEPARTMENT OF EDUCATION AND SCIENCE (1984) *Curriculum Matters 1: English from 5–16*, London, HMSO.

DEPARTMENT OF EDUCATION AND SCIENCE (1985) *Education for All* (The Swann Report), London, HMSO.

DEPARTMENT OF EDUCATION AND SCIENCE (1986) *Curriculum Matters 1: English from 5–16*, second edition (incorporating responses), London, HMSO.

DEPARTMENT OF EDUCATION AND SCIENCE (1988) *Report of the Committee of Inquiry into the Teaching of English Language* (The Kingman Report), London, HMSO.

DEPARTMENT OF EDUCATION AND SCIENCE (1989) *English from ages 5–16* (The Cox Report), London, HMSO.

DEPARTMENT OF EDUCATION AND SCIENCE (1990) *National Curriculum: Modern Foreign Languages Working Group*, Initial Advice (The Harris Report), London, HMSO.

DABYDEEN, D. (1988) *A Handbook for Teaching Caribbean Literature*, London, Heinemann Education.

EVANS, E. (1992) *Reading Against Racism*, Buckingham, Open University Press.

FISHER, S. and HICKS, D. (1985) *World Studies 8–13: A Teacher's Handbook*, Edinburgh, Oliver and Boyd.

GARSON, S. *et al.*, (1989) *The World Languages Project*, London, Hodder and Stoughton.

GRIFFITHS, P. (1987) *Literary Theory and English Teaching*, Milton Keynes, Open University Press.

GUNNER, E. (1984) *A Handbook for Teaching African Literature*, Oxford, Heinemann International.

HARRIS, J. and WILKINSON, J. (1990) *A Guide to English Language in the National Curriculum*, Cheltenham, Stanley Thornes.

HOULTON, D. (1985) *All Our Languages: A Handbook for the Multilingual Classroom*, London, Edward Arnold.

JOYNER, J. (1989) *Materials for Bilingual Learners in English Classes*, London, English and Media Centre.

LEACH, S. (1992) *Shakespeare in the Classroom*, Buckingham, Open University Press.

LINC (1992) *Language in the National Curriculum-Materials for Professional Development*, London, Hodder & Stoughton.

LINGUISTIC MINORITIES PROJECT (1985) *The Other Languages of England*, London, Routledge and Kegan Paul.

RALEIGH, M. (1981) *The Languages Book*, London, English and Media Centre.

SARLAND, C. (1991) *Young People Reading: Culture and Response*, Buckingham, Open University Press.

SAWYER, W., WATSON, K. and ADAMS, A. (1989) *English Teaching from A–Z*, Milton Keynes, Open University Press.

SAVVA, H. (1990) *The Multilingual Classroom*, in HARRIS, J. and WILKINSON, J., *A Guide to English Language in the National Curriculum*, Cheltenham, Stanley Thornes.

SEELY, J. (1991) *Language Live!*, Oxford, Heinemann Educational.

START, K. and WELLS, S. (1972) *The Trend of Reading Standards*, Slough, NFER.

STIBBS, A. (1987) *Teaching English and Language in a Multicultural Society*, Sheffield, National Association for the Teaching of English.

STYLES, M. (1989) *Collaboration and Writing*, Milton Keynes, Open University Press.

WATSON, K. (1987) *English Teaching in Perspective*, Milton Keynes, Open University Press.

Chapter 5

Science

Michael J. Reiss

The cessation of motion is due to the opposing force...If there is no opposing force...the motion will never stop. This is as true as that an ox is not a horse

in the *Mo Ching*, the collection of writings of a school of philosophers in China in the third or fourth century BCE. (quoted by Temple, 1991, p. 161)

Introduction

The last ten years have seen an increasing acknowledgment that the science taught in schools is narrow in its approach and one-sided in its implicit assumptions. During the 1980s it was realized that most school science was essentially 'male' in focus, teaching style, content and assessment. It is generally agreed that this has been a factor contributing to the relatively small numbers of girls opting to choose physical sciences at 'O' level/CSE/GCSE. By now it is increasingly being accepted that most school science is not only male but Western. The model of science held, the way science is taught and the specific content matter are all too often restricted in outlook.

The consequences of a narrow, male, Western view of school science are far reaching and of two main sorts. First, many pupils feel alienated or marginalized from science and drop it once they can. Secondly, the minority that continue science into the sixth form or its equivalent continue to learn an impoverished form of science. A valid science education for a pluralist society would encourage and permit greater equality of standing between science as carried out and perceived by different cultural, ethnic and religious groups. It can be contrasted with the present prevalent model of science education which leads to non-Western non-atheistic science simply being ignored (Ditchfield, 1987; A.S.E. Multicultural Education Working Party, 1990; Reiss, in press).

In this chapter I begin by asking who scientists are and what science is. A consideration of the scientific method leads into an examination of the relevance of the history of science to school teaching. I then examine to what extent the Science National Curriculum hinders or helps attempts to arrive at a more balanced and less parochial science curriculum. Finally, I discuss the relationship between multicultural and anti-racist science teaching and give some specific suggestions for classroom practice in the teaching of particular topics.

Who are Scientists?

A few months before writing this, I happened to see the new Royal Mail stamps titled 'Scientific Achievements' on sale in my local post office (Date of issue: 5 March 1991). If you haven't seen them, or thought much about them, spend a few moments imagining what you might expect to see on four stamps under the umbrella title Scientific Achievements.

Well, whatever you think, the Royal Mail produced four stamps under this heading with the captions *Faraday — electricity*, *Babbage — Computer*; *Radar — Watson-Watt* and *Jet engine — Whittle*. I find it difficult to imagine a narrower conception of what science is and who does it (Reiss, 1991). The image seems to be that real science is hard physics, with military applications, done by males who were white and worked on their own between about 1820 and 1940.

No wonder so many students drop science at school as soon as they have the chance. As ten years of consistent research findings by the CLIS (Children's Learning in Science) group at Leeds and other studies have told us, children come to school science lessons with clear impressions of what science is, how it operates and who does it (Driver, Guesne and Tiberghien, 1985; Osborne and Freyberg, 1985; Scott, Dyson and Gater, 1987). There is a limit to what science teachers can realistically be expected to achieve in terms of challenging social perceptions and changing received wisdom.

It seems sad that the Royal Mail can produce a set of stamps that portray such a biased view of science. One hopes that the next set of stamps to feature scientists will convey the notion that women do science, that science didn't start in the nineteenth century and finish around the time of the Second World War, that it isn't a Western construct, that it is done by people working in groups and that it permeates every area of life.

Countless examples could be given of the way we are all, including students in school, bombarded with messages about who scientists are, but one more will suffice. The BBC World Service recently broadcast a major series called 'They Made our World'. To quote from the book that accompanies the series '[The series was] broadcast around the world in 26 episodes Autumn 1990–Spring 1991. It features a gallery of great scientists, engineers, inventors and thinkers who contributed massively to the development of world (sic) we live in today' (Hamilton, 1991). One might have thought that a World Service Series would at least have striven to be international in flavour, but the list of chapter titles is so distinctive that it is worth giving in full:

Sir Francis Bacon (1561–1626)
Sir Isaac Newton (1643–1747)
Joseph Priestley (1733–1804)
Antoine-Laurent Lavoisier (1743–1794)
Michael Faraday (1791–1867)
James Clerk Maxwell (1831–1879)
Sir Charles Lyell (1797–1875)

Charles Darwin (1809–1882)
Father Gregor Mendel (1822–1895)
Edward Jenner (1749–1823)
Louis Pasteur (1822–1895)
Sir Alexander Fleming (1881–1955)
James Watt (1736–1819)
George and Robert Stephenson (1781–1848) (1803–1859)
Sir Alexander Graham Bell (1847–1922)
Thomas Alva Edison (1847–1931)
Wilbur and Orville Wright (1867–1912) (1871–1948)
Henry Ford (1863–1947)
Professor Wilhelm Röntgen (1845–1923)
Guglielmo Marconi (1874–1937)
John Logie Baird (1888–1946)
Leo Hendrik Baekeland (1863–1944)
Alan Turing (1912–1954)
Albert Einstein (1879–1955)
Ernest Rutherford (1871–1937)
Robert Oppenheimer and the Manhattan Project (1904–1967)

Of the twenty-eight people listed, none is a woman and none comes from outside Western Europe and the USA. Now, the point I wish to make is that who a great scientist is largely depends on one's point of view. There are no absolute or universal criteria by which scientific excellence can be judged. This means that the Royal Mail and the BBC World Service are guilty of sins of omission, rather than of comission. And, of course, all that such institutions do is to reflect society's view of who scientists are. Powerful organizations such as the BBC and the Post Office both reflect and perpetuate myths.

The effect that all this has can be seen by asking children to draw or describe a scientist. The results are consistent (Ward, 1986; Wyvill, 1991; Solomon, pers. comm.). Most scientists are portrayed as being white, male, middle-aged to old and wearing white coats. To determine whether or not this is a distortion or an accurate reflection of the community of scientists, we need to go beyond the question 'Who are scientists?' and ask 'What is science?'

What is Science?

The popular view of what science is and how it proceeds probably goes something like this:

> Science consists of a body of knowledge about the world. The facts that comprise this knowledge are derived from accurate observations and careful experiments that can be checked by repeating them. As time goes on, scientific knowledge steadily progresses.

Such a view persists, not only among the general public, but among science teachers and scientists, despite the fact that it is held by most historians of science, philosophers of science, sociologists of science and science educationalists to be, at best, simplified and misleading and, at worst, completely erroneous (Collins, 1985; Latour, 1987; Fensham, 1988; Woolgar, 1988; Wellington, 1989; Longino, 1990; Harding, 1991).

It is not too much of a caricature to state that science is widely regarded as *the* way to truth. It is generally assumed that the world 'out there' exists independently of the particular scientific methodology used to study it. The advance of science then consists of scientists discovering eternal truths that exist independent of them and of the cultural context in which these discoveries are made. All areas of life are presumed amenable to scientific inquiry. Truth is supposed to emerge unambiguously from experiment like Pallas Athene, the goddess of wisdom, springing mature and unsullied from the head of Zeus.

This view of science is mistaken for at least the following reasons:

1 Scientists have to choose on what to work. These choices are controlled partly by their background as individuals and partly by the values of the society in which they live and work. Most scientific research is not pure but applied. In particular, approximately half of all scientific research funding is provided for military purposes. To give just one specific example of the way society determines on what scientists should work: the last ten years have seen a drastic reduction in Great Britain of research into systematics, taxonomy and nomenclature (the classification, identification and naming of organisms). This is a direct result of changes in government funding which now, for instance, requires the Natural History Museum in London, the major UK centre for such research, to generate much of its own income. As a result, the number of scientists working there in these disciplines has more than halved, as such scientists generate very little income.

Now, my point is not specifically to complain at the demise of systematics, taxonomy and nomenclature in the UK, but to point out that society and individual scientists have to choose on what to work. To a very large extent that choice is not determined on scientific criteria, but by political machinations and by the quirks of funding bodies.

2 Scientists do not discover the world out there as it is. Rather they approach their topic of study with preconceptions. There is no such thing as an impartial observation. In the classroom this is seen to be the case every time a group of pupils is asked, for the first time, to draw some cells under the microscope. It isn't possible until you know what to draw. Unless you know that a leaf of pondweed consists of numerous small brick-like structures, all you can see is a mass of green with lines and occasional air bubbles. Expecting a child to draw regular epidermal cells is like expecting Michelangelo, if transported to the twentieth century, to appreciate a Picasso, a Mondrian or a Lichtenstein. The human mind needs to organize what it perceives through its senses.

Instances where we can look back and see how scientists have unconsciously interpreted what they have seen in the light of their cultural heritage are legion. One must suffice. In his book *Metaphors of Mind* Robert Sternberg points out that much of the present confusion surrounding the concept of intelligence stems from the variety of standpoints from which the human mind can be viewed (Sternberg, 1990; see also Eysenck and Kamin, 1981; Gould, 1981). The geographic metaphor is based on the notion that a theory of intelligence should provide a map of the mind. This view dates back at least to Gall, an early nineteenth century German anatomist and perhaps the most famous of phrenologists. Gall investigated the topography of the head, looking and feeling for tiny variations in the shape of the skull. According to Gall, a person's intelligence was to be discerned in the pattern of their cranial bumps. A second metaphor, the computational metaphor, envisions the mind as a computing device and analogizes the processes of the mind to the operations of a computer. Other metaphors discussed by Sternberg include the biological metaphor, the epistemological metaphor, the anthropological metaphor, the sociological metaphor and the systems metaphor. The point is that what scientists see and the models they construct to mirror reality depend very much on their point of view.

3 Once a scientist or group of scientists have discovered something or produced a new model to interpret a phenomenon, it is necessary for their work to be disseminated in some form, usually through publication. Getting work published, read, cited and recognized depends greatly on the personalities of individuals involved and on what society values.

As a single example of the importance of society's world view, consider the acceptance of William Harvey's ideas on the circulation of the blood. Although the circulation of the blood had been established in China by the second century BC at the latest, in Europe the idea was proposed by Michael Servetus (1546), Realdo Colombo (1559), Andrea Cesalpino (1571) and Giordano Bruno (1590). These men had read of the circulation of the blood in the writings of an Arab of Damascus, al-Nafis (died 1288) who himself seems to have obtained the idea from China (Temple, 1991). Harvey published his 'discovery' in 1628. It is possible that the early seventeenth century accounts of a huge diversity of pumping engines for mine drainage and water supply caused the scientific community and general public to be in an appropriate frame of mind to accept the notion of the heart as a mechanical pump (cf. Russell, 1988a).

4 The notion as to what constitutes science differs over time and between cultures (Ingle and Turner, 1981; Hiatt and Jones, 1988). Attempts by certain historians and philosophers of science to identify a distinctive scientific method which demarcates science absolutely from other disciplines have not proved successful. Although certain principles, such as testability and repeatability, may be central to modern science, it is now widely held that the question 'what is science?' can only be answered 'That which is recognized as such by a scientific community'. Although this answer, being somewhat tautologous, may appear distinctly unhelpful, its truth may be seen by examining what other times and cultures include in science.

Figure 5.1 shows a standard classification of Islamic science (Nasr, 1976). To many readers the inclusion of grammar, dictation, recitation, prosody, jurisprudence and theology may appear surprising. But one should remember that throughout the Middle Ages Western philosophy operated within a framework of the seven liberal arts. These consisted of the verbal arts (the trivium) — grammar, rhetoric and logic or dialectic — and the mathematical quadrivium — arithmetic, music, geometry and astronomy (Wagner, 1983). The twentieth century Western understanding of science is just that — a twentieth century Western understanding. In particular, science is now seen as separate from the creative arts despite the fact that practising scientists, historians and philosophers of science agree that creativity is of prime importance in science. Science is also often seen in conflict with religion despite the fact that other models of the relationship between science and religion exist and many outstanding scientists have a religious faith (Peacocke,

Figure 5.1   The classification of the sciences according to the Iḥṣā' al-'ulūm of al-Fārābī.

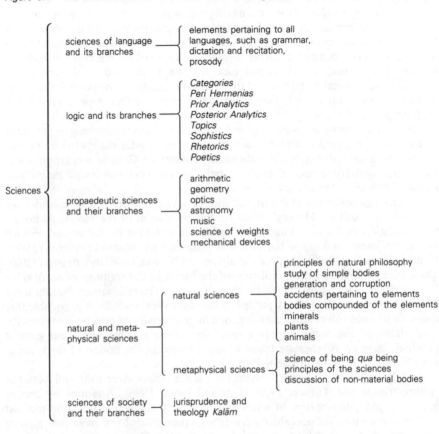

Source: Figure 4a of Nasr (1976).

1979; Polkinghorne, 1983; Barbour, 1990; Poole, 1990; Wilkinson, 1990; Brooke, 1991).

The Science National Curriculum

The story of science in the National Curriculum has been one of a successive diminution of the centrality of multicultural and anti-racist science in official publications.

The June 1988 report of the National Curriculum Science Working Group contained much of value with respect to multicultural and anti-racist science. In particular, there was an entire chapter titled 'Science for All' with a significant section of some 600 words on 'Science and cultural diversity' which included such statements as:

. . .interpretation of the nature of Science may vary from culture to culture.

It is important that the pupils' own experiences should be used as a basis for learning so that they can genuinely be agents of that learning. Science readily lends itself to the use of different social contexts, for example, in relation to diet, nutrition, energy, health, the ecosystem, and cultural diversity could thus help to enrich the quality of science education for all pupils provided the teacher does not adopt a narrow view of 'correctness' — for example in a discussion about diet or alternative technologies.

. . .the science curriculum must provide opportunities to help all pupils recognise that no one culture has a monopoly of scientific achievement — for example, through discussion of the origins and growth of chemistry from ancient Egypt and Greece to Islamic, Byzantine and European cultures, and parallel developments in China and India. It is important, therefore, that science books and other learning material should include examples of people from ethnic minority groups working alongside others and achieving success in scientific work. Pupils should come to realise that the international currency of Science is an important force for over-coming racial prejudice. (DES and the Welsh Office, 1988, p. 92)

The Science National Curriculum as it eventually emerged contained none of this section on 'Science and cultural diversity'. However, the Attainment Target on 'The nature of science', which the Working Party had proposed, was included and many teachers found this a most powerful vehicle for multicultural and anti-racist science teaching as the heading of this Attainment Target read as follows:

Pupils should develop their knowledge and understanding of the ways in which scientific ideas change through time and how the nature of these ideas and the uses to which they are put are affected by the social, moral, spiritual and cultural contexts in which they developed; in doing so, they should begin to recognise that while science is an important way of thinking about experience, it is not the only way. (DES and the Welsh Office, 1989, p. 36)

Even though Attainment Target 17 only started at level 4 and was omitted from the shorter model B of the Science National Curriculum (intended to lead to only a single GCSE in Science), the inclusion of this Attainment Target, with specific Statements of Attainment, accompanying Programmes of Study and Non-statutory Guidance) was most encouraging.

Unfortunately the reduction in the number of Attainment Targets from 17 to 4 (DES, 1991) has led to a significant reduction in the importance attached to multicultural and anti-racist science. Although explicit references to multicultural science still feature in the Programmes of Study (such as to 'encourage the use of non-standard measures, for example hand-spans' and 'explore how to make and experience sounds by speaking and singing, striking, plucking, shaking, scraping and blowing, using familiar objects and simple musical instruments from a variety of cultural traditions'), they are essentially absent from the Attainment Targets and associated Statements of Attainment. This is the case even though the NCC's evaluation of the proposed changes showed that 41 per cent of respondents believed that issues of ethnic and cultural diversity were not properly addressed (NCC, 1991). Further, the same NCC evaluation contained a summary of advice on assessment from the School Examinations and Assessment Council which states, *inter alia* that

> There will be difficulties if there are elements of a programme of study that do not appear to match any statement of attainment. Such elements are present in the proposals. Evidence shows that teachers and pupils underemphasise the parts of any curriculum which they think are not to be assessed. (NCC, 1991, p. 118)

It is sad, but probably valid, to conclude that many pupils are likely to learn more of the international and human nature of science in history and in technology than in their science lessons. Another worry is that the move to 'paper and pencil' national tests may further disadvantage pupils whose first language is not English. The National Union of Teachers' evaluation of the 1991 Key Stage 1 SATs found that over 70 per cent of the teachers who had bilingual pupils in their classes said that the SATs were not suitable for them (National Union of Teachers, 1991). Preliminary indications are that many teachers felt the same about the 1992 Key Stage 3 science tests.

Multicultural Science

Multicultural science education starts from the fundamental premise that the science taught in most schools is too narrow in its focus (Williams, 1983; Science for a Multicultural Society Group, 1985; Turner and Turner, 1989; Secondary Science Curriculum Review, n.d.). Specifically:

1 School science is often divorced from its historical and international context.
2 When science is put in an historical context in school, that context is often biased, with the work of white scientists being overrepresented.
3 Despite recent curricular initiatives, school science is still often portrayed in such a way that traditional activities such as agriculture, cooking, the making of clothes and the design of homes are not seen to fall within its remit.

Multicultural science emphasizes the work of non-Western scientists. This is an important part of good science teaching. Most pupils have no idea of the contributions made to science by non-Western cultures. To give just some examples from China, the following were all known about, invented or used in China hundreds of years before they were 'discovered' in the West:

> the compass, magnetic remanence and induction, the iron plough, the 'modern' horse harness, the multi-tube seed drill, sunspots, quantitative cartography, solar wind, 'Mercator' map-projection, cast iron, the crank handle, deep drilling for natural gas, the suspension bridge, underwater

salvage operations, paper, the wheelbarrow, sliding calipers, the fishing reel, the stirrup, porcelain, biological pest control, the umbrella, matches, chess, brandy, whisky, the mechanical clock, printing, paper money, the spinning-wheel, endocrinology, diabetes, immunology, use of thyroxine, the decimal system, zero, negative numbers, 'Pascal's' triangle, 'Newton's' first Law, the seismograph, phosphorescent paint, the kite, the parachute, masts, hermetically sealed laboratories, chemical warfare, the crossbow, gunpowder and the rocket.

The only way to improve one's teaching so as to include more examples of non-Western science is first to spend a lot of time reading and making notes. The following books are particularly helpful: Nasr (1976), Hayes (1983), Ronan (1983), Nasr (1987), Qadir (1988), Solomon (1989), Mutasa (1991), Temple (1991), Burns and Morgan (n.d.) and Jones (n.d.). (Full details are given in the references where the most valuable sources for classroom teaching are asterisked.)

Although important, considerable care needs to be taken in incorporating examples of multicultural science into one's teaching. First, any appearance of tokenism may be self defeating. Second, appearing to push a particular line may be counter productive. Third, many pupils are not especially interested in the history of science. Finally, few science teachers are likely to have a background in the history of science. As Russell points out:

> While not wishing to become embroiled in a discussion of the philosophy or purpose of history (which are just as lively as the similar debates about science), there does seem to be agreement that genuine historical under-standing is achieved when the events of a particular period are under-stood within the context of that period. Accepting this line of argument would mean that the proper analysis of, say, Pasteur's work on the germ theory of disease would require his life and ideas to be fully integrated into his background in mid- and late nineteenth-century France. Most science students have little or no formal historical training and little in-terest in the broader aspects of history so that a 'proper' job on Pasteur involving a course on late nineteenth-century French culture and politics would obviously be wholly inappropriate. One must therefore accept that the history you can teach and which your students can learn cannot be the rigorous stuff of serious study. They can only be expected to become aware of some rather general historical points and one must accept that the analysis will be partial and will not pass muster as the real thing. (Russell, 1988b, p. 48)

Measuring Time

As an example of how a multicultural approach to science can enrich a topic and lead to better science being taught and learned, consider the topic of the passage of time mentioned in the Programme of Study at Key Stage 1 of the Science National Curriculum (DES and the Welsh Office, 1991; DES, 1991). I will list some background information about time (taken from Ronan, 1983; van Sertima, 1983; Bedini, 1991; Temple, 1991 and Jordan, pers. comm.) and then consider a range of possible teaching strategies that relate to this background information (based partly on Kent, 1990).

Background information
By 4241 BCE the Egyptians had a calendar of 365 days. Each day was divided into 24 hours. Around 3500 BCE Sumerian people (present day Iraq) made the first known shadow clocks. They used a moving shadow produced by the Sun to divide the day into hours. Water clocks were used in Egypt around 2000 BC. The oldest sundial known (Egyptian) dates back to 1500 BCE.

Mechanical clocks involve getting something, usually a wheel, to turn at the same speed as the Earth. Once this is achieved, the wheel behaves as a mini-Earth, as the hour of the day is nothing more or less than how far the Earth has turned today. The mechanical clock was invented in China and first completed in 725 AD. It was built by the Tantric Buddhist monk and mathematician I-Hsing. It was driven by water which caused a wheel the size of a room to describe a single revolution every 24 hours.

Incense timekeepers played an important role in early Chinese and Japanese social and technological history, in addition to their use for time measurement. They were used in temples for religious rites, in agricultural regions for regulating water for irrigation, in palaces, in government offices and in the studies of scholars.

Galileo Galilei (1564–1642) was an Italian who became a Jesuit novice at the age of fourteen and then enrolled as a medical student. While studying medicine Galileo noticed that the time taken for a pendulum to complete a swing is independent of the angle through which it travels. This discovery was made by using his pulse to time the swings of a chandelier during church services. Galileo realized that the regular swing of a pendulum could be the basis of an accurate clock.

Possible teaching strategies
Brainstorm ideas as to how we can measure time. Some of the methods listed below will be suggested by the children; others may need to be introduced.

- On a sunny day, push a stick into the ground so that it casts a shadow. Every hour mark where the end of the shadow falls. This is a shadow clock.
- Similarly, make sundials.
- Make water clocks. Bore a hole in the bottom of a tin and time how long it takes the water to reach a specified height in a container placed beneath the tin.
- Make candle clocks by timing how long it takes a candle to burn down a specified amount.
- Count one's pulse (approximately five pulses every four seconds).
- Make hour glasses using sand to fall through a fine hole.
- Make pendula. The shorter the pendulum, the less time it takes for each swing.
- Count tree rings on the stump of a tree (one ring every year).
- Explain how day and night occur by moving a spherical object (the Earth) on its axis, a fixed distance from a lamp (the Sun).

Anti-racist Science

At a whole school level, considerable agreement exists as to what constitutes anti-racist education. Fundamentally, anti-racist education seeks actively to challenge educational inequalities based on race, ethnicity, culture or religion. It aims to counteract and combat attitudes and behaviours which lead to prejudice, discrimination and injustice (Troyna, 1987; McLean and Young, 1988; Grinter, 1989; Maitland, 1989; NUT, 1989; Bishop, 1990).

Anti-racist science education tries to help achieve these aims through science teaching (Lindsay, 1985; Gill and Levidow, 1987; Reiss, 1990; Brophy, 1991; Reiss, in press). All I can attempt in the space available is to give a few examples of anti-racist science teaching, avoiding such well discussed topics as food, sickle-cell anaemia and the concept of race itself. Each teacher has to decide for her or himself whether such examples are appropriate for their particular class(es) and, if so, how they should be introduced. The teaching of controversial issues is not always straightforward, but must not be avoided because of that.

- When teaching the topic of human populations, challenge the widely held view that overpopulation is the fault of people in 'third world' countries. Few pupils appreciate the many factors which affect average family size, or realize that most 'first world' countries support a greater density of people that do most 'third' world countries — the average density (people per square kilometre) of Belgium is 324, of the United Kingdom is 233, of France is 102, of China is 113, of Kenya is 40 and of Brazil is 17.

- Use role play, drama, creative writing or discussion to explore inequality. Many people (including pupils) enjoy writing and acting out scripts or character descriptions — though undue stereotyping needs to be guarded against. Here is a typical example that could be used when teaching about water or energy:

  > Franca stood up and stretched. She felt tired. She had got up at five o'clock in the morning and by now it was four o'clock in the afternoon. Time to go home. It was the sowing season. Franca and the other women had spent about eight hours that day sowing manioc, a very important food plant in Zaire.
  >
  > Now it was time to stop sowing and start collecting firewood. About 30–40 kg of firewood would have to be collected for the preparation of the evening meal. Nowadays collecting firewood seemed to take Franca and the other women longer than it used to. Franca preferred collecting the water. At least then she could walk to the well with her friends, even if it did take a long time. Her family of seven would need about 40–50 litres of water daily. Franca could carry about 10–15 litres on her head at a time, so she would have to make four trips to the well. The well was two kilometres from her home.

- Ask *why* certain things are so:
  - Why is fuel consumption so much higher in the USA than in other countries?

73

- Why has malaria been eradicated from Europe but not from Africa?
- Why are cash crops planted?
- Why do famines happen?
- Why are most known scientists white and male?

Conclusion

Science education has to choose between being monocultural or being multicultural. There is no such thing as a universal science education, equally applicable to all people. Good science teaching encourages pupils and students to learn about the natural world, to undertake scientific activities, and to enable themselves to shape their own scientific thinking. These aims can best be realized by the full adoption of a multicultural and anti-racist perspective on science.

The story of science in the National Curriculum over the years 1988–1992 has been one of a move away from multicultural and anti-racist science playing a pivotal role in official publications. Nevertheless, this chapter has argued that within the Science National Curriculum there is still great scope for a science education that is appropriate for a pluralist society. Indeed, without such education, we are less likely to arrive at such a society.

References

Those references that are especially recommended as an aid to classroom teaching are marked with an asterisk.

A.S.E. MULTICULTURAL EDUCATION WORKING PARTY (1990) *Race, Equality and Science Teaching: A Discussion Pack Prepared for the 1991 A.S.E. Annual Meeting, University of Birmingham*, Birmingham, Association for Science Education.

BARBOUR, I.G. (1990) *Religion in an Age of Science: The Gifford Lectures 1989–1991, Volume 1*, London, SCM.

BEDINI, S.A. (1991) *The Trail of Time: Time Measurement with Incense in East Asia*, Cambridge, Cambridge University Press.

BISHOP, A.J. (1990) 'Western mathematics, the secret weapon of cultural imperialism', *Race and Class*, **32**(2), pp. 51–65.

BROOKE, J.H. (1991) *Science and Religion: Some Historical Perspectives*, Cambridge, Cambridge University Press.

BROPHY, M. (1991) 'Global science', *School Science Review*, **73**, 262, pp. 59–66.

*BURNS, C.J. and MORGAN, G.J.D. (n.d.) *Hey! Science is Global! An Introduction to the History of Science and the Contribution of Black Scientists*, available from Local Studies Project, c/o The Alumwell Community School, Primley Avenue, Walsall WS2 9UA.

COLLINS, H.M. (1985) *Changing Order: Replication and Induction in Scientific Practice*, London, SAGE Publications.

DEPARTMENT OF EDUCATION AND SCIENCE (1991) *National Curriculum: Draft Order for Science laid before Parliament in December 1991*, London, HMSO.

DEPARTMENT OF EDUCATION AND SCIENCE AND THE WELSH OFFICE (1988) *Science for Ages 5 to 16: Proposals of the Secretary of State for Education and Science and the Secretary of State for Wales*, London, HMSO.

DEPARTMENT OF EDUCATION AND SCIENCE AND THE WELSH OFFICE (1989) *Science in the National Curriculum*, London, HMSO.

DEPARTMENT OF EDUCATION AND SCIENCE AND THE WELSH OFFICE (1991) *Science for Ages 5 to 16 (1991): Proposals of the Secretary of State for Education and Science and the Secretary of State for Wales*, London, HMSO.

DITCHFIELD, C. (Ed.) (1987) *Better Science, Curriculum Guide 7: Working for a Multicultural Society*, London, Heinemann Educational Books & Association for Science Education, Hatfield, for the School Curriculum Development Committee.

DRIVER, R., GUESNE, E. and TIBERGHIEN, A. (Eds) (1985) *Children's Ideas in Science*, Milton Keynes, Open University Press.

EYSENCK, H.J. and KAMIN, L. (1981) *Intelligence: The Battle for the Mind*, London, Pan.

FENSHAM, P. (Ed.) (1988) *Developments and Dilemmas in Science Education*, London, Falmer Press.

GILL, D. and LEVIDOW, L. (Eds.) (1987) *Anti-racist Science Teaching*, London, Free Association Books.

GOULD, S.J. (1981) *The Mismeasure of Man*, Harmondsworth, Penguin.

GRINTER, R. (1989) 'Anti-racist strategies in the National Curriculum', *Multicultural Teaching*, **7**(3), pp. 34–8.

HAMILTON, J. (Ed.) (1991) *They Made Our World: Five Centuries of Great Scientists and Inventors*, London, Broadside Books.

HARDING, S. (1991) *Whose Science? Whose Knowledge? Thinking from Women's Lives*, Milton Keynes, Open University Press.

*HAYES, J.R. (Ed.) (1983) *The Genius of Arab Civilization: Source of Renaissance*, 2nd ed., London, Eurabia.

HIATT, L.R. and JONES, R. (1988) 'Aboriginal conceptions of the working of nature', in HOME, R.W. (Ed.) *Australian Science in the Making*, Cambridge, Cambridge University Press, pp. 1–22.

INGLE, R.B. and TURNER, A.D. (1981) 'Science curricula as cultural misfits', *European Journal of Science Education*, **3**, pp. 357–71.

*JONES, L. (n.d.) *Science and the Seeds of History*, 2nd revision, available from 134 Egerton Road South, Chorlton Cum Hardy, Manchester M21 1XJ.

KENT, G. (1990) *Practical Guides — Science: Teaching within the National Curriculum*, Leamington Spa, Scholastic.

LATOUR, B. (1987) *Science in Action: How to Follow Scientists and Engineers through Society*, Milton Keynes, Open University Press.

LINDSAY, L. (1985) *Racism, Science Education and the Politics of Food*, All London Teachers Against Racism and Fascism Occasional Paper No. 1, available from ALTARF, Room 216, Panther House, 38 Mount Pleasant, London WC1 0AP.

LONGINO, H.E. (1990) *Science as Social Knowledge: Values and Objectivity in Scientific Inquiry*, Princeton, New Jersey: Princeton University Press.

MCLEAN, B. and YOUNG, J. (1988) *Multicultural Anti-racist Education: A Manual for Primary Schools*, Longman.

MAITLAND, S. (1989) *Multicultural Inset: A Practical Handbook for Teachers*, Hanley, Stoke-on-Trent, Trentham Books.

*MUTASA, N. (1991) *Black Scientists and Inventors*, Nottinghamshire Afrikan and Caribbean Education Team, available from Afrikan and Caribbean Education Team, Glenbrook Mangement Centre, Wigman Road, Bilborough, Nottingham NG8 4PD.

*NASR, S.H. (1976) *Islamic Science: An Illustrated Study*, World Of Islam Festival Publishing Company.

NASR, S.H. (1987) *Science and Civilisation in Islam*, 2nd ed., Islamic Texts Society, 5 Green Street, Cambridge CB2 3JU.

NATIONAL UNION OF TEACHERS (1989) *Anti-racism in Education: Guidelines Towards a Whole School Policy*, London, National Union of Teachers.

NATIONAL UNION OF TEACHERS (1991) *Miss the Rabbit Ate the 'Floating' Apple! The Case Against SATS: A Report on the 1991 Key Stage 1 SATs by the National Union of Teachers*, London, National Union of Teachers.

NATIONAL CURRICULUM COUNCIL (1991) *Science in the National Curriculum (1991): A Report to the Secretary of State for Education and Science on the Statutory Consultation for Attainment Targets and Programmes of Study in Science*, York, National Curriculum Council.

OSBORNE, R. and FREYBERG, P. (Eds.) (1985) *Learning in Science: The Implications of Children's Science*, Heinemann Education.

*PEACOCK, A. (Ed.) (1991) *Science in Primary Schools: The Multicultural Dimension*, Basingstoke, Macmillan Education.

PEACOCKE, A.R. (1979) *Creation and the World of Science: The Bampton Lectures, 1978*, Oxford, Clarendon Press.

POLKINGHORNE, J. (1983) *The Way the World is: The Christian Perspective of a Scientist*, London, Triangle.

POOLE, M.W. (1990) *A Guide to Science and Belief*, Oxford, Lion.

QADIR, C.A. (1988) *Philosophy and Science in the Islamic World*, London, Routledge.

REISS, M.J. (1990) 'Whither multicultural science?', *Journal of Biological Education*, 24, pp. 1–2.

REISS, M.J. (1991) 'Science (?) on stamps', *School Science Review*, 73(263), pp. 139–40.

*REISS, M.J. (in press) *Science Education for a Pluralist Society*, Milton Keynes, Open University Press.

*RONAN, C.A. (1983) *The Cambridge Illustrated History of the World's Science*, Feltham, Newnes Books & Cambridge, Cambridge University Press.

RUSSELL, N. (1988a) 'Teaching biology in a wider context: the history of the discipline as a method 2: worked examples', *Journal of Biological Education*, 22, pp. 129–35.

RUSSELL, N. (1988b) 'Teaching biology in a wider context: the history of the discipline as a method: 1', *Journal of Biological Education*, 22, pp. 45–50.

SCIENCE FOR A MULTICULTURAL SOCIETY GROUP (1985) *Science Education for a Multicultural Society*, Science Curriculum Review in Leicestershire, Leicestershire Education Authority.

SCOTT, P. DYSON, T. and GATER, S. (1987) *A Constructivist View of Learning and Teaching in Science*, Leeds, Centre for Studies in Science and Mathematics Education.

SECONDARY SCIENCE CURRICULUM REVIEW (n.d.) *Multicultural Education Through Science: A Resource and Workshop Pack for Science Teachers*, Secondary Science Curriculum Review East/Central Region. Available from Ms S. Barnes, c/o Cistel, Manchester Polytechnic, 9A Didsbury Park, Didsbury, Manchester M20 8RR.

*SOLOMON, J. (1989) *The Search for Simple Substances*, Hatfield, Association for Education.

STERNBERG, R.J. (1990) *Metaphors of Mind: Conceptions of the Nature of Intelligence*, Cambridge, Cambridge University Press.

*TEMPLE, R. (1991) *The Genius of China*, London, Prion/Multimedia Books.

TROYNA, B. (1987) 'Beyond multiculturalism: towards the enactment of antiracist education in policy provision and pedagogy', *Oxford Review of Education*, 13, pp. 307–20.

TURNER, S. and TURNER, T. (1989) 'An international dimension to the teaching of science — opportunities in the National Curriculum?', *Multicultural Teaching*, 8(1), pp. 34–9.

*VAN SERTIMA, I. (Ed.) (1983) *Blacks in Science: Ancient and Modern*, New Brunswick, New Jersey, Transaction Books.

WAGNER, D.L. (Ed.) (1983) *The Seven Liberal Arts in the Middle Ages*, Bloomington, Indiana, Indiana University Press.

WARD, A. (1986) 'Magician in a white coat', *School Science Review*, 68, pp. 348–350.

WELLINGTON, J. (Ed.) (1989) *Skills and Processes in Science Education: A Critical Analysis*, London, Routledge.

WILKINSON, D.A. (1990) 'The revival of natural theology in contemporary cosmology', *Science and Christian Belief*, **2**, pp. 95–115.

WILLIAMS, I.W. (Ed.) (1983) *Third World Science: Resource Materials for Science Teachers*, available from The Centre for World Development Education, Regent's College, Inner Circle, Regent's Park, London NW1 4NS.

WOOLGAR, S. (1988) *Science: The Very Idea*, Chichester, Ellis Horwood.

WYVILL, B. (1991) 'Classroom ideas for antiracism through science in primary education', in PEACOCK, A. (1991) *Science in Primary Schools: The Multicultural Dimension*, pp. 11–27.

Chapter 6

History

Martin Booth

The History Working Group Final Report

Of all the subjects in the National Curriculum, history has aroused the fiercest controversies and the widest debate. The reasons for this are not hard to find — for history is, above all, a political subject, creating as it does views and attitudes about humankind's past, present and future; a government which controls the content, assessment and thus to a large extent the teaching of history in schools can mould its future citizens.

Part of this debate has focused on the need to produce a history curriculum appropriate for a multicultural society. The Final Report of the History Working Group History for Ages 5 to 16 (DES, 1990), from which the Statutory Order now in force was derived, gave clear recognition of this by stating that one of the purposes of school history is 'to contribute to pupils' knowledge and understanding of other countries and other cultures in the modern world. Education in British society should be rooted in toleration and respect for cultural variety. Studying the history of other societies from their own perspectives and for their own sake counteracts tendencies to insularity, without devaluing British achievements, values and traditions' (DES, 1990, p. 1).[1]

This view of school history for a multicultural society is then developed in the statement on multicultural education which is given in DES, 1990, Chapter 11, p. 184. It is based first of all on the premise that in an ethnically diverse society teaching a substantial element of British history will act as a cohesive factor and will aid integration; thus nearly fifty per cent of the content to be covered relates to the history of England, Wales, Scotland and Northern Ireland from Roman times to the present day. Guidance from the government to the Working Group made it clear that this was a prime objective:

> The programmes of study should have at the core the history of Britain, the record of its past and, in particular, its political, constitutional and cultural heritage. They should take account of Britain's evolution and its changing role as a European, Commonwealth and world power influencing and being influenced by ideas, movements and events elsewhere in the world. (DES, 1990, p. 189)

Yet the message which comes across on reading the British study units is that British history is essentially about the white indigenous people and is the whiggish story of the political and economic improvement of the great British people. There is little to direct the history teacher to multicultural themes such as the impact of and response to the waves of invaders and refugees that have come to Britain or the attitudes towards black people from the sixteenth to the twentieth centuries. Unit titles such as 'Medieval realms: Britain 1066 to 1500', 'The making of the United Kingdom: Crowns, parliaments and peoples 1500 to 1750' or 'Expansion, trade and industry: Britain 1750 to 1900' certainly give the impression of a top-down view of our past which moves inexorably towards prosperity, unity and democracy.

Emphasis on British History

This emphasis on British history inevitably overshadows the idea of cultural pluralism which the Report attempts to promote — that teaching about other cultures and peoples in their own right and from their own perspectives will encourage a healthy respect for different societies.[2] Thus in Key Stage 2 the early invaders are studied together with the the ancient civilizations of Egypt and Greece; Key Stage 3 history study units deal with the Roman Empire, a non-Western culture such as Islamic civilization or Imperial China and the Americas; Key Stage 4 students have to study the history of a non-Western culture such as Japan or China in the twentieth century.

There is a third important element which underwrote the Working Group's view of the role of history in a multicultural society. History is seen as a subject which encourages openmindness and objectivity, which questions easy assumptions and encourages reasoned arguments. It is also a discipline which has no final truth to offer but where our view of the past is constantly being reshaped in the light of new or reinterpreted evidence. Such historical skills and attitudes, the working party considered, 'should assist in identifying, and thus combatting, racial and other forms of prejudice and stereotypical thinking' (DES, 1990, p. 184). This approach to history is enshrined in the attainment targets which the Working Group described as 'the backbone of the National Curriculum' (DES, 1990, p. 7); and in their Final Report the Working Group identified four Attainment Targets (ATs) — Understanding history in its setting; Understanding points of view and interpretations of history; Acquiring and evaluating historical information; Organizing and communicating the results of historical study.

The weight of the Report, therefore, emphasizes integration of ethnic minority groups through a common cultural heritage. It makes a gesture towards the notion of cultural pluralism by demanding the study of non-western societies at Key Stages 2, 3 and 4, and it believes that the development of the habits of toleration and disinterested objectivity will be encouraged by the critical use of historical sources. It is, of course, an approach to the issues of ethnic diversity that some would challenge. They would see the common cultural heritage presented in the British study units as the story of the dominant white majority; they would label the study units dealing with non-western societies as 'tokenism'; they would ask for the evidence that the critical study of historical sources will lead to greater toleration and understanding. Godfrey Brandt, for example, in his book *The*

Realization of Anti-Racist Teaching (Brandt, 1986) rejects the assimilationist, integrationist and cultural pluralist traditions as inherently racist in that they stem from the dominant white culture and are designed to maintain the racial *status quo* and power relationships between black and white in Britain, not challenge or change them. Brandt argues throughout his book that the only approach, the only focus for education in a multicultural society, should be anti-racist. The content of a history syllabus should deal with the roots and development of racism in society; teaching styles should be collaborative with group-centred learning.

The Secretary of State's Consultation

The dissatisfaction which many felt about the History Working Group's Final Report prompted the Secretary of State to conduct his own consultation process before sending the document to the National Curriculum Council in July 1990. Most of those concerns centred not on the multicultural dimension (indeed, the National Curriculum Council reported of their consultations that 'few respondents disagreed with the sections of the report concerning history and multicultural education' (NCC, 1990, p. 11)), but on the issues of the amount and balance of content to be covered, the balance between knowledge, skills and understanding, and the wording of the attainment targets and their associated statements of attainment at ten different levels. In the event, the Secretary of State reduced the number of units to be studied and cut the attainment targets from four to three by deleting the fourth target, 'organizing and communicating the results of historical study'. The first target was renamed 'knowledge and understanding of history'. In the light of these amendments and of further public consultations, the National Curriculum Council issued its own Report to the Secretary of State on History in the National Curriculum (NCC, December 1990).

Statutory Order: The History National Curriculum

It is this document which forms the basis of the Statutory Order for History *History in the National Curriculum (England)* (DES, 1991a); on first reading, it makes a marked contrast to the Final Report of the History Working Group. In the first place, both NCC Report and Statutory Order deal only with the attainment targets and the programmes of study; all the Working Group's sections on the essence of history, the general rationale for school history, 'bringing history to life' or the relationship of history to the rest of the school curriculum have been omitted. Thus the Report and Order have nothing explicit to say about the role of history in a multicultural society. Second, the attainment targets have been slimmed down to three and renamed to make them more immediately intelligible. The first is 'knowledge and understanding of history' — a target which essentially deals with ideas of chronology, time, change, cause and consequence in history and the necessity of understanding events, issues and people within the context of their times and circumstances. The second is 'interpretations in history', and the third 'the use of historical sources'. The statements of attainment at ten levels which accompany the three ATs have been simplified and made more obviously hierarchical.

The third major change concerns the programmes of study. In place of the detailed lists of names and events which characterized the units for Key Stages 2–4 in the Final Report, the twelve core study units for Key Stages 2, 3 and 4 of the Order sketch broadly the themes to be covered (the core study unit for Key Stage 1 remains much as it was in the History Working Group Final Report: a general demand that 'pupils should be given opportunities to develop an awareness of the past and the ways in which it was different from the present. They should be introduced to historical sources of different kinds' (DES, 1991, p. 13)); the rigid PESC formula which detailed the content of each unit under the headings of 'political, economic, social and religious and cultural and aesthetic history' has been abandoned though it remains as part of the general introduction to the programmes of study for Key Stages 2–4. The supplementary units (three or four for Key Stage 2, three for Key Stage 3 and two for Key Stage 4) leave even more scope for the teacher.

Similarities with the History Working Group Final Report

How far is all this a real advance for the teacher of history in a multicultural society? First, though the programmes of study have been slimmed down and simplified, British history remains the core of the curriculum. Seven of the ten core study units in Key Stages 2 and 3 deal specifically with British history; the core study unit in Key Stage 4 deals, *inter alia*, with the development of British democracy and economic, social and cultural change in Britain. The supplementary study units in Key Stage 2 demand one unit on local history and at least one thematic unit dealing with, for example, ships and seafarers or land transport, in which the links between local, British, European and world history have to be made clear. At Key Stage 3 the supplementary units demand at least one which extends the core of the British units — for example, by studying Britain and the Great War 1914–1918. The impression of a white, middle class and meliorist view of a common cultural heritage giving integration to ethnic diversity still underwrites the curriculum. Secondly, the attainment targets and their associated statements are still concerned with understanding the past within the context of particular periods, with debate, enquiry and the critical use of sources. Here again is the liberal, democratic approach to history — history as the great emancipator through its critical, objective study of the past — but enshrined in more accessible language. Thirdly, there is the requirement that at Key Stages 2, 3 and 4 pupils study at least one supplementary unit covering the history of a non-European society. A tokenist gesture towards cultural pluralism still seems to be part of the curriculum. Finally, history can now be given up in favour of geography at the end of Key Stage 3; the idea of a coherent, progressive 5 to 16 history curriculum has been abandoned.

The Statutory Order, therefore, seems to be underwritten by the same approach to history in a multicultural society as was made explicit in the Final Report of the History Working Group; the anti-racist lobby will feel that there is little to encourage them. Many people too will deeply regret the fact that history is no longer a foundation subject to the age of 16. Yet in two ways the Orders are a significant advance: the curriculum is less obviously content driven than the one which was being proposed by the History Working Group, and it does now give history teachers more opportunity to choose content areas, teaching styles and to shape their pupils' learning. In whatever way some would interpret the multicultural message of the Statutory Order, the reality is that history teachers concerned with the issues of ethnic diversity now have considerable latitude to choose and emphasize themes and topics they consider important.

The issue of specified content had been at the heart of much of the debate over the history curriculum. A vociferous lobby argued that far too much history teaching was concerned with skills and the dubious notion of empathy; children should be taught good, solid facts. The then Secretary of State, Mr John Macgregor, seemed to endorse this position in a letter to the Chairman of the School Examinations and Assessment Council commenting on the History Working Group's Final Report (DES, 1991a, pp. ix–x):

> I attach great importance to the assessment of knowledge. . . . I look to the Council to consider and let me know whether assessment against the attainment targets, as recommended in the report, will reliably reflect a pupil's level of knowledge within each study unit.

Certainly the Final Report's study units detailed knowledge under four essential information columns (political; economic, technological and scientific; social and religious; cultural and aesthetic) but the attainment targets and their associated statements of attainment made no mention of the specific knowledge which was to be drawn on in order to show mastery of a particular level. This position was endorsed by the History Committee of SEAC; and the Statutory Order has also adopted this position. Pupils, of course, will have to deploy their historical knowledge in order to show the level they have attained in any one attainment target, but there is no question of stating what this knowledge should contain, other than that it should be 'drawn from the historical information in the programmes of study'.

Room for the Multicultural Dimension

Yet the Statutory Order goes further than this, for the programmes of study are so broadly drawn and organized on thematic issues that there is plenty of scope for teachers to organize content along the lines that they consider most appropriate. This is particularly so with the supplementary study units where the units are described either with a simple title (Domestic life, families and childhood) or even more generally with an injunction to the teacher, for example, to devise 'a unit which extends the study of the core British study units for this key stage' (Key Stage 3). The only other criteria in this instance are that the 'unit should relate to the history of the British Isles before 1920 and involve either study in depth or the study of a theme over a long period of time'. It would therefore be perfectly legitimate for a teacher to plan a course round the theme of black settlers in Britain from the sixteenth to the early twentieth centuries, using as a source and text book Nigel File and Chris Power's *Black Settlers in Britain 1555–1958* (File and Power, 1981), materials which have been used with Year 9 mixed ability groups. This would extend the theme of social and economic change in Britain which is part of Key Stage 3 core study unit 4 (expansion, trade and industry: Britain 1750–1900).

Another approach to this particular supplementary unit would be to take the theme of Britain and her relationship with her colonies with particular reference to Africa, sixteenth to early twentieth centuries. This would be a study which would extend the theme of Britain's world-wide expansion which is also part of core study unit 4. The local study supplementary unit which teachers have to design for their Key Stage 2 pupils could focus on the issue of the impact on a locality over a period of time of ethnic minority groups. The London Borough of Newham, for example, has developed a splendid teaching pack of materials entitled *People Who Moved to Newham*, which documents the range of peoples who came to Newham in the last two thousand years or more and the immense contributions they have made to the area. But even with the British core study units there is still great scope for the multicultural teacher. Take, for example, core study unit 1 in Key Stage 2 'Invaders and settlers: Romans, Anglo-Saxons and Vikings in Britain'. This could be approached from a number of perspectives. Pupils could address the diversity of the cultures each invading group encompassed (for example, that slaves and soldiers from every part of the Roman empire came to Britain during the time of the Roman occupation — there was a division of black Roman soldiers defending Hadrian's wall in the third century AD; that the Vikings had a sophisticated and flourishing culture which certainly makes us modify the popular picture of boorish warriors raping and pillaging). Pupils could also study the issue of institutionalized racism — master/mistress and slave, conqueror and conquered — which each group of invaders brought with them. Or in core study unit 3 in Key Stage 3, 'The making of the United Kingdom: Crown, parliament and people 1500 to 1750', emphasis could be put on the sixteenth and seventeenth century ideas of hierarchy and superiority within and between religious, social and economic groups. A particular study could be made of the impact of black people on Britain in the sixteenth, seventeenth and eighteenth centuries and the reaction of the government, or the coming of the Huguenots in the late seventeenth century.

Of course there are issues other than those described above which need to be covered in these two core study units; but the point that I am making is that there is plenty of scope to address multicultural or racial issues in the History National Curriculum, even within the context of the British core study units. There is moreover a further important point to make. In the NCC Report and Statutory Order, unlike the Final Report of the History Working Group, the attainment targets and their statements of attainment at ten levels come before the programmes of study. Whatever the rhetoric of the History Working Group, the impression given by the eighty-nine pages which describe the forty core and option history study units (DES, 1990, pp. 34–113) is that content dominates the curriculum. Each unit whether compulsory or optional is spelt out in detail; coverage and chronology seem to rule. Gaby Weiner, in a paper presented to the annual conference of the British Educational Research Association in 1990 which analyzed the Interim and Final Reports of the History Working Group (Weiner, 1990), emphasized this when she commented:

Throughout this paper I have constantly alluded to the content-led nature of the documentation. In my view, enormous emphasis has been placed on what teachers should teach and what pupils should know but little on *how* teachers might 'deliver' the syllabus.

She goes on to quote a letter to the *Times Educational Supplement* in which Michael Armstrong considers this to be a fundamental weakness in the National Curriculum documentation generally.

> It is the fatal weakness of the national curriculum that it isolates. . .two sorts of questions — what to teach and how to teach. In practice, any curriculum is necessarily an attempt to resolve the interminable conflict between received wisdom, as represented by the established orthodoxies of scholarship, and naive enquiry, as represented by the developing interests and purposes of children. The excitement of teaching is the excitement of having continually to re-examine and revise one's own understanding of subject matter in response to children's understanding as it emerges from their engagement with that same subject matter.
>
> There is no hint of excitement in the reports of the working parties [sic], no sense of challenge to knowledge that is inherent in the practice of education. Theirs is a comfortable, overdetermined world in which the intellectual confusion of the classroom, inseparable from its vitality, is never permitted to disturb the confident and shallow prescriptions. (Weiner, 1990, p. 17)

Many of these objections, it seems to me, are met by the History Statutory Order. Teachers are given a great deal of flexibility over content; and with attainment targets placed first, the emphasis is put on conceptual understanding, process, debate, the use of a wide range of source materials and the many-sided nature of our view of the past. These are now at the forefront of the agenda; the teacher is at once encouraged to adopt a range of teaching styles.

A Post-modernist Curriculum

The History National Curriculum, therefore, though it may at first sight appear to be underwritten by a particular philosophy, in fact presents a syllabus which in many ways is neutral. Indeed, some would argue that whatever the intentions of the politicians, the curriculum is post-modernist in that it is devoid of the old organizing frameworks and that it allows teachers and pupils to have power over the past (Jenkins and Brinkley, 1991). The challenge to the teacher lies in fleshing out the bare bones of the document and turning rhetoric into the hard currency of classroom practice. When choosing material and teaching approaches for history in a multicultural society, there are, I would suggest, a number of points to bear in mind. First, is the topic significant in itself or in its relation to wider issues or has it merely been chosen because it can serve as a vehicle for multicultural or anti-racist teaching? Brandt, for example, in his book *The Realization of Anti-Racist Teaching* (Brandt, 1986), describes with approval a history lesson he had observed. The lesson which was based on a piece of primary source material describing Tacky's Rebellion in Jamaica, 1760, had been preceded by two lessons on the Maroon wars of the 1730s, in Ashanti (modern Ghana). The focus in these lessons had been on Nanny, an obeah or wise woman who became the leader of the Maroons. The document for the observed lessons was a graphic and bloodthirsty account of the slave Tacky's rebellion and its brutal suppression. I don't doubt the writer's comments that the Year-nine children were absorbed with the work and challenged by the teacher's style (Brandt says that 'the whole lesson was punctuated with questions such as: 'Do you believe it? Do you think it true?. . . . think about it!'); but it does seem to me that the incidents with which the material dealt are not intrinsically significant or of particular importance; they had principally been chosen as vehicles for advancing a particular message.

Equally important are the ways in which the topic chosen is presented to the pupils — the teaching approaches and materials to be used. I would suggest that the cause of multiculturalism and anti-racism — and indeed of school history in general — is much better served if the emphasis can be on pupil involvement and collaborative learning. Didactic teaching can easily lead to special pleading, indocrination and propaganda. The style of teaching in the history lesson which Brandt observed (Brandt, 1986) is described as 'didactic', though the observer is at pains to emphasize that '. . . though on the one hand [the teacher] was reading [the primary document on Tacky's rebellion of 1760] with great authority, he was *obviously* standing back from the material and inviting or rather encouraging the students to question and evaluate the matter presented'. The reader gets more than a hint that there was a strong message which was being conveyed with almost religious fervour by the attitude and style of the teacher; anti-racist teaching can easily turn into propaganda. Collaborative learning and pupil involvement, on the other hand, through debate, role play and group work, can lead to a real sense of pupil commitment to the issues they are studying and a willingness to address them in a deep and serious manner.

Teaching Styles Appropriate for a Multicultural Approach

Let me give four practical examples which could be used within the context of the History National Curriculum which I would argue avoid the pitfalls of propaganda, yet would engage the children and challenge them to address multicultural issues. The first concerns a topic which could well form part of Key Stage 3 core study unit 2, 'Medieval Realms: Britain 1066 to 1500'. Much of the emphasis of the teaching for this study unit could focus on the idea of a foreign power with an alien language and culture imposing itself by force on the Anglo-Saxons. Attainment Target 1, 'knowledge and understanding of history', would form the major attainment target with the statement of attainment 6c, can 'describe the different ideas and attitudes of people in an historical situation', as the level to be aimed for. The impact of the conquest could be explored in a number of ways, but the Domesday Survey of 1086 could serve as a particularly graphic example. Pupils might start by considering what a foreign ruler, having subdued most of England, might want to do next; a role play of King William (the teacher) with his Council is an effective way of doing this. The king is an impatient and autocratic ruler; he wants information quickly about his territories, at last under his control after twenty years of fighting. Can the Council advise him? What sort of information might he require? How might it be collected? What difficulties might be encountered? The children might then go on to examine part of the Domesday Survey which relates to their own part of the country. A facsimile of the original could be compared with its transcription and some guesses could be made about what some of the words, abbreviations or Roman figures might mean. A translation could then be examined. What can we tell about the community in the time of King Edward before the Norman conquest? What has happened to it in the last twenty years? Role play could again be used to explore the impact of the survey.

The class could be divided into a number of small communities in the area, with each group given details of their inhabitants, land, who the new Lord of the Manor is, cattle, mills and so on. The Norman commissioners will shortly be visiting them and cross-examining them under oath. Few of the commissioners speak Saxon — they'll be using interpreters; and their manner will be overbearing and arrogant. How are the Saxon villagers going to react? Will they try to hide the truth and make out that they are poorer than in fact they are? The penalties for hiding information will be severe! A vital part of the exercise is the debriefing after the role play. Here again the emphasis could be on the relationships between conquered and conquerors, Norman and Saxon. What do they think of the new regime? Has it brought any benefits? What are their reactions to the Saxon girl who's just married a Norman soldier?

The clash of cultures can be explored in a study of the crusades which could form a supplementary, teacher-designed unit for part of Key Stage 3. The crusades are often studied simply from the European point of view, but teachers concerned with the multicultural dimension will want their children to think about the impact of the invasions on the Muslims. Graphic material for this is provided in Book 1 of the Collins Education series *Past into Present* (Culpin and Linsell, 1988, pp. 96–108). The pictorial and written material on pp. 104–5 explore what Turks and European crusaders thought of each other. Pupils could discuss what constitutes opinion in each written source and what fact. They could consider the usefulness of the evidence to historians studying the crusades and the ways in which such evidence can be useful. Here the focus would be on Attainment Targets 2 and 3, 'interpretations of history' and 'the use of historical sources'.

A third example reflects work I undertook with Year-8 children in a mixed ability class. We had taken as our theme for the term the Pilgrim Fathers — a topic which could be taught as supplementary study unit A (the teacher has to devise a unit which extends the study of the core British study units at Key Stage 3). Working closely with the drama department who had agreed that the children's weekly drama lesson should also explore the topic, we studied the original departure of the Pilgrims from Lincolnshire, their settlement in the Netherlands and the factors which made them feel that their only hope lay in the New World. Much of this work was based on role play; but this was closely linked to a study of source material. Thus, for example, speculation about the type of stores and equipment they might want to bring to the New World was modified in the light of study of a seventeenth century list of recommended items. Attainment Targets 1 and 3 were thus the particular objectives of the lessons. The arrival off Cape Cod and the feelings of the Pilgrims gave splendid opportunities for empathetic work based on sources of evidence. In particular, we focused on the first meetings between the indigenous population and the Europeans. We know from Bradford's journal that in the early Spring of 1621 an English-speaking Indian, Samoset, visited the Pilgrims' settlement and befriended them. How did the two sides view each other? The children were asked to invite Samoset (played by a student teacher) into their huts. What would they show him? How would they react to him? The Pilgrims were amazed that Samoset would not use a chair but sat cross-legged on the ground; he in turn could not understand the notion of a god contained in a book — an object which the Pilgrims seem to prize highly. Later Samoset took them into the country and taught them the arts of trapping and fishing. How lacking the craftsmen were in these essential skills! How grateful they were to Samoset for passing on his expertise! Indeed, what price could now be put on so-called European superiority?

The final example I want to give also comes from Key Stage 3 — the core study unit entitled 'The era of the Second World War'. An aspect of this unit focuses on the Holocaust which, as Carrie Supple and Nick Hudson emphasize (Supple and Hudson, 1990), can form a graphic topic for exploring a multicultural theme. Supple and Hudson argue that the Holocaust has too often been seen as something which is part of the Jewish experience alone. In fact 'it involved people of all nationalities, whether as perpetrators, victims, bystanders, rescuers, resisters or collaborators' (Supple and Hudson, p. 42). The Holocaust should raise issues of racism and its nature, power and propaganda, obedience, conformity and responsibility. In order to explore these ideas, Supple and Hudson brought together twelve students with four people who had lived through the Nazi/Holocaust period, creating a situation for open dialogue and discussion. The results have been filmed and the moving video (which is available as a teaching resource) could serve as an excellent basis for class discussion.

I've done work with fourteen and fifteen-year olds on Rudolf Hoess, the commandant of Auschwitz from 1942–44 which raises similar issues. I introduce the topic by telling the story based on the affadavit of Hermann Graebe of the mass execution he witnessed at Dubno, Ukraine, in 1943 (The account is recorded in the proceedings of the International Military Tribunal, 1946). It's a horrific story of the callous indifference of the executioners and the pitiful helplessness of the condemned. I remind the class that this is no imaginary account but based on sworn evidence; how was it that a nation which had produced some of the world's greatest artists, musicians, composers, writers and engineers could engage in such acts? Perhaps a study of Rudolf Hoess can shed some light on the problem. The work centred on two written documents — part of the testimony Hoess gave to the Nuremberg tribunal in 1945 and an extract from his autobiography which he wrote in prison in Poland while awaiting trial and execution. We spent a lot of time thinking about the words or phrases we might use to describe Hoess on the basis of the coldly clinical evidence he gave at Nuremberg ('The Camp commandant at Treblinka. . . . used monoxide gas and I did not think his methods were very efficient. . . . I used Cyclon B. . . . It took three to fifteen minutes to kill the people. . . . We knew the people were dead because their screaming had stopped. . . . Another improvement that we made on Treblinka was building our gas chambers to accommodate 2,000 people at a time' (taken from Noakes and Pridham, 1974). Were there any aspects of Hoess' character as revealed in the witness box of which we could approve? We role-played how he might have stood in the dock giving his testimony and the tone of voice he might have used. What might have led a man like this to have become Commandant of a death camp? We then turned to Hoess' autobiography (Hoess, 1959). This emotional and self-justificatory document is quite a revelation. He is devoted to his wife and family; he wishes he had more time to play with his children; he loves animals and is never happier than when he rides through the forest. He was repelled by the mass exterminations; duty, however, demanded that he carried out his superiors' commands without flinching. What words do we now wish to use to describe Hoess? In what ways has our previous view of him been modified? I remember in one particular class a boy making the point that the litany of self pity with which Hoess describes how day in, day out as Commandant he had to observe the

mass murders in every detail, was really a cry for help: 'each Jew died only once
— I died a thousand deaths every day. I deserve your sympathies just as much as
the victims of Nazi tyranny' — a mature and telling point from a fifteen-year-old
which led on to the whole issue of responsibility for actions taken.

Teaching and Assessing the History National Curriculum

My argument is that whatever the appearances, there is, in fact, plenty of scope
within the History National Curriculum to develop a syllabus appropriate for a
multicultural society and to adopt teaching styles which address fundamental
issues of cultural diversity and racism. My examples make clear that my own
preference as far as the latter is concerned is to use drama, role-play and story-
telling, approaches which I have found can generate real commitment and understanding, providing the work is based firmly on historical sources and information.
I can, however, hear my critics challenging me on two counts. First, my stance
is nothing more than the typical, white liberal view which operates within the
status quo and is thus inevitably tainted with racism. I have accepted the curriculum
imposed from above by a government determined to preserve existing structures,
not change them. But I have argued throughout this chapter that the History
National Curriculum can be regarded as a neutral document and indeed through
its attainment targets encourages debate and a range of views and approaches. Its
effective delivery — and indeed the nature of what that delivery shall be — is
dependent on the history teacher.

This leads me to the other criticism which may be made. Even if it is conceded
that the history teacher appears to have a fair degree of flexibility, surely the
national, centralized assessment of the curriculum through the standard assessment tests will, to a large extent, determine what is taught and how it is taught.
Again, I think this is to see some sinister conspiracy where none exists. In the first
place, there will be no statutory tests in history in Key Stages 1 and 2; teachers
will be responsible (as they are at the moment) for the assessment and recording
of the achievement of their pupils, though non-statutory tests will be available if
they wish to make use of them. For Key Stage 3 it seems that a statutory test or
tests will be imposed; a contract for the development of these tests has been
awarded, although at the time of writing no test material has appeared.

We are therefore unsure as to what a statutory test in history at Key Stage 3
might look like. It will certainly be less formidable than many teachers fear,
probably occupying no more than two hours during the first few weeks of the
summer term. The questions will be straightforward and fairly conventional; it
has been suggested that a teacher should be able to mark a set of thirty scripts in
less than three hours. The statutory test may have to be tied to a particular core
study unit (perhaps 'Expansion, trade and industry: Britain 1750 to 1900') so that
all schools are operating within a common framework; assessment, however, will
be in terms of the attainment targets and statements of attainment, which means
that the knowledge needed to demonstrate attainment at a particular level will not
be specified. All that will be required is that it is drawn from the core study unit in
question. It may even be that a 'hollow test' is developed — that is, an assessment
framework focusing on the attainment targets which the teacher can use within
the context of any Key Stage 3 study unit, core or supplementary. One thing we
can be sure of: no test at the end of Key Stage 3 can cover the entire syllabus; once

again teachers will largely be in charge of the measurement and recording of their children's achievement. Indeed, I would argue that, whereas in the past such assessment has sometimes been ill-conceived and perfunctory, we may now have far greater guidance both from the History National Curriculum with its attainment targets and statements of attainment and from the non-statutory guidance issued by the National Curriculum Council and the School Examinations and Assessment Council, as to what we mean by progress in history and how it can be recorded.

Conclusion

The Swann Report of 1985 ennunciated the principle of 'education for all', an education which must 'reflect the diversity of British society'. . . . and. . . . 'help pupils to understand the world in which they live and the interdependence of individuals, groups and nations'. History, above all, is a subject which can focus on these issues and there is nothing in the History National Curriculum which can prevent this. Research does indicate that teaching about race relations can affect attitudes and increase tolerance; Stenhouse, Verma, Wild and Nixon, for example, undertook some interesting work in schools using a variety of teaching styles which supports this view, though interestingly, their research casts some doubts on the effectiveness of drama as a strategy for teaching about race relations (Stenhouse *et al.*, 1982). My own research in the mid-1970s indicated that an enquiry approach to the teaching of history based on the use of source materials also aids the development of more tolerant attitudes (Booth, 1983). Yet clearly at the heart of it all are the schools, the departments and the teachers who take on the task of teaching for a multicultural society. There is an increasing body of research to show what good schools can do (for example, Rutter, 1979; Smith and Tomlinson, 1989) and a growing recognition following the Swann Report that education for a multicultural society must not be confined to schools with ethnic minority groups alone. It is easy to dismiss the History National Curriculum as a document which does little to promote multicultural education, yet its attainment targets which stress debate and pupil enquiry and its core study units which demand the study of other cultures, other nations and its opportunities through the supplementary units for teachers to develop special interests and concerns could give school history a renewed vigour and help it to contribute to the proper education of a multi-ethnic nation. Let us recognize and exploit these opportunities, squeezing the new history curriculum for all its multicultural potential.

Acknowledgments

I am most grateful to Mrs Maggie Holling, General Inspector with particular responsibility for history and humanities, Cambridgeshire, and Mr Richard Matthews, Advisory Teacher (History), Cambridgeshire Curriculum Agency, for their perceptive and helpful comments on an early draft of this chapter.

Notes

1   The discussion in this chapter relates throughout to the publications of the English History Working Group and the Statutory Order for England. The Welsh had

their own History Working Group (as did Northern Ireland) and the Welsh Office has published the Statutory Order for Wales (Welsh Office, 1991). The Welsh history documents are similar to the English documents. Both Statutory Orders, for example, have the same Attainment Targets and Statements of Attainment. The Programmes of Study are similar; the Welsh Programmes, however, stress Welsh rather than British history.

2 This tension between developing in pupils a national identity and the need to prepare them for a European and international world, is greater in the Welsh National History Curriculum, where the focus is on Welsh, rather than British, history. Whereas it is hard to identify a specifically *British* culture, Wales has a strong cultural identity, underlined by language, literature, religion, custom and economy. Dafydd Elis Thomas, then a Welsh Member of Parliament, argued in a public lecture in December 1991 that the ideal history curriculum would promote a federal world view while at the same time advocating strong ethnic, local and regional history — a case perhaps of trying to have one's cake and eat it! But certainly the Welsh Order, like the English, gives considerable opportunity for choice, for emphasizing particular themes and for adopting a range of teaching styles.

References

BOOTH, M.B. (1983) 'Skills, concepts and attitudes: The development of adolescent children's historical thinking', *History and Theory*, Beiheft 22, pp. 101–117.

BRANDT, G. (1986) *The Realization of Anti-Racist Teaching*, Lewes, Falmer Press.

CULPIN, C. and LINSELL, D. (1988) *Past into Present Book 1: 43 AD–1400*, London, Collins Educational.

DEPARTMENT OF EDUCATION AND SCIENCE (1990) *History for Ages 5 to 16*, London, HMSO.

DEPARTMENT OF EDUCATION AND SCIENCE (1991a) *History in the National Curriculum (England)*, London, HMSO.

DEPARTMENT OF EDUCATION AND SCIENCE (1991b) *History in the National Curriculum (Wales)* London, HMSO.

FILE, N. and POWER, C. (1981) *Black Settlers in Britain 1555–1958*, London, Heinemann.

HOESS, R. (1959) *Commandant of Auschwitz*, English edition, London, Weidenfeld and Nicolson.

INTERNATIONAL MILITARY TRIBUNAL (1946) *International War Tribunal*, Vol XIX, London, HMSO.

JENKINS, K. and BRINKLEY, P. (1991) 'Always historicise: Unintended opportunities in National Curriculum history', *Teaching History*, No. 62, pp. 8–14.

NATIONAL CURRICULUM COUNCIL (1990) *Consultation Report: History*, York, National Curriculum Council.

NOAKES, J. and PRIDHAM, G. (1974) *Documents on Nazism*, London, Jonathon Cape.

RUTTER, M. (1979) *Fifteen Thousand Hours: Secondary Schools and Their Effects on Children*, London, Open Books.

SMITH, D.J. and TOMLINSON, S. (1989) *The School Effect: A Study of Multi-Racial Comprehensives*, London, Policy Studies Institute.

STENHOUSE, L., VERMA, G.K., WILD, R.D. and NIXON, J. (1982) *Teaching About Race Relations: Problems and Effects*, London Routledge and Kegan Paul.

SUPPLE, C. and HUDSON, N. (1990) 'Learning about the holocaust: Using video to develop empathy', *Multicultural Teaching*, 8(3), pp. 42–3.

WEINER, G. (1990) *The Framing of School Knowledge: History in the National Curriculum*, paper presented at the annual conference of the British Educational Research Association.

Chapter 7

Geography

Rex Walford

The linkage of the teaching of geography in schools to the multicultural dimension of education is inescapable. Geography lessons frequently deal with other parts of the world beyond the home nation and put the understanding of environment, economy and social structure in a spatial context. Other cultures come under scrutiny, are explored, analyzed and compared with our own.

Similarly, in dealing with the home nation, geography lessons seek to describe and explain the physical and human background. Over thousands of years waves of immigrants have left varying cultural imprints on British life; in recent times there have been significant arrivals and contributions from the New Commonwealth nations, who now form part of an increasingly multicultural society.

The task of dealing with this dimension is not a simple or obvious one. Teachers, even with the best of intentions, reveal varying degrees of sensitivity and understanding. Some work from ethnocentric viewpoints which make it difficult to understand or present cultures different from their own. Others deliberately seek to eschew some of the issues raised by concentrating on (supposedly) neutral and factual material. Pupils, on the other hand, may also subvert the worthiest of efforts. Those in the 'white heartland' may make hasty and ill-informed judgements about other cultures based on unfamiliarity, fear or misunderstanding; those in multicultural areas may bring existing grievances, prejudices and hostilities to classroom work.

At least the matter has been extensively aired within the world of geographical education over the past two decades, even if definitive answers have not been produced. But past generations of geography teachers sometimes looked at other cultures through glasses of curious colours. . .

Early Geography Textbooks

The earliest books used in geography classrooms were those of travellers' tales brought back by explorers and adventurers. Brave though their voyages and marches may have been, they were usually coloured by a reaction of 'otherness' and strangeness in relation to the peoples with whom the authors came in contact. The habits and cultural patterns of such peoples were judged rigidly against the standards and customs of our own.

These views were taken on by later writers who sought to disseminate a growing body of world knowledge. One clergyman author writing at the start of the nineteenth century for schools (Goldsmith, 1815) could comment in his 'General facts worthy to be remembered' that:

The most civilised and intelligent quarter of the world is Europe:
the most barbarous is Africa.
The preponderance of civilization is in the northern hemisphere:
there have been no distinguished nations in the southern hemisphere.

The passing of Forster's Elementary Education Act (1870) and Scott Keltie's influential Report to the Royal Geographical Society (1884) stimulated the spread of geography teaching in schools at the time when Imperial ambitions and perspectives were rising quickly to their zenith. Thus it was not surprising that texts of this period extolled the virtue of British rule and power and demonstrated proudly that the 'map was being painted red' in many parts of the world. Poring over school atlases to learn basic world knowledge schoolchildren quickly imbibed this message through the power of cartography.

Some writers see the Imperial legacy as little more than a naked extension of rapacious capitalism, searching for ever more resources and markets, and bringing chauvinism, militarism and racism in its wake. But the simplistic forcing of the Imperial period into a Marxist framework almost certainly underestimates the complexity of a phenomenon in which idealism and self-interest, naïvety and low-cunning were inextricably (and unconsciously) mixed. It undoubtedly led, however, to a series of school textbooks in which those in other lands ('the colonized') were seen as needing the civilizing influence of the colonial powers, British, French, Dutch, Italian, German, Belgian alike. Light was brought to the Dark Continents in this reading of events.

Terminology, even where kindly, was patronizing. Pictures of inhabitants of other countries were captioned as 'smiling piccannies' or 'sturdy kaffirs'. Those who lived by codes other than those which recognized the concept of land ownership and property were judged simple. Indigenous peoples were subtly demeaned by being referred to as 'native tribes'. Yet, as William Bunge was later to point out, 'Natives are the people who were once called Settlers by the people who were there before *them*' (Bunge, 1984).

The danger of stereotyping can lie as much with those who criticize the books as with the books themselves. The so-called 'Bombo of the Congo syndrome' became a fashionable term to deride a whole approach to geography in the primary school which began with simple case-studies of children from other lands, supposedly because of its dangerously picturesque and unrepresentative material. But a re-examination of the books, from which this phrase originated (Archer and Thomas, 1936) by postgraduate students of geography over fifty years later, failed to produce the expected dismissive responses; indeed, many of the group of twenty (on a PGCE course) commented with favour on the vividness and sympathetic approach of the book — including some who had themselves lived and travelled in Bombo's country of origin.

There were, however, some books which carried their cultural superiority like a badge. One writer, as late as 1948, could say in a secondary school text,

'The inhabitants of the savannas are superior to the forest tribes, who have many degraded customs and superstitions. . .'

Books which described the geography of Africa, South-East Asia or the Caribbean often implied that the coming of plantation agriculture was an undoubted benefit to all concerned; Europeans provided business know-how, efficiency and entrepreneurial expertise, whilst 'natives' provided the perspiring labour (which, it was implied, was the best that could be expected of them). The extraction of resources from one country, for the benefit of another at favourable rates of purchase, was scarcely questioned. By implication, Western culture was accorded a favoured position.

The Emergence of Concern

Concern about these images and attitudes in geography textbooks began to emerge publicly in the late 1970s. One of the first to draw attention to the matter was David Hicks, himself a former geography teacher, who had become a researcher in a funded project at Lancaster. Hicks wrote a major article considering images of the world as presented in geography textbooks for the *Cambridge Journal of Education* in 1981 (Hicks, 1981). Though written mainly in a concern for the context of development education, it included a considerable amount of material about multicultural issues.

One part of the article which drew particular attention was a diagram in which Hicks classified a range of popular contemporary school textbooks on two scales. One scale was related to the supposed 'geographical paradigm' on which the book was judged to be based; it ran between Radical — Liberal — Status Quo. The other scale was related to supposed 'perspective' and was calibrated between Racist — Ethnocentric — Non-racist — Anti-racist. Some authors thus found themselves unfortunately and damagingly classified, without any evidence adduced in print to support the judgement, nor any chance to respond or explain concerning their own books. There is little doubt that Hicks was impeccably intentioned, and the article was generous in other ways. But it set some dangerous precedents for later debates when the temperature on these issues was being raised — (some would say, justifiably).

At the conclusion of his article Hicks urged that:

1 We urgently consider how to bring the 'relevance revolution' into school geography. . .
2 Educational publishers need to develop checklists and guidelines on ethnocentric bias in geography textbooks a) to use themselves and b) to be used by authors.
3 Educational publishers need to commission new textbooks to rectify the deficient images already noted in this survey.
4 Teachers and study groups need to make known praise or blame for textbooks and make their comments and criteria known to publishers and colleagues.

This put into play some key issues, and also set the scene for a major controversy in the world of geographical education.

Dawn Gill's Schools Council Report

In 1982 the Schools Council made headlines in the educational press when they declined to publish a report which they had commissioned in the previous year. The Report, designed to highlight the problems of assessment in a multicultural society with special reference to geography, was one of a series commissioned by a project team. The Geography Report was commissioned from Dawn Gill, then Head of Geography at Quintin Kynaston School in St John's Wood, London.

The Project lead officer, Geoff Bardell, maintained later that 'Miss Gill received detailed and critical comments on her work. . .and was asked to take on board some/all of the criticisms. . .(but that) some two months later the steering group received a virtually unchanged report and reluctantly reached the decision not to recommend publication'. Gill had chosen to interpret her brief widely, taking on board not only examination issues but also those of geography syllabuses in general. She concluded that many syllabuses were inherently racist in the way in which they tackled matters. Her criticisms included the accusations that geography syllabuses failed to discuss colonialism and its effects fully, that developing countries were exclusively seen as 'problems'; that other countries were defined in what 'they' could provide for 'us'; and that there was an undesirable Eurocentricity in much of what was studied.

The Schools Council admitted that there was much of value in the report but felt that it was partial in coverage and too negative and critical to influence examination boards into change — the original purpose of the exercise. The decision not to publish precipitated the report (and Gill herself) into national prominence.

The Education Officer of the Commission for Racial Equality (CRE), Gerry German, ascertained that Gill had kept the copyright on her own work and then shrewdly offered to make the report freely available to those who wished to see it. A press conference, radio appearances and a flurry of correspondence in the educational press made the issue something of a *cause célèbre*, and it was given further publicity at a conference held at the London Institute of Education in March 1983 and backed by the CRE and the Multi-Ethnic Inspectorate of ILEA.

The focus of Gill's criticisms was on the immensely successful Geography for the Young School Leaver Project (GYSL), an approach to geography 14–16 which had been called the jewel in the Schools Council's crown and was certainly an immense influence on many geography teachers in the 1970s and 80s. It had been powerfully disseminated post-1976, and its well-produced materials and ideas stimulated many teachers beyond those who picked up its particular GCE and CSE-related examination syllabuses.

Gill criticized particular resource sheets in the material of the project (see Example in Figure 7.1) for their approach and their implicit Eurocentric bias: accusations of racism were made in forthright terms. GYSL co-directors subsequently invited Gill and some of her colleagues to a consultation about the materials and to the 1984 GYSL Conference at Homerton College, Cambridge. But a further dispute then ensued about whether or not GYSL themselves had acknowledged the materials as 'racist' and whether or not such material should go on being published and circulated. Following the Conference Dawn Gill and Ian Cook circulated a letter to conference members accusing GYSL of lack of action to correct perceived inadequacies and saying 'We have no alternative but to withdraw from co-operation with the project'. They likewise refused an invitation to

Figure 7.1

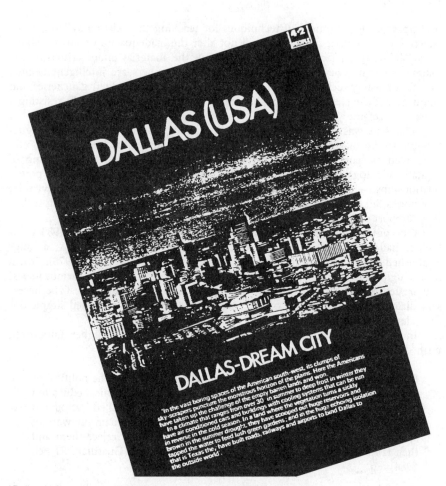

'*Dallas U.S.A.*' (Resource Sheet 4.2 Cities and People Unit)
Dallas is presented as a 'dream city' which has three problems:

* Dallas is a visual mess — fine new buildings jostle rundown shacks, unsightly parking areas blot the town, festoons of garish advertising defile the walls, and raw, unfinished or abandoned building sites proliferate. ** The crime rate is also a disgrace and has been growing at three times the rate of population increase. *** Nineteen per cent of the population is negro and economically deprived — though by most American standards the 'deprived' negro is well off.	It is a visual mess; the crime rate is a disgrace; and 19% of the population is negro. These statements are juxtaposed on the resource sheet.

Are criminal behaviour and skin colour necessarily related? If not, why the juxtaposition of these statements? Although economic conditions are mentioned, there is no attempt to link explicitly the incidence of crime with that of economic or social deprivation, with relative powerlessness or the acquisitiveness associated with low social status in a consumer oriented society. In fact skin colour is presented as the only relevant factor, because although the American negro is economically deprived, 'by most American standards, the deprived negro is well off'. What does this phrase mean? One of the consequences of using this resource sheet in the classroom without questioning the underlying assumptions and the juxtaposition of these statements may be that racism is fostered unintentionally.

participate in development of techniques for teaching the existing syllabus more effectively. 'Cosmetic alterations will not alter the inadequacies of this syllabus.'

GYSL did, in fact, eventually withdraw the material under criticism, but maintained that 'Our line has always been that teachers are intelligent beings, capable of using such materials with care'. They acknowledged gaucheries and language deficiencies in some of their early worksheets whilst stoutly resisting a charge of racism.

The issue was complicated by the wider issues which Gill and her colleagues brought to the analysis of the materials. A set of six newer textbooks from GYSL were seen as 'part of a subtle system of indoctrination' and the 'fostering of capitalist ideology to the exclusion of alternatives'. 'The current system of power relationships — globally and nationally — is presented as natural and inevitable. The books fail to encourage critical questioning of these power relationships, thus they support an inequitable status quo in world affairs.'

One notable non-sponsor of the London Institute of Education 1983 Conference had been Michael Storm, the Geography Inspector of ILEA, a long-established writer and commentator on Third World topics (Storm, 1978). Storm now sought to disentangle matters of fact from matters of debate in various issues, and argued that Gill's analysis was tendentious and over-simplified. 'The necessary dialogue is not advanced by stereotyping (teachers) as misguided simpletons or malevolent National Front recruiting agents.'

In reply John Huckle, a lecturer at Bedford College of Higher Education, pushed the context ever wider:

> Dawn Gill and others. . .are seeking to raise awareness of the political or ideological role of much that currently passes for geographical education in schools. . .geographical education is inevitably political education and its goals are not served by 'professionals' who either remain unaware of structuralist explanations of society and inequality, or reject them and then fail to give them any mention in the classroom. (Guardian, 21 Feb 1984)

Elsewhere, Huckle had written openly of the need to progress 'towards a socialist approach to school geography' (Huckle, 1983).

This heavy political baggage was counter-productive in some ways. Teachers who acknowledged the cogency and legitimacy of some of Gill's criticisms of school materials did not necessarily share the radical and Marxist analysis of education which accompanied them. The highly politicized context recruited some enthusiasts to the cause, but the strident and indiscriminate tone of some of the criticisms alienated other potential supporters. The original basic issues (notably in relation to multicultural perspectives) became bound up in complex ideological arguments.

Two other factors contributed to an eventual loss of impact of these viewpoints. First, the whole tide of educational thinking was swinging away from 'progressivism' as the 80s proceeded. The liberal educational establishment which had dominated thought and action from the Plowden Report onwards found itself being uncomfortably wrong-footed by a Government-led response which invoked the viewpoints and influence of parents, governors and employers. This quest for 'traditional values' — a return to emphasizing the basics, a concern for standards exemplified by more rigorous testing, a creation of a National Curriculum — was adopted as enthusiastically by Labour and Liberal Democrat politicians in a re-markable tri-partisan volte-face, following the espousal of reconstructionist ideals in the previous twenty years. Educators, faced with challenges to their philoso-phies (and some hard evidence about their relative ineffectiveness), sometimes reacted with strategies perilously close to those of Canute.

This, allied to a shrinking school population (which in turn meant that there were fewer promotional opportunities for young, radical teachers), provided a much less favourable climate for change than in the expansionist 60s and 70s. Quite apart from the merits of the case, the circumstance was not propitious for radical reforms.

Second, it must be said, Gill and her colleagues took some curious strategic options. Having set up the Association for Curriculum Development in Geo-graphy (ACDG) in the wake of the 1983 Conference, the nucleus of a coherent group of idealists was identifiable. The ACDG produced a highly-readable maga-zine, *Contemporary Issues in Geography and Education*, which was generously and sympathetically reviewed, even by those who had reservations about its ideo-logical position. The first two issues concentrated on 'Geography and education for a multi-cultural society' and provided provocative and stimulating reading.

But the Journal brooked no viewpoints other than those which it endorsed as ideologically pure, even to the point of eschewing advertisements for books which had not been endorsed by it. It successively began to search for other targets, change its format, and become more 'academic'. Labouring under an entirely voluntary editorial team, its frequency became more and more erratic and whilst originally intended to be thrice yearly, it published only eight editions in eight years. A letter in February 1991 to the remaining band of dwindling subscribers regretted that it was no longer possible to publish through lack of money (a substantial ILEA grant having eventually run out). 'We regret particularly that we have to discontinue publication at a time when the need for a radical educa-tional journal in Geography is especially acute. . . . we will continue to work as individuals towards the aims which we held as a collective and hope that you feel that the work which we have done over the past few years has not been entirely wasted. . .'

It is tempting to speculate what might have happened had the ACDG sought to become involved with both the GYSL Project (as invited) and The Geographical Association, whose larger membership and substantial infrastructure of committees and salaried administrators could have provided fertile ground for a group with enthusiasm and purpose. (A similar situation had occurred twenty years earlier when the spatial-analysis dominated London Schools Geographical Group had been taken on board by the GA as a Models and Quantitative Techniques Committee and very successfully disseminated its views to an initially sceptical wider audience).

The Geographical Association did, in fact, respond to the impact of Gill's writing by setting up its own Working Party with a membership drawn widely across educational sectors and geographical areas. After a year's work it produced a Report, *Geographical Education for a Multi-Cultural Society* (Walford, 1985), which was published and extensively circulated. There is no doubt that the cogent criticisms of the ACDG and its analysis of both textbooks and pedagogies played an important part in the deliberations of the Working Party (see Figure 7.2).

Figure 7.2 Synopsis of the Report of the Geographical Association Working Party, 1985

The Report of the Geographical Association Working Party

Synopsis

The Working Party believes that:-

1 it is unhelpful and inadequate to make a response such as "This is not my problem because I don't have any black/Irish/Muslim, etc. . .pupils in my school";

2 there is a distinctive part for the geography teacher to play in educating for life in multi-cultural Britain;

3 geography teachers, through their concern to develop a multi-cultural perspective for pupils, should be concerned to give controversial issues full consideration in their programmes of work and to facilitate rational and informed debate and discussion about them;

4 teachers should subscribe to a GA originated statement which seeks to oppose racist practices in schools and classrooms;

5 teachers should be prepared to examine thoroughly their own classroom practices and resources and ensure that there is representation of different cultural viewpoints;

6 teachers should seek to develop strategies of teaching and learning which exemplify multi-cultural realities in practical ways. For example:

if the diversity of races and cultures across the world is to be considered it should not be in hackneyed stereotypes or rooted in the picturesque;

more than one source of information should be used in teaching about our own and other cultures wherever possible;

a move to increase experiential (in addition to informational) teaching should be encouraged;

the development of good relationships between pupils and between teachers and pupils in the classroom can be the most effective demonstration of how the outside world should be.

Associated with the Report itself were checklists for teachers, as Hicks had suggested, a set of teaching examples, and an extensive bibliography. The Working Party also drew up an Anti-Racist Statement which the GA adopted in June 1984 as its official policy.

Beyond this, the whole debate in geographical education was being generally stimulated. Starting tentatively with general issues of multiculturalism, it extended into the harder-edged debate about racism and anti-racism. The consciousness of many geography teachers was raised on the issue, and this helped to stem some of the more insensitive expressions of cultural bias.

Prompted and made uncomfortable by Gill's diligent exposés, publishers and authors became much more aware about the criticisms which she and her colleagues in ACDG were raising (Storm, 1987). Almost inevitably, whilst extreme radical viewpoints were not generally adopted, the general thrust which lay behind them was accepted. They had the ability to lay bare the inadequacies of much which was being unconsciously perpetrated with good intentions. The relative status and visibility of ethnic minorities in books, pamphlets and worksheets was assessed. Techniques for the analysis of publications were developed and demonstrated. Associated issues (particularly those associated with gender bias) were raised and brought into full public debate at geography conferences and in-service sessions for teachers.

Thus the apparent demise of an organization, a journal and a movement cloaks an ultimate success. Though Gill's full-blooded reconstructionist philosophy for geographical education was not widely adopted, the essence of some of her original criticisms had its effect. Various houses were subsequently begun to be put in order.

The Advent of the National Curriculum

Most of this furore had (fortunately?. . .) died down by the time the National Curriculum was mooted in the late 1980s. The multicultural issue did not figure prominently in the discussion about whether or not geography should be a National Curriculum subject; geography became one of the ten foundation subjects in the proposals of the Education Reform Bill which passed through Parliament in 1988. Nevertheless, the members of the National Curriculum Working Group appointed by the Secretary of State for Education and Science to draft the geography curriculum in detail were well aware of the landscape of the recent past, and by no means disposed to ignore it.

The Terms of Reference given to the Group on its institution in May 1989 included the injunction to 'identify the contribution which geography could make to the overall school curriculum' using the given structure of Attainment Targets, Levels of Attainment and Programmes of Study already formulated by the Task Group on Assessment and Testing (DES, 1990).

It was suggested that the group should take account of

the contributions which geography can make to learning about other subjects and cross-curricular themes. . .and which they, in turn, can make to learning about geography. (DES, 1990)

Multicultural education did not figure prominently in the priorities for cross-curricular themes listed by the National Curriculum Council, and of these environmental education was the one more specifically targetted for geography's consideration in the Terms of Reference. The 'Supplementary Guidance' from the DES for the Chairman of the Working Group did make more open reference to multicultural matters, however.

The study of geography in schools should enable pupils. . .to develop an informed appreciation and understanding of the world in which they live. (DES 1990; Annex B, para. 4)

Geography should also help pupils to gain a knowledge of ways of life and cultures other than their own, and to understand the similarities and differences. (DES, 1990; Annex B, para. 5)

It should also help them to understand the physical, economic, political and cultural relationships that link people living in different places throughout the world. (DES, 1990; Annex B, para. 5)

It will be important to bear in mind that the curriculum should provide equal opportunities for boys and girls; the group should also take account of the ethnic diversity of the school population and society at large. (DES, 1990; Annex B, para. 16)

The underlying message of both the formal Terms of Reference and the more informal advice offered by the DES, however, was of the need to ensure that the curriculum was returned to a clear base of knowledge. The present *status quo* (often process-dominated) was deemed unsatisfactory, and the implication was that the Working Group should ensure that a broad basis of factual content was specified. More ambitious intentions need not be stifled but must work from a secure underpinning.

The *general* significance and relevance of the multicultural issue meant that it would be bound to surface, whatever the emphases of the initial guidance. Almost at once the over-riding concern about how to understand other cultures with insight arose in the discussion on the form and structure of possible Attainment Targets. The DES Secretariat provided a memorandum on 'The Geography Curriculum and Ethnic Diversity' and the Group spent a half-day discussing matters specifically related to it. The GA's Multicultural Report was circulated to all members for background reading, and a reference commending it for further information and study stayed in the Draft of the Final Report for a long time, until excised near publication for reasons of textual congruence.

Multiculturalism in the Final Report

The Final Report of the Geography Working Group included a separate section on 'Geography in a Multicultural Society' within a Chapter titled 'Geography for All'. The subsequent document produced by the National Curriculum Council after organizing a Consultation on the Report noted that

Few respondents disagreed with the sections of the Report concerning geography in a multicultural society, but some considered that the Report could have done more to challenge racism, and others that the proposals could have put greater emphasis on cultural awareness. (NCC Consultation Report on Geography 2.21, November 1990)

Such criticisms were unsurprising, given the variety of viewpoints held by teachers, and the various constraints which operated on the Working Party.

The Final Report made positive multicultural moves in asserting that geography in schools should help to educate all pupils for life in a culturally diverse society by introducing pupils to the reality of cultures and ways of life in other countries, *and by dealing with cultural diversity in Britain* (DES, 1990, para. 8.2).

But perhaps the most significant paragraph in this sphere was 8.5:

Geography is controversial. It cannot avoid dealing with cultural and ethnic issues. The existence of differences, the reasons for them, peoples' attitudes towards them, and their implications are as likely to arise in work on the home area or region, or on the United Kingdom, as on work on other countries or in human geography. The geography curriculum provides the context in which the questions can be asked and the issues raised in rational and informed debate. (DES, 1990)

The wholesale implication of geography in multicultural matters is clearly asserted in that statement. It was an injunction not to duck out on the issues.

But, it must be remembered, the accompanying text of the Final Report was not to be part of the statutory legal framework which was to pass through Parliament. The proper test of such sentiments was to see if the curriculum which passed into law allowed (or encouraged?) the kind of context and controversy to which 8.5 refers. The proposals of the Working Group (and the subsequent amendments proposed by the National Curriculum Council) suffered some change on the way to becoming Draft Orders and then Final Orders for enactment in law. By Christmas 1990 Kenneth Baker had moved on, John McGregor had come and gone, and Kenneth Clarke was now in office as Secretary of State for Education. He had expressed some irritation about the advice being offered by both SEAC (School Examinations and Assessment Council) and NCC in the months before, and so he no doubt looked at the geography Proposals on his desk with a critical eye.

In explaining his decision to make some changes Clarke wrote:

The Secretary of State recognizes that geography lessons will sometimes deal with conflicting points of view on important geographical issues. However, he considers that the main emphasis in the statutory requirements should be on teaching a knowledge and understanding of geography, rather than on the study of people's attitudes and opinions. Some statements of attainment, which appeared to concentrate on attitudes and opinions rather than geographical knowledge and understanding have therefore been removed. (*Draft Orders for the National Curriculum in Geography*, DES, 1991)

Some anguished pleading from all quarters of the geographical community restored one or two statements to the Final Orders, but it was clear that the Government wished geography (like all other core and foundation subjects in the National Curriculum) to be based on a knowledge component.

The Secretary of State consolingly pointed out that a reduction in the number of statements to be tested would reduce overloading in the curriculum. He also pointed out that he had no wish to curtail discussion of issues, but that it was quite another matter to have them tested within statutory frameworks. Given previous uncertainty about the validity of testing in the affective domain, there was some weight in this argument.

On reflection, it could also be appreciated that the National Curriculum was a base-line entitlement for pupils rather than a global umbrella to describe all that should be taught. Statements concerning the appreciation of other cultures or the promotion of anti-racism were unlikely to figure in a restricted and ultimately test-driven scenario, whatever DES views were about them.

Figure 7.3 Combining the attainment targets

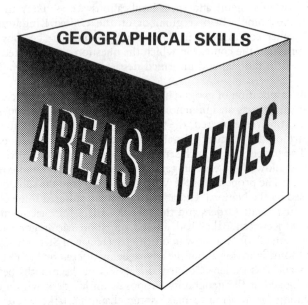

Opportunities for multicultural education and anti-racist teaching have not been closed off. But given the DFE's present reluctance to commit much effort or influence into cross-curricular initiatives until the 'building blocks' are established, it is likely that such opportunities must be explored primarily within individual subject frames in the next few years.

The question then arises; what opportunities does the statutory Geography National Curriculum give?

The Final Orders in Geography (DES, 1991) clearly reflect the expressed wish for a defined knowledge base for pupils between the ages of 5 and 16. That wish was endorsed by the Working Group for quite *non*-political reasons. Lay members of the group expressed their disquiet with some of the present situations, and their views were supported by HMI surveys and other evidence considered by the Group. Consequently the move to a content-driven specification — rather than a skills-based or mode-of-enquiry based formulation — was knowingly done.

The frame finally adopted centred around 5 Attainment Targets;

AT 1   Geographical skills (centring on mapwork and fieldwork)
AT 2   The knowledge and understanding of places
AT 3   Physical geography
AT 4   Human geography
AT 5   Environmental geography

The heart of the subject was expressed by reference to a cube (see Figure 7.3) which represented the interlocking nature of skills, themes and area studies. The subtext of this framework included the coining of 'Environmental Geography' as a new term (and Attainment Target) to link both physical and human aspects of geography and focus on current environmental issues. The study of places was also re-emphasized as an important part of school geography.

The feeling was that there had been too little place-study in some schools in recent years and that some students passed through their school education without anything but the fragmented understanding of some concepts, skills and themes which drew randomly and insecurely on a locational base. The hoisting of 'places' into greater prominence clearly benefits multicultural objectives. In some primary schools, for the first time for many years, some specific geography will now be undertaken. A study of a locality *beyond* the home area is now required in Key Stage 2. The ghost of 'Bombo of the Congo' may hover over this move, but hopefully the study of overseas places will not be in picturesque and antique vein.

The programme of study for Key Stage 2 requires that:

> Pupils should study. . .a locality in an economically developing country. They should be taught:
> * to investigate features of other localities. . .and how these features might affect people's lives;
> * to describe the features and occupations of other localities studied and compare them with those of the local area;
> * to identify and describe similarities and differences between their local area and other localities;
> * how the localities have changed as a result of human actions;
> * to investigate recent or proposed changes in a locality;
> * to examine the impact of landscape, weather and wealth on the lives of people in a locality in an economically developing country.

All this adds up to a reasonably comprehensive case-study of another culture, grounded in the reality of small-scale study — family and community life in a village or other small settlement. It should help to dispel ignorance and prejudice about other life-styles, and may quite likely be related to the countries of origin of some children in the particular class.

A further case-study — this time at national scale — is required in Key Stage 3. Here students are required:

> to study the geographical features and conditions of an economically developing country selected from Bangladesh, Brazil, China, Egypt, Ghana, India, Kenya, Mexico, Nigeria, Pakistan, Peru or Venezuela;

> to describe the features and occupations of a locality in the country selected and compare them with the local area; how the locality has changed as a result of human actions; and to investigate recent or proposed changes in the locality;

> to examine the impact of landscape, weather and wealth on the lives of people in a locality in the country selected;

> to discover how the occupations, land-use and settlement patterns of a locality in the country selected are related to the country's environment and location;

to outline the distribution of population in the country selected and how this is influenced by the features and conditions in the country;

to evaluate the extent to which the country displays the characteristics of development.

Thus it can be seen that this is a broadly complementary study to be undertaken at a more wide-ranging scale with equal opportunity for the study of another culture in some depth.

Statements of Attainment in the Human Geography Attainment Target also offer potential in the multicultural sphere.

At Key Stage 2 children should be taught

why some parts of the world contain very few people while other parts are densely populated;

why people move homes;

how land is used in different ways.

At Key Stage 3

to examine and seek reasons for changes in the population size of regions and countries; to examine the global distribution of population, and to give reasons as to why some regions have high population density whilst others have low population density;

to compare differences in economic development and welfare in different parts of the world;

to analyse the causes and effects of a recent large-scale migration of population.

At Key Stage 4

to examine at different geographical scales some reasons for, and the consequences of, differences in the structure of populations;

the roles of decision-makers in processes affecting urban and regional development;

the causes of uneven economic development in and between countries and to appraise actions intended to redress such imbalances;

the causes and geographical consequences of the distribution of ethnic, religious or linguistic groups in particular areas (Level 9);

to evaluate international differences in levels of economic development, and international strategies for improving the quality of life in economically developing countries (Level 10).

These proposals do not, in general, address multicultural issues as directly as some would have preferred; but, if properly carried out, they provide some of the essential background knowledge needed to counter ignorance, indifference and prejudice about other cultures.

Pedagogy: The Critical Factor

The written injunctions of the National Curriculum will eventually be tested by as yet unknown forms of assessment; the critical factor in exploiting their possibilities will be the pedagogy used in the classroom. The general pattern of National Curriculum formulations has been to leave this matter to teachers as far as possible, the encouragement being to knead Programmes of Study into various units of classroom work using whatever teaching approaches seem suitable to the individual practitioner. There is clear acceptance that this should not necessarily mean uniform methods in every classroom.

In this context, the Secretary of State's expressed concern about 'overloading' may be seen in its most beneficial light. However supposedly vital its content, an overpacked curriculum would cause teachers to resort to 'pressure-feed' methods. Thus, the considerable literature about classroom approaches to multicultural issues is not put out of play by the shift to prescribed content. Specifically in relation to geography lessons, the publications of the Association for Curriculum Development in Geography and The Geographical Association offer ideas for classroom use.

The ACDG materials have proved difficult to purchase since the demise of the Association in 1991, but the GA's Multicultural Report remains available in print. The two major teaching handbooks produced by the Association (Mills, 1988; Boardman, 1986) are rich repositories of classroom ideas, many of which relate to teaching about other countries and cultures.

Another useful source of material has come from the continuing work of projects concerned with development education, world studies and global studies. This derives its roots from work done in personal, social and religious education as well as in history and geography. Robin Richardson was a significant and continuing influence in these areas in the 1980s and, through the World Studies Project, a co-author of two important collections of classroom ideas (Richardson, 1979; Richardson, Flood and Fisher, 1980).

The work of the World Studies Project was continued by David Hicks and others, and further publications developed general classroom approaches in a number of related topics. (Hicks and Fisher, 1985; Hicks and Steiner, 1988). The Centre for Global Education at York has been another contributor to this field (Pike and Selby, 1988).

Mention should also be made of the stream of ideas (usually encompassed in short magazine or newspaper articles) which have emanated from David Wright, the geographer in the School of Education at the University of East Anglia. He was one of the earliest to draw attention to the partiality and deficiency of textbook images of other cultures (Wright, 1979; Wright, 1982).

What these pedagogic approaches have in common is a strong commitment to active participation by pupils in classrooms and a concern for the affective as well as the cognitive domain. Richardson's work was particularly concerned with fostering effective discussion in classrooms so that pupil viewpoints and perspectives about multicultural issues could be revealed (Richardson, 1982). Hicks, and Pike and Selby, have developed many examples of group activities in which students have a chance to complete unfinished sentences with thoughts of their own choosing, or make comparisons between apparently opposing points of view. Another fruitful way of developing insight and concern for other cultures is through the use of simulations, role-plays and games. There is now a considerable general literature in this field, a flourishing national journal, which combines insights from different disciplines, and numerous practical examples in print (see references for examples). The situation is long past when teachers regarded such activities only as end-of-term revels or interesting curiosities.

Two classic examples may bear mention here, both originated by Garry Shirts, a professional American game-maker. *Starpower* involves students getting into three groups of 'Squares', 'Circles' and 'Triangles' and trading together. The group which trades most successfully is given the ability to change the rules of trading at various times — and they usually do so to their own advantage. The game goes on until some signs of disaffection from the unsuccessful groups begin to show. . . . The teacher is then required to debrief the situation and explore the mechanisms and motives of what was going on, while the groups explain, justify (and confess) to each other. Issues of cultural solidarity and misunderstanding usually loom very large on the agenda.

BA'FA BA'FA (also known in a European version as *Outsider*) has even more cultural import. The Game Manager sets up two 'cultures' in different rooms, one friendly but ritualistic and secretive (Motto: Keep smiling); the other wealth-oriented and given a path to achievement through hard trading (Motto: Keep trying). Groups from each society visit the other, successively as Tourists (looking through the windows of the other room), Anthropologists (being allowed to scrutinize at close quarters) and then Migrants (given the wherewithal to survive but no other instructions). At the end of the session the two groups are asked to explain to each other what they thought was going on in the other culture; the usual result is considerable misperception and misunderstanding. Migrants have often had an uncomfortable time. The simulation is an effective tool in pointing out the ease with which one culture can misunderstand another, and in giving students a strong experience of being in someone else's shoes in this context.

Not all simulations have to be as large-scale as these two activities, however; it is possible to involve students in exercises which last only a few minutes in which they imaginatively 'put themselves in other people's shoes' in facing particular situations. Some games such as *The Paper Bag Game* (Christian Aid, 1981) involve simple practical work; others such as *Aid Committee* (Oxfam, 1980) involve group discussion and decision-making. There are also a number of simple games such as *Caribbean Fisherman* (Walford, 1986), which can be operated within a single school period and which help to provide insight into ways of life in other countries. Role-plays and games usually have strong empathetic intentions, but they need careful management. If used sensitively they can be powerful tools in developing multicultural understanding and are in no way irrelevant to the more generalized National Curriculum objectives listed above.

Given the current emphases in National Curriculum statutes, geographers have also to ensure that *knowledge* about other cultures is effectively transmitted. Here, textbooks and teacher-talk need to be effectively enhanced by other approaches. Geography has always had a strong tradition of audio-visual teaching, and recent developments in video and computer-based learning offer great opportunities to learn in depth about other cultures. The Cambridge-based 'Sahara Project' for instance, expects to publish soon an inter-active video disc concerning life in Mali, which will encompass thousands of slides and hundreds of hours of video and audio tape to aid in-depth understanding of the region. Such resources allow pupils to pursue their own interests and enquiries as well as provide comprehensive and thorough background as an antidote to stereotypes.

The use of less hi-tech resources can also bring its dividends. Artefacts from other cultures can form the basis of investigation and understanding. Visitors from another country do not have to be skilled teachers in order to represent their cultures effectively. Rather than being asked to give a talk, a person from another culture may be much better used in answering the usual stream of questions which a school class will ask if given a little time to think and prepare. Such simple human interaction goes a long way towards removing fears and misconceptions and improving multicultural understanding.

Conclusion

Opportunities do not have the same impelling force as legal requirements, however. If teachers choose to interpret the need for a knowledge base in geography (as implied by the National Curriculum) as an indication to return to a limited set of didactic, information-processing strategies, it will be a disappointing response (and short-sighted analysis) of the situation. The hope must surely be that there is adequate time given to the subject for its National Curriculum obligations (the Working Group predicated 60–65 hours of time each year) so that lack of time does not become the excuse for a narrow back-to-basics approach. The new consciousness engendered by the lively controversies of the 1980s (and described in the first part of this chapter) must surely inform and enhance the transmission of essential content.

Multicultural dimensions remain an important part of school geography. The fact that they are not precluded by the present shape of the National Curriculum may be a modest achievement but, in the present climate, not an entirely unworthy one.

References

ARCHER, A.B. and THOMAS, A.G. (1938) *Geography; First Series Books 1–4*, London, Ginn.

ASSOCIATION FOR CURRICULUM DEVELOPMENT IN GEOGRAPHY (1983–91) *Contemporary Issues in Geography and Education*, London, Association for Curriculum Development in Geography.

BOARDMAN, D. (Ed.) (1986) *Handbook for Geography Teachers*, Sheffield, Geography Association.

BUNGE, W. (1984) 'Racism in Geography', *Contemporary Issues in Geography and Education*, **2**, Spring, pp. 10–11.

DEPARTMENT OF EDUCATION AND SCIENCE (1990) *Geography for Ages 5 to 16; Final Report of the Geography Working Group*, London, HMSO.

Rex Walford

DEPARTMENT OF EDUCATION AND SCIENCE (DES) (1991) *Geography in the National Curriculum; Statutory Orders*, London, HMSO.

GOLDSMITH, J. (1815) *An Easy Grammar of Geography for Schools and Young Persons (47th edn)*, London, Longman.

*HICKS, D. (1981) 'Images of the world: what do geography text books actually teach about development?', *Cambridge Journal of Education*, **11**, 1, Cambridge, pp. 15–35.

HICKS, D. and FISHER, S. (1985) *World Studies 8–13; A Teachers Handbook*, Edinburgh, Oliver and Boyd.

HICKS, D. and STEINER, M. (1989) *Making Global Connections: A World Studies Workbook*, Edinburgh, Oliver & Boyd.

HUCKLE, J. (Ed.) (1983) *Geographical Education; Reflection and Action*, Oxford, Oxford University Press.

MILLS, D. (Ed.) (1988) *Geographical Work in Primary and Middle Schools*, Sheffield, Geographical Association.

NATIONAL CURRICULUM COUNCIL (1990) *Consultation Report on Geography*, York, National Curriculum Council.

PIKE, G. and SELBY, D. (1988) *Global Teacher, Global Learner*, London, Hodder & Stoughton.

RICHARDSON, R. (1979) *Learning for Change in World Society; Reflections, Activities and Resources*, World Studies Project.

*RICHARDSON, R. (1982) 'Talking about equality: the use and importance of discussion in multi-cultural education', *Cambridge Journal of Education*, **12**, 2, Cambridge, pp. 101–14.

RICHARDSON, R., FLOOD, M. and FISHER, S. (1980) *Debate and Decision: Schools in a World of Change*, World Studies Project.

SIMULATION (1980-present) *Simulation Games for Learning*, London, Kogan Page.

STORM, M. (1978) 'Multi-ethnic education and geography' in *Schooling and Culture*, Issue 3, Autumn.

STORM, M. (1987) 'Geography and antiracist teaching', *ILEA Geography Bulletin*, 25, Spring, pp. 6–10.

WALFORD, R. (Ed.) (1985) *Geographical Education for a Multi-Cultural Society: A Report*, Sheffield, Geographical Association.

WALFORD, R. (1986) *Caribbean Fisherman*, Cambridge, Cambridge Publishing Services.

WRIGHT, D.R. (1979) 'Visual images in geography texts: The case of Africa' in *Geography*, **64**(3), July, Geographical Association, pp. 205–10.

WRIGHT, D.R. (1982) 'Colourful South Africa?; An analysis of textbook images' in *Multiracial Education*, **10**(3), pp. 27–36.

Chapter 8

The Design and Technology Curriculum in a Multiethnic Society

John Eggleston

Technology, of which Design and Technology constitutes 80 per cent, is now a compulsory subject from the age of five to sixteen for all children in state schools in England and Wales. Moreover, there is every sign that many, if not most, independent schools are following suit. Yet the precise identity of this new subject is still being defined and is still unclear to many teachers who have not encountered it in their professional training or in their experience to date.

Design and Technology is unique in the school curriculum. It is the one subject directly concerned with the individual's capacity to design and make and to solve problems with the use of materials. The easiest way to define Design and Technology is by reference to *Technology in the National Curriculum* (Department of Education and Science, 1990a). Essentially this is specified in four Attainment Targets. The fifth Attainment Target in National Curriculum Technology is Information Technology: this is the subject of Chapter 9. Though National Curriculum Technology is under review at the time of writing the Attainment Targets are likely to remain intact with Planning and Making having the heaviest emphasis.

Attainment target 1: Identifying needs and opportunities.
Pupils should be able to identify and state clearly needs and opportunities for design and technological activities through investigation of the contexts of home, school, recreation, community, business and industry.

Attainment target 2: Generating a design.
Pupils should be able to generate a design specification, explore ideas to produce a design proposal and develop it into a realistic, appropriate and achievable design.

Attainment target 3: Planning and making.
Pupils should be able to make artefacts, systems and environments, preparing and working to a plan and identifying, managing and using appropriate resources, including knowledge and processes.

Attainment target 4: Evaluating.
Pupils should be able to develop, communicate and act upon an evaluation of the processes, products and effects of their design and technological

activities and of those of others, including those from other times and cultures.

Some teachers have seen all this as a 'Design and Make' process, but it is much more than that, as the Working Group Report and the ensuing Regulations and illustrative material make clear.

Although the National Curriculum provides a useful working basis, it cannot and does not attempt to be the authoritative and complete definition of Design and Technology. At the simplest level it has two components, Design and Technology, in close relationship. It consists of using technology to achieve solutions that satisfy sound design criteria and using design to achieve solutions that satisfy sound technological criteria. Most secondary schools have, for a very long time, offered a range of technology and design activity in areas such as food, fashion, work with wood and metal, applied science, business education and much else. The importance of this relationship and integration is strongly emphasized in the Working Group Report on Design and Technology (DES, 1989) sections 1/20 and 1/21 which read:

1.20   The activities of Design and of Technology overlap considerably. As we said in the Interim Report, 'most, though not all, design activities will generally include technology and most technology activities will include design'. However, we believe that the core of knowledge and skills as encompassed by our programmes of study, taken alongside the four attainment targets we detail, cover the significant aspects of design.

1.21   That is not to say that the knowledge, skills, values and processes of designing cannot be used and developed in other subjects. For example, in environmental design pupils will rarely be involved in creating a totally new environment, but will need to appraise what already exists, explore needs and devise ways of organising and achieving change. In pursuing their ideas, they will develop their sense of historical and cultural continuity and a recognition that the new has to grow out of the old. There are clear opportunities here for work in history, but also for other subjects such as geography, to build on and develop these ideas.

The close integration of Design and Technology is emphasized by Statutory Orders for National Curriculum Technology (DES, 1990a). They require that pupils' Design and Technological capability is to be developed at each Key Stage through:

- A broad range of practical activities. In each key stage, pupils should design and make:
  artefacts (objects made by people); *systems* (sets of objects or activities which together perform a task); *environments* (surroundings made, or developed, by people) in response to needs and opportunities identified by them.
- five broad contexts of work (situations in which design and technological activities take place): home, school, recreation, community, business and industry. Work should progress from familiar to unfamiliar contexts.

- working with a broad range of materials including textiles, graphic media (such as paint, paper, photographs), construction materials (such as clay, wood, plastic, metal) and food.
- a breadth of knowledge, skills, understanding, attitudes and values required in the attainment targets and programmes of study. In addition, 'pupils should be taught to draw on their knowledge and skills in other subjects, particularly subjects of science, mathematics and art, to support their designing and making activities'.
- personal development through activities in Design and Technology. 'Pupils should be taught to discuss their ideas, plans and progress with each other and should work individually and in groups.' 'They should be taught to take reasonable care at all times for the safety of themselves and others', 'Activities should also reflect their growing understanding of the needs and beliefs of other people and cultures, now and in the past'.
- progression of individual capability. 'As pupils progress, they should be given more opportunities to identify their own tasks for activity, and should use their knowledge and skills to make products which are more complex, or satisfy more demanding needs.'

National Curriculum Technology is particularly sensitive to the way issues of culture and race can be incorporated into a rigorous curriculum and also be firmly based within the educational objectives of the subject.

The Non-statutory Guidance for Technology quotes these passages from *Design and Technology for Ages 5–16* (DES, 1989):

Cultural diversity has always been a feature of British life. [Providing] a richer learning environment for all. . .the teaching of design and technology will require perceptiveness and sensitivity from teachers [to take account of] different beliefs and practices, especially when food, materials and environmental designs are involved. . . .

And it goes on to observe:

. . .there are rich opportunities here to demonstrate that no one culture has the monopoly of achievements in design and technology.

The Report urges that this be emphasized as much in white as in culturally diverse schools and affirms that Technology has 'an important part to play in preparing pupils for life in a multicultural society'.

Klein (1993) comments:

The Technology Working Group, then, has gone further in overtly addressing teachers' attitudes and teaching practice than most foundation subject working groups. It remains for classroom teachers to extend these recommendations to other National Curriculum areas.

But even though there is abundant opportunity for development it remains true that few schools have presented their curriculum in a way that fully incorporates all that Design and Technology offers. In many schools Technology and

Design are still seen as lesser areas of activity — taking place in workshops and studios respectively, being predominantly practical in nature and largely unrelated to the other subjects in the curriculum. As recent HMI surveys have shown, there is even evidence that there are shortcomings in the practical achievements available to many children.

A particular problem is the distribution of opportunity in schools. In many areas of Design and Technology, male achievement far outstrips that of female; white achievement exceeds that of black. As there is no evidence that overall capability in Design and Technology is distributed according to gender or ethnic variables there is an urgent need to examine this problem — not only on the grounds of justice, but also on the grounds of economic necessity, to satisfy the growing need for technological capability in modern society.

In principle, the problem should be solved by the very legislation that has brought the National Curriculum into being, for this prescribes that Technology should be taught to all children, black and white, male and female. But this will be an incomplete solution until we understand the sources of the powerful social pressures that have, for generations, differentiated technological achievement by race and gender.

Let us begin the analysis by briefly referring to gender; the issues of gender and race are analogous and research is more abundant in the former. It is easy to say that Technology is a male subject and that the images of Technology generally portray men doing the physically and intellectually demanding technological activities. Even very young children already perceive the subject in this way. Smithers and Zientek (1991) undertook a national survey of 259 boys and 247 girls, all aged five. They showed, for example, that car repairs and woodwork are seen as almost exclusively the province of men, and mending and washing clothes the domain of women. Both the boys and the girls saw it that way.

But of course the popular definition of Technology on which the male image is based is an incomplete one. For example, food technology, fashion and office skills, are all part of technology and are predominantly undertaken by women. Even when this is recognized, it is still true that there has been much gender stereotyping within technology. National Curriculum Technology, including Design and Technology, embracing Home Economics and Business Studies, Craft, Design and Technology and Art and Design is, however, remarkably free from such stereotyping and the broad definition of Technology in the National Curriculum is wholly welcome. But embracing subjects that were previously female areas of the curriculum may make it all too easy for schools to deliver Technology to boys and girls in separate ways that are little different from when the boys did woodwork and the girls cookery and needlework. The only difference would be that they would now be by 'choice' and not by imposition. As most school administrators know, choice can be a very effective strategy for achieving differentiation by apparently democratic means. It is all too easy to build on the perceptions of the 5-year-olds that Smithers and Zientek surveyed.

On the face of it the existence of racial differentiation in schools is a very different matter from gender differentiation, but the outcomes in terms of a selection of children based upon irrelevant and unnecessary expectations is very similar. The linkage has been identified by a number of writers, notably Banks (1987).

Fewer studies have been undertaken on the ethnic dimension of opportunity in Design and Technology, but much has been written on the ways in which ethnic minority children perceive their ability, experience and generally lower level of achievement in schools than their fellow pupils. Gillbourn (1990) has usefully reviewed the literature and shows that the differential expectations that so powerfully affect girls' and boys' achievement are paralleled by similar expectations that determine the experience of black young people and that their expectations are, if anything, more persistent than those surrounding gender.

It may be argued that a rapidly growing subject area such as Design and Technology could and should provide, not only equal, but enhanced opportunities for young people who have, so far, not found it easy to succeed in the more traditional areas of the curriculum. In particular, it should present opportunities for black young people to compete on more equal terms with white children for the new examination, higher education and career opportunities being opened up through Design and Technology.

Certainly some progress has been made. Black children have full access to Design and Technology classes; there is no sense in which their participation is excluded. Yet, sadly, ethnic disadvantage in access to examination classes and examination successes seems, in many schools, to be just as marked in Design and Technology as it does in other subjects. In a subject area in which long established 'success paths' do not exist to inhibit 'outsider groups', in which formal written English is relatively less important and in which creativity, flair, imagination and style are at a premium, why are black children not able to compete on at least equal terms? Why, one may even ask, are they not sometimes at an advantage?

In suggesting answers one begins to assemble a picture in which children may be disadvantaged in all aspects of schooling — not just in specific aspects. Perhaps at the simplest level of explanation may be the latent, even benign, but unmistakably racist orientations of the school culture which has spread over into the Design and Technology class. Visits to a range of Design and Technology classes by the author yielded ready examples:

Teacher to class, 'This is a messy job and you'll get your hands dirty. . .but that won't worry you, Winston, will it?' (White majority pupils smile, Winston, an Afro-Caribbean origin pupil, is clearly discomforted.)

Teacher to a group of black boys, 'Now then you lads, come down off the banana trees and get on with your work.'

Teacher to a group of black girls using an acid bath, 'Now then girls put your aprons on please; you don't want to mess up your grass skirts do you?'

There is no evidence that these teachers were intentionally or consciously racist. In discussions with these teachers after the incidents it was clear that they saw it as part of the everyday banter of the classroom, much the same as the banter of the pub, the sports club, the shop or the factory. Moreover some teachers even claimed that it was 'their duty' to expose their pupils to 'the reality of the world outside'. Such remarks were not confined to Design and Technology teachers, on investigation they were characteristic of many of the staff of the schools. Yet, that the effects of their remarks were unmistakably playing a part in generating and perpetuating racially linked assumptions for black and white pupils showed clearly in the response of both groups. There was some evidence that school anti-racist policies, where they existed and were implemented, reduced but did not entirely eliminate this kind of teacher behaviour.

Perhaps a more fundamental problem lies in the selection of children for examination streams. Research has shown that black children, particularly of Afro-Caribbean origin, are often less likely to be given a place in the examination streams leading to high status 'negotiable' qualifications. Even able black children are denied access because of beliefs that they will lack motivation, be handicapped by language, lack the appropriate cultural backgrounds, fail to understand the system, not 'know how to work hard', or will have behavioural problems and be disruptive. Many of these beliefs, alas, have a tragically self-fulfilling effect (Eggleston, *et al.*, 1986).

Design and Technology teachers, like other teachers, do not always challenge these assumptions; but they may fail to do so for a special reason. After years of being seen as offering a convenient haven for the pupils defined by the school as non-academic, non-motivated or otherwise of low status, Design and Technology teachers, encouraged by the newly won standing for their subject, are now enthusiastic to recruit academic, high status pupils to their courses. Sadly, in many schools many black children are not yet in or perceived as being in that category. As one Design and Technology teacher put it, 'after years of having to accept the low status kids why should we continue to do so now that we can have the high status ones for the asking?'

A final, and in the short run perhaps insoluble problem, is the attitude of black parents. They, often more keenly than white parents, want their children to succeed in the educational system. The motivation is understandable; they know that for their children educational success is even more crucial than for many white children because they have fewer alternative paths to achieve adult success. Brown (1984) and many other writers provide abundant evidence of racial discrimination in the work place and the paths to it. The studies are reviewed in Chapter 2 of Eggleston, *et al.* (1986). Not surprisingly, therefore, they view with suspicion new and alternative courses, as yet unproven in occupational and higher education achievement, and fight zealously for places on the traditional high status academic courses.

This was confirmed by a study of ethnic minority pupils' response to the Technical and Vocational Education Initiative (TVEI) conducted for the Training Agency (Eggleston and Sadler, 1987) in which the preferences of black pupils for 'main stream courses' was very clearly demonstrated. In part this preference was reinforced by poor communication between school and home. Many parents assumed, for example, that the work placement for children during the course was an indication of the job they were likely to get after completion of the TVEI programme. Many of the placements in jobs such as canteen assistant and supermarket shelf filler were seen as inferior and unacceptable. Similarly, schools failed to explore the extent of ethnic minority parental ambition and support, with regular Saturday school attendance, encyclopedias, computers and books in the home and much else.

The Report (Eggleston and Sadler, 1987) concludes with a number of recommendations which, though specific to TVEI, apply generally to the delivery of

Design and Technology in a multicultural society. Indeed, readers may care to substitute Design and Technology for Technical and Vocational Education Initiative in the paragraphs that follow. These include:

> Written communication must be accessible to parents in style and language and expert assistance should be used, as appropriate, to ensure this. The presence of more community language speakers on the staff of schools — as teachers or ancillaries — is an urgent need. The assistance of community leaders and teachers in the communication process should be used wherever possible. The appointment of 'home-school liaison officers' may be an attractive way forward.

> Communications should not be confined to factual information but should address parents' proper concerns about the status and opportunities afforded by TVEI. Clear indicators about the career and life chances offered by TVEI for pupils are now available and should be presented by the school. In particular, the concept of TVEI as a component in the overall change in the curriculum for all pupils — including those seeking to follow professional careers — should be presented fully and clearly. The ways in which TVEI can enhance academic courses rather than provide an alternative to them is a message of particular importance for parents and clear and unambiguous information should be given.

> Similar attention must be paid to the even more difficult task of ensuring that parents have adequate opportunity to communicate with the school so that programmes may be enhanced by a knowledge of home and community, parental experiences, concerns and aspirations, out of school education and the full richness of the children's cultural and community backgrounds. (Eggleston and Sadler, 1987, p. 42)

For similar and perhaps other reasons, we are witnessing a failure to grasp a new and real opportunity for black children to 'make it' in the education system — a failure symbolized by the worryingly low proportion of black children in TVEI schemes in many parts of the country. Design and Technology teachers who have played a major role in delivering TVEI must now take urgent steps to work with parents, pastoral and careers guidance colleagues and community leaders to overcome the problem of delivering National Curriculum Technology before yet another manifestation of disadvantage becomes established.

Fortunately some encouraging strategies are being developed. One promising initiative is the National Curriculum Council's 'Initiating Activity Through Other Cultures' which is a component of the BBC Television Programme *Design and Technology 11–16: Ways Forward*. The programme notes (NCC, 1991) state:

> Attainment Target 4, level 5, requires that pupils should be able to:

> Understand that artefacts, systems or environments from other times and cultures have identifiable characteristics and styles and draw upon this knowledge in design and technological activities.

The staff at the Holyrood School, Somerset, addressed other cultures and other times. Being a rural school, staff felt that pupils had little experience of the needs and values of other cultures. To broaden pupils' understanding, visitors from Tanzania and India spoke to all Year 7 pupils and gave displays of Indian dancing.

Following this presentation, pupils studied and evaluated clothing, textile design and food products and authentic musical instruments were made from plastic tubing. The effectiveness of these outcomes was assessed in many ways. Food was eaten and discussed in relationship to taste, visual appeal and nutritional value; clothing was modelled by pupils and evaluated with consideration of colour, style, cultural requirements and manufacturing processes. The sounds created by the musical instruments were adapted by the BBC to create the musical composition accompanying this programme.

This example opens up a prospect of opportunities still only incompletely recognized in many schools. It involves a recognition of the rich cultural tradition in Design and Technology that many ethnic minority children bring from their families and communities. Properly recognized in schools it could enable many black children to experience high achievement in Design and Technology and, as the Holyrood example shows, to obtain recognition from their fellow pupils in the process.

Another useful initiative comes from the Commonwealth Institute (1992) which has developed three resource packs to support technology 'across cultures'. All three address cultural perspectives in technology, making them useful for cross-curricular approaches in areas such as art, mathematics, and religious education. They provide stimulating material for a wide range of activities covering all four attainment targets. Although designed for Key Stages 2 and 3, they can be used effectively with Key Stages 1 and 4.

The packs are aimed at technology teachers who may know little about Islamic technology. The approach is one of guided discovery, sense and experimenting with new applications of known skills. Also available are the Intermediate Technology publications such as *Rural Blacksmith, Rural Businessman* (1992) on making and selling metal goods in Malawi.

Conclusion

The experience and achievement of pupils in Design and Technology is still often differentiated on grounds of race and ethnicity. In general this differentiation is arbitrary and bears no necessary relationship to the basic abilities, capacities and aspirations of the individuals. The self-fulfilling prophecy in all aspects of education is very powerful, and it is all too easy for teachers, employers, parents and pupils themselves to create expectations which make the differences seem real and justifiable. Constant vigilance is needed. However, the National Curriculum requirement to commence Design and Technology at the age of five gives the opportunity to challenge more readily the assumptions that are often firmly in place by the time secondary education begins. The new beginnings currently taking place in

Design and Technology give a window of opportunity through which to build real equality and enhanced achievement for all pupils.

References

BANKS, J.A. (1987) *Teaching Strategies for Ethnic Studies*, (Fourth Edition), Boston, Allyn and Bacon.

BROWN, C. (1984) *Black and White Britain*, London, Policy Studies Institute.

COMMONWEALTH INSTITUTE (1992) *Islam Technology Packs 1–3*, London, Commonwealth Institute.

DEPARTMENT OF EDUCATION AND SCIENCE (1989) *Design and Technology for Ages 5–16* (Final Report of the Working Group on Design and Technology), London, HMSO.

DEPARTMENT OF EDUCATION AND SCIENCE (DES) (1990a) *Technology in the National Curriculum*, London, HMSO.

DEPARTMENT OF EDUCATION AND SCIENCE (DES) (1990b) *Circular 3/90*, London, HMSO.

EGGLESTON, J. and SADLER, E. (1987) *The Participation of Ethnic Minority Students in TVEI*, Sheffield, Training Agency.

EGGLESTON, J., DUNN, D. and ANJALI, M. (1986) *Education for Some*, Stoke-on-Trent, Trentham.

GILLBOURN, D. (1990) *'Race' Ethnicity and Education*, London, Unwin Hyman.

INTERMEDIATE TECHNOLOGY (1992) *Rural Blacksmith, Rural Businessman*, Shaftesbury, I.T. Publications.

KLEIN, G. (1993) *Education Towards Race Equality*, London, Cassell.

NATIONAL CURRICULUM COUNCIL (1991) *Design and Technology 11–16: Ways Forward*, York, National Curriculum Council.

SMITHERS, A. and ZIENTEK, P. (1991) *Gender, Primary Schools and the National Curriculum*, London, Engineering Council.

Chapter 9

The Cultural Dimension of Information Technology

Brent Robinson

IT has a critical role in enhancing the learning process at all levels and across a broad range of activities including, but going beyond, the National Curriculum. Through the use of IT in the curriculum, schools will also be helping pupils become knowledgeable about the nature of information, comfortable with the new technology and able to exploit its potential. (DES, 1989a, para. 7)

Within the National Curriculum the use of information technology (IT) has become mandatory. It features within Technology (DES, 1990a) as an attainment target in its own right. It also features largely among the attainment targets and programmes of study of all the subjects. Indeed it is expected that children's acquisition of IT skills will occur very much through their acquaintance with the technology across the whole curriculum. This is recognition of the significant part which IT can play in the enrichment of learning experiences in many subject areas, not least in those learning situations where a cultural dimension is involved.

In a multicultural society, it is important to include aspects of a range of cultures right across the curriculum so that children can understand different and often unfamiliar cultural traditions with an open mind unhindered by stereotyped beliefs. Information technology offers itself as a useful resource to this end. There are now several computer programs published specifically to present material from community and other cultures. Typical topics include Diwali, the Festival of Lights celebrated by Asian communities throughout the world, Chinese New Year and religious and secular images of Christmas. These software applications are often very simple but useful; disks containing images centred on particular themes which can be printed out and included in pupils' work or imported into other computer-based work children are embarked upon — like desk top publishing. The images can also be loaded into graphic programs if pupils wish to alter them in any way before using them. *Ramayana Tales*, a program which focuses on Diwali, offers children a disk-based picture library and special graphic characters which they can call upon to combine with text they type in to form the pages of an electronic book.

The use of databases, like word processing and desk top publishing, is frequently promoted within the subject orders of the National Curriculum. Publishers are producing an increasing number of interesting data collections which will be useful in a multicultural context. *World Development Database* provides a rich source of information with social and economic statistics on one hundred and twenty five countries. Databases also offer the possibility for children and teachers to enter their own data. This makes them very adaptable to suit many classroom topics. Databases can contain cultural material provided by the teacher or drawn by pupils from their own knowledge and experience of home and community. Once constructed, a database can be used as an information source in a variety of otherwise non-computer related activities. It can also be used to allow children to interrogate and test out hypotheses. A database in which a class, for example, has been entering data about themselves and their home backgrounds can be used to highlight interesting social and cultural patterns worthy of discussion in class.

There are now newer electronic media using interactive video and CD disks to store moving images, sound (including multilingual sound tracks) and many thousands of pages of text written in any script. These storage media will greatly enhance the amount and quality of resource material available to teachers and pupils. Aspects of culture previously impossible to record with computers will become accessible in large quantities to enrich the types of learning opportunities which databases currently offer.

Electronic communication adds a totally new dimension to the provision of multicultural materials in the classroom. A school computer can be attached to a conventional telephone line via a small piece of extra technology called a modem. With this in place, a user can dial up one of an increasing number of large databases available on mainframe computers both here and overseas. Pupils can gain access to authentic contemporary materials from a number of cultures. Electronic communication is promoted — most noticeably within the English (DES, 1989b, para. 9.11) and Modern Languages (DES, 1990b, para. 8.35) curricula — because it offers the potential for direct contact between the members of different communities. This should make it attractive in several subject areas. Electronic mail is the most common form of electronic communication currently available to schools. With a computer attached to a telephone line via a modem, it is possible to send messages typed at the keyboard (or previously word processed) to be stored on a remote central computer until another school also accesses the remote central computer to have the messages forwarded to its own computer. The messages can be read on screen as they come in, stored on disk or printed out. With this technology, pupils are able to contact pupils in other schools who may be very distant geographically and culturally from themselves. No matter where in the country the electronic mail is addressed, users pay only the cost of a local telephone call so there is no great financial burden in making contact over large distances. As new electronic communication networks become established and as the existing ones improve and expand, it becomes a viable technological and financial option to communicate directly overseas.

Electronic mail offers two further advantages. It is very fast compared to conventional postal services. A message transmitted from a school computer to the remote central computer will arrive and be stored there in seconds. It can then be accessed and fed down to the receiving school in as many seconds. Alternatively, the message can remain in the central computer just as long as necessary — the receiving school dialling up the host computer whenever it is convenient for it to do so. This means that international communication is facilitated even between time zones. Children in a British school can send messages during their lessons. The messages wait to be picked up by children on the other side of the world when they are next in school. These children then respond to the message and the response is awaiting the British children the next time they have a lesson — at most two days after the original letter was sent.

The possibility of quick direct communication with such a diversity of new correspondents in close proximity and further afield provides exciting opportunities for widening pupils' perspectives and offers new cultural experiences. Internationally there have been a number of interesting projects, and there now exists an organization *Computer Pals across the World* to facilitate day to day communication and more structured curricular projects between school children in many countries. Closer to home in Northern Ireland, an electronic mail project funded by the National Council for Educational Technology (NCET) has allowed children from Protestant and Roman Catholic schools to contact each other and collaborate on school projects in ways which would have been impossible without the technology (Anketell, 1990; Keep, 1991). In England, another NCET project allowed children in schools which are ethnically very different from each other to communicate and work together. In Northumberland, pupils from city and rural populations have shared views on language and on fairy tales and other stories with which they are familiar (Keep, 1991). In the Distant Muse Project (Robinson, 1992) children in two culturally different areas of Bradford similarly exchanged views on the stories and myths with which they have grown up. In this project, the children also communicated electronically with a professional writer to compose together their own modern myths.

Electronic mail has now been joined by the newer technologies of facsimile transmission (Fax) and satellite communication. These enable the transmission of images, sound, written output and print in any language, increasing the range of cultural material which might be exchanged. Electronic mail gives little away about the true nature of its users. Obvious physical attributes like age, sex, colour or disability are invisible and do not get in the way of communication. Users of electronic mail must make assumptions about their correspondents or keep an open mind. They are sometimes surprised when they realize the true identity of those with whom they are communicating. This realization may not come for some time until it is forced by something that is said or by the accumulation of a series of small clues. Such realizations, the assumptions which preceded them, the attitudinal changes which may follow and the practical issue of how the correspondence should continue open up fruitful possibilities for discussion in the classroom.

Computer simulation is one application of the technology which has been successfully used to focus explicitly on the cultural dimension of the curriculum. The rationale for simulations is the educational principle that learning through doing is more effective than learning through formal didacticism. It requires pupils to examine issues from the perspective of a participant, assuming a role within a model and then following through the effects of actions determined. *Sand Harvest* is a computer simulation designed to encourage empathy with the individuals and cultural groups to be found in the Western Sahel. In this simulation, children operate as nomads, villagers or government officials within an economic, political and cultural context. In the *Mali Cattle Game*, children pose as cattle farmers, while in *Rat Attack* they are faced with an Indian grain store under constant attack. Computer simulations can help children understand distant cultures. Nearer to the children's own experience, when simulations are used with groups which are not homogeneous, they can provoke very different responses, revealing the markedly different cultural assumptions and attitudes which might exist among a group of users. In these circumstances, children will need to adopt cooperative attitudes and to listen, persuade and negotiate with others. A sensitive and attentive teacher will encourage tolerance, understanding and cooperation as the children work through a simulation. The teacher might also focus explicitly and constructively on the differing cultural perspectives which emerge among users as they interact with the software.

The same technological advances which we are now beginning to see in relation to databases are also enhancing computer simulation. Compact and video disks can store more complex models, making simulations far more sophisticated. These technologies can also provide a greatly increased store of factual data, sound and action video to enhance the presentation of a simulation. *Living in the Sahel* is a pilot interactive video disk providing 50,000 pictures, sounds and video. Users of the disk can find out about the region and its different groups of inhabitants and then participate in a simulation making full use of the storage and presentational facilities of the medium.

Some computer simulations do not involve the technology for the entire presentation of the simulation but just for the management of its conduct in the classroom. *Conflict and Compromise* is one such program written to manage role played negotiations. There are a number of published negotiations available, each one a file to be used with the program. Some negotiations involve issues to do with cultural minorities like travellers, but the program also allows teachers to set up their own issues for negotiation involving whatever role play groups they wish. Once the teacher has chosen a negotiation to be enacted, the computer takes the teacher through a setting up process in which the machine is informed about the groups to be involved and the objectives to be pursued by each group. The objectives are given weightings, as are each of the possible agreements, which may be made between the protagonists. A time limit is also set. Away from the computer, the teacher prepares background briefing information for the users. When the program is run, the students obtain from the computer the objectives they are to seek. They go away to talk to other groups to reach agreements, coming back to the computer to record any successful agreements they reach. Working on the weightings already keyed in by the teacher, the computer then urges the groups to gain support from further parties or points them in the direction of another objective. So the negotiation proceeds until a time limit is reached. At that point, the teacher can gain a printout of how the negotiations have proceeded, who has achieved which agreements with whom, as a basis for a debrief of what happened in the role play.

Electronic communication provides new possibilities for simulation and role play in the classroom. It facilitates communication between groups or real individuals allowing, for example, monoethnic or homogeneous cultural groups to interact with a diversity of groups not found in the classroom, or for one ethnic minority group to contact another similar group elsewhere. This introduces an element of authenticity into a simulation. If the communicators are acting in role then the opacity of the medium for its users adds verisimilitude to any role play. Electronic communication allows for a direct and fairly speedy dialogue, but since the actors do not meet face to face, they can assume with credibility very different characters from their own — including changes of sex, age and colour. Moreover, in composing a message to send or in responding to one received, there is time available for users to think carefully about what to write and how to write it — perhaps, if they are in role, making use of language and ideas which are unfamiliar to them.

Within the National Curriculum, information technology exists not only to support learning across the curriculum but also as a subject of study in its own right. It has its own attainment targets and programmes of study laid out in the Technology Order (DES, 1990a). Within the Order there are five aspects or strands to the IT capability which children are to acquire. The first strand is concerned with developing ideas and communicating information, the second with information handling. In these two strands, information technology is seen as an enabling facility. Using applications like word processors, electronic communications and databases in the ways described earlier, the technology can be harnessed as a resource medium or as a productive tool to foster cultural awareness. Modelling is a further strand and within it, simulation, as a specific realization of a model, finds a place. From the modelling strand it is apparent that pupils should be introduced to simulations at an early age progressing quickly to those presenting situations drawn from real life. This could, and possibly should, include simulations which present cultural aspects.

If we think of the way that children will interact with technology in these three strands of IT capability, and in particular of the National Curriculum's insistence that all children should be given the opportunity to acquire specific skills in the use of electronic technology, some important issues arise. The National Curriculum specifies that in using technology there should be 'equal opportunities for all pupils regardless of gender and of ethnic, cultural or linguistic background' (DES, 1989c, para. 3.13). The non-statutory guidance issued to schools reiterates the imperative that 'All pupils, regardless of race or gender, should have the opportunity to develop IT capability' (NCC, 1990, para. 5.1). The guidance draws attention to the fact that steps may need to be taken to overcome the cultural bias implicit within the technology. One might first think of the content of software as the most obvious locus of bias. This may indeed be true since so much software is Anglocentric in content. Even simulations have a tendency to present an Anglocentric perspective on the situation modelled. But the non-statutory guidance focuses on the form rather than the content of software. It draws attention to the linguistic bias of software and the ways in which users interact with the technology. Software is typically presented in English, but there should be room for programs which give users information in other languages. It is not just the content of software which is Anglocentric. Even content-free software like word processors or databases reveal cultural bias. Again, the non-statutory guidance suggests that ethnic minority children in school should be provided with programs like word processors which enable writing with a range of alphabets. Luckily, there are such word processing programs available. *Folio* is one of the most popular word processors in schools. In addition to versions in European languages there are also versions in community languages like Punjabi, Bengali, Gujarati and Hindi. Together, programs like *Folio* and *Ramayana Tales* (mentioned earlier) are beginning to cater in content and form for the needs of ethnic users of software. When used alongside more conventional software they begin to present a more culturally diverse perspective for the benefit of all, not just minority, users.

Even databases can depict and encourage the same cultural myopia. It is not simply that most published datafiles fail to utilize content drawn from other cultures or to present multi-ethnic subject matter. The very structure of a database exhibits a particular culturally dependent way of categorizing experience, presenting it and making use of it. A database imposes constraints upon the kind of data which it can store, possibly forcing its users to perceive experience in a particular way or to record experience in quantifiable form. It encourages the identification of that which conforms to its structures to the neglect of that which does not. The way a database program enables information to be stored — the balance of text, numerical data and graphic input; its use of a hierarchical structure or its use of records and fields (with the selection of particular types of search facilities available to access and interrogate them) and the ways in which it allows interrogated information to be presented — all impose a model of recording, ordering and presenting experience. Within the confines of any one database program with its model built upon particular cognitive and phenomenological assumptions, any one datafile — with its own specific levels and pathways characteristic of a hierarchical database or with its own particular fields and records characteristic of a relational database — manifests the compiler's particular way of structuring the world. It indicates too the ways in which the compiler expects future researchers to interrogate the information, the types of data they are interested in, the types of hypotheses they wish to pursue and the ways in which they wish to pursue them.

It is very easy when working with electronic technology to forget that the way a computer manipulates and presents information is a construct, in part socially determined and only one among many. We know from anthropology and from social linguistics that different cultures think and communicate differently. There is a view (Trudgill, 1983, p. 24) that a speaker's native language sets up a series of categories, which act as a kind of grid through which the speaker then perceives the world, and which constrain the way in which speakers categorize and conceptualize different phenomena. A language can affect a society by influencing or even controlling the world-view of its speakers. The computer may operate in the same way. For the majority of users in the Western world within which the technology has been developed, the computer may present patterns familiar within the culture. For some other users, even those within the same society, computers may present unfamiliar and novel ways of perceiving and thinking. This can provide a fruitful and constructive opportunity for enlarging the cultural repertoire of some users. For other users, computers might present the world from such an alien perspective, remote from their own culture, that without intervention and mediation the technology poses considerable barriers to thought and communication.

Like word processors or databases, art and design programs can also exhibit cultural bias. Through the computer, images may be created and then modified freely and rapidly using a complex range of effects. The use of computer systems enables pupils to refine many of the formal skills that are required in practical designing and making. But it must be remembered that while the technology may be redefining certain aspects of the dominant visual forms of our society, this is not true of all cultures within or beyond that society. Computer technology is better disposed towards some artistic processes and forms than others. An over reliance on technology removes the potential for exploration of art and design from non-technological cultures. It forces all children to work within one particular cultural frame and presents that frame as the dominant one. It will be important to remember these constraints when using graphics programs in the classroom.

We have to remember that we are concerned with hardware as well as software.

Computers are not neutral. As Boyd-Barratt (1990, paras. 2.20–2.22) points out, the design of both software and hardware reflects particular values and choices, which in turn embody a wide range of considerations, including economic, political, social and ideological ones. Computer hardware is a product largely controlled by a few multi-national companies. Increasingly too, the same can be said of software. After a brief period in which there was a remarkable flood of educational software produced in the United Kingdom, by the end of the 1980s it became obvious that the indigenous British educational market was too small to sustain such production. Many software publishers disappeared, and there has been a marked shift of focus onto the acquisition of the more flexible commercial, often international, products — word processors, spreadsheets and databases — which are still available because of the larger market which is open for them. The type and range of hardware and software which exist for school use therefore reflect the values of the market context in which the products were manufactured and the needs of the commercial purchasers in those markets. Computers are presented as beneficial, economically competitive, efficient, growing in importance and essential for national economic advancement. Missing from this cluster of values are the less positive or competing views for what some may see as cultural imperialism: that a market economy is not the only economy; that there are other areas of life and experience felt by some to be more important to a healthy individual or nation; that there are aspects of life to which the application of computers, though possible, may not be socially desirable; that computers may be far too expensive for some social groups or nations and thus that the advance of technology simply widens the gap between these groups and disadvantages yet further those with less technology.

Computers are well established in popular culture. Boyd-Barratt claims they convey both positive and negative sets of associations or significations to do with such abstractions as rationality, efficiency, status and progress, as well as ruthlessness, mindlessness, futurism and 'yuppiedom'. Computers are the focus of mini-cultures that have grown up around them, or in opposition to them. Supportive user groups and computer enthusiasts have their own values and jargon. The technology therefore highlights different assumptions and expectations among different groups of users. It affects not only the way that different groups approach and respond to the technology but also brings into sharp focus more fundamental cultural differences between such groups. An extreme example of this occurred in 1988 when Information Technology was first proposed as a statutory component of the National Curriculum. One religious sect appealed to the Secretary of State for Education claiming that computers were diabolic engines to which their children should not be given access. The Secretary of State reiterated the statutory obligation for all children in state schools to receive an IT education. If parents wished to deny their children this entitlement, he stated, then they should remove them to a denominational school or establish one of their own which did not have to conform to the new statutory curriculum.

The tenacity of Government in relation to information technology in schools is a complicating factor which needs to be scrutinized. Goodson (1990) on claims that the Government's introduction of IT in schools in the early 1980s and its continued support for the use of computers via the National Curriculum must be seen as a process of symbolic action. In presenting the currency of symbolic action, Goodson quotes, by way of example, the Labour leader talking about the party's campaign for election: 'The campaign deliberately selects symbolic policies — such as under-fives provision, cervical cancer screening, a ban on lead in petrol, and home improvement grants — to illustrate our commitment to general values'. Goodson claims that the introduction of computers in schools can be understood as an example of symbolic action illustrating and invigorating commitment to particular values. Two implications follow from this. In the first place, information technology can be seen as a symbol endowed with powerful connotations. All societies view their educational systems as means of transmitting cultural values and national identity. The very appearance of a computer in a school becomes a vehicle in this process. This again will affect the way in which some groups of children approach the technology or the ways in which teachers perceive that they should approach and work with it. Secondly, if this is primarily symbolic action — and the present Government's financial commitment to the number of machines introduced, to training in their use and to empirical research into learning benefits suggests that it can be little more — then the extent to which IT can be used in the classroom to effect the types of learning described in the opening pages of this chapter is severely curtailed.

Within the National Curriculum these issues can be faced directly. In addition to the strands of information technology capability concerned with communication, information handling and modelling, there is an important emphasis within the capability on another strand focusing on awareness of the applications and effects of technology. Pupils should be able to stand back from technology and evaluate its impact on themselves, other individuals, organizations and society. The eventual aim by Level 10 is that students should be able to discuss the ethical, moral and social issues raised by the technology. The sorts of macro-issues I have identified seem entirely appropriate to discuss with pupils in a direct and constructive manner.

At the more immediate level of direct personal experience, the National Curriculum Technology Order allows for attention to the sorts of issues I have raised in relation to the diverse ways in which different cultural groups may view or make use of technology. At the most rudimentary level, Level 1, the attainment target specifies that pupils should be able to cooperate with others in their use of information technology. Because children are often given group rather than individual access to computers, teachers can use the technology to develop communications and social skills through these group activities. When working collaboratively, pupils must learn how to listen, persuade, negotiate and accept the viewpoint of others. Group work with a computer necessitates cooperative attitudes and tolerance. It also offers an opportunity to create an understanding of the human and moral dimensions of what has been learned. Sensitive attention to the type and range of software presented, both its content and its form, to suit different cultural needs or to encourage greater understanding of those needs across cultures can greatly enhance this aspect of learning. By Level 2 pupils should be encouraged to talk about their use of information technology at home and in school. The opportunity thus arises at a very early age to begin to address the very different technological expectations and assumptions which different communities may hold. By Level 3 pupils should be able to describe their use of information technology and compare it with other methods. By encouraging children to compare media they can be better equipped to make sensible choices about which medium to use to suit their own personal circumstances and dispositions. Encouraging a frank exchange in the classroom can help children appreciate and ultimately value the very different technological needs and expectations, often culturally induced, they each might have. By Level 4 pupils should again be reflecting upon their own use of technology but also considering further application in the outside world. Again, the opportunity arises for pupils to share their very different experiences of the technology and their perception of how information technology can and should be used in society as they see it.

These particular elements of the information technology curriculum principally define areas of content rather than skills. There is a coherence given to them by concepts in the social, political, economic and moral domains. They would thus be well placed in personal and social education or in religious studies (DES, 1989a, paras. 46–48, 81–83). Design and Technology also offers a place for an examination of the nature and function of the technology. Design can vary in significant ways from culture to culture, and children from different ethnic backgrounds may bring to design activities very different proposals and solutions reflecting different beliefs and practices (DES, 1989c, para. 1.45). Information technology is involved as a production tool and as a product in the design process. Children should become more aware and critical of its nature and function as they identify needs and opportunities to demonstrate that no one culture has a monopoly of achievements in design and technology. The same is true of what is expected in the new curricula for Science (DES, 1991a, p. 44) and Art (DES, 1991b, paras. 11.2–11.5).

Art and English are well placed to consider many of the issues since they relate very much to media literacy. Media education within English, which is concerned with computerized sources of information as well as with other media, aims to create more active and critical users who will demand and could contribute to a greater range and diversity of media products (Bazalgette, 1989). In relation to the visual aspects of the media, the proposals for Art highlight the rapid progress of information technology and the need for young people to acquire the skills of visual communication. Visual images carry information and ideas within popular culture. Analysis will reveal the way that images and artefacts are influenced by the culture from which they derive.

It would be a pity if explicit attention to the cultural dimension of information technology did not permeate the whole curriculum. Like the rest of information technology capability, the issues to be covered in the attainment targets concerned with applications and effects should be encountered across the curriculum wherever information technology is applied. They match many of the subject frameworks. But in addition, from the arguments put forward, it should be seen that there are many cultural issues to be considered whenever technology is used in the curriculum. Multicultural awareness should be pursued not just through software written specifically or adapted for the task. So often when we use software or hardware in the classroom there are cultural issues of content, form, function and perception to be examined and potential for cultural awareness to be developed. The same questions about the use of information technology and opportunities for explication relate to this medium as to any other we use in the classroom. In some ways, the issues are more pertinent here than with other media. It would be a great loss if teachers confined their efforts to software developed specifically with cultural awareness in mind while they failed to analyze and exploit the cultural dimension of so much of the hardware and software currently used in so many areas of the curriculum and beyond.

References

a)   Computer Applications

Computer Pals across the World, c/o John Meadows (Hon. UK Director), South Bank
Polytechnic, 13–16 Borough Road, London SE1 OAL.
Conflict and Compromise, Cambridge University Press, The Edinburgh Building,
Shaftesbury Road, Cambridge CB2 2RU.
Folio, Tedimen Software, PO Box 23, Southampton SO9 7BD.
Mali Cattle Game, Christian Aid, PO Box 100, London SE1 7RT.
Ramayana Tales, BBC Soft, PO Box 22, Wellingborough NN8 2RE.
Rat Attack, Christian Aid, PO Box 100, London SE1 7RT.
Sand Harvest, Centre for World Development Education, Regents College, Regents
Park, London NW1 4NS.
World Development Database, Centre for World Development Education, Regents
College, Regents Park, London NW1 4NS.

b)   Literature

ANKETELL, R. (1990) 'Northern Ireland: Joint work in the environment', in MARSHALL,
D. (Ed.) *Campus World 1990/91*, Cambridge, Hobsons Publishing.
BAZALGETTE, C. (Ed.) (1989) 'Primary media education: A curriculum statement',
quoted in DES (1989) *English for Ages 5 to 16*, London, Department of Education
and Science, para. 9.7.
BOYD-BARRATT, O. (1990) 'Educational computing in context' in *Communication and
Education: Course EH 207*, Milton Keynes, Open University, Unit 28 (Revised
edition).
DEPARTMENT OF EDUCATION AND SCIENCE (1989a) *Information Technology from 5 to 16:
Curriculum Matters 15*, London, HMSO.
DEPARTMENT OF EDUCATION AND SCIENCE (1989b) *English for Ages 5 to 16*, London,
HMSO.
DEPARTMENT OF EDUCATION AND SCIENCE (1989c) *Design and Technology for Ages 5 to
16*, London, HMSO.
DEPARTMENT OF EDUCATION AND SCIENCE (1990a) *Technology in the National Curriculum*,
London, HMSO.
DEPARTMENT OF EDUCATION AND SCIENCE (1990b) *Modern Foreign Languages for Ages 5
to 16*, London, HMSO.
DEPARTMENT OF EDUCATION AND SCIENCE (1991a) *Science for Ages 5 to 16*, London,
HMSO.
DEPARTMENT OF EDUCATION AND SCIENCE (1991b) *Art for Ages 5 to 16*, London, HMSO.
GOODSON, I. (1990) *Computers in Schools as Symbolic and Ideological Action*, Research Unit
on Classroom Learning and Computer use in School (RUCCUS), University of
Western Ontario, unpublished.
KEEP, R. (1991) *On-Line*, London, National Council for Educational Technology.
NATIONAL CURRICULUM COUNCIL (1990) *Non-Statutory Guidance: Information Technology
Capability*, York, National Curriculum Council.
ROBINSON, B. (1992) *The Distant Muse* (unpublished report), Cambridge, Cambridge
University Department of Education.
TRUDGILL, P. (1983) *Sociolinguistics* (Revised edition), Harmondsworth, Penguin Books.

Chapter 10

Music: Respect for Persons, Respect for Cultures

Marjorie Glynne-Jones

This chapter was written during the statutory consultation period following the publication of Music for Ages 5 to 14 *(DES/WO, 1991), the final report of the National Curriculum Music Working Group, and updated when the separate Orders for music in England and Wales came into force, and non-statutory guidance was published by the respective Curriculum Councils. The final report of the Working Group proposed three attainment targets with related end of Key Stage statements for Key Stages 1, 2 and 3, and programmes of study. The provisions under the Orders relate to two attainment targets for England and three for Wales. As the Group worked towards its final report the brief was modified to take account of the Secretary of State's decision that music and art should be optional subjects in Key Stage 4. Unlike the core and other foundation subjects of the National Curriculum, the Orders for music, as for art and physical education, do not include statements for ten levels of attainment, although, as originally briefed, the Group prepared these as non-statutory guidance for each of the three attainment targets proposed. These statements were not included in the Music Non-Statutory Guidance from the National Curriculum Council (NCC, 1992c) nor in the Non-Statutory Guidance for Teachers from the Curriculum Council for Wales (CCW, 1992).*

By Statute: Music 5–14

There are stories about how music came to be a foundation subject in the National Curriculum. Whatever the credibility of these, music teachers and other music educators are delighted that it's in, and prefer to interpret events as an affirmation of entitlement! This formalizing, by statute, is, as stated in the final report of the Working Group, a 'momentous development' (DES/WO, 1991). But we should not forget that it is also a logical outcome of development work in music education over the last thirty years which has focused on all pupils' entitlement to music experience and development throughout their schooling. However, the amendment to section 3(2) of the *Education Reform Act* (1988) removing music and art from the foundation subjects to be studied in Key Stage 4 is of serious concern. It is therefore appropriate to look first at issues in relation to Key Stage 4.

**Equal Access to Musical Achievement Across Cultural
Traditions and Styles: Key Stage 4 and Post-16**

The argument for the arts as essential to the educative experience of all children
and young people, 'crucial elements in a balanced curriculum' and 'of vital importance in the balanced growth and development of the child' is cogently made in
The Arts in Schools (Gulbenkian Foundation, 1982), from which these quotations
are taken. To consider that this balanced growth can be adequately realized through
the curriculum 5–14 (finished off by 14!) is, of course, woefully to miss the point,
if indeed, given the demands of logistical expediency, the point was allowed to
surface. As far as music is concerned the Key Stage 4 imperative is that the
curriculum must provide for those young people who wish to take music and for
those for whom music is a main interest and talent. They may wish to study
music by itself or as a main element within performing arts; in GCSE, or in
certificated vocational courses as these come increasingly on stream in Years 10
and 11. As the Working Group stated in the final report the main concern was
'to safeguard the opportunity to study music in Key Stage 4 in depth' (DES/WO,
1991). It was emphasized that this depth should correspond to the level applicable
to the study of other foundation subjects in Key Stage 4, and, therefore, that
alternative optional courses 'should be offered only in those schools which also
offer the option of a full GCSE course in the subject' (*ibid*). We should be clear
that the Key Stage 4 issue is an equal-access issue: that during their schooling
pupils who wish to study music 14–16 and post-16 should, by order, have access
to appropriate curriculum provision in Key Stage 4 in order to permit such progression. The appropriateness of the provision and its level is critical; it must
include the range of music styles and traditions in which the expertise and commitment of young persons may manifest itself. It is helpful that the Welsh Minister
of State for Education asked the CCW to develop a non-statutory programme of
study for Key Stage 4, clearly, to take further the additional advice given to the
Secretary of State for Education and Science on music non-statutory programme
of study material for Key Stage 4 (NCC, 1992b). At the time of writing no similar
intention had been announced in England.

The question of 'what progression and for whom', continues to be a vexed
one. Despite the earnings which Britain receives from the arts and entertainment
industries, and from music in particular, the contribution of music and the other
arts to pupils' work experience, and the career opportunities the arts provide, have
generally lacked attention, except in relation to established routes to further study
via A-level courses. There are some further and higher education courses which
focus on popular music, light music and jazz, but these are few though growing
in number. But what of the opportunity to achieve excellence through further and
higher education in, for example, Indian classical music, or an African music?
Where are the courses? Are they, like the late lamented Indian music course at
Dartington College of the Arts, which was discontinued in 1991, courses on
which female and male students, and students of differing ethnic origins, are
encouraged to enrol? What of the opportunity to achieve excellence in Western
music for students of Asian, African or Caribbean origin? What is the ethnic
profile of music students in the music colleges, universities and colleges of higher
education? Does the ethnic profile of students who play in county/borough youth
orchestras and other performance activities organized through LEA music support

services or other agencies reflect the local student population? These questions are to do with provision and with access to it. A survey of LEA instrumental provision by the National Foundation for Educational Research (Sharp, 1991) found that:

> A minority of LEAs provided tuition on instruments for the performance of music outside the Western tradition (steel band, tabla, harmonium and sitar). Steel band tuition was provided by about a quarter of LEAs. It was most commonly taught in London authorities:. . . Provision of tuition on Indian instruments followed a similar pattern, being most commonly taught in London authorities.

A year later the picture may well be very different as the management of LEA monies under Local Management of Schools is affected by budget reductions. There is a need to monitor which aspects of instrumental provision are affected in relation to equal-access issues.

Equal Access to Achievement in the Arts for All Pupils Across Cultural Traditions and Styles: Key Stage 4

It is generally accepted that the Key Stage 4 curriculum suffers from overload. The view in music education of the way forward for the arts is that the curriculum for *all* pupils should, by order, require that an arts course is taken through Years 10 and 11. This could be through discrete courses in arts disciplines, courses/short courses in the arts which combine or integrate two or more arts in some way, or a combination of these, perhaps achieved through modular structures. The rationale for this is to do with experiences which civilize, which educate sensibility, which enhance individuals' sense of self and of others, and which can be a potent force in promoting respect for the values and preferences of others, and respect for differing styles and traditions. Those transferable skills which engagement in the arts promotes, as well as the employment possibilities offered by the arts industries, were presented in relation to music in the final report of the Working Group (DES/WO, 1991), but, regrettably, receive no attention in the non-statutory guidance available at the time of writing.

Access to Musical Achievement for All Pupils: The Influence of GCSE

A rueful smile might be appropriate when we remember that there was a time in the early 70s when 'music for all' carried very negative connotations; many, both inside and outside music education, had difficulty with the idea of all pupils having musical abilities, and with the idea of a music curriculum being essentially a practical curriculum. Music education has moved a long way since then. The music proposals of the Working Group properly reflected the strong commitment of music teachers to all pupils' music experience and development, a commitment which was established for many as a result of implementing GCSE courses and the three assessment criteria of composing, performing and listening. The Working Group confirmed these criteria through identifying the main aim of music education in schools as being 'to foster pupils' sensitivity to, and their understanding and enjoyment of, music, *through an active involvement in listening, composing and performing*' (italics mine), (DES/WO, 1991). Following the development of music GCSE HMI, in *Music 5 to 16* (DES, 1985) advised that 'Music education should be mainly concerned with bringing children into contact with the musician's fundamental activities of performing, composing and listening'. Since then the marked increase in the take-up for GCSE courses has clearly signalled the appropriateness (and timeliness) of the reform, radical though it seemed to those outside music education — and to some in it — while it was taking place! What has happened subsequently is persuasive evidence of the untapped musical potential of young people, not only as demonstrated by pupils in Years 10 and 11, but by those in the first three years of secondary schooling as well. For GCSE has impacted on the whole music curriculum offered in many secondary schools and the three assessment criteria are being used as a basis for planning schemes of work. Pupils have benefited from GCSE approaches, particularly from the fact that these approaches have been developed at a time when the parallel development of music technology has permitted a growing number of children and young people to demonstrate their capability for handling musical ideas and acquiring technical skills in music. To put it another way, GCSE approaches have been developed at a time, when, alongside other factors, the use of music technology in education has challenged long held notions of what counts as musical ability and achievement. As a consequence, the provision of appropriate hardware and software becomes a key equal-access issue in ensuring resource provision which matches in range pupils' style/tradition commitment and its associated technical requirements. These are also key questions in relation to acoustic instrument technologies. For, although GCSE has offered pupils the opportunity of meeting the assessment criterion of performing on an instrument of their choice, the event of it being interpreted in the widest sense is rare enough to warrant a headline in the educational press about two pupils taking 'GCSE in Indian music' through tabla playing. (That they were also younger than 16 did, of course, contribute to the newsworthiness of the event!)

Equal Access to a Full Range of Music Experience: What Attainment Targets, and How Many?

Although by the time this book is published the Order for music will have been in force for a number of months, I think it will be useful to consider the process of its development as it relates to aspects of entitlement. The Working Group, having proposed four attainment targets in the interim report (Performing, Composing, Listening, Knowing) (DES/WO, 1990), argued strongly for the three-target formulation proposed in their final report (Performing, Composing, Appraising) (DES/WO, 1991). This advocacy was in part a response to the Secretary of State's view that four targets would make for a 'more complex assessment and reporting structure than the other two subjects (art and physical education)' (DES/WO, 1991). The Group's final report went some way to acknowledge the overwhelming body of opinion among music educators that the attainment targets should match the GCSE criteria of Composing, Performing and Listening. These have served the music curriculum well. Where they were in need of revision was helpfully identified through the debate about musical knowledge stimulated by the interim report. Performing, Composing and Appraising, the statutory attainment targets for Wales and, with Listening, the components of the statutory attainment targets for England, will serve the music curriculum even better, and make a strong contribution to the next phase of development in GCSE music.

Following receipt of the final report the Secretary of State asked the National Curriculum Council 'to advise on whether the detailed structure of the attainment targets might be simplified and clarified, possibly with two attainment targets. . .' (NCC, 1992a, p. 11). The final formulation closely resembled the two targets proposed by the (then) recently formed Music Curriculum Association (Making music, and Understanding music) in its response to the interim report. In January 1992 the National Curriculum Council Consultation Report for Music proposed two attainment targets: Performing and composing, and Knowledge and understanding. One of the comments by way of rationale, which, on the evidence of the detail of the Order (England) might be viewed in part as mere rhetoric, was that the Council considered that the Working Group placed insufficient 'emphasis on the history of music, on our diverse musical heritage and on an appreciation of a variety of other musical traditions' (NCC, 1992a, p. 7). In the period following the publication of the NCC report and the draft Order for music quite unprecedented lobbying took place by professional musicians of national and international repute, and by national organisations, arguing for the practical emphasis to be reinstated, and for recognition of the dynamic of cultural influence and heritage. A last minute compromise resulted in changes to the titles of the two targets (to Performing and composing, and Listening and appraising), greater weighting (double) to the practical target, and subsequent reworking of the end of Key Stage statements for Attainment Target 2.

The equal-access issue here was, and is, quite critical. Any formulation of attainment targets which, either implicitly or explicitly, took as an assumptional basis that there were (possibly many) pupils 'with a real appreciation of music but perhaps a limited aptitude for its practice' (letter from the Secretary of State to the Chair of the Working Group, published in the interim and final reports (DES/WO, 1990, 1991)) or, that suggestions (for attainment targets) should 'accommodate those children who will not be performers or composers, but who may well enjoy the musical heritage to which they are heirs' (response to the interim report from the Music Curriculum Association, 1991) seriously risked selling children and young people short. The concerns of music educators were twofold. First, that in the two-target model advocated, the principle that 'knowledge about music should be taught in the context of practical music activities' (Interim Report, DES/WO, 1990) might be lost in a return to curriculum methodology in which theory and history were separated from practice. The majority of teachers would have considered this to be a retrogressive step indeed. One which would have put at risk the capability of the music curriculum to meet the needs of all pupils, with possible loss of the ground gained in the last decade. Although it was touch and go on this, the Orders for Music and Non-Statutory Guidance do reflect the Working Group's view of the relationship between practice and theory. 'This practical approach does not reflect a denial of the value of knowledge and understanding in music; on the contrary it reinforces the view. . .that knowledge and understanding are more effectively gained in the context of performing, composing and listening to music' (CCW, 1992). The National Curriculum Council's comment (NCC, 1992c) was 'Music is a practical subject, but one to which subject knowledge — the theory — makes a significant contribution. The two ATs need to be closely aligned. The consequences of integration in terms of planning, teaching and assessing need to be discussed amongst the staff ' (F2, 4.1).

The second concern was that composing might have become lost in a general target of 'Making music' or be seen as an alternative to performing. Composing is, after all, the area which has most recently been developed, and it may have appeared at first to be too specialized for a general music curriculum — particularly to persons who have not worked with children and young people in creative music making situations. If there is a problem with composing it is certainly not a pupil's problem; the evidence is that where opportunities are created for composing work, all are able to handle 'the raw materials of music' (DES, 1985) effectively. However, the key point is that composing is significant in children's learning and development in *all* areas of music activity. To make a piece — to craft it, shaping the sounds you have chosen to express what you want, is, as it were, to get inside music, and to discover how it works in the most direct way. Pupils' performing and appraising capability is enhanced by their composing experience. Therefore the question of how many attainment targets there should be, and whether composing should be a separate one, should not have been looked at merely as a matter of organizational expedience, nor determined on the grounds of economic caution — given the music curriculum training (composing training in particular) which the majority of primary teachers will need. The issue was and is quite critically to do with children's potential levels of achievement in music. Without composing as either a separate target or strand pupils' access to the experience of a full range of the ways in which persons engage with music could be denied, and their development of understanding and skill consequently limited. This would in effect institutionalize musical disadvantage.

There is a further point. The processes pupils are involved in as they compose

> are no different in kind to those undertaken and experienced by composers and performers. They are to do with having ideas; identifying intentions; drawing on experience, on feeling, knowledge and skill; seeing possibilities; appraising alternatives; recognising solutions; making decisions of selection; seeking best present outcomes. . . . pupils need opportunities to be engaged in these processes for themselves, *from start to finish*, or from the start as far as the ideas go should a decision to abandon a piece be made; or from a slow or hesitant start to the finish, recognising that ideas do not always come quickly or easily. (*Observation and Intervention in Music Teaching* (Glynne-Jones, 1985))

Experiencing these processes, as an individual, as a member of a group, as a member of different groups at different times, and sharing the outcomes in performance as a performer/composer or a listener, gives pupils a rich opportunity to learn — and teachers a rich opportunity to teach them:

- to discern the distinctiveness of individual and group composing styles and the similarities and differences between the range of styles found, for example, in one class; (through working in this way pupils do, indeed, develop their own composing styles);

- to make critical appraisals of a composition or performance taking proper account of the context, because the contexts and the makers are known well;
- to acknowledge that persons may take different views about the music they hear and have different preferences;
- to value the music made by others (composed and/or performed) and respect the selective decisions that went into the making;
- to appreciate that musical quality can be found in both simple and difficult music, in playing/singing by persons with differing levels of technical expertise, and in diverse styles.

Throughout the Key Stages composing work should be followed by performance and discussion, although, as pupils become skilful at memorizing their music, or storing it in other ways, this need not necessarily take place in the same session. Teachers who are working in this way have noted that, as members of a class play their compositions to each other, there is almost always total attentiveness — even if as the last note is sounded pupils re-engage in less focused activities! The fact that the composer(s) knows the composition intimately, and understands it, enables her/him/them to hold the listeners' attention, and draw them into the music. This, together with the fact that the listeners know the players well, and have themselves been involved in the same making processes, helps them to be active listeners, listeners seeking to make sense of the piece and to get the feel of the music. Their shared experience is one of open-ended possibility. Thus, pupils learn to discern, not only the particular way in which an individual or group crafts a piece of music and the features of the music which has been made, but also the particular expressive quality which that person or group brings to it. They learn to recognize, and respect, differing forms of musical expression and to understand how these are special to the individuals and the groups who made them. This is genuinely to take a pluralist stance on what counts as music. The extension of this active response to the range of music they listen to and perform has a powerful contribution to make to the development of respect for cultural traditions and styles in the context of world musics.

However, such experiences will only be possible if under the second requirement of the General Provisions for all Key Stages pupils are given opportunities to 'work individually, in groups and as a whole class' (DES, 1992; WO, 1992). There is very little in the non-statutory guidance to help teachers plan for a balanced opportunity for pupils to work in these three ways. Indeed, the *Non-Statutory Guidance for Teachers* (CCW, 1992) suggests quite the reverse. For example, in a check-list of questions about developing units of work the sole question relating to this requirement is 'How will. . .pupils be grouped?' And in the twelve examples of units of work which follow, under the heading of 'Class organization', seven do not include individual work, four include one entry of individual work of a non-musical nature, and one includes three entries of individual work as an alternative to group work. The picture is no different in the *Music Non-Statutory Guidance* (NCC, 1992c) although the General Provisions are quoted at the beginning. No attention is given to this requirement in the planning advice given other than a box headed 'General requirements' on the exemplar planning proformas. In the two examples given, using attainment target strands as a framework for planning, one involves a four-week unit of class work for Year 2, and one a four-week unit of group work for Year 6 (Diagrams 5 and 6). A third example for a six-week unit for Year 7 makes no reference to class organization although the text indicates class and group work (Diagram 8). There is no mention of this requirement under the heading of 'A Balanced Programme of Activities' (D.4.0).

Equal Access to Musical Achievement: Key Stages 1 and 2

Although in primary schools the commitment to all children's music experience is a longstanding one, this commitment has been matched neither by provision, nor by training. HMI have reported in *Aspects of Primary Education, The Teaching and Learning of Music* (DES, 1991) that 'All the primary schools visited included music in their curriculum, but the content of the music teaching and the quality of the musical achievements of the children varied considerably within and between schools'. Also, that 'More than in other subjects, the quality of the work in music depended on one or more teachers with specialist expertise' (*ibid*). In looking to the future, HMI suggested in the concluding section that 'Within that framework [the National Curriculum for music] the guidance offered should help teachers to overcome two persistent and related weaknesses in the music curriculum of many primary schools; a lack of progression in the work, and under-expectation of the children's musical abilities' (*ibid*). Schools will need to consider how they will ensure that children have access to musical expertise in differing traditions and how teachers will be supported in identifying appropriate world music resources in terms of instruments, singing and listening repertoire, and other learning materials.

Composing offers a particular challenge in primary schools in terms of children's equal access to musical achievement. HMI reported that 'Composing was the least well-developed aspect of the work' in the schools surveyed. 'Very few schools gave sufficient attention to experimental work or allowed children to explore the properties of sounds, experiment with rhythm patterns and thus develop their ability to compose' (DES, 1991). However, the challenge derives not only from the particularity of composing as an activity, and its newness as a curriculum component for many teachers, but, as I have said earlier, from the significance of composing in promoting 'open ears' and open-mindedness, as well as in contributing to pupils' development in performing, listening and appraising. Music residencies, and other projects involving local and professional groups and musicians working creatively with children and teachers, have much to offer here in broadening children's experience of handling musical ideas from differing cultural traditions and styles in composing activities.

Individuals' Access to Musical Achievement

For individual pupils, particularly in primary school, the National Curriculum for music is indeed a 'momentous development'. It enables schools to develop approaches to children's learning and development in music which focus on individual achievement — each individual's achievement — and not merely on the general achievement of pupils in class listening, class singing, and class playing activities. As has already been discussed it is now a statutory requirement that 'In all Key Stages, pupils should be given opportunities to. . .work individually, in groups, and as a whole class' (DES, 1992; WO, 1992) although this is quite inadequately reflected in non-statutory guidance. Interestingly, some aspects of the proposals in the final report were surprisingly hesitant in this respect. For example, the introduction to the end of Key Stage statements for Performing included the following: 'It is expected that pupils will be able to meet the re-quirements of the statements for attainment target 1 at key stages 1 and 2 by performing in a group or within their class, although some may engage in indi-vidual activity' (DES/WO, 1991). A similar statement introduced the end of Key Stage statements for Composing, with the addition of 'At key stages 3 and 4, they [pupils] will be expected to compose both individually and in a group' (*ibid*). The proposals for the (statutory) programmes of study stated, under the general provisions: '[These] planned situations and activities should include: whole class and group work, with individual work being undertaken *where appropriate* [em-phasis mine] at key stages 1 and 2, and from key stage 3 by all pupils' (*ibid*).

The trouble here was that the arrangements for the taught curriculum had somehow become confused with the arrangements for assessment, and it was not made clear by what criteria teachers could establish what 'where appropriate' might mean in practice. The formulation was flawed in that individual work was seen as characteristic of pupils who achieve higher levels of attainment than would normally be expected in the primary school years. Perhaps it was felt by the Working Group to be unrealistic to expect that all primary aged children could sing, play and improvise on their own — that it would be too difficult for them. Yet, spend time listening to the vocal utterances of nursery children at playtime, and listen to their instrumental utterances in the classroom, which are either improvisatory (Composing) or which recall pieces (or parts of pieces) — usually songs — that they have learned (Performing), and it becomes absolutely clear that they confidently sing and play and improvise on their own, as well as alongside other persons. HMI remind us that 'As with other subjects, it would be foolish to assume that (children) enter school with, as it were, a "blank slate" in music. The skilled teacher uses [their] previous experience to develop children's abilities in music' (DES, 1991).

In both the Music Orders (DES, 1992; WO, 1992) this was rectified as out-lined earlier. Had it not been it could have led to performing and composing activities in primary schools being organized solely on a whole-class basis, an approach which, even at best, would not allow for the planned differentiation being developed in other National Curriculum subjects. A further result would have been greatly to limit children's experience of the different ways in which sounds can be shaped into music, and so to miss opportunities for promoting their appreciation of what can count as music, that is, their appreciation of musical diversity. Although the published non-statutory guidance from the NCC and CCW does not include statements of ten levels of attainment as had been presented by the Working Group in their final report, the Group's thinking is pertinent here. It is of concern that they only identified 'confidence' as part of the assess-ment of achievement in Performing, in the (non-statutory) statements of attain-ment for levels 7, 8, 9 and 10. The implicit assumption here, that confidence is an important factor only in the work of pupils who reach the higher levels of attainment, has to be challenged. The reality is that children's confidence in music situations is, in all Key Stages, an essential condition for successful music learning (as it is essential for successful professional activity in music) and needs to be encouraged and promoted at all times by teachers. All too often the confidence shown by under-5s can be put off course, and perhaps lost, if the music situations they find themselves in at primary school do not continue to give them an opportunity to make musical utterances — to sing and play — on their own. It is also important that pupils use their voices as they work in music, as a way of modelling possibilities or making suggestions for interpretation. A maxim might be 'Voice across the music curric-ulum'! What was proposed, far from being supportive of children's development, would, in fact, have inhibited it. This would be particularly true of individual vocal development if singing were only ever organized on a whole class basis.

There is a further point. Individuals have distinctive speaking and singing voices, and this is as true of pupils of school age as it is of adults. The quality of a voice(s) evokes an immediate response in listeners; if they are not used to hearing different voices they may find particular vocal timbres difficult, and the experience can become a negative one for singer and listener alike. On the other hand where children have the opportunity to listen to each other's voices as a normal part of their work in music they are more easily able to develop a respect for individual vocal differences. This in turn helps them learn to appreciate differences in the vocal tone, characteristic of different musical cultures, which they should have an opportunity to experience both live, in performance and workshops, and through recordings.

Other Inhibitors of Equal Access

The programme of study (England) for Attainment Target 1: Performing and composing, Key Stage 1, includes

> viii) explore and use a range of sound sources including their voices, bodies, sounds from the environment and instruments, tuned and untuned. (DES, 1992)

Attainment Target 2 (Wales): Composing, Key Stage 2, includes

> iv) develop and refine musical ideas through improvising, composing and arranging

and the end of Key Stage statement (Wales) for Attainment Target 3: Appraising, Key Stage 3, includes

> b) evaluate live and recorded performances, drawing on their experience of a range of musical traditions, styles and cultures. (WO, 1992)

May I ask the reader to look at the previous paragraph again and to imagine the look and the sound of the activities it describes, particularly the sound. Sounds, caused and received, and sounds imagined, must be the pervasive features of a music curriculum since hearing and making sound are the ways in which people engage with music. The 'need to express and share feelings, thoughts and ideas by ordering sounds into forms which symbolize and interpret people's experience' (Interim Report, DES/WO, 1990) is a universal human characteristic. Music as a phenomenon is universal. Each manifestation of that phenomenon is particular to the society or group — and the time and place — from which it stems. There are many musics. To come back to your sound images, as you imagined the sound of children exploring a range of sound sources or refining a musical idea, or the sound of some music a class group may have listened to, there are a number of assumptions that you could have made. For example, that the music matched in style your home music tradition/language, or your preferred music style or tradition. That the music children were listening to was the sort of music you listened to when you were a pupil in school — if you listened to any at all! On the other hand you may have felt that you needed to 'hear' a musical style that would be appropriate for the group of pupils you 'saw', appropriate, perhaps, in relation to ethnicity. You may, of course, have had to wrestle to get the sound images going, possibly because this is not a skill which you practise very often, or because you may have insufficient experience of listening to children's own composed (made-up) music to draw on. Your images could also have been influenced in two further ways: perhaps because some vestige of an attitude persists which views children as either musical or unmusical, or because in coming to have a clear view of your own musical preferences you have not sought to broaden your experience of musical styles and traditions. The former would make it difficult to conceive of the music activity of a (musically) mixed-ability class group; and the latter might invoke some feeling of unease at the possibility of receiving unfamiliar sounds.

It may well be that many persons would bring to this imagining task some of the preconceptions and stereotypes to which I have briefly referred. In looking toward the National Curriculum to promote individual achievement in music we should be aware of the attitudes which could hold this back. Teachers will wish governors and parents to be fully aware of these issues. They are particularly difficult ones because of the profound and immediate way in which persons are affected by sound qualities, and because of the strength of allegiance to the music which is known and loved! This awareness will be promoted by the music ethos of the school, the way in which, in all aspects of the school's life, the place and value of music are evident and celebrated. For example, in all school documentation, from the brochure to reports on individual pupils; in the organizational and management decisions of the school; through the statutory contribution to other subjects, for example history, taking account of performing and composing as well as listening and appraising; through being an integral part of the visual environment in classroom and thoroughfare display; in the school calendar of curriculum and extended curriculum events; through the range of persons with musical expertise who visit the school and work with pupils — parents, and community and professional musicians; in the care taken to ensure that visiting musicians and instrumental teachers present non-stereotypical role models in terms of music roles and music styles; through the care taken to achieve appropriate acoustic environments in the school; in the way all staff and pupils talk about music and respond to its sound presence; in the way in which each pupil contributes to musical activities and events, in a variety of following and leadership roles, and a variety of music roles; and in the range of musics and musical works pupils, and other members of the school community, come to know well.

Equal Access to World Musics

The general requirements for programmes of study in the Order (England) state that 'Pupils should perform and listen to music in a variety of genres and styles, from different periods and cultures', and continue 'It [the repertoire] should include examples of works taken from:

- the European 'classical' tradition, from its earliest roots to the present day;
- folk and popular music;
- music of the countries and regions of the British Isles;
- a variety of cultures, Western and non-Western.
  (DES, 1992)

The general provisions of the Order (Wales) for all Key Stages state that 'Pupils should perform and listen to music in varied genres and styles, from different periods and cultures. . . . It should include examples taken from:

- the European 'classical' tradition from its earliest roots to the present day;
- folk and popular music;
- the music of Wales;
- other musical traditions and cultures.
  (WO, 1992)

These categorizations taken, with some amendment, from the final report responded to earlier criticism that not enough reference was made in the interim report to Western music, while at the same time taking account of the European dimension and going some way to acknowledge the consensus among music teachers that the only defensible approach in Britain in the 1990s is a world musics one. The amendments made to the introduction to the four categories given in the final report are significant; it had included 'It [the repertoire] should, however, be a broad one,. . .; it should reflect musical trends and influences, and include reference to composers and performers who have proved influential in shaping and refining the language of music; and it should include a balanced selection of examples of works from all the following categories' (DES/WO, 1991). The sensitivity of this issue was reflected in a question included in the National Curriculum Council response questionnaire for music: 'Whether the examples given in the programmes of study make appropriate reference to our cultural heritage?' (Consultation Report Response Form, NCC, 1992a). This question was clearly influenced by some of the responses to the interim report, for example, from the Music Curriculum Association which commented:

> . . .no part should be given to non-western music in the statutory attainment tests before Key Stage 4, and even there it should not be central. We do not believe that schools should be made to feel that they are selling pupils short by omitting it, but equally schools should not be prevented from teaching it additionally, provided that they have the requisite skills to do so. (Music Curriculum Association, 1991)

Reference has already been made to the Association's proposal for two attainment targets for Key Stages 3 and 4. The second 'Understanding Music' comprised listening, basic skills, and history of music. Pupils would be tested, for example, on

> Familiarity with well-known repertory pieces by composers in the western classical tradition such as JS Bach, Handel, Mozart, Beethoven and Tchaikovsky (questions would concentrate on principal and popular works such as the Brandenberg concertos, *Messiah*, the *Water Music*, Beethoven's Fifth Symphony, *Romeo and Juliet* etc; repertory works might include topically familiar pieces such as *Nessun dorma*. (*ibid*)

The Association's rationale for these proposals was summed up,

> In making the western classical tradition the core of history of music and also central within the other prescribed components of school music, we do not disparage other traditions. We simply recognize the fact of our own cultural and historical identity. Western classical music is one of the greatest achievements of our civilisation, an achievement we, as educators, have a duty to transmit to our pupils. . . . . . (*ibid*)

In the letter to the Secretary of State introducing the National Curriculum Council's Consultation Report the Chairman stated that 'Council has strengthened the content of the curriculum in the areas of the history of music, our diverse musical heritage and the appreciation of a variety of musical traditions. Although this concept is included in the Working Group's rationale, the choice of repertoire and periods to be studied has been very largely left to teachers. We consider that National Curriculum music should ensure that children have studied major periods of music history and are aware of the major music figures although we do not consider that the statutory Order should define particular musicians by name' (NCC, 1992a).

To go back to the NCC response question, the broadest view of 'our cultural heritage' would be that it is all of the categories required in the programmes of study, although I would wish to edit the description of the fourth category to read: 'the traditions and cultures of Africa, the Americas, Asia and Australasia'. There are a number of reasons. To use 'other' or 'non-' to define a category is, in this context, divisive, and, in my experience, leads to a view of 'different but not equal'. Not to identify by name the great traditions of world music is to fall into that trap. Not to identify them is to allow for the possibility of pupils receiving a restricted experience of the world music heritage, and runs the risk of stereotypical choices of music for listening and performing on the basis of 'matching' the ethnic profile of pupils. Of course, in the amended form of the Order, even with my fourth category, the list cannot reflect the interaction and two-way influencing of the musics listed.

The thing about ears is that they don't have ear-lids as eyes have eyelids! Even if we are not consciously listening to music we are, neurologically speaking, receiving it and being influenced by it. It has ever been thus that one music is influenced by another, and in turn influences another. This is acknowledged by the fact that identifying influences is considered an essential aspect of academic study and criticism of musical works. The world phenomenon at the end of the twentieth century is not only that children and young people are, to differing degrees, surrounded by music, but that music is surrounded by other music in a similar way. As a result of international communication and travel systems music cultures now have a mobility across the world, and, through satellite broadcasting, immediate impact. In Britain, for example, we are beginning to learn of the wealth of music languages stemming from the great traditions of Africa and Asia. The need to raise levels of awareness that there are many music languages was reflected in the title of the 1992 World Conference of the International Society for Music Education held in Korea: 'Sharing Musics of the World'. Against this reality the Music Curriculum Association's wish to clap a preservation order on European music of the eighteenth and nineteenth centuries is, at the very least, disconcerting; and the reference to all the rest of the musics in the world as 'it', that is, non-Western music, beggars description.

In making their final proposals the Working Group had taken account of the political context in which their advice was being given while also aiming to ensure that the music curriculum would have a world musics perspective. On the face of it the latter is embodied in the Orders. The general introduction to the end of Key Stage statements for Attainment Target 2: Listening and appraising (England) describes 'The development of the ability to listen to and appraise music, including knowledge of musical history, our diverse musical heritage, and a variety of other musical traditions' (DES, 1992). The equivalent statement for Attainment Target 3: Appraising (Wales) is closer to the Working Group's advice: 'Pupils should develop the skills and knowledge needed, as audience listeners, to respond to the elements of music from a wide range of styles and from different cultural traditions; to make reasoned judgments about and evaluate performances and compositions; and to bring to bear, in doing so, relevant knowledge of the historical and cultural background of the music concerned' (WO, 1992). This is what is on the statute. However, apart from repetitions of these statements there is nothing in the non-statutory guidance for England which suggests that they should be taken seriously or which helps teachers to make them a reality in curriculum planning. For no guidance or example of the non-Western aspect of the fourth statutory repertoire category is given, although a brief note about achieving a balanced programme of activities by 'a musical repertoire which genuinely reflects the European 'classical' tradition, but allows for non-Western, folk and popular music as well' (NCC, 1992c, D.4.1) is included. By contrast, in the twelve exemplar units of work given in the non-statutory guidance for teachers in Wales, two are concerned with the fourth category; 'Music from around the World', involving music from Africa, the Americas, Asia, Australasia and Europe, and 'Chinese Music' (CCW, 1992).

In the Orders themselves, the non-statutory examples for programmes of study, as well as the programmes themselves, do, of course, declare an assumptional stance, explicitly or implicitly. The statements which explicitly address (or appear to address) the issue of the fourth category in the Order for England are:

1 '. . .learn to recognise some different characteristics in music from different times and places' (statutory programme of study v), AT2, KS1, Listening and appraising) with the non-statutory example of 'sing folk songs from different parts of the world and discuss their similarities and differences';

2 'understand the principal features of the history of music and appreciate a variety of musical traditions' (statutory end of Key Stage statement b), AT2, KS2, Listening and appraising) with, in the statutory programme of study iv), 'listen to the work of influential composers and learn something of their social and historical context and importance to the development of musical traditions', but in the non-statutory examples with one reference to jazz, and, by name, to twelve Western European composers and seven works;

3 'compose an instrumental piece using gamelan modes and structures' as a non-statutory example of 'compose, arrange and improvise music, developing ideas within musical structures' (statutory end of Key Stage statement d), AT1, KS3, Performing and composing);

4 'recognise and talk about traditions such as Scottish fiddle music, Indian raga or Indonesian gamelan' as a non-statutory example of 'show a knowledge of the historical development of music, and an understanding of a range of musical traditions from different periods and cultures' (statutory end of Key Stage statement b), AT2, KS3, Listening and appraising), with reference by name to nineteen Western European composers and six works, and four jazz/popular musicians (DES, 1992).

The fourth repertoire category is handled very differently in the Order for Wales through the end of key stage statements and programme of study for Attainment Target 3, Appraising:

- For Key Stage 1; 'Pupils should be able to: a) listen attentively to a variety of music and recognise and respond to its main elements' (EKSS); with 'Pupils should be taught how to iv) listen attentively to, respond to and talk about live and recorded music of a variety of styles, times and cultures' (PoS).

- For Key Stage 2; 'Pupils should be able to: b) discuss and evaluate a variety of music, including their own compositions' (EKSS); with 'Pupils should be taught how to: ii) listen attentively and respond to music of different styles, times and cultures, and relate it to its historical and cultural background. iii) identify the characteristics of music from different styles and cultures' (PoS); with 'Pupils could: recognise and respond to the characteristic rhythms and instrumental sounds of music from Africa, South America, India and the West Indies' (Examples of PoS).

- For Key Stage 3; 'Pupils should be able to: b) evaluate live and recorded performances, drawing on their experience of a range of musical traditions, styles and cultures' (EKSS); with 'Pupils should be taught how to: ii) listen to and recognise the distinctive characteristics of music from a broad range of styles and genres, composed for different media and for various purposes' (PoS, WO, 1992).

It will be through discussion of the variety of music they have heard, and the contexts in which it was made, that pupils will become not only informed about world musics, but also come to have an understanding of and respect for differing, and changing cultural values, and differing, and changing personal preferences. As previously discussed, this begins with children being curious about, and developing an active respect for each other's music through listening to it. An active respect seeks to understand, and goes further, I think, than the 'cultural tolerance' referred to in the Working Group's Final Report (1991). To achieve this the planned curriculum must give pupils opportunities to get to know a number of pieces of music well, which is quite different from making their acquaintance through one hearing. Repeated hearings over a period of time are needed so that pupils can get to know the music well enough to mutter, hum or tap along with it as it is being performed; and later, to do so from memory (recall it) without it being played. Pupils will be helped to do this in the early stages of learning to listen, if short, whole pieces, as well as short extracts, are chosen; if, when a new piece or new style is being introduced, the piece/extract is played a number of times on the first occasion so that their relationship with it begins to develop. The planned curriculum must therefore give pupils opportunities over time to get to know different musical styles well and so become attuned to the musical expression of different cultural traditions. The approach taken in the Order for Wales is helpful in that 'category four' is treated as a strand permeating the programmes of study for all Key Stages, whereas in the Order for England this consistency of approach is not taken. The content of the programmes of study for Wales is expressed in a way which permits implementation through each of the four repertoire categories, with a Key Stage 2 example which sets a world musics context, as previously mentioned, and references to Welsh music (category three) in the examples for each Key Stage. This flexibility is not permitted in aspects of the programmes of study in the Order for England which are limited to implementation through the ideas and works of the European 'classical' tradition (category one). However, both programmes of study involve a comprehensive set of activities which are capable of being delivered through using, in performing and composing activities, the characteristic patternings of different musical styles and cultures, although none of the examples given in the National Curriculum music documents themselves (for England, for Wales), or in the non-statutory guidance from the respective curriculum councils are premised on such an approach. Rather, albeit in different ways, the guidance takes a one-off approach.

The Final Report helpfully recognized that no one music teacher would have the range of expertise needed for the delivery of the National Curriculum. The need is, therefore, to establish ways in which expertise in different musical styles and traditions can be made accessible to pupils, for example, through instrumental teaching, through musicians in residence schemes, and through school-based projects involving professional and community musicians. When musicians who are based in this country, or visiting from abroad, present an African or Asian music in performances in schools the situation and the context are obviously different to those in which the particular music originated, or is usually performed. The audience in school will bring its own experience of music to the presentation, and will listen with different ears from audiences elsewhere, those different ears being affected by the cultural mobility to which I have previously referred. The view that particular musics should not be taught unless all the cultural conventions surrounding their performance, or their teaching, in the home country can be somehow replicated, as if that were possible, is, I think, misguided. It reflects a conservationist view of culture rather than recognizing that cultures are organic things which change, develop — and travel!

While regretting the lamentable myopia of a view of musical culture which fails both to perceive this dynamic and to conceive of its potential for promoting respect for persons and respect for cultures, and 'respect for the cultural achievements of individuals in all parts of the world' (Blacking, 1986), the music national curriculum for England, as many have said, is not very bad — although it is not very good either! The curriculum for Wales is not so shortsighted. Finally, of course, it will be the teachers who manage and deliver the music curriculum: they will need to plan for a balance between the (statutory) four repertoire categories and between (statutory) individual, group and class work, and for each of these to be included, alongside the others in the Orders, as strands in the programmes of study; and, to support this, they will need to ensure that pupils experience, both live and on recordings, the expertise of a range of musicians. It is a challenging prospect, but a positive one!

References

BLACKING, J. (1986) *Culture and the Arts*, National Association for Education and the Arts.

CURRICULUM COUNCIL FOR WALES (1992) *Music in the National Curriculum, Non-Statutory Guidance for Teachers*, Curriculum Council for Wales.

DEPARTMENT OF EDUCATION AND SCIENCE (1985) *Music from 5 to 16*, London, HMSO.

DEPARTMENT OF EDUCATION AND SCIENCE (1988) *Education Reform Act*, London, HMSO.

DEPARTMENT OF EDUCATION/WELSH OFFICE (1990) *Music Working Group Interim Report*, London, HMSO.

DEPARTMENT OF EDUCATION AND SCIENCE (1991) *Aspects of Primary Education, The Teaching and Learning of Music*, London, HMSO.

DEPARTMENT OF EDUCATION AND SCIENCE/WELSH OFFICE (1991) *Music for Ages 5 to 14*, London, HMSO.

DEPARTMENT OF EDUCATION AND SCIENCE (1992) *Music in the National Curriculum (England)*, London, HMSO.

DUST, K. and SHARP, C. (1991) *When Every Note Counts*, Slough, NFER.

GLYNNE-JONES, M.L. (1985) *Observation and Intervention in Music Teaching*, Western Australia, International Music Education.

GULBENKIAN FOUNDATION (1982) *The Arts in Schools*, London, Calouste Gulbenkian.

MUSIC CURRICULUM ASSOCIATION (1991) *Recommendations to the Working Group*, Music Curriculum Association.

NATIONAL CURRICULUM COUNCIL (1992a) *Consultation Report, Music*, York, National Curriculum Council.

NATIONAL CURRICULUM COUNCIL (1992b) *Additional Advice to the Secretary of State*, York, National Curriculum Council.

NATIONAL CURRICULUM COUNCIL (1992c) *Music Non-Statutory Guidance*, York, National Curriculum Council.

WELSH OFFICE (1992) *Music in the National Curriculum (Wales)* London, HMSO.

Chapter 11

The Visual Arts

Sudha Daniel and Rachel Mason

Historical Overview of Multicultural Curriculum Reform in Art

Art education has been slow to respond to the call for multicultural reform. As long ago as 1972, Brian Allison chastised art teachers for their superficial understanding of Third World arts and for the fact that non-European art hardly ever entered into school programmes. At the same time, Anne Taber, working with the children of Indian-Asian settlers in a reception school, found that her teacher training had left her ill-equipped for teaching them art. By 1986, some black artists in Britain were labelling Government Arts policies and practices racist and establishing separate cultural centres in which to operate artistically in ways they claimed were denied them. Shortly after, Lashley (in Mason, 1988, p. 76) produced the following as evidence of Eurocentric attitudes and practices in art teaching in schools.

- Pupils' work displayed on classroom walls did not reflect the multi-racial mix of contemporary British Society.
- Art teachers tended to rely solely on visits from out-of-school experts for teaching non-Western art.
- They engaged pupils in unrecognized practice of non-Western art forms.
- They failed to take into account the role art plays in minority ethnic community life.

These criticisms remain valid today.

One explanation could be the persistence of psychological and technical conceptions of art curricula. By the former we mean approaches that place a premium on children's individual growth and self-development and emphasize the psychological benefits of art-making; by the latter, approaches that emphasize the acquisition of technical skills related to artistic production. In both approaches the curriculum focus is almost exclusively on children's artistic performance rather than on knowledge and understanding of art and design.

Another explanation must surely be the lack of leadership from DES/DFE. While the Arts Council has clearly sought to bring about multicultural curriculum reform in the school system through, for example, the injection of funding for non-European artist residencies,[1] DES reports such as the Swann Report (DES,

1985) of major enquiries into the education of minority ethnic pupils have been noteworthy for their failure to address the subject. Meanwhile, HMI documents and case studies targeted at the subject have omitted to make reference to cultural pluralism in the arts and to ethnic minority needs and concerns.

Significant multicultural innovations have taken place at grass roots level however. Examples are the *Ethnographic Resources for Art Education Project* located in the Department of Art at Birmingham Polytechnic (now the University of Central England), the work of the *Art as Social Action* Development Education group in South East London, projects emanating from Bradford City and Leicestershire Museums, the *Afro-Caribbean Education Resources Project* and the British Film Institute. Since these initiatives have tended to be small scale and have been carried out by local groups operating outside mainstream education, their influence has been slight.

The National Curriculum Final Report for Art

The National Curriculum Final Report (DES, 1991) was a welcome glimmer of light in a bleak official scene. First, it clearly was not seeking to perpetuate psychological or technical conceptions of art curricula. The rationale for art stressed the acquisition of a language which is conceptual and the importance of children understanding the meanings of the visual symbols and conventions they and other image makers use. Because most schools pay inadequate attention to looking at and thinking about art, the working party decided to include an attainment target called Understanding (altered to Knowledge and Understanding in the Statutory Orders) which incorporated two components, namely, (A) Responding practically and imaginatively to the work of artists and designers and (B) Exploring art, craft and design in a wide historical and cultural context. Two other attainment targets were labelled 'Making' and 'Investigating' respectively.[2]

Second, it contained a comprehensive policy statement demonstrating commitment to cultural pluralism. Paragraph 10.10 stated unequivocally that

- All pupils should be given some access to good art, crafts and design from a number of cultures.
- Teaching should be aimed at bringing non-Western art into the mainstream.
- Pupils should be encouraged to appreciate and value in its own right, art, craft and design from other cultures and should be introduced to the work of a variety of artists, craftsworkers and designers currently working in the United Kingdom.

Commitment to cultural pluralism was spelt out in a chapter called 'Art for all' and by supporting examples of arts from outside the European context in the recommended programmes of study.

The Final Report was not without problems. A pluralist definition of art embraces not just fine art but all sorts of designed forms such as architecture, film, clothes and domestic crafts. The pronounced emphasis on drawing and painting in the examples of programmes of study was worrying. We noticed a tendency to impose Western ideas about form or aesthetic qualities on arts from outside the European context. We remained unconvinced by the argument for three attainment targets since Investigating (AT3) logically appeared to us a part of Understanding

(AT1) and Making (AT2). The conception of the artistic process it promoted, which afforded a key role to drawing from observation, recording from first-hand experience or following through a problem-solving design process, is peculiarly Anglo-European.

Cultural Bias in Art Teacher Preparation

In many non-Western societies people rarely engage in 'Art for art's sake'; indeed often they do not have a designated word for art, as there is no need for it. Nevertheless, art is very much a part of their everyday lives — in, for example, the way they beautify their homes, adorn themselves and embellish their sacred things. Anthropologists and philosophers agree that it is a historical fact that all cultures and societies have manifested their attitudes and beliefs in their art. Art in this sense incorporates design and can be taken to mean human-made objects and images and to include everything from pictures to cathedrals, bicycles, aeroplanes, jewellery and statues. Individual cultures or societies produce visual images and forms which are unique and peculiar to themselves. Even where they appear similar, images and forms in other cultures or societies invariably have different meanings attached to them (Allison, 1986).

The Final Report stated that art education should provide opportunities to 'help all pupils to recognize that no one culture has a monopoly of artistic development' (p. 114). We wholeheartedly support this aim but think it will be difficult to implement in the absence of art teacher training reform. It is important to remember that the specialist route to art teaching is via the three year BA Art and Design course, the main thrust of which is professional training for a career as a fine artist or commercial designer.[3]

The legitimate artworlds of the fine artist and commercial designer cater for the aesthetic needs and wants of a small but dominant taste-public in British society. Participants in this taste culture — the majority of whom are highly educated people of upper- and upper-middle class status employed in academic or professional occupations (Gans, 1974 and Bourdieu, 1980) — tend to downgrade the aesthetic needs and wants of alternative taste-publics while subscribing to an excessively individualistic theory of the production of art.[4]

Gundara (1987, p. 2) has described BA art history courses as 'locking student-teachers into a cultural prison'. Instead of teaching history of art from a world perspective, they locate it uncritically in a tradition of European high culture and Western civilization. The contribution of the art of Phoenicians and Egyptians to the origins of this civilization in Greece is undervalued. Other civilizations, traditions and art forms receive scant attention. The art history of Africa, for example, is not considered very important, nor are the civilizations of Australasia and the Americas. Student-teachers learn very little about the great artistic traditions of China or India.

A black British woman (Haque, 1988) commented on her experience of professional training in architecture as follows:

> I was unprepared for being not only the one Asian woman but also the only Black woman on the course. Coming from a working class background also made it difficult for me to participate fully in the discussions

and debates about art and architecture. The lectures particularly reinforced the dominance of western art and architecture and portrayed them
as the most important influence on architectural design. Other significant
forms such as Islamic and African architecture were relegated and merely
seen as precursors for the more important western traditions.

Whole academic terms were, for example, spent studying Renaissance architecture, whereas a two-hour morning lecture was deemed
sufficient to cover Egyptian and Islamic architecture. African and Asian
architecture were completely negated in the curriculum. When I reached
the third year I decided to deal with this negation by doing a dissertation
on the influence of sufism in Islamic architecture. Working on this dissertation gave me a sense of the wealth of an alternative knowledge and
history of architecture, which up until then had been denied me. However, my personal tutor openly stated that he could give me no help on
the subject, not only because he knew nothing about it, but also because
he was not interested.

Another example of Eurocentric bias and arrogance was when two
Nigerian male students submitted work for the formal crit procedure
using models from their particular experience of housing in Nigeria. The
tutors refused to acknowledge this experience and pressured them to
re-submit the work using European models. This attitude forced one of
them to drop out of the course. The other persevered but, like me, faced
a catalogue of indifference and arrogance. During his last year he explored
the possibility of developing a health centre in Nigeria for his comprehensive design study. From the outset, he was actively discouraged
and told to base his model on European architecture and buildings here.
(Haque, 1988, p. 56)

Sociologists have noted that cultivated Western taste (the taste for visiting
fine art galleries and museums, for example) is characterized by an aesthetic
disposition which hinges on an ability to distance art from everyday concerns
(Bourdieu, 1980). In the process of developing this disposition during their subject training, student-teachers acquire a formalist conception of art which they
assume is universal.

As the anthropologist, Geertz, has noted (1983), Western art theorists have
developed a specialist vocabulary about art's technical aspects. In addition, they
have managed to convince themselves that this is sufficient for a complete understanding of aesthetic and artistic phenomena. Art critics, for example, frequently
talk as if 'the whole secret of aesthetic power is located in formal relationships
between sounds, images, volumes, themes, or gestures' (Geertz, p. 95). The lay
person in the West and most people everywhere do not share this vocabulary, but
make sense of art in their terms by relating it to localized cultural concerns or
linking it to the general dynamic of human experience.

We understand that aesthetic value is manifest in undiluted form in the creation
and appreciation of works of fine art and pursuit of artistic excellence for its own
sake. But we think it important that art teachers acknowledge the aesthetic as just
one of any number of basic fields of human interest which are a fundamental part
of everyone's everyday experience of life. Concern for aesthetic value is apparent
in our enjoyment of nature and in our making and appreciating whatever is added

beyond practical and intellectual need to things in our daily affairs (Rader and Jessup, 1976). For example, in our appreciation of practical excellence in useful articles or in the care we take in arranging furniture in the home.

Fundamentals of a Pluralist Curriculum for Art

A genuinely pluralistic curriculum that responded to cultural diversity in contemporary British society would have to embrace alternative conceptions of art, art history and aesthetic value. It should embrace the concept of artist as shaman, for example, peasant and folk artists, child artists and naive artists; the classical artisan, mediaeval guildsman, renaissance genius, artist as revolutionary and artist as bohemian (Feldman, 1982) not just the gallery idol and commercial designer. Popular culture, rural crafts and the non-institutionalized artworlds and art heritages that have particular meanings for different kinds of ethnic minority groups in Britain would have to be taken at least as seriously as the institutionalized worlds of fine and commercial art. Examples are the Celtic art heritage for Irish, Welsh and Scots, New Year processions for the Chinese community and costume design and decoration in the context of Greek-Cypriot, Bengali, Polish, Serbian folksong and dance performances and plays.

Art history courses would have to focus on art and peoples in processes of change which are not necessarily sequential. The traditional approach which identifies characteristics of art within a particular period of social and political history and classifies it by peoples and periods (for example, ancient Greek art, German romanticism, contemporary black British art, etc.) tends to encourage stereotypes and gives student-teachers only a part of the knowledge they need. A priority would have to be the study of similarities and differences in art and life among various periods and peoples (McFee and Degge, 1977).

Most importantly, student-teachers would have to treat artworks as the products of collective action, not just of individual artists or designers. In teaching about art in any given social or cultural context, aesthetic values would have to be related to other human interests — political, economic, environmental and religious.

Teaching Art and Design in a Wider Context

Not surprisingly, we view successful acquisition of learning related to exploring art, craft and design in a wider context (AT1-B in the Final Report, 1991) as the key to pupils achieving a genuinely pluralist understanding of art. But it is vital that it takes place alongside learning associated with making and investigating. What would this mean for teaching a unit on Indian art and art heritage?

Example 1: Indian Art and Art Heritage

It must be stressed, first of all, that in Indian art, as in most non-European art, there is no marked distinction between fine art, decorative art and crafts, such as is typical in a Western conception. We have chosen Indian art and art heritage for the following reasons:

1   India has a civilization more than 5,000 years old, rich in artistic traditions dating back from the times of ancient Egypt, but European Art History textbooks frequently omit to treat it as a serious tradition in its own right.

2   The peoples of the Indian sub-continent (India, Pakistan, Bangladesh and Sri Lanka) living in Britain today are here because of the close relations between Britain and India following British rule of that area for more than 100 years before 1947. Historical links with the Indian sub-continent and the fact that the two cultures are inextricably entwined should not be ignored.

3   Almost every town in Britain has an Indian restaurant decorated in a way that conjures up a visual and aural atmosphere and confirms Indian cultural identity and has supermarkets selling a variety of Indian foods. Thus, the average person in Britain is exposed to an important aspect of Indian culture.

4   About 10,000 children, the majority of whom visit their parents' and grandparents' Villages of origin, go from Britain to India every year on holiday.

5   Most Indians of all creeds continue to adhere strictly to Indian religious beliefs and values (marriage customs and traditions, worship, moral and ethical codes) and these are directly connected to a system of aesthetic values in dress, interior decoration, music, dance and drama.

6   The study of artistic traditions enables ethnic minority pupils to identify with their culture of origin and take pride in it. For the majority population it provides knowledge and understanding and celebrates the rich diversity of the arts.

An important contextual consideration for teachers and pupils is the multi-credal, multi-lingual, multi-ethnic/racial nature of Indian society. They should be taught to recognize differences of visual representation between Islam, Sikhism and Hinduism, for example. In Islam imagery is predominantly non-figurative, for fear of idolatry and because holy persons cannot be directly represented in art. In Hinduism images of gods and goddesses are directly portrayed in both two and three-dimensional form — as are portraits of revered gurus in Sikhism. Calligraphy is one of several distinctive Islamic arts. The homes of pupils from Muslim family backgrounds in Britain are likely to have carpets or wall hangings incorporating calligraphy from the holy Qur'an together with architectural representations or stylized, geometrical motifs. In contrast, visual representations in Hindu homes are likely to depict scenes from their sacred scriptures, such as incidents from epic stories such as the Ramayana or Mahabharata. It is important that art teachers and pupils are sensitive to this.

A distinction would have to be made between rural and urban art. This could be followed by comparisons of interior and exterior house decoration, costume, transport, household utensils, jewellery and furnishings. Villagers in many parts of India hand-paint the walls of their homes using natural pigments. Cotton is grown, spun, woven and decorated locally and garments are made for local consumption and for sale in towns. Costume varies from locality to locality and for men, women and children. Women, especially the elderly, spend months handmaking a wedding trousseau for a daughter or granddaughter. Garments are beautified by means of elaborate techniques such as shisha (mirror) embroidery, woodblock printing on fabric and tie-dye, each of which has a centuries old tradition. Each village craft such as pottery, the weaving of mats, basketry, the making of toys and of musical instruments is a vital living tradition which serves both functional and aesthetic purposes in the home and an economic purpose (such as trade in the village fair).

In towns, by comparison, the well-off purchase works of art for their walls, together with artefacts for daily living. These may have been made in rural areas of India or overseas. Art and design processes are different in towns. Textiles are mass produced and manufactured, as are national images and symbols such as the lotus, peacock and the Taj Mahal. Japan has been successful in cornering the manufacture of saris for sale in the Indian market, yet there are international Indian fashion and film industries with world-wide circulations of glossy magazines. Fine art has become institutionalized in Indian museums, galleries, art colleges, art associations and patronage.

An important point for consideration generally is the increasing interest by Third World artists in the production of art for exhibition in international fine art galleries (Grigsby, 1977). Fine art works from all over the world displayed in New York, Lagos or Tokyo often focus exclusively on technical rather than human concerns and reveal nothing of the geographical, racial, or religious identity of the artists. Pupils' attention could be drawn to an important distinction in post-colonial societies between inwardly directed arts (those that are made to be appreciated and used by peoples within that society) and arts made for an external dominant world of colonizers. Tourist or souvenir arts provide a useful focus for examining the effects of interaction with Western society on traditional or inwardly directed arts. For reasons of profit-making, crude and trivial representations of traditional forms are produced in mass. While these tend to be despised by art connoisseurs, they nevertheless have some significance in presenting to the outside world an ethnic image that projects a distinctive cultural and artistic heritage (Graburn, 1976).

A different kind of debate concerns appropriate forms for contemporary art in post-colonial societies. One component of this discourse centers upon the efficacy of abstract expressionism and its attending aesthetic (process painting and non-objective imagery) and questions its authenticity with regard to modern African art. In southern Africa some art critics consider this kind of artistic production 'too foreign', calling it a kind of American imperialism. In Zimbabwe and South Africa, however, it has quite an extensive tradition as an alternative form of local imagery — one which expresses inner feelings which were not understood by minority (white) regimes. Ironically, it has been disparaged on grounds of inacessibility. The artists in question who are urban dwelling and have considerable exposure to and tuition in contemporary fine art, continue to be outraged that art specialists cast such judgements along racist lines and dictate to them what they, as blacks, ought to be painting. One of their aims has been to get away from 'township pity' or ghetto realism. Nonetheless, while most African Abstractionists fervently believe that their expressions are locally inspired, a few do claim internationalism.

While we have emphasized historical and cultural knowledge in the above discussion, we do not believe it can be assimilated through rote learning or presentation of facts. Pupils need opportunities to engage with cross-cultural concepts in concrete learning situations involving practical art activities and contact with professionals. The following introductory unit on Indian art is offered as an example of how Knowledge and Understanding and Making and Investigating can all be combined at Key Stage 2.

Broad aims covering all ATs for a unit on Indian art are:

- to develop appreciation, knowledge and understanding of Indian textile traditions and
- to study the decorative character of Indian art.

Specific objectives are:

- to introduce the concept of border patterns through Indian costumes and fabrics
- to study their design elements and
- to copy them accurately.

Primary resource materials needed to illustrate Indian motifs and patterns include a sari, an Indian mirror-decorated skirt, a decorated door-hanging (toran) and a block-printed fabric. These materials should be displayed in the classroom throughout the unit. In addition, a supply of small Indian wooden fabric printing blocks is needed. (All the above can be obtained from Indian textile and gift shop dealers in London, Leicester, Bradford and many other cities; also from some local authority teachers' resource centres or from museums.) Other more standard equipment includes pencils, A4 and A3 size cartridge paper, newsprint, liquid ready-mix poster paint and ink pads improvised out of thin rubber foam.

Lesson one has two main activities. In the first, the teacher provides brief introductory information on the environmental, social and cultural aspects of each of the primary source materials. Ideally this should cover:

- Place of origin, natural environment, raw materials used in manufacture, etc.;
- Who made it and used it. (Were they rich or poor? Was it an urban or rural context? Was it used in everyday life or for special occasions?);
- The artifacts' aesthetic qualities — beauty of material, texture, line, colour, form, motifs, proportion, symbols etc.;
- Religious or other special significance.
  Teachers should direct pupils' attention to the importance of the decorated border patterns also.

In the second activity, pupils working in groups of five are instructed to produce accurate copy drawings of one or two border patterns concentrating on repetition of line and shape solely from direct observation of the costumes and fabrics on display. If necessary, the teacher could demonstrate ways in which border patterns are constructed out of simple motifs by focusing on single examples, such as paisley.

In *lesson two* pupils produce patterns on paper to decorate their borders using the wooden printing blocks. In *lesson three* they study other motifs visible on the primary source materials; these are used as a basis for decorating the areas within the borders. In *lessons four* and *five* they invent their own border patterns and experimental designs. While they are instructed to reproduce the Indian motifs accurately using the wooden blocks, they are afforded an opportunity to experiment with their arrangement and rearrangement. The way line and shape are treated in lessons one to five can be developed progressively to cover the other design elements (shape, colour, form, proportion, texture, motif and symbol) using a range of materials and techniques. For example, pupils could progress to an exploration of colour in paint, or texture and surface decoration simulating mirror work in collage and embroidery.

Each lesson should last at least one to one and a half hours. We advocate beginning all these lessons with a short question and answer session relating to the primary source materials, to ensure that contextual learning underpins art production. We also advocate the extensive use of visual aides in the form of slides, posters, pictures and books to assist teaching related to AT1.[5]

Example 2: Gypsy Wagon Painting

Our second unit of study features one of a number of contemporary British folk arts that go unrecognized, because they are self-taught and have little market potential. Gypsy wagon painting is a twentieth century phenomenon which has replaced the earlier carving. It is part of a rich culture going back to fairground design. Wagon painters draw on a repertoire of motifs including the running scroll, ribbon work, coach lining and horse's head, buckled belt and horseshoe. Not only is it a unique art form (Smith, 1989), but it is an integral part of traveller identity and a statement of ethnicity.

We end this section by arguing for a theory of art education that explains all art forms, including those of European 'high culture', as products of collective action (Becker, 1972). Pupils should learn that art works are seldom simply the products of an individual artist or designer's endeavours, although an artworld can and does routinely make and unmake an artistic reputation. Instead, their production is typically dependent on networks of people whose co-operative activity, organized by their joint knowledge of conventionalized means of doing things, produces the kind of works a particular artworld is noted for.

Potential of Art for Challenging Ideas of Cultural Superiority and Inferiority

Over the past fifteen years a number of art curricular strategies have been developed with the aim of challenging ideas of cultural superiority and inferiority.[6] The 'anti-racist strategy' is exemplified by reference in the interim report (ATI Key Stage 2) to pupils investigating the issue of racial stereotyping through analysis of European fine art[7] and mass media imagery but was omitted in later reports and orders.

Instructional materials on stereotyping for use in Media Education are plentiful. The British Film Institute's packs are designed to teach children that visual images are constructions and to convince them it is worth asking questions about how photographic meaning is produced. Analysis of media images of black people, for example, in the form of advertisements, news photographs or film stills, is encouraged as a means of addressing important social issues including racial prejudice and black 'otherness'. Involving children in exercises in which they analyze and discuss a series of images depicting changing perceptions of black people over time is suggested as a means of getting them to look more closely at the ways in which certain stereotypes have become popular (for example, black sambo, black face minstrel, savage or brute stereotypes) or to examine the myths they have projected. A similar stance can be taken to media representation of Irish people.

We believe that discussion about racism and ethnocentricism in contemporary British society should be situated historically. Analysis of the popularity and need for ethnocentric models and racial myths during the eighteenth and nineteenth centuries is particularly important. Historical images from boys' adventure books of this period could be analyzed in terms of ways in which they served as a justification not only for European imperialism and the domination of other lands and peoples but also for the slave trade. Such images present white European culture as more civilized and, therefore, better than non-European cultures; their dominant image of Africa is of a barbaric continent. Racism and stereotyping are sensitive issues, however, and we recommend that teachers focus on cultures other than those represented by pupils in class when dealing with them.

A second curriculum strategy stresses the significance of interpersonal dialogue and the exchange of subjective accounts of experience in the development of understanding and respect for people whose cultures are different. It has been labelled 'a human relations approach'. Teachers applying it promote expressive art production as an instrument of intercultural learning. They encourage pupils to produce artwork (paintings, photography, puppets, etc.) that takes as its subject-matter their own experience of their everyday worlds. Following this they create the necessary conditions for intercultural dialogue to occur by exchanging the work with that of pupils from different cultural backgrounds. Finally, they encourage both sets of pupils to share and accept each other's experience by engaging in critical discussion of each other's work. It is important to note that there is an extensive range of expressive themes (favourite foods, places to go, hobbies) which can be employed for this purpose, and it is a mistake to limit the art form to representational painting and drawing. For example, one group of pupils in a multiracial school studied body adornment and decoration in Papua New Guinea prior to communicating their experience of their hobbies to other children through the medium of cut paper work and body costume. A second group used realist fiction to express their community experience using the medium of animated film.

Too many visual images of minority or Third World societies paint a negative picture of their peoples and art. We support a human rights perspective, which emphasizes the use of positive images, expressing the dignity of the individual and of all forms of art. Pupils should learn that although art starts with individuals it takes forms that have meaning for many people. In this way it becomes a communication system. A culture or society's beliefs and values are conveyed through their art. For example 'the subject matter of art illustrates the status and roles of people, what is important to observe in nature, what critical ideas need to be considered. The style of art tells us whether people are more objective or subjective in their view of the world' (McFee and Degge, 1977, p. 7).

Afro-Caribbean street carnival is a particularly good illustration of an art form that offers positive affirmation of minority cultural identity (Owusu and Ross, 1988, p. 16) past and present. On the one hand, it celebrates the liberation of Caribbean peoples from slavery in the past; on the other it functions as a symbol of black aspirations in contemporary Britain. Carnival masquerades often celebrate the glory and splendour of West African civilizations. They centre on important themes frequently inspired by direct research into African cultures and necessitate year-long community preparation and involvement.[8] Notting Hill Carnival, which has become Europe's biggest street festival, is unique in its display and expression of almost all art forms (music, dance, costume, sculpture and poetry). It provides not only a basis for teaching essentials of art and design (Owusu and Ross, 1988, p. 7 described one such carnival as culminating in 'high moments of inspired creativity transforming wire, cane, paint, leather, paste, card and cloth into objects of beauty'), but also exemplifies the interdisciplinarary character of many art forms outside the European tradition. We agree with the view put forward in the Final Report that the subject of art should not be subsumed under expressive arts, but timetabling or other practical difficulties should not be used as an excuse for total avoidence of interdisciplinary arts projects or cross-curricular teaching.

Non-European arts should not be viewed through European spectacles. Their insider perspectives are valuable because they communicate alternative viewpoints. Protest art by oppressed peoples of the world is a particularly useful resource for analytical and creative work in class (Walters, 1990). The phenomenon of Chilean *arpilleras* provides an example. These are patchwork pictures made of scraps of waste cloth and wool backing cut from flour sacks by groups of women in the poor areas of Santiago. The images give expression to the direst realities which the Chilean working class have experienced after the military coup of 1973 (Brett, 1987). These messages of resistance are unsigned and are valued by their makers both for the money they can bring into the home and the stories they carry to other parts of the world. They have received a remarkably wide international circulation.

Contemporary black artists often identify themselves with past and present oppression of black peoples. Hence, much of the fine art they produce shares a common preoccupation with the culture and civil rights of black people everywhere; its subject matter, imagery and symbolism represent relationships between the oppressors and oppressed. The ATs provide wide scope for exploring the significance of such art in all the Key Stages. Resources for teaching about black British art are in limited supply, but catalogues of recent exhibitions such as *The Other Story* (Araeen, 1990) and *Art Pack: a History of Black Artists in Britain* (Chambers and Joseph, 1988) are important instructional resources supplying insider perspectives. Contemporary protest art produced by black visual artists in America often depicts heroes of political resistance during the Civil Rights movement.

Because British arts models tend to be urban, a case has been made for the study of rural deprivation. A recent inquiry sponsored by the Gulbenkian foundation (Bailey and Scott, 1990) found that concern for rural culture is well understood in Ireland, Scotland and Wales, but less so in England, where indigenous members of rural communities increasingly liken themselves to ethnic minorities in a period of drastic social change. The report advocated support for any art activities that can increase rural children's understanding of their place in the society in which they live — both past and future. It called for an end to patronizing attitudes to rural crafts and questioned whether the way a farmer lays a hedge is any less an art than making a musical instrument or painting a picture.

Finally, the Western tradition of observational drawing can be utilized as a means for exploring similarities and differences in people's physical appearance in positive ways. The ACER curriculum development group (ACER, 1981) have developed instructional materials for art at primary level designed to elicit more accurate visual representations of non-European hair styles, facial features and skin colour in pupils' paintings and drawings. While one of their stated aims was to improve the quality of portrait work, another was to address the issue of stereotyping and misrepresentation of black peoples.

Problems with Assessment

The emphasis on art assessment to date has been on developing strategies to assess production rather than learning about art in a wider context. Strategies for assessing production have, typically, been underpinned by European models of representation and imagery. For example, we noted earlier the priority afforded drawing from observation, Western perspective, a problem-solving design process and individual self-expression through art.

The dominance of Western cultural perceptions was well illustrated in some GCE examinations. Leary's report of a survey in 1984 noted art appreciation papers with no questions on anything other than essentially British themes. Calligraphy and lettering papers examined skills based on a knowledge of Roman letter forms, but neglected to include questions for Muslim candidates familiar with Arabic and related non-European scripts.

There are more seminal objectives for learning in the cultural domain which the National Curriculum working party and others involved in developing formal assessment procedures for art have yet to accept. There is a need specified by Allison (1986) that pupils learn about sources of imagery and symbolism, and that they understand that these sources vary from the ritualistic, mythical and magical to representations of visual responses to the environment. They must learn how artists and designers in one culture derive symbols and images from other cultures and attach new meanings to them (Allison, 1986, pp. 23–4).

If, as seems probable, art systems have their own fundamentally different ways of seeing, feeling and being, an unsolved question for National Curriculum assessment is whether the pictorial rules and order of one system can, in fact, be translated and comprehended by another without causing considerable distortion.

The criterion of originality in assessing practical work in art can and should be reassessed, however. Perpetuation of tradition is rated more highly in some cultures than creation of new ideas. (This is the case with living traditions in Europe such as icon painting in Greece and Jain temple art in Britain, not just of ancient cultures.) Classical purists of such traditions may object to contamination. In cross-cultural art projects, credit should be given first to knowledge and understanding of the non-European art form in its cultural context. Second, accurate representation of source material should be rewarded to make the point that perpetuation of tradition is regarded as important and desirable. Equal merit should be given to minority ethnic pupils' efforts to integrate their own cultural experiences and traditions into contemporary art forms, in whatever way they try to represent them. It is important that teachers neither covertly nor overtly direct them into Western European modes of representation and imagery as if it was simply a matter of normal development (Allison, 1986, p. 22).

Resources for Multicultural Art

How can teachers without relevant training deliver a multicultural National Curriculum for art? We subscribe to a definition of the term 'culture' in its popular sense which includes history, language, customs and traditions, religion, beliefs and values, arts and crafts, music, costume, dance, food, and leisure activities as a way of life that is shared by a particular group of people. It would be useful for teachers to acquire or have access to a range of primary source materials, such as artefacts and objects from any one culture representing all the above aspects. This would enhance the teaching of the subject in its own right and provide a sound basis for cross-curricular work.

We recommend extensive use of authentic and original primary sources including the environment and everyday artefacts. These can often be obtained locally from pupils' homes, dealers, museums and teachers' resource centres. They should be supplemented with secondary source materials, such as slides, film strips, videos, films, posters and postcards plus background information from local libraries.

The quality of any formal discussion about art depends on an understanding of certain key concepts and the phenomena to which they refer. These basic concepts include types of art forms and types of products, media forming processes, aspects of design, perceptual qualities, inferred qualities, subjects or themes, symbolism, stylistic features and functions or purposes (Chapman, 1982). In addition, ability to read meanings in visual imagery is effected through learning a method or system of critical response. Methods of art criticism have been summarized in art education literature. Feldman's strategy which organizes discussion about artworks under the headings description, analysis, interpretation and judgement has been widely disseminated. From our multicultural perspective we favour the more anthropologically-based approaches which emphasize discussion of a work's function, environment, meaning, relationships with other symbol systems, etc..

Interpreting messages communicated in art necessitates speculation about ways in which different elements in a work affect each other from the standpoint of design and intended meaning. For example, ways in which artists, designers and craftspersons combine certain colours, textures and shapes, and ways in which film makers utilize sequencing, camera placement and lighting, provide clues about the kinds of effects they are trying to create and how they feel about their subjects.

Many museums and galleries now have a multicultural policy and use this as a basis for enriching their collections of exhibition and loan materials. A recent HMI report (DES, 1989) investigated the use that schools make of local museums for learning about ethnic and cultural diversity. Their aims for this included developing an awareness of and respect for different cultural traditions, developing pupils' self-respect and providing them with an opportunity to value their own cultural heritages, rejecting stereotypical images of people, appreciating reasons for migration and settlement and recognizing the nature and effects of racial prejudice and discrimination. Preparation for such visits was considered to be important and museum sessions which had the most impact were those where pupils were able to handle artefacts, see documentary material and have access to artists, dancers and storytellers working in museum galleries. Art-based projects which centred on two exhibitions were described as follows:

Schools which visited the Yoruba exhibition at Ipswich Museum had the opportunity to hear a Nigerian giving background information about his country and demonstrating traditional Yoruba dance steps. In the exhibition area, younger pupils were told stories about Shango, god of thunder, to explain some of the traditional artefacts on display; they made drawings and took part in a game based on Yoruba textile patterns. The follow-up work included clay models and painting masks where some features were exaggerated in the style of Yoruba masks.

A group of nursery children with physical disabilities briefly visited *The Golden Treasury* at Bradford's Cartwright Hall. During the workshop they had an enjoyable session handling and wearing pieces of jewellery. The children were encouraged to describe each piece they tried on and were then able to make models of the jewellery using clay. They were photographed by the teacher so that they could see the results. GCSE art and design classes used this ethnographic material after an introduction which drew attention to recurring design themes and techniques in making jewellery. (DES, 1989, p. 5)

National Museums such as the Commonwealth Institute, Museum of Mankind, British Museum and the Victoria and Albert Museum provide a wealth of multicultural art resources. Some have mounted exhibitions specifically designed to get teachers and pupils to question stereotyped attitudes to non-Western art (e.g. *Lost Magic Kingdoms*, 1987).

Practising artists, designers and craftspeople are important human resources for multicultural artwork also. Minority Arts Associations have compiled registers of artists experienced in or anxious to work with children in schools. The Arts Council of Great Britain has been instrumental in funding such residences both regionally and nationally. Descriptive accounts of residencies and their effects on multicultural art curriculum development in schools can be found in publications by Mason (1988) and Taylor (1986) and in reports emanating from National Curriculum development and research projects such as the Arts Education for a Multicultural Society (AEMS) Project, the Schools Council Curriculum Development Committee's (SCDC) Arts-in-Schools Project and a publication based on the findings of a two year research project funded by the National Foundation for Educational Research (Sharp and Dust, 1990). Additionally, ethnic minority contributions from parents and community representatives with artistic skills are an undervalued resource.

Finally, liaison with local authority advisors with a multicultural brief is advantageous, in terms of strategies and resources, as is use of multicultural teachers' resource centres. Teachers can take advantage of the intensive in-service training courses provided by many galleries, regional arts associations and museums which focus on exploration of art traditions from outside the European context.

Examples of Good Multicultural Practice in Art

We end this discussion of multicultural dimensions of art curricula with a checklist of good practice. Evidence of good practice might include:

- Displays of artwork from a variety of cultural traditions in the classroom and around the school;
- recognition of a variety of functions for art and design;
- contact with non-European artists;
- efforts to extend the knowledge base of art forms derived from cultures and modern developments outside Europe;
- study of the interrelationships between art, music and dance forms in cultural traditions outside Europe;
- use of outside and community agencies to widen pupils' expressive art experience;
- encouragement for minority ethnic pupils to portray their own experience and those of their communities in their art;
- examination of visual imagery for racism and prejudice in contemporary and historical contexts;
- use of art for studying similarities, inter-connections and differences between cultures in a positive light;
- curriculum development relevant to areas of concern such as race relations and discrimination;
- resources for teaching art and artistic conventions from within their cultural contexts.

We agree with Congdon (1986, p. 146) that pupils today cannot avoid the fact that there are differences in people's value systems. Art lessons need to give them greater choices by allowing for and expanding on their expressions and perceptions. Middle-class students growing up in surburbia should learn more about the arts, values and life-styles of working-class inner-city and isolated rural populations as well as those of fine artists and critics. Similarly, both urban Asian and Welsh mountain children should have the opportunity to perceive and verbalize in the abstract manner of fine artists and critics. It should not be our aim to create cultural conformity in art production, appreciation or criticism. Rather it should be our purpose to demonstrate that all human beings strive to fulfil the same needs for security, identity, self-worth and acceptance; it is the problem-solving approaches and value systems utilized towards these goals that vary. They need to be recognized and encouraged.

Notes

1   It is worth pointing out that some of the strongest critics of the Arts Council's ethnic arts policies are so-called minority ethnic artists.
2   This chapter was substantially written prior to the publication of the statutory Orders for Art. The statutory Orders for England contain two attainment targets only — namely, Making and Investigating and Knowledge and Understanding, while the statutory Orders for Wales have retained three. References to cultural pluralism have been much reduced and there is an increased emphasis on Knowledge and Understanding of Western European artistic heritage in both the programmes of study and examples.
3   The art component in preparation for teaching at primary level is often so miniscule as to be negligible. When it is offered as a major subject, the model approximates specialist training for secondary teachers.

4 The theory of reputation is as follows: (1) Specially gifted people (2) create works of exceptional beauty and depth, which express profound human emotions and cultural values. (3) The work's special qualities testify to its maker's special gifts, and the already known gifts of the maker testify to the special qualities of their work. (4) Since the works reveal the maker's essential qualities and worth, all the works that person makes, but no others, should be included in the corpus on which his/her reputation is based (Becker, 1972, pp. 352–3).

5 Useful books in print for teaching this unit include the following: Nicholson, J. (1988) *Traditional Indian Arts of Gujurat*, Leicester, Leicestershire Museum Publications; Lloyd, B. (1988) *Colours of India*, London, Thames & Hudson.

6 Surveys of multicultural curriculum initiatives in art have uncovered a number of value orientations with different implication for curriculum change (Mason, 1988). They are:

- The global or internationalist orientation in which reformers attempt to promote cultural diversity by expanding art education goals and content to include a wider variety of cultures than the dominant or typically Anglo-European approach generally allows. (Many of these initiatives have focused on the development and dissemination of resources for teaching and learning about traditional crafts of so-called Third World countries.)
- The ethnic arts or single studies orientation in which reformers seek to develop units or courses for study about the experience and cultures of minority ethnic groups in Britain. (Arts Council policy and funding for contemporary ethnic arts initiatives such as residencies and use of adults from the community to teach traditional African and Indian crafts, for example.)
- The anti-racist orientation concerned not only with broadening the curriculum to take account of cultural diversity but also with preparing pupils to take action against social inequality and oppression of people of colour.
- A human relations orientation in which reformers emphasize the need to improve communication between people of different cultural backgrounds and devise curricula designed to improve pupils' understanding of culturally different peers.

7 David Dabydeen's work on representation of black people is a good resource for this. (*Hogarth's Blacks: Images of Blacks in Eighteenth Century English Arts* (1987) Manchester, Manchester University Press.)

8 The Burkinabe culture in West Africa provided the inspiration for the theme 'When the spirit moves me' at one Notting Hill Carnival (Owusu and Ross, 1988, p. 16). The imagery and symbolism were drawn directly from the natural and social environment. Deep brown colour symbolized soil, jaded yellow for fallen leaves and lustrous pink for sundown. Costumes were made of leather, wood and tall blades of grass which functioned as work clothes and camouflage for hunters as they pursued their game. As they hunted they reproduced sounds to synchronized movements described as 'evoking a fusion of work and creativity'. The significance of interaction with nature as the source of life was manifested in this carnival.

References

ACER (1981) *Words and Faces*, Afro-Caribbean Resources Project, London.

ALLISON, B. (1972) *Art Education and Teaching about the Art of Asia, Africa and Latin America*, London, Voluntary Committee on Overseas Aid and Development Education Unit.

ALLISON, B. (1986) 'Values in art and design education', in TOMLINSON, P. and QUINTON, M. (1986) (Eds) *Values Across the Curriculum*, London, Falmer Press.

ARAEEN, R. (Ed.) (1990) *The Other Story*, London, South Bank Centre.

BAILEY, T. and SCOTT, I. (1990) *Rural Arts*, London, Gulbenkian Foundation.

BECKER, H. (1972) *Artworlds*, Berkeley, University of California Press.

BOURDIEU, P. (1980) 'The aristocracy of culture', *Media, Culture and Society*, **2**, pp. 225–54.

BRETT, G. (1987) *Through Our Own Eyes: Popular Art and Modern History*, London, GMP.

BRITISH MUSEUM (1987) *Lost Magic Kingdoms*, London, British Museum Publications.

CHAMBERS, E. and JOSEPH, T. (1988) *Art Pack: A History of Black Artists in Britain*, Norfolk, Thetford Press.

CHAPMAN, L. (1982) *Instant Art, Instant Culture*, New York, Teachers College Press.

CONGDON, K. (1986) 'The meaning and use of folk speech in art criticism', in *Studies in Art Education*, **27**(3), pp. 140–48.

COURT, E. (1990) 'Pachipamwe 11: The avant-garde in Africa', unpublished paper, London, University of London.

DABYDEEN, D. (1987) *Hogarth's Blacks: Images of Blacks in Eighteenth Century English Art*, Manchester, Manchester University Press.

DEPARTMENT OF EDUCATION AND SCIENCE (1985) *Education for All: Report of the Committee of Enquiry into the Education of Children from Ethnic Minority Groups* (The Swann Report), Cmnd 9543, London, HMSO.

DEPARTMENT OF EDUCATION AND SCIENCE (1989) *A Survey of the Use Schools Make of Museums for Learning about Cultural Diversity*, Stanmore, DES Publications Despatch Centre.

DEPARTMENT OF EDUCATION AND SCIENCE (1991) *Art for Ages 5 to 14*, London, HMSO.

DEPARTMENT OF EDUCATION AND SCIENCE (1992) *Art in the National Curriculum (England)*, London, HMSO.

FELDMAN, E. (1982) *The Artist*, New Jersey, Prentice Hall, Inc.

GANS, H. (1974) *Popular Art and High Art*, New York, New York: Basic Books.

GRABURN, N. (Ed.) (1976) *Ethnic and Tourist Arts*, Berkeley, University of California Press.

GRIGSBY, J. EUGENE JR. (1977) *Art and Ethnics*, Dubuque, William C. Brown.

GUNDARA, J. (1987) 'Art history in a multicultural society', unpublished conference paper, Bergen, Netherlands.

HAQUE, S. (1988) 'The Politics of Space. The Experience of a Black Woman Architect', in OWUSU, K. (Ed.) *Storms of the Heart: An Anthology of Black Arts and Culture*, London, Camden Press.

LLOYD, B. (1988) *Colours of India*, London, Thames & Hudson.

McFEE, J. and DEGGE, R. (1977) *Art, Culture and Environment*, California, Wadsworth.

MASON, R. (1988) *Art Education and Multiculturalism*, Beckenham, Croom Helm.

NICHOLSON, J. (1988) *Traditional Indian Arts of Gujarat*, Leicester, Leicestershire Museum Publications.

OWUSU, K. (Ed.) (1988) *Storms of the Heart: An Anthology of Black Arts and Culture*, London, Camden Press.

OWUSU, K. and ROSS, J. (1988) *Behind the Masquerade: The Story of the Notting Hill Carnival*, London, Arts Media Group.

RADER, M. and JESSUP, B. (1976) *Art and Human Values*, New Jersey, Prentice Hall Inc.

SHARP, S. and DUST, K. (1990) *Artists in Schools: A Handbook for Teachers and Artists*, London, Bedford Square Press.

SMITH, D. (1989) 'The decorative tradition in English gypsy wagon and cart painting', unpublished paper presented at conference at Sarajevo.

TAYLOR, R. (1986) *Educating for Art*, London, Longmans.

WALTERS, S. (1990) *Anti-Racism and Art in Britain and South Africa*, Art and Development Education Project, distributed by Oxfam Education Department.

Chapter 12

Physical Education and Dance

Maggie Semple

To fling my arms wide
In the face of the sun, Dance! Whirl! Whirl!
Till the quick day is done.
Rest at pale evening. . .
A tall, slim tree. . .
Night come tenderly
Black like me. (Langston Hughes quoted in Kennedy, 1989)

We know that for centuries Britain has been a culturally diverse society. When the Venerable Bede (673–735 AD) described London as 'an emporium of many people coming by land and sea' (The Guardian, 1990), he was referring to the variety of people from different cultures who were already a feature of British life, gathered in the great ports and trading centres. Nevertheless a subtle discriminatory practice is still at work, over 1250 years later. Seeing a black performer in large scale arts productions in large scale arts venues and seeing black athletes in prestigious sports fixtures continues to startle the dominant white aesthetic. In contrast, the perception of a black performer is beautifully outlined in the opening quotation from a poem by Langston Hughes.

When players from Cameroon scored enormous success in the early stages of the 1990 World Cup, they were greeted with scorn and disbelief by those English television viewers who perceive excellence in football as essentially English. This was compounded by a startling degree of geographical ignorance and a media response which centred on archive photographs of the Cameroon team with only one pair of boots between them.

When black dancers perform, their audiences are invariably enthusiastic and responsive to a new aesthetic. However, reviews feature phrases that leap off the page exclaiming about: 'native dances', 'women meet with playful swings of the backside', 'people just had to walk to show that a sensuous rhythm was right in their bones'. As educationalists it must be our express concern to ensure that subsequent generations of sports and arts audiences have fundamentally different initial responses.

The National Curriculum Council document, *The Whole Curriculum*, gives guidance to schools on Cross-Curricular Elements; that is, those areas which should permeate the curriculum: Dimensions, Skills and Themes. It is in the Dimensions section that we read:

> In order to make access to the whole curriculum a reality for all pupils, schools need to foster a climate in which equality of opportunity is supported by a policy to which the whole school subscribes and in which positive attitudes to gender equality, cultural diversity and special needs of all kinds are actively promoted. (NCC, 1990, p. 3)

Over the last forty years, educationalists in Britain have coined many terms to categorize various groups of pupils or students. Multicultural, multi-ethnic, ethnic minorities and cultural diversity, to name but a few — all have something in common, quite apart from the over use of hyphens. These phrases present a semiotic challenge because they do not only raise questions about race, culture and ethnicity; they are used subtly and interchangeably to describe a group of people by the colour of their skin. Cultural diversity is about recognizing that *everyone* belongs to a cultural group, and *everyone* simultaneously belongs to several groups. We may list these as, for example: gender, religion, age, class, languages spoken, sexuality, race. The debate becomes more complex, however, when race is the *only* criterion used for judging cultural diversity. Assumptions are then often made about those whose cultural values are maintained through and because of their skin colour.

Issues of cultural diversity and the establishment of multicultural education are not only pertinent to schools with large numbers of children from ethnic minorities. The question, 'is a multicultural approach inappropriate in areas with very few immigrants?' is asked of me too often. That question displays a lack of understanding about what multicultural education is, and what it is not. It is not to do with immigrants, whoever they happen to be. Multicultural education is *good education*. It values everybody and the contribution they make. If we accept one of those hyphenated definitions I mentioned above, then multicultural equals only the colour of your skin and, in those areas which we call white, we would have to say that there is no diversity of cultures. This would be a very sad situation, I think, for teachers. It is important that good education practice is multicultural and pluralist by definition. It is only pluralist teaching that is true to the nature of all curriculum subjects, and we must work to erase the notion that there is any such thing as valid education which is not fundamentally of that kind. There is no *separate* multicultural education, just good practice which is therefore multicultural — education for difference.

All educators need to be involved in shaping multiculturalism. The National Curriculum documentation gives us the opportunity to establish multicultural practice not as an aspect of our work, but as integral to it. In drawing up National Curriculum documentation, working groups addressed Government policy; that ethnic minority pupils should have the same opportunity as all others to profit from what schools can offer, and that schools should preserve and transmit values in a way which accepts Britain's ethnic diversity and promotes tolerance. The DES National Curriculum Working Group for Physical Education took the opportunity in its final report to comment on cultural diversity issues. As a member of this group and a dance specialist, I recommended that the Programme of Study should reflect a belief that dance needed to be understood within a broad cultural context (DES, 1991, p. 75, Appendix D, 6).

Equal opportunities was a guiding principle in the working group's final report and was identified as a cross-curricular dimension which should permeate all subjects.

> For physical education this means that all children should be allowed access to and given confidence in the different activities involved, regardless of their ability, sex, or cultural/ethnic background. (DES, 1991, p. 15, 6.2)

> Working towards equality of opportunity requires that teachers should treat all children as individuals with their own abilities, difficulties and attitudes. All children have their own individual gifts to contribute, some of which may be derived from their backgrounds, and which may be used to enrich the experience of the group. But they should never be used as a basis for restricting access to, or opportunity for, any part of physical education. (DES, 1991, p. 15, 6.4)

In August 1991 the group reported and the National Curriculum Council undertook wide consultation on the group's recommendations. In December 1991 the NCC published its response and suggested to the Secretary of State the content of the final statutory orders. These make rather stark reading and teachers will need the working party's final report to help them deliver aspects of the Physical Education curriculum.

How are teachers to implement and monitor National Curriculum cross-curricular dimensions generally; more specifically, how do we establish cultural diversity as integral to our teaching? A helpful start might be to examine further what is meant by cultural diversity; to consider the ways in which non-white contributions have been made invisible and appropriated, how this continues in contemporary accounts pertinent to physical education and dance, and, finally, to give two interpretations of cultural diversity and suggest an alternative perspective.

Martin Bernal, in his account of the politics of knowledge, *Black Athena* (1987), sets out to restore the credibility of what he calls the Ancient Model of the beginnings of Greek civilization. His historical reconstruction is fascinating, but the value of the book lies in a demonstration of how scholarly views of the past are repeatedly modified by the changing political environment.

He discusses two models of Greek history: one viewing Greece as essentially European or Aryan, the other seeing it rooted in Egyptian and Semitic black African cultural areas. These he calls Aryan and Ancient models. By the nineteenth century, the Ancient model had been replaced by the Aryan model — the one I certainly learned at school. The Ancient model was overthrown for entirely external reasons:

> for 18th and 19th century Romantics and racists it was simply intolerable for Greece, which was seen not merely as the epitome of Europe but also as its pure childhood, to have been the result of a mixture of native Europeans and colonizing Africans and Semites. Therefore the Ancient model had to be overthrown and replaced by something more acceptable. (Bernal, 1987, p. 2)

At this point the contribution of black scholars to European civilization was made invisible.

Black artists continue to search for black art forms in Britain which have been subsumed in the ideologies and histories of Eurocentrism. In Britain there is both the long strand of creativity and artistic sources, touched on by Bede above, stretching from the black Roman emperor Septimus Severus and the indigenous art of Africa, Asia and the Caribbean. The search has produced many examples of the appropriation of black art. It is central to European movements like Cubism and Surrealism. There is a joke, casually passed on, of Picasso's 'discovery' of African artefacts in a shop. Eurocentric attitude often trivializes and denies the profound. Commenting on contemporary fashion, Nadir Tharani writes in *Storms of the Heart* of appropriation assertions that:

> permit Jean Paul Gaultier to dress his models in the South Indian *lungi* (similar to the sarong) on the cover of *Harpers and Queen* and 'stun' Paris; or allow designer Laurent Goldstein to present the male garb of Pakistan in *The Observer*, 22 March 1987, and to describe it as being inspired by Mozart's *Requiem*. (Tharani, 1988, p. 44)

The work of black artists and their experiences of education, crystallizes the legacies of Britain's past. In the same collection of writing, Shaheen Haque, a black woman architect, tells us that architecture is informed by the politics of space; power wielded by white middle-class architects who make up the body of the profession in Britain:

> They create the physical environment in which we live and reinforce through their designs their problematic definition of women, Black people and the working class. . . . Inevitably the buildings they produce reflect a limited response to the arts and to the social life of the people they design for and, by doing so, limit the life choices of the Black and working class. (Haque, 1988, p. 55)

Let us not, as teachers, be guilty of a similarly limited outlook.

Some research continues to be confused by what has been taken for self-evident truth concerning race and sport. The confusion stems from work conducted in the 1920s and 1930s in 'sport science'. Studies focused on variations in height, weight, body composition (in terms of bone, muscle and fat) measurement of arm and hand, legs, feet and trunk. From this period (and later) also comes the 'heavy bone theory' that attempts to explain black children's supposed inability to swim.

Just as much of the hypotheses and research, catalogued by Karl Murray (1985) in a thesis called *Sports, Power and Black Participation*, leaves one incredulous, so do the answers to questions posed in his research: Why is the arena of sport so appealing to black pupils? Why is it that so many young blacks are seen to achieve in the arena? Why have many black people performed better by world standards in track and field and boxing events than in most other sports and games?

Murray's research cites a general belief that because black people are under-represented in traditional high-status and high-income professions outside sport, many young black people see sports as being more open and attainable than other

areas of high-reward work. There are still, long after Darwin, those who pro-
pound the view that black people have a natural propensity for sport, that it is part
of our natural genetic make-up!

The currency of these views was expressed well in a recent Channel 4 television programme, 'Great Britain United' (Critical Eye Channel 4, 1991). Who
was Ron Noades, Chairman of Crystal Palace Football Club, talking about here,
do you suppose?

> I don't think too many can read the game. . . . You get an awful lot,
> great pace, great athletes, love to play with the ball in front of
> them. . .when it's behind them, it's chaos.

You guessed it, black footballers! He elaborated further:

> . . .when you're getting into the mid-winter in England, you need a few
> of maybe the hard white men to carry the artistic black players through.

This is a man who presides over the the club's recruitment policy and is armed,
therefore, with considerable powers to hire and fire. The Ron Noades' quotes
form part of a response to a (white) interviewer's inquiry as to the fitness of black
English players to fill positions of team manager at the end of their playing days.
His views exemplify the absurdly stereotyped yet enduring contention that black
footballers are routinely equipped with more speed, agility and more flair (heard
the one about 'natural rhythm' in your staffroom recently?) than most white
counterparts, but are not considered capable of the strategic aspects of the game.
Speed, agility and flair do not count for much when considering management
potential.

The programme also interviewed black players who suggested that attitudes
in the dressing room were rather more considered than those in the boardroom,
that they (players) were frequently the subject of verbal and physical abuse by
their supporters when on the field, that in one instance the only circumstance in
which the player could allow his mum to attend a match to watch him play was
if he secured a seat for her in a private box, in case she heard the chants of abuse.
The opinions of Mr Noades were all the more disturbing because they were not
delivered with any obvious malice or derision. They were uttered with the blunt
certainty which characterizes the repetition of received wisdom, without fear of
challenge. He was challenged, but remains a powerful chairman.

It is less easy to challenge directly the reactions of established dance reviewers
to performances by black dance companies. Their writing often reflects, not only
a particular perception of dance, but also inappropriate use of language. Physical
Education and dance teachers will provide opportunities for pupils in the development of appropriate language. The meaning of words is illustrated in action and
the ability to talk about what pupils do and see, to describe using technical and
non-technical language to express ideas, to organize themselves and others and to
give instructions, should all be fostered. I detect some differences in the way PE
teachers and dance teachers use language; dance language may be less instructional
based, more rooted in the imaginative and creative domain.

Let us examine a few examples of those other professional users of language, dance critics. They are all considering performances by Adzido Pan African
Ensemble. In a review headed *Riotous Energy*, Anne Pickles writes:

Drums and dance transported Leeds into deep African heatwave last night, with a joyous celebration of music and movement. . .the ensemble dropped into the city. . .drummers and dancers made their journey across a continent with a riotous, raw energy. . . . In a rush of colour and a breathtaking fury of movement, they told their tale. (Leeds Evening Post, 1989)

Innocuous enough, perhaps, a bit of purple prose, but consider carefully some of these phrases. When did we ever see similar expressions applied to Western European dance, say ballet? Is it possible that something which has 'riotous, raw energy' can also be controlled, choreographed, with clear dance form and attention to detail?

In another review of Adzido, called *Excitement of African Ballet*, Sid Eliner (Worksop Guardian, 1988) produces some more confused analysis. Sid Eliner is a 'follower of classical ballet' and 'decided to give it a go, as they say'. Further comparison with ballet follows: 'If ballet is the art of telling a story by dance movements, then I have witnessed African ballet. The major difference however, simply no orchestra: just the rhythm of drums and associated beads and metals, plus, of course, the enthusiastic voices of the cast'. Would Sid Eliner say of a ballet performance, 'where did they get their energy? How can they learn so many intricate steps and perform them with such ease?'

In the capital, Adzido played at Sadlers Wells Theatre and were reviewed by Edward Thorpe (Evening Standard, 1988). Here 'Coming Home' is 'a simple odyssey' featuring the people of 'that huge continent who express themselves in dance almost as freely — and frequently — as they do in conversation. . . . This propensity to dance is exuberantly illustrated by the 29 dancers of Adzido. . . surprisingly, many of his (George Dzikunu, founder) were born in Britain'.

By contrast, let us consider the writing of Rex Nettleford, founder of the National Dance Theatre Company of Jamaica, which is now thirty years old.

Is the Caribbean capable of achieving a cultural synthesis out of its disparate elements? Jamaica's National Dance Theatre Company believes it is and therefore has pursued a course to demonstrate this in earnest. To the joy of hundreds of thousands of viewers all over the globe the Company has sometimes taken flight. In the future, contact with the implosive energy of ancestral hearths and the vigour of contemporary reality must be continually reviewed so that even greater heights can be reached. (Nettleford, 1985, p. 279)

Rex Nettleford continues an analysis of this emerging cultural synthesis by expressing the need for the Company to create its own logic, notion of excellence and understanding of cultural diversity. The different modes of expression — traditional, classical, contemporary — are in a symbiotic relationship, each mode feeds from the others. Dance is not only a performing art, it is a community effort that 'proclaims the virtue of cooperation over unrestrained individualism'. (Nettleford, 1985, p. 21)

In discussing the identification of cultural diversity, he directly addresses the problems hinted at by the reviewers of Adzido. The process is similar to the creation of new, diverse art forms anywhere.

167

The question becomes not whether European classical ballet is superior to American modern dance or to Broadway jazz dancing or whether Western dance expressions in general are better than other types of dance, such as the great dance theatre traditions of Africa, India and Asia. The questions were best posed in terms of the nature and meaning of definitive expressions developed by the genius of separate civilizations. What then are the characteristic features of such expressions that make them different from one another so that they are all within the realm of the art of dance? When Europeans write about international dance, areas like the Caribbean, the Orient and Africa, all great dancing regions of the world, are for the most part ignored — no doubt through genuine ignorance but also through ethnocentric arrogance. (Nettleford, 1985, p. 172)

Learning about these new perspectives is not comfortable. The process will generate feelings of inadequacy when having to re-examine our practices, and there is also a risk that performance previously regarded as successful may lose its currency because of the application of new criteria. When prevailing assumptions are challenged, there is often genuine surprise and resentment, and the adoption of suitable strategies to achieve change causes disagreement. I want to draw together some of the issues which we, as educationalists, must address. These are practical issues, central to our multicultural educational practice.

Multicultural Issues in Physical Education, a paper produced by Cambridgeshire County Council, recognizes that any change is a developmental process which involves staff progressing through a number of stages, probably at different rates. The stages may include:

- raising awareness of the issues involved
- developing understanding: looking at the issues in more depth
- implementation: putting the planning into practice
- evaluation: assessing the outcomes
- dissemination of successful materials/strategies/experiences to other colleagues.
  (Cambridgeshire LEA, 1990, p. 2)

Among other issues that educators need to address is the need to ensure that participation of some pupils is not limited by religious and cultural observances. As boys and girls mature, sensitivity is required over arrangements for changing and showering and wearing of suitable clothes for PE and dance. For example, Muslim girls are required by their religion to cover their limbs. Schools should ensure that their clothing requirements do not conflict with customs of particular ethnic minority pupils, and this should be an established procedure so that the class teacher is not left having to make a hurried and possibly ill-considered decision in their lesson. Schools should therefore seek to be as flexible as possible over religious and cultural concerns, for example, by allowing pupils to wear track suits for PE, making special arrangements for Muslim pupils to shower in the absence of separate cubicles, providing single-sex swimming lessons and allowing pupils to wear costumes which cover legs and arms, and arranging for pupils to be taught by a PE teacher of their own sex. By sympathetic responses of this kind it should be possible to develop full access by all pupils to PE and dance.

Some pupils of Afro-Caribbean origin find within PE an opportunity to excel and develop self-esteem. Be aware of the difficulties caused by stereotyping, and do not assume, nor let other teachers assume, that all pupils from Afro-Caribbean groups are good at PE and poor at other curriculum studies. Both are false and prejudiced assumptions.

Some other issues are particularly concerned with dance. Some Muslim groups have advocated the withdrawal of Muslim pupils from dance lessons, because of dancing with boys or dance perceived as a 'performance'. There are no statutory rights of withdrawal from elements of the secular school curriculum, but schools should be alert to possible parental concerns about dance and should also involve local religious leaders in disseminating the curriculum content and methodology of dance and PE; schools should be willing to explore ways in which dance may be taught without offending religious principles. Similarly, recognition and understanding of pupils undertaking periods of fasting should lead schools to modify PE and dance programmes during times of fasting; pupils may be able to participate through observing, commenting, umpiring and choreographing.

Language used in describing action should be non-technical, or technical, as appropriate and relevant to the pupils helping to broaden their vocabulary. The level of participation in PE and dance of some pupils whose mother tongue is not English, particularly those in primary years, may be adversely affected by their limited command of English; they may do the wrong things or copy others badly. Copying can be useful in the process of acquiring physical competence, but we must ensure that the relationship between an action and the language used to initiate, describe or refine it are understood. Establishing clear practices and procedures within PE and dance through which racism can be tackled and be seen to be tackled is important. Personal or individual racism (racist remarks, racist jokes, name-calling in lessons) and institutional racism (failing to recognize and respond to particular needs of a group of pupils in PE and dance or ignoring and undervaluing the contributions that other cultures make) must both be addressed.

Finally, I want to look at two interpretations of cultural diversity and suggest an alternative model. For me the arts have a significant role in the fusion of body and intellectual domains. The arts have an ability to:

- seduce, persuade, subvert, reflect, celebrate and confront attitudes and behaviours;
- challenge or maintain the dominant aesthetic;
- act as powerful cultural agents;
- establish and maintain an individual's sense of cultural identity.

The arts are an effective means of conveying messages, in that they can shift perceptions through the use of symbolic forms. Engaging in dance is to feel the power of dualism:

i   because it enables the exploration of the private and public domains of the individual;
ii   because it presents a body of unique knowledge which can be applied to investigate a range of issues.

Cultural diversity and arts education have had a relationship which can be encapsulated in two models of practice. The first I call the European model, which suggests that European knowledge is at the centre of educational philosophy and that any other World philosophies are of secondary importance. This basis of knowledge, based on the principle of omission, suggests that there is only one 'correct' view. Dancer Shobana Jeyasingh illustrates this when she states that classical Indian dance techniques:

> appear totally opposed to Western ones. When a ballet dancer extends her leg and points her foot, she does so in the happy knowledge that to the majority of people the long slim line she creates is the acme of elegance. To flex the foot is a comic inversion of the Western norm. One of the primary stances of *bharatha natyam* is the exact opposite of what is understood by the word elegance. The body in a demi plié position goes earthwards with an outstretched leg ending in a firmly flexed foot. When the foot touches the ground, it is with the precision and effect of a clap of thunder. No doubt in many centres of 'alternative' dance there are challenges to the dominance of ballet. However *bharatha natyam* with its two thousand years of history wears the title of 'alternative' awkwardly and with irony. (Jeyasingh, 1988, p. 273)

Educators in dance training institutions have the responsibility to ensure that they do not perpetuate a myopic view of dance, which stifles development of the subject. We must ensure that when studying European and American influenced dance genres, dance content is placed within a context that promotes the understanding that both European and American dance resulted because of an interaction between a wide range of cultures.

A second model for cultural diversity and arts education I will call the Ethnic model. A few years ago this would have meant a teacher attending a short course, usually in African or Indian dance, which would then be taught in the school context. More recently there has been a trend for a dancer to visit a venue and be expected to be the sole purveyor of a particular culture. The dancer will not only teach and perform but might be asked to cook and give a brief humanities talk, in order to contextualize the workshop! Whilst this way of working may be mutually negotiated, the work has no chance of being truly contextualized if it is not placed within a whole curriculum scheme. The experience, undeveloped, places the work outside of the normal curriculum and is inevitably seen as tokenistic and exotic.

Some educators justify use of the Ethnic model by quoting the numbers of students, or lack of students, from diverse cultures in their educational environment. In my last teaching school, it would have been difficult to select dance experiences solely on geographical heritage, language, religious or skin colour criteria, for example. Policy was actively put into practice which ensured that pupils were given the opportunity to participate in a range of activities across the spectrum of dance and the arts.

We must encourage people to understand, value and appreciate differences, not simply to acknowledge all these differences, while not allowing them to become part of our own development. We do not want people to appropriate either. We *do* want people to value and appreciate the importance of diversity, so it becomes part of their lives. It must be something without which we are fundamentally deprived.

It would be opportune for us, as we explore the cross-curricular potential of dance, to take the best from the European and Ethnic models outlined above to form a Fusion model — the alternative interpretation I would like to suggest for cultural diversity. I like this word, Fusion, because it has immediate parallels in the world of art, music and dance. Those black artists, who we followed as they uncovered their art buried in Eurocentrism, are now free to develop a fusion that reflects their discovery and their sense of being British. Musicians continually and easily explore fusion of styles. Perhaps the Fusion model is idealistic, but it is a model which allows the rediscovery of hidden black scholarship, arts and history so that it may be placed within a non-hierarchical structure of knowledge. Elements of classical Indian dance, for example, would become an essential part of *any* dance training because without it a dancer's training would be incomplete.

I suspect that educators like myself, trained in the European model, will need guidance on how to work towards the Fusion model as it challenges deeply held beliefs and assumptions. We can easily seek help, however, from groups of professional artists, who practise outside of the European tradition and who are experienced in extending educators' knowledge. Many of these artists work through a variety of media, see their work as serving both functional and decorative purposes and forge creative links, collaborations and alliances in order to make sense of their work in Britain. As Pitika Ntuli reminds us:

> (It) is more than a fusion of all art forms. It is the conception and reality of a total view of life. It is a capsule of feeling, thinking, imagination, taste and hearing. (Ntuli, 1988, p. 215)

All civilizations by definition share certain modes of artistic manifestations, which are categorized broadly as ancestral-traditional, popular-contemporary and classical. These three aesthetic modes interrelate symbiotically: traditional forms influence the classics, popular expressions eventually establish themselves as traditional and the classics even draw on pop culture.

The Fusion model depends for its success on an interaction between artist and educator. Both need to be acquainted with the resources available and with each other's perspectives, so that genuine permeation of cross-curricular dimensions can underpin practice. That fusion process must inform all of us, as it did the American poet Ntozake Shange, who recalls in *Nappy Edges*:

> my mother and father went to europe, cuba, haiti and mexico. they kept their friends around me from nigeria, togo, haiti, cuba, india, the philippines, france, mexico. i heard so many languages, so many different kinds of music. we used to have sunday afternoon family variety shakespeare, countee cullen and t.s. eliot, my dad would play congas and do magic. (Shange, 1987)

References

ARMSTRONG, N. (Ed.) (1990) *New Directions in Physical Education* 1 Leeds, Human Kinetics Books.
BERNAL, M. (1987) *Black Athena*, London, Free Association Books.

CAMBRIDGESHIRE LEA (1990) *Multicultural Issues in Physical Education*, Cambridgeshire County Council.

CRITICAL EYE CHANNEL 4 (1991) *Great Britain United*, 12 September.

DEPARTMENT OF EDUCATION AND SCIENCE (1991) *Physical Education for Ages 5–16*, London, HMSO.

EVENING STANDARD (1988) *Coming Home*, performance at Sadlers Wells Theatre, London, England, 9 December.

THE GUARDIAN (1990) 'Saxon London is Phantom of the Opera', 3 March.

HAQUE, S. (1988) 'The politics of space. The experience of a black woman architect', in OWUSU, K. (Ed.) *Storms of the Heart: An Anthology of Black Arts and Culture*, London, Camden Press, pp. 55–59.

HUGHES, L. 'Dream Variations', in *The Negritude Poets* (1989) KENNEDY, E.C. (Ed.) New York, Thunders Mouth Press.

JEYASINGH, S. (1988) 'The flexed foot', in OWUSU, K. (Ed.) *Storms of the Heart: An Anthology of Black Arts and Culture*, London, Camden Press, pp. 271–274.

LEEDS EVENING POST (1989) Review of *Riotous Energy*, performance at Leeds Civic Theatre, 23 February.

MURRAY, K. (1985) *Sports, Power and Black Participation* (unpublished thesis), London, University London Institute of Education.

NATIONAL CURRICULUM COUNCIL (1990) *Curriculum Guidance Three- The Whole Curriculum*, York, National Curriculum Council.

NETTLEFORD, R. (1985) *Dance Jamaica*, New York, Grove Press.

NTULI, P. (1988) 'Orature: A self-portrait', in OWUSU, K. (Ed.) *Storms of the Heart: An Anthology of Black Arts and Culture*, London, Camden Press, pp. 209–218.

SHANGE, N. (1987) *Nappy Edges*, London, Methuen.

THARANI, N. (1988) 'Heads under the sands. Western appropriation of South Asian Arts', in OWUSU, K. (Ed.) *Storms of the Heart: An Anthology of Black Arts and Culture*, London, Camdon Press, pp. 39–46.

WORKSOP GUARDIAN (1988) Review of *Excitement of African Ballet*, performance at Nottingham Royal Concert Hall, 10 June.

Chapter 13

Foreign Language Teaching and Multicultural Education

Michael S. Byram

Let us begin with an anecdote. One day in May 1990 I was sitting with a group of English schoolchildren on a patch of grass under the Eiffel Tower in Paris. It was lunchtime, and we were eating our sandwiches before going off to explore Paris — all part of an annual trip organized to introduce my students, future teachers of French, to the necessities and joys of taking pupils to France. I suddenly overheard the end of an argument between two passers-by. One of them spoke French with a North-African accent and appeared to be an Arab. As they parted, and as the final insult, the first shouted at the other '*Etranger!*' (foreigner!)

At first glance this might be dismissed as just another example of the racism suffered by North-African immigrants. But there were several questions which occurred to me as I sat with a group of other foreigners. Why shout 'foreigner' and not one of the other insults for North-Africans or Arabs? Would he have insulted us with the same word — or would he have shouted 'tourists!'? Did the pupils realize that they might be just as unwanted? That they were foreigners? Was I still a foreigner?

Clearly it would be unwise to read too much into this small incident — which passed unnoticed by others in our group — but it nonetheless points to one of the fundamental purposes of foreign language teaching. Learning a foreign language is learning about otherness, about foreigners, and that we too are foreigners, we too are different and *other*.

The purpose of this chapter is to explore this dimension of language learning, to examine its position in the foreign language teaching envisaged in the National Curriculum and to suggest how it might be further developed in the daily and annual work of the foreign language teacher. It will be obvious from my choice of anecdote that the otherness and foreignness to which language teaching might and should address itself is not only 'over there' — by which people refer to places beyond the sea, our natural boundary marker — but also 'over here', within our natural, and national, boundaries.

'Them' and 'Us'

The power of the distinction between in-group and out-group is evident at different levels of social interaction. It is, however, a distinction which rests on a capacity to discriminate: we are 'we' because we are 'not them'; our awareness of ourselves crystallizes only when we encounter others. Yet we often find that our similarities are as great as our differences, and in order to clarify and sustain our own identity, we need to emphasize some specific characteristics which mark us out from them. This is particularly important when we are in a position of weakness, of being a minority in numeric or qualitative terms. The affirmation of minority identity is familiar enough to those of us from a majority who take an interest in the music of Afro-Caribbean minorities in Britain, for example. It is less familiar and more of a shock when members of a majority suddenly find themselves in a minority and cling to their habits in their new environment. The Englishman abroad who insists on familiar food is not just keeping to the same tastes and textures but is also marking his Englishness and maintaining a secure boundary around himself in an unfamiliar situation of weakness.

Food is, however, only one of a large number of potentially distinctive features. The choice — not a fully conscious act — of what to use to emphasize difference and identity is made more complex and mutable by the effects of commercial fashion and international marketing which import foreign music, food, clothing, inside the boundaries of the in-group once so secure. Language remains a special case.

For language is not simply a symbol of adherence to a group. It is the means by which individuals become members of a group. The internalization of language (Vygotsky, 1971) is simultaneously the internalization of the values, practices and modes of thinking of the group. Individuals acquire their cultural identity, their familiarity with what it is necessary to know and believe in order to be acceptable as a member of the group (Goodenough, 1964) in the process of acquiring their language. They learn 'how to mean' (Halliday, 1975) in a specific social group, initially within the confines of the family, and therefore primarily within those values and modes of thinking and acting which the family shares with other members of a social group. In complex societies this is unlikely to be identical with socialization into the whole of a society, and this second stage begins in earnest as the child enters school.

Socialization in the School

It is in the school that a child is most likely to meet for the first time the values and modes of thinking and acting — the culture — which are 'chosen' as the markers of a society's identity. In contemporary societies, this is the same as marking a national identity, for in an age of nation-states, national identity is emphasized at the expense of regional, racial or socio-economic identities. And, though ethnicity is claimed as their token of identity by minorities, — racial and regional alike — it has been hi-jacked by the nation. Although minorities are vociferous in their claims to specific identities, nations hold the power to impose a national identity through the institutions of the state. An inhabitant of France has a French identity — and a French identity card — irrespective of allegiance to Breton, Basque, Alsacien or other identities. The Welsh and the Scots have a British passport imposed by a 'British' — synonymous with 'English' — government. Children are expected to attend a 'state' school with a 'national' curriculum, unless they belong to the social elite which can be relied upon to impose national culture without legal obligation.

This situation is by no means peculiar to England/Britain, even though it is only in the current decade that it is becoming as explicit in England/Britain as it has been elsewhere for many years. The control over the curriculum, and therefore over the culture which it embodies, is firmly held at the centre by other nation-states. The haste with which the British government has sought to catch up is the consequence of the threat to nationhood, implicit in the development of a supranational European community which is also willing to support the claims of regional and (im)migrant minorities. The irredentism or revival of the minorities would be of no concern to the nation-states if they were not bound — in principle, if not in practice — to follow the directives from Europe. The success of the nation-states in coping with and suppressing minorities in the past would otherwise indicate they could continue to do so, were they not caught between the minority and the supra-national. The response has not, however, changed: the nation-state continues to treat minorities as abnormalities which have to be tolerated until they can be absorbed into the homogeneous whole, until assimilation or integration is complete.

The school is the prime instrument. It is used to homogenize the society within national boundaries and mark the boundaries with other nations (Barth, 1969). It presents a culture which has been inherited, and, by insisting that national history and literature should be taught, a national government creates a national ethnicity. For ethnic identity is a function of inheritance and of adherence to a territory. English ethnicity is reinforced by English history. This may be the last life-struggle of the nation-state in decline, but it will probably continue for many years, and, in the meantime, generations of children are acquiring an 'English' identity.

The Language(s) of Schooling

Language again plays a special part. Although the internalization of language and culture begins in the family — or its equivalent — the school is the location where the process is continued, in the formal and the informal or hidden curriculum. The language acquired in school embodies the cultural values and is the means by which they are internalized. For some children the development is unidimensional, a continuation of the process of language and culture acquisition begun in the home. For others there is a gap to be jumped, and their academic success depends on it.

Government insistence that the language of school and of schooling or secondary socialization, should be 'standard' English, ensures that 'standard' cultural values are purveyed. Children 'learn to mean' in standard English and learn to accept the culture which sustains the nation-state. Failure to do so is accompanied by academic failure, and the latter ensures that individuals with other than 'standard' cultural values do not reach positions of power and influence. The longevity of the nation and the creation and maintenance of a national ethnicity is largely dependent on a standard language. National governments have seldom sought to hide their motives, even though debates have often been confused. The thread is clear from the revolutionary government of post-1789 France — which suppressed any attempts to revive regional languages — through Mitterand's refusal to support Breton, to Kenneth Baker's declaration that the English language is 'the essential ingredient of the Englishness of England' (cited in Jones and Kimberley, 1991, p. 17).

It is therefore scarcely surprising that languages other than English are not granted entry into the National Curriculum. The Swann Report disappointed many by not advocating bilingual education for bilingual children, but this was already pre-figured in the preface where the 'common language' is given equal standing with a common political and legal system as the means to give a society 'a degree of unity and its members a form of "corporate membership" ' (DES, 1985, p. 4). The same underlying argument can be found in later reports (Kingman (1988), Cox (1989)) although it is often disguised in terms of giving children greater access to educational opportunities through a standard language. The argument is occasionally tempered by playing down the monolithic import of one standard, national language and discussing the significance of spoken varieties. Government nonetheless seizes the opportunity to insist upon standard language also in speaking.

In this situation the position of foreign languages is anomalous. They are the — potentially insidious — international abnormality in a national curriculum. It is also the position into which the non-standard, non-national languages of the minorities have been forced, despite their status as bilingual languages. Only in the majority within a majority — Welsh in Wales — is a non-national language given access to the national curriculum. Here, of course, the national government has to give way to substantial political pressures. Essentially the position of foreign languages could be treated, at least until recently, as marginal, holding no threat to national identity. More recently, however, political pressure from supranational Europe — agreements to have foreign languages, preferably two, in the curriculum — and perhaps more powerful economic pressures to find non-English speaking markets, have led to foreign languages becoming a foundation subject. It remains, however, insignificant in terms of national identity as long as it is seen as an economic instrument, as a necessary gesture towards a European community, and as a means of creating tolerance of those who are not English.

Foreign Languages — An Alternative View

Every foreign language is a native language for someone else, and as such is the embodiment of their native culture, the way in which they learned how to mean. It offers, therefore, an alternative, another means of experiencing the world. It requires an even greater jump than the one which some pupils will have made from dialect to standard on entering school, the process of secondary socialization. For in this case it is not simply a development or expansion of the cultural values and mode of thinking and acting, it embodies a complete alternative to everything that has been acquired so far. At the simplest level it involves a different way of 'telling' or conceptualizing the time, for example, in German *dreiviertel vier* in English 'quarter to four'. At a more advanced stage, it involves a cognitive and affective understanding of the historical and contemporary resonances of political terms, in German *die Wende*, the word used to describe the breakdown of the German Democratic Republic, which has no equivalent in English. If the individual is led, through learning the foreign language, to acceptance and integration into his own concepts and value-system of the value system and concepts of another mode of thinking and acting — another culture — he can be said to have achieved a stage of 'tertiary socialization' (Byram, 1990; Doyé, forthcoming).

Tertiary socialization is not merely tolerance of difference and otherness; it involves a modification of learners' existing culture, their existing modes of thinking and acting, as a consequence of confrontation with the culture of others. It does not require an acceptance of or identification with the culture of others; it involves a critical review of the values and modes of thinking and acting of others and of oneself. It involves a critical analysis of self and others which is essentially political, because it challenges and relativizes the taken-for-granted naturalness of existing systems in both own and foreign culture (see Doyé, 1991). As such it takes individuals beyond the concept of the nation-state, for it opens to them a perspective which is dependent neither on the one nor the other, but which does not deny — and could not, even were it desirable — the significance and power of socialization into one environment as the basis of linguistic and social identity.

This view of language teaching — let it be said immediately — is not widespread, although it is entirely consonant with the professions of aims for language teaching common to many countries. Those aims include reference to tolerance, acceptance, insight, with which the vast majority of language teachers would concur. What is proposed here takes these aims as the basis for a fuller understanding of the necessary nature of foreign language learning.

The more widespread view of language teaching takes its origin from another commonly held purpose: to promote a capacity for communication. This, though clearly not incompatible with the others, is seen as primary, in the pursuit of which 'tolerance', 'insight' and 'acceptance' will doubtless emerge. There may well be justification for this standpoint, insofar as exposure to a foreign language — especially when it is presented in contexts from a foreign country, which is not always the case — leads inevitably to increased awareness of otherness. Does it also lead to cognitive change, to modification of existing concepts, to affective change and the modification of existing values and attitudes? Our earlier research has indicated that it does not necessarily do so (Byram, Esarte-Sarries and Taylor, 1991). It is useful therefore to keep a distinction between 'awareness' and 'understanding', between 'tolerance' and 'acceptance', in the following discussion of the role foreign language teaching and learning might play in multicultural education.

Foreign Language Learning and Multicultural Education

The argument presented thus far can be summarized as follows: primary and secondary socialization into the norms of a society based on the nation-state takes place primarily through the acquisition of a standard language and culture. Other languages are excluded from the major instrument of secondary socialization, the school, since they embody other and foreign norms. The only access to other norms is through 'Foreign Languages', which include the non-standard-English languages spoken within the society by bilinguals. Foreign Languages could therefore be a means to introduce otherness, not only to make learners aware that otherness exists, and has to be tolerated, but also to confront and modify learners' perceptions of otherness and of self by acquisition of another language and cultural perspective.

By introducing this chapter with an anecdote about immigrants to France,

Michael S. Byram

I wanted to demonstrate from the outset that otherness outside the nation's boundaries is closely related to otherness within it. The experience of extra-territorial otherness should not be separated from understanding of otherness within national boundaries. Despite this implicit conceptual relationship, however, there are institutional and political pressures to keep them separate. Even where inner-territorial languages such as Gujurati or Modern Greek are classified as part of Foreign Languages, links are administrative rather than conceptual and in practice such languages are learned mainly by bilingual pupils as 'home', 'community' or 'second' languages. If Foreign Languages is to have a practical relationship with inner-territorial otherness, there has to be a deliberate effort by Foreign Language teachers.

Such an effort has indeed already been made in some parts of the profession. Under the umbrella term Language Awareness, teachers have developed courses which introduce all pupils to one or more of the languages spoken by their bilingual peers. Such introductions have to remain brief and can only serve to make pupils aware, rather than give them the opportunity to acquire (part of) the language and the culture it embodies. It is unlikely that pupils are led to any degree of understanding through cognitive and affective change in such short courses. There is also a tendency to place the emphasis in Language Awareness courses on the comparison of syntactic and morphological systems in different languages. This fulfils a legitimate aim of language teaching — to help pupils to understand the nature of language — but it is unlikely to contribute to a major degree to the development of cultural awareness and understanding.

The National Curriculum will not encourage any extension of Language Awareness courses, either in the sense of more courses introducing the languages of bilinguals, or in the sense of broadening the concept to Language and Culture Awareness. The pressure to reach new attainment targets will probably lead teachers to spend all available time on the foreign language. And, with respect to the broadening of the concept, the discussion of awareness of language by the Working Group (DES, 1990, p. 50) does not go beyond what they call 'linguistic processes'. It is nonetheless important that awareness of language has been given at least this degree of recognition, for it is a necessary part of reflection upon the otherness of other languages and cultures.

Another area in which efforts have already been made is the representation of inner-territorial otherness in foreign societies. The significance of the textbook in many dimensions of foreign language teaching is evident here too, for it is in the selection of contexts in which to present the foreign language that there is oppor-tunity to make the connections. The interpretation of language teaching as a preparation for a visit as a tourist to the foreign country militates against the presentation of minorities. It is nonetheless possible to find good examples of textbooks which challenge the tourist view. In *Orientations* (Aplin, Miller and Starkey, 1985) not only are minorities, including the North-Africans, part of the content, but they are represented in a way which deliberately challenges popular stereotypes. In fact the challenge is broader than this, since stereotypes of sex roles and middle-class norms of behaviour are also the target of the authors' subtle use of irony and the genre of the 'roman-photo'.

The Working Group were also quick to endorse and encourage this kind of effort. They point out that the National Criteria for the General Certificate of Education already stressed the importance of using material which incorporates the linguistic and cultural diversity of society. They warn against stereotyping, even as a source of humour, and suggest that 'members of all nationalities and cultures should be portrayed' (DES, 1990, p. 81). They go on to emphasize that the portrayal should be 'in ways which show them to have the same common human qualities and needs, whatever the physical and cultural difference may be'. Laudable though this may at first sight appear, it unfortunately implies that otherness is superficial and can be passed over. Although it would be unfair to over-interpret this subordinate clause in a whole chapter on 'Equal Opportunities in Modern Language Learning', it is nonetheless an indication that further thought is needed.

Although the detailed proposals for attainment targets have been amended, the Working Party's report remains a significant contribution to the debate on foreign language teaching, and I propose to refer to it as well as to the Statutory Order published in December 1991.

In its report incorporated in the proposals of the Secretary of State, *Modern Foreign Languages for ages 11 to 16* (DES, 1990), the Working Group took as its baseline the 'educational purposes' already familiar to teachers from the National Criteria for the GCSE — with one important addition. They added the following purpose: 'to develop pupils' understanding of themselves and their own culture'. This small addition, to seven other purposes, opens the way for an important shift in the focus of foreign language teaching which hitherto has been directed, by silent consensus, towards the foreign country exclusively. The change is then carried through into the Programmes of Study in a series of statements.

Learners should therefore have frequent opportunities to. . . .

- appreciate the similarities and differences between their own and cultures of the communities/countries where the target language is spoken;
- identify with the experience and perspective of people in the countries and communities where the target language is spoken;
- use this knowledge to develop a more objective view of their own customs and ways of thinking. (DES, 1990, p. 36)

It becomes clear, therefore, that a different, alternative view of their own culture (and socio-political environment?) is to be provided in Foreign Languages. There is still a need to explicate what psychological processes are implicit in terms such as 'appreciate' or 'develop a more objective view' or 'identify with'. A similar lack of clarity of methodology is implicit in the subsequent references to comparisons, but the emphasis on reflection on self as well as, and as a consequence of, reflection on otherness is clear enough:

Without the cultural dimension, successful communication is often difficult (sic). . . . The context of the language community. . .plays a substantial role in classroom activities. In this, comparisons between the learners' own way of life and that of the other language community are an essential means to better understanding of both. (DES, 1990, p. 37)

The Statutory Order appears to accept the shift of emphasis, although the formulation is less explicit. There is acceptance of the notion of developing cultural awareness, and a methodology is proposed which is based on comparison: 'In learning and using the target language pupils should have regular opportunities to:. . .consider and discuss the similarities and differences between their own culture and those of the countries and communities where the target language is spoken.' (DES, 1991, p. 26)

This shift of focus would, however, be insignificant without a change in the contexts in which it is proposed to teach the foreign language. The concentration in the GCSE on a picture of the foreign country in terms which appeal to the tourist would be an inadequate basis for comparison with the learners' own culture. It is the introduction of new Areas of Experience which provides the potential for meaningful comparison with learners' own experience of their own culture and society. These seven Areas of Experience form the content of the foreign language curriculum, including 'everyday activities', 'the world of education, training and work' and 'the world of communication', for example. It is possible to find here the opportunity to make explicit reference to inner-territorial otherness, combining the specifications of Area of Experience B with the suggestion that there should be comparison between own and target culture/community.

In Area of Experience B, Personal and Social Life, it is stated that pupils should explore 'topics which deal with. . .social attitudes, customs and institutions which are relevant to them', and as non-binding examples, the Statutory Order document suggests 'attitudes towards religion, politics and society (including stereotyping and equal opportunities)' (DES, 1991, p. 28). The final phrase refers implicitly to the chapter in the Working Group's report already mentioned above.

In their discussion of 'equal opportunities' the Working Group addresses directly the issue of 'reflecting diversity'. Here they state quite categorically, in paragraph 14.22, the potential for foreign languages in multicultural education, although here again the use of terms such as 'appreciation and enjoyment' and 'presenting and interpreting' beg many questions:

> One of the most potent agents in combating prejudice is the appreciation and enjoyment of diversity. This is particularly true of cultural and ethnic diversity. Of all the subjects in the National Curriculum, the study of a foreign language most directly addresses the existence of other cultures, opening up areas of knowledge and understanding which extend far beyond the way in which the language is spoken and written. Language teachers are therefore frequently involved in presenting and interpreting the experiences and identities of people in other communities. In doing so they inevitably find themselves dealing with questions such as:
>
> - does the depiction of different ethnic groups faithfully present their perspective and their voice?
> - do all pupils, as a natural part of their language course, learn about culture and experience of groups other than their own?
>
> Schools which have pupils from a diversity of backgrounds will have no difficulty in recognising the importance of these questions. Pupils in schools without this advantage have an even greater need to be made aware of the rich cultural diversity which is a part of all modern societies. (DES, 1990, pp. 81–2)

This is clearly an invitation to ensure that, at the very least, the lead given by textbooks such as *Orientations* (Aplin, Miller and Starkey, 1985), should be followed in the future.

The Working Group also turned its attention to the position of bilingual pupils. It is in a sense a diversion from the main argument of this chapter, which is concerned with the role of foreign language teaching in opening new cultural perspectives for all pupils. It is nonetheless important to note that, though the Working Group does not challenge the nation-state's policy of diverting inner-territorial languages into the marginal position of Foreign Languages, they are concerned that bilingual pupils should be given the best opportunities within this policy. They state quite clearly that

> the foreign language attainment targets and programmes of study that we are proposing here have been developed with reference to all pupils in Key Stages 3 and 4. It is our hope that they have been formulated in such a way as to facilitate productive and appropriate learning for any bilingual pupils who opt to study their home language. (DES, 1990, p. 84)

They then point out the implications: 'The inclusion of bilingual pupils in modern language classes inevitably broadens the range of language attainment that the teacher has to address' (DES, 1990, p. 84). Unfortunately, the import of this was lost on many teachers who have little or no contact with bilingual pupils, some of whom could easily have reached the attainment targets proposed. The lowering and reduction of the targets as a consequence of consultation must be seen as a disappointment for those teachers, few though they may be, who could have pushed their bilingual pupils to significant achievements. On the other hand it is clear, that for the vast majority of teachers and pupils, the languages are indeed 'foreign' and not 'home' or 'second', and the problem is essentially one of the policy of treating the latter as if they were the former.

A further disappointment to bilingual pupils and their teachers must be the Working Group's response to the Section 3 Order. The Order established two lists: one containing the eight EC working languages and another containing eleven other languages, including those widely spoken by bilingual pupils. Under the terms of the Order schools *must* offer a language from the first list and may offer, in addition, a language from the second. Although they recommend that all languages which might be offered in schools should be named as one single list, they still give clear priority to EC languages, by saying that if a school offers only one language it must be an EC language. The attempts to soften the blow by referring to possibilities of diversification and 'split-year models' do not hide the political priorities and the marginalization of bilingual pupils' languages.

Turning back to the proposals which affect all pupils, we have so far identified a number of encouraging statements and points for potential development. It must be acknowledged that, with the exception of paragraph 14.22, there are no unequivocal indications that the Working Group or the Statutory Orders have the possibility of a dual focus on otherness within and without national boundaries at the heart of their concerns. To this must be added a general criticism of the Areas of Experience which have no apparent theoretical rationale. There is, first, no definition of 'culture' or 'way of life' — both phrases are used — in the discussion of 'cultural awareness' (DES, 1990, p. 36). Nor is the relationship between language and culture adequately discussed; it must be inferred from the following: 'Cultural awareness is developed through: i) a combination of topic content and knowledge of linguistic conventions, in which learners are encouraged to reflect on the similarities and contrasts of cultures and on language as a tool for communication. . .' (DES, 1990, p. 38). Further on it is suggested that 'learners become increasingly aware: that the other language is a means of communication like their own. . .: of cultural attitudes as expressed in language.' There appears to be a recognition that language and culture acquisition are inseparable, but, given the lack of familiarity amongst most language teachers with the notion of cultural awareness, the failure to be explicit is lamentable.

The Areas of Experience themselves, through which cultural awareness is to develop, are a selection from the culture/way of life of 'topics' which are above all 'familiar' to pupils. There is no attempt at a theoretical justification for this kind of selection, although they doubtless have a face-value appeal to teachers and, hopefully, to pupils through the notion of familiarity and relevance. It is odd to imply that Area E, The world of communications and technology — which means such things as 'informal and formal letters', 'advertising' and 'benefits and dangers of technology' — is of the same order and nature as Area B, Personal and social life, under which such fundamental social issues as 'family relationships, national customs and ways of behaving' and 'religious life' are included. The Statutory Order reduces the number of examples but does not improve on the underlying problem. Much clearer guidance is needed if the potential for cultural analysis — and therefore understanding rather than simply awareness — is to be realized. Teachers and textbook writers may be tempted to interpret cultural awareness in a superficial way and the hopes expressed in the Working Group's paragraph 14.22 will scarcely be realized.

Strategies for the Classroom and Beyond

I have argued that because foreign language learning is an introduction to otherness and the perspectives of others on oneself, it is, in general, a significant contributor to an education which is looking beyond and within national boundaries, at the cultures of other minorities and majorities. I have also argued that the National Curriculum allows, more explicitly than in the recent past, for a focus on the acquisition of language and culture as an indivisible process. The opportunity to turn the focus on inner-territorial minority cultures is also available, at the very least through comparison with minority cultures in other nation-states. There is little guidance as to how these opportunities are to be realized, partly, I suspect, because the Working Group and the Statutory Order do not have a firm grasp of culture, cultural awareness or the relationship between language and culture.

As is often the case in foreign language teaching, the realization of the possibilities will be in the hands of teachers and textbook writers. For, by omitting any attempt to assess cultural awareness in the proposals for attainment targets, the Working Group and the government in its Statutory Orders have handed the responsibility to others.

Elsewhere (Byram, 1989), I have proposed a general model of language and culture teaching which proposes, for cultural awareness, a combination of experiential and reflective learning. The most important adaptation of the National Curriculum areas of experience will be to develop a systematic approach to topics which realize these areas, a system which includes the combination of experience and reflection and, by returning to the same topic at different stages in the course of language learning, allows for greater degree of abstraction and critical analysis. This applies to every topic, but can be exemplified in terms of the one which allows direct reference to inner-territorial minority cultures.

As suggested above, it is in Area B that pupils can be introduced to social attitudes towards inner-territorial minorities. At an initial stage, pupils should meet texts which give an accurate factual account of the position of minorities in the foreign country. For example, a text on demographic statistics for the whole country and another charting the history of immigration and emigration are within the grasp of beginners (in the first two years of secondary schooling) and could be combined with learning numbers and dates in the foreign language. Parallel information about the pupils' own country would be provided for explicit comparison. At an intermediate level, a narrative text about people from one of the minorities would be linguistically and conceptually more demanding, as pupils might be asked to comment on social attitudes implicit in the text, and to find parallel examples from their own society. At the more advanced level a suitable text would be one which gives expression to prejudice and its effect on its victims. Such a text could deliberately draw upon the experience of minorities in the pupils' own culture as expressed in poetry and music and commented on by someone from the foreign language society. All of these clearly open up the possibility of parallel work in other subjects: demography and immigration in geography, response to prejudice in the arts in English or music. Appropriate texts are not always easy to find as this schematic example suggests. They may have to be a combination of specially-written and authentic texts. The role of the textbook writer is crucial, since the teacher cannot spend the necessary time on text construction and selection.

The reference to links with other subjects echoes the views of the Working Group. My earlier suggestion that cultural learning must be in part experiential also reinforces the views of the Working Group and the Statutory Order that 'pupils should have regular opportunities to: come into contact with native speakers in this country and (where possible) abroad' (DES, 1991, p. 25). The power of the experience of a sojourn in the foreign country to relativize and even destabilize pupils' perceptions of themselves as normal and the others as foreign cannot be overestimated. Elsewhere (Byram and Esarte-Sarries, 1991), we have suggested ways in which ethnographic techniques can be used to help pupils see the foreign culture from within during a school trip. It is, in the final analysis, this experience for which much classroom learning should be preparation and post-sojourn analysis. For it is on such occasions that pupils who belong to a monocultural majority learn what it is like to be 'other', to be the recipient of the insulting epithet *étranger*.

For some pupils the memory of such an experience is unpleasant, as we discovered when interviewing 3rd Year pupils — as they were at the time — in research on the effects of language learning on their perceptions of other people (Byram and Esarte-Sarries, 1991). The sense of isolation in a foreign culture can be very strong:

Interviewer: Can you describe it a little?

Pupil: Like, you thought you were alone, and things like, you couldn't get to know things. You thought someone was talking about things you couldn't understand, just like wondering what they were talking about.

I: What did you feel like then?

P: Can't describe it.

I: You felt alone you said.

P: Yes.

I: Makes you feel alone?

P: 'Cause everyone else is French and, like, surrounded by French people. They really don't understand things there.

The tendency to attribute the problem of understanding to others, when the pupil himself is the outsider, is one means of maintaining self-confidence. The lack of understanding is clearly the most destabilizing factor in the experience, as another pupil describes it:

I: What did that feel like when you heard people around you speaking French for the first time then?

P: I was scared. I thought I was lost, really. When I said to my friends, if a person came over on the beach I would be lost, because I was just playing football with them and when we went for an ice-cream or something like that, I was scared.

Of course, the reaction depends on other factors such as personality, previous experience of visiting other countries or even other parts of Britain.

I: You have been abroad quite a number of times now. Have you ever had that moment when you felt like a foreigner, as though you didn't belong in the country?

P: No. I just forgot I was in another country.

The significance of being able to speak the foreign language, however little, was mentioned again and again by pupils, and in the following example is clearly linked with being an outsider:

I: Have you heard people speak French?

P: Yes.

I: What's it feel like?

P: I don't know what they're talking about. You just feel left out. 'Cause you don't know what they're saying. You can catch some of it but most of it, you don't know what they're talking about.

I: So what did it feel like?

P: Just feels like you're talking, like. . .they're not, like, talking to you at all. When they try and talk to you in a foreign language, you don't think they're talking to you 'cause you don't know what they're on about. I don't know really, it's hard to explain.

This is the pupil's attempt to explain the experience of being the *other*, which only the immersion in another culture can give.

The final word can be left to another pupil who identifies the significance of learning a foreign language:

P: ...all different nationalities are the same to me. Like, French was just the same till we started learning it really.

I: Until you started learning it?

P: Yes.

I: Now that you've been learning about it, do you see the French differently then?

P: Well, say, they're different to a lot of countries, 'cause like I can understand the French a bit now.

Understanding is clearly not simply a matter of linguistic decoding and encoding. There is here the articulation of a differentiation, so that the simple category of *other* is broken down and an insight into the world of the French begins to appear. This is the significance of successful language learning.

References

APLIN, R., MILLER, A. and STARKEY, H. (1985) *Orientations*, London, Hodder and Stoughton.

BARTH, F. (1969) *Ethnic Groups and Boundaries*, London, Allen and Unwin.

BYRAM, M. (1989) *Cultural Studies in Foreign Language Education*, Clevedon, Multilingual Matters.

BYRAM, M. (1990) 'Intercultural education and foreign language teaching', *World Studies Journal*, **7**(1), pp. 4–7.

BYRAM, M. and ESARTE-SARRIES, V. (1991) *Investigating Cultural Studies in Foreign Language Learning*, Clevedon, Multilingual Matters.

BYRAM, M., ESARTE-SARRIES, V. and TAYLOR, S. (1991) *Cultural Studies and Language Learning*, Clevedon, Multilingual Matters.

DEPARTMENT OF EDUCATION AND SCIENCE (1985) *Education for All: Report of the Committee of Enquiry into the Education of Children from Ethnic Minority Groups* (The Swann Report) Cmnd 9543, London, HMSO.

DEPARTMENT OF EDUCATION AND SCIENCE (1990) *Modern Foreign Languages for ages 11 to 16*, London, HMSO.

DEPARTMENT OF EDUCATION AND SCIENCE (1991) *Modern Foreign Languages in the National Curriculum*, London, HMSO.

DOYE, P. (1991) 'Erziehung zu internationaler Verstandigung als Aufgabe des Fremdsprachenunterrichts. Ein Beitrag zu politischer Bildung' in DOYE, P. (Ed.) *Grossbritannien: seine Darstellung in deutschen Schulbuchern fut den Englischunterricht*, Frankfurt, Germany: Diesterweg.

DOYE, P. (forthcoming) 'Fremdsprachenunterricht als Beitrag zu tertiarer Sozialisation'.

GOODENOUGH, W.H. (1964) 'Cultural anthropology and linguistics,' in HYMES, D. (Ed.) *Language in Culture and Society*, New York, Harper and Row.

HALLIDAY, M.A.K. (1975) *Learning How to Mean*, London, Edward Arnold.

JONES, C. and KIMBERLEY, K. (1991) *Intercultural Perspectives on the National Curriculum for England and Wales*, London, University of London, Institute of Education.

Michael S. Byram

KINGMAN, J. (1988) *Report of the Committee of Inquiry into the Teaching of English Language*, London, HMSO.
NATIONAL CURRICULUM COUNCIL (1991) *Modern Foreign Languages in the National Curriculum: Consultation Report*, York, National Curriculum Council.
VYGOTSKY, L.S. (1971) *Mind in Society*, Cambridge, Massachusetts: Harvard University Press.

Chapter 14

Religious Education and the Multicultural Perspective

Peter Mitchell

The Education Reform Act and RE

At last religious education can no longer be criticized as being the only subject made mandatory by statute in English and Welsh schools. This is not because the status of RE has been altered — for all practical purposes it has not — but because of the advent of the National Curriculum. Indeed, the tables have been turned and RE now has greater freedom from central direction than the rest of the compulsory curriculum. Its syllabuses are still firmly under local control, and it remains the duty of local Agreed Syllabus Conferences on religious education, with their carefully balanced membership and voting rights, to decide what the RE curriculum should be and the place, if any, that programmes of study and attainment targets ought to have in it.[1]

In fact, local control has been enhanced. Under the 1988 Act all Local Education Authorities (LEAs) have also had to set up permanent Standing Advisory Councils for Religious Education (SACREs) with well defined duties and memberships. Such councils may be largely advisory and their influence variable in different parts of the country, but they are obliged to publish annual reports of their work and have the right to enquire into the state of RE in their area, to offer advice on teaching methods and materials and to request the drawing up of a new agreed syllabus.

Significantly the membership of such Councils includes teacher representatives but puts them in a minority. The greater part of the membership must come from the various religious groups in the area and from locally elected councillors. This has one important consequence for multicultural education. Where SACREs and Agreed Syllabus Conferences are operating properly, the various faith communities can, through their representatives on such bodies, make their voices heard on what is to be taught. Even if this is still much too heavily biased against minority faith communities (Mabud, 1992), it contrasts favourably with the core and foundation subjects of the National Curriculum.

However, one important qualification has to be made to this portrayal of local freedom. The 1988 Education Reform Act lays down new statutory obligations about the content of RE which seem to run counter to the pluralist spirit of our times. Any new Religious Education syllabuses will have to 'reflect the fact that the religious traditions in Great Britain are in the main Christian'. Schools are required to continue to provide daily acts of collective worship, but this collective worship has to be 'wholly or mainly of a broadly Christian character'.

Of course, closer inspection shows that the story is far less monocultural than these bare bones suggest. The Christianity concerned is to be of a broad, non-denominational kind. Confessional teaching, i.e. advocacy of any particular form of Christianity or indeed any other religious denomination, is, in LEA schools, strictly ruled out. Religious education has also, for the first time, a legal obligation to take 'account of the teaching and practices of the other principal religions represented in Great Britain'. Part of the membership of any conference concerned with the drawing up of an agreed syllabus of religious education must by law 'appropriately reflect the principal religious traditions in the area'. When devising acts of collective worship schools must allow for the family background of the pupils as well as their ages and aptitudes. Schools can also, if they so request, be exempted in whole or in part from the requirements for Christian worship. As in the 1944 Education Act, any pupil can be withdrawn from all or part of religious education lessons and acts of collective worship, and teachers continue to have similar rights of exemption.

The Act in its provisions for Religious Education in relationship to the pluralism of our society seems therefore to embody ambiguity. On the one hand, for the first time, an Education Act specifically states that an understanding of Christianity shall be part of the educational entitlement of all pupils attending state schools. Yet it does so in a highly qualified way, whilst also accepting the legitimate place for the study of alternative points of view or for no study at all.

It is, therefore, not so easy as is sometimes supposed to decide whether or not the requirements of the 1988 Education Reform Act governing RE are conducive or constrictive so far as the multicultural dimension of education is concerned. Some light is thrown on this puzzle when we consider the origin of the most significant clauses concerned with RE in the Act. They were not part of the government's plans as set out in the original Bill, where there was a brief desultory mention of RE, leaving the subject largely as it was in 1944 and in the wider context of the Bill marginalized almost to extinction. Instead, the present legislation was the outcome of pressure and sharp debate in the House of Lords and was essentially a political compromise between very different points of view (Alves, 1991).

It is not surprising, therefore, that such a law was almost inevitably framed in a way that leaves it open to a variety of inconsistent interpretations and uses. Yet, as one lawyer has recently suggested, 'the emergence of (such) inconsistency does not necessarily mean that the law is defective. Rather it may demonstrate that policy and practice have been left free to adapt and develop creatively' (Harte, 1991). Indeed Harte further argues, 'the provisions of the Education Reform Act 1988 concerned with religion in schools are part of a wider trend of modern legislation to use the law as a framework within which decision-makers are forced to reconcile competing and constantly developing ideologies and aims'. It is worth noticing that the same clauses were later passed by very large majorities in the House of Commons. The compromise could be read in different ways by different interests.

RE and the Act's Interpreters

We have, therefore, to turn to the decision makers themselves to see if they have chosen to interpret the Act in the realm of religious education in a way that is compatible with a multicultural perspective. In one sense the jury is still out. Sufficient time has not yet elapsed for the full implications of the Act to have been worked out, especially since we are dealing with an essentially local phenomenon with many different LEAs acting at remarkably different speeds. Nevertheless, there are enough pointers to show how things are likely to develop.

Decision makers exist at different levels. The first is the Secretary of State for Education, whose powers are severely curtailed so far as RE is concerned. He is, however, the last court of appeal to whom parents and others can make representations about RE and school worship after they have exhausted the local complaints procedures newly set up under the 1988 Act. So far, these powers have been used largely to support a non-partisan interpretation of the Act. Thus Kenneth Clarke, the then Secretary of State for Education, in response to a complaint from a parent that the act of worship at their child's first school was not 'wholly or mainly of a broadly Christian character' because it was multifaith, writes that worship under the Act is in his opinion 'clearly intended to be such that pupils of a non-Christian background can take part' (TES, 2.8.91).

The Education minister's legal powers over new agreed syllabuses are even more ill defined. He can rule on complaints made about them, and he has powers to determine when a new syllabus shall take effect. This means that in practice he is able to object to such a syllabus if, in his opinion, it fails to comply with the law. He has, however, no power to amend syllabuses, though he can return them to the LEA for further consideration. This he has recently done in two cases, to the London Boroughs of Ealing and Newham. The main reason in these instances appeared to be a failure to set out exactly what aspects of Christianity and what elements of the other principal religions were to be taught. These views were expanded in a general letter sent at the same time to all Chief Education Officers (DES, 1991).

The sharp public debate that occurred over these ministerial pronouncements illustrates the tightrope on which ministers walk in matters concerned with RE and how easily the topic can be exploited by those with ideological axes to grind. At the time much of the press took the view that this was a welcome attempt to reassert the cultural hegemony of Christianity. Yet the wording of the letters and the legal advice they enshrine hardly reads as such straightforward partisan directives. Rather they assert that new syllabuses must give sufficient detail of what is to be taught about both Christianity and the other principal religions represented in Britain. Indeed, the advice given goes so far as to state that 'an agreed syllabus which conforms with Section 8.3 [of the 1988 Education Reform Act] cannot confine itself exclusively to religious education based on Christian traditions' (DES, 1991). All this may indicate a regrettable departure from recent developments in agreed syllabus construction, where increasingly aims and objectives are set out and decisions about specific content are left to individual schools. But it hardly constitutes an attempt to assert the innate superiority of Christianity (Hull, 1991a and 1991b).

The minister can also issue circulars and draft circulars to LEAs and schools showing how he interprets the Act and indicating how he intends to exercise his various powers. He has done this for RE and collective worship by issuing Circular no. 3/89 (DES, 1989). Once again it is possible to define government policy in a benign way. 'The Government believes that all those concerned with religious education should seek to ensure that it promotes respect, understanding and tolerance for those who adhere to different faiths' (DES, 1989, para. 8). The Circular also accepts, though in a somewhat qualified way, that it is both possible and legitimate to 'teach RE in an integrated form along with other subjects' (DES, 1989, para. 43).

A similar sensitivity is apparent when it deals with parents' rights to withdraw their children from RE. It recognizes that the discussion of religious issues is not confined to timetable periods of RE. It acknowledges that a parent could not 'insist on a child being withdrawn every time issues relating to religion and spiritual values were raised' (DES, 1989, para. 44). Nevertheless, 'the Secretary of State will expect head teachers to establish with any parent wanting to exercise the right of withdrawal a working understanding of the religious issues about which the parent would object to his or her child being taught, directly or indirectly; the practical implication of withdrawal; and the circumstances in which the school can reasonably be expected to accommodate parental wishes' (DES, 1989, para. 44). Withdrawal here seems to be allowed for more than just specific periods labelled RE. This is something which could have far reaching implications for objectors, such as those Muslim parents who on grounds of religious belief oppose the provision of sex education for their children by schools, though whether this is a correct interpretation of the law is open to dispute.

It is, of course, possible to deconstruct the provisions of the Act and its accompanying documents and read them in a far from benign way. How, for example, is the phrase 'different faiths' to be understood? In an egalitarian, personal way? Does it mean teaching tolerance and understanding of those who differ in their beliefs from one's own, no matter what these might be? Or is it a paternalist reference to non-Christian faiths with the implication that what is normal and to be expected is Christian belief? Why all the complex talk about rights of exemption and withdrawal? Might it not be that behind an educational smoke-screen the real intention of the Act is an induction into Christianity and a reassertion of the hegemony of one religion over all others? This is certainly the way some Muslim commentators see the Act and Circular (Sarwar, 1991).

Such an interpretation is certainly possible. The ideological context of any government policy, whatever its political hue, is not to be ignored. Nevertheless, whatever its origin, the actual legal import of the Act and its ministerial interpretations is to delegate the crucial decisions about religious education to others. Indeed, for better or worse, the aims and methods of teaching RE and the way of delivering collective acts of worship remain largely in the hands of individual teachers and their schools. The recent promise of a new circular and fresh legislation on religious education and collective worship does not seem likely to disturb these basic arrangements (Hansard, 1992, col. 278, and DFE, 1992, p. 37).

The NCC and Religious Education

Unfortunately, little guidance in this area has been forthcoming from the NCC, though its brief as expressed in the provisions of the 1988 Act certainly includes RE. It has, for example, 'to keep all aspects of the curriculum for maintained schools under review' {section 7(3)(a)}. Up until recently it seemed resolutely determined to have little to do with the subject. Now, however, the NCC has appointed a professional officer for RE and has published the first summaries of the reports which SACREs are required to send to it. It also commissioned the NFER to analyze these first reports in greater detail (Taylor, 1991) and has itself produced a document offering guidance to SACREs based on NCC's experience of attainment targets and programmes of study in other curriculum areas (NCC, 1991). Nevertheless, the NCC continues to make it abundantly clear that any guidance it offers is to be strictly circumscribed. Local control must remain inviolable.

SACREs

What then of SACREs, the apparent intended vehicles of local initiative and enterprise and one of the most important innovations in the 1988 Act so far as RE is concerned? Unless these show vigour and enterprise, the prized local control may turn out to be a disadvantage. The lack of mandatory attainment targets nationally assessed could easily reinforce the marginal nature of RE as part of the compulsory curriculum.

The NCC analysis of the first two years of SACRE reports and Monica Taylor's more detailed research of their first year's working suggests that such bodies are still feeling their way, and that with such diverse memberships there is often an inevitable tension between very different view-points. Indeed Monica Taylor's report indicates that in some cases the elected members (i.e. the politicians) are 'ill-informed on educational matters and especially on the place of world religions in the RE curriculum and RE's contribution to multicultural education' (Taylor, 1991, p. 170). On the other hand at least 90 per cent of SACREs include representatives of at least one religion other than Christianity. Nevertheless, in a sample extending to a quarter of their total number, approximately half the LEAs 'could be said to have a low profile for RE' (p. 182). In such a context SACREs have a very daunting task if they are to be a major instrument in raising the status and effectiveness of RE, let alone in making it a major contributor to the multicultural scene.

Agreed Syllabuses

SACREs offer advice and encouragement. Agreed syllabuses have statutory force. One encouraging outcome of the ERA has been a much more vigorous pursuit by LEAs of Agreed Syllabus revisions. The NCC analysis suggests that nearly a quarter, and Monica Taylor reports that, of her sample, over a third of LEAs are now reconsidering or reviewing their Agreed Syllabuses. The reasons given for such revision are various. Some syllabuses are said to be outdated — and some are shockingly so — or out of print! Others fail to reflect recent changes in the make-up of local populations. Yet more do not meet the requirements of the ERA and in particular do not link with the programmes of study, key stages, attainment targets and assessment arrangements of the National Curriculum. It is not surprising that the government in the 1992 White Paper on education promises to make it obligatory for all LEAs to revise their agreed syllabuses in the light of the requirements of the 1988 Education Reform Act (DFE, 1992, p. 37).

It is inevitable, however, given so many LEAs with such different political and social contexts, that the quality and appropriateness of even the most recent revisions should vary enormously. However, in spite of recent ministerial pronouncements mentioned above, there are few signs as yet that the influence of the 1988 Act has hindered in any appreciable way the modern developments of RE as reflected in the best of such syllabuses produced in recent years. If anything, the experience of looking afresh at what is supposed to be taught in schools is proving in many cases to be a salutary experience. Howarth (1991) in a recent analysis of seven new Agreed Syllabuses published since 1988 suggests that all of them recognize that to reflect the terms of the Act they must be 'multifaith'. Even more importantly they read the Act as requiring an emphasis on present day expressions of religious belief and practice. 'All seven syllabuses expect the content to cover a broad spectrum of material in which the contemporary expressions of religious belief and practice are essentially part and parcel of the religious education programme in every stage of schooling and in every key stage' (Howarth, 1991, p. 164).

The Situation of RE in Schools

What these agreed syllabuses all refuse to do is to be strictly prescriptive over the balance that should be struck between the space given to Christianity and that to other faiths. This is left firmly in the hands of individual schools. Teachers and individual schools can therefore still decisively affect the range, the quality and the balance of the RE offered to pupils. Statutory requirements, ministerial pronouncements, Agreed Syllabuses, SACREs and the like provide a legal and advisory framework within which it is still possible for schools to plan and deliver an RE which can enhance the education offered to pupils in our pluralist society and which can properly embody a multicultural perspective.

In a large number of schools, if HMI reports on individual schools are to be taken seriously, this, it has to be admitted, is not happening. One informed commentator, describing the situation revealed by HMI inspections just before the 1988 Act writes of RE as a subject 'dangerously near one of terminal decline' (Orchard, 1991). Present pressures on the timetable because of the demands of the National Curriculum, the higher status accorded to core and foundations subjects with their nationally regulated programmes of study and forms of assessment, the continuing shortage of qualified RE staff, and a lack of will by some LEAs and senior management tend to reinforce such a pessimistic diagnosis. Indeed, in a minority of institutions years of neglect and an ideological antipathy to religion have combined to all but kill any serious religious education.

However, it is possible to point to contrary and much more optimistic evidence. There are a sufficient number of places where the subject is both popular and thriving to suggest that, given sufficient resources and competent staff, such gloomy prognostications for the subject are unwarranted. There is also an increasing amount of teaching material produced both commercially and by various resource centres which can enrich the teaching of the subject in a way inconceivable even a few years ago. Much of this material is not only of very high quality, but is also far from being parochial, covering the whole range of world religions and is often extremely sensitive to the attitudes and aspirations of the various faith communities in a markedly non-paternalist way.

Pluralist Religious Education

We can therefore legitimately claim that, even given its present legal and social parameters, religious education can contribute positively to the group of educational tasks which fall under the general title multicultural education. Of course there are those who would abjure any such intention. For them religious education is inextricably linked to nurture in a particular faith. However, whilst the 1988 Education Reform Act and its accompanying documents recognize the right of individual parents, if they so wish, to educate their children in this fashion, they point schools in a very different direction. LEA schools have been given an opportunity to provide for their pupils a religious education that can widen their horizons and understanding to that which lies beyond the province of their own upbringing.

That there are good educational reasons for so doing is something which is rehearsed in other parts of this book. In the case of religion it is especially important. To understand properly our pluralist world necessarily involves knowing something of its major faiths, for the diverse religions of humankind have an unavoidable presence in the political and social maelstrom of today's world. Yet, whether it casts them in an heroic mode engaged in humanitarian relief or in a more malevolent role as agents of conflict and oppression, the mass media almost inevitably distorts the picture it gives of religions. We owe it to our pupils to give them a more balanced and informed understanding of those different patterns of belief and behavior, both religious and non-religious, which help shape the lives of the world's inhabitants.

Individuals also need to be able relate sensitively and without prejudice to their neighbours, whatever the varied beliefs and cultural mores of these might be. Without such understanding and sensitivity, it is extremely unlikely that pupils will ever come to enjoy the benefits or be able to respond positively to the challenges which diversity in culture and belief bring. Indeed, if education insists on ignoring the place of religions in the life of humankind, it can hardly expect to counter the prejudice and racist attitudes that have so often marred the western approach to cultural pluralism. Pupils as individuals need to be given the social space and intellectual skills to appraise their own beliefs and attitudes to religious and other life styles and to ascertain the possible value for themselves of this area of human experience. Religious education so understood has a crucial role to play in the education of the young, broadening their horizons and making them aware of those diverse religious motivations which help to explain so much of the pluralist world in which they live.

We must not ignore the dark side of the human story with its record of cruelty and exploitation in which religion has tragically shared. Such an education does not imply the bland acceptance of human frailty or evil. It also involves an education in justice with its attendant values of compassion and personal responsibility. Sensitivity on its own is never enough.

This, however, brings us to the heart of the challenge facing religious educators. On the one hand they are not in the business of depreciating or belittling the faith stance of any pupils or their families. Indeed, amongst the sharpest criticisms voiced by some of the leaders of the faith communities in our society is that the secularist tone of much of the total school curriculum does just this by ignoring or minimizing the faith perspective in what is presented to pupils

(Islamic Academy, 1991). Yet, on the other hand, religious educators are, as *educators*, committed to an open approach that encourages pupils to explore, appreciate and inevitably evaluate for themselves human diversity. As the Swann Report earlier expressed it, 'Education has to be something more than the reinforcement of the beliefs, values and identity which each child brings to school' (DES, 1985, p. 769). But this has to done in a way that does not undermine these same beliefs, values and sense of identity. Teachers have to strike a delicate balance between helping pupils to gain a fuller knowledge of their own cultural roots and to feel a legitimate pride in their own personal identity as members of a specific community, whilst at the same time providing them with wider cognitive perspectives and encouraging in them a deepening sensitivity to the views and feelings of others.

Of course, these are values and attitudes which ought to be shared by all teachers engaged in education in a pluralist society. They are especially important for religious educators because they, above all, are engaged in the direct study of religions and their impact on human life. The religious educator cannot avoid meeting head on the challenges and demands of multicultural education.

Strictly speaking, therefore, religious educators cannot be neutral. Not only does their teaching have to exhibit a commitment to the substantive ideals of justice, compassion and personal responsibility, but it also has to embody respect and sensitivity to a wide range of beliefs and cultural and religious behaviour. The latter is of particular significance, since for many faith communities questions of etiquette, diet and dress are often inextricably linked to deeply held religious convictions.

All this is made doubly difficult because it is idle to suppose that many teachers can for long conceal their own personal commitments from their pupils. Indeed, artificial attempts to do so can create in pupils a sense of educational hypocrisy. One reason why the idea of the teacher as a neutral chairperson, so popular in the seventies, proved almost impossible to sustain was that pupils often knew their teachers too well! The attitude of religious educators to faiths and belief systems other than their own thus becomes an important substratum to all their teaching. Respect for and sensitivity to the beliefs of others has to become ingrained in the fabric of their thinking as well as in the structures of their lessons. Without such attitudes informing their teaching, even the most professionally produced and religiously illuminating materials can prove to be ineffectual in the classroom.

This is not to minimize the value of well designed and appropriate materials and schemes of work, examples of which can be found at the end of this chapter.[2] What is important is to recognize is that no material or scheme produced by others can perfectly fit the particular needs and backgrounds of an individual class or group of pupils. As any experienced teacher knows, flexibility and adaptability are necessary hallmarks of the successful educator.

Teaching Methods and Materials for Pluralist RE

There are certain criteria worth applying to any teaching methods and materials that are to be used in the pluralist religious education being advocated here. The first is the absolute necessity of accuracy. We have to ask, 'Is this a true picture of the phenomena to be studied?' Too often in the past text books have presented caricatures, especially of non-Christian religions (Islamic Academy, 1986). One useful test is to ask whether or not an adherent would recognize the authenticity of the religion being portrayed. This is not so simple as it seems. Often the adherent's view needs interpretation and amplification, if it is to become intelligible to pupils in today's schools. Some books are now being co-authored by adherents and non-adherents to provide this double perspective.

Second, teachers have to achieve some kind of balance in their treatment of the various religions. It is this that both statute and agreed syllabuses leave firmly in the court of the schools themselves. Admittedly it is not easy to achieve. Attempt too much and pupils can become confused. Concentrate on too little and the richness of the religious phenomena is missed. Individual teachers will, no doubt, evolve different practical solutions to this problem, depending on their own knowledge and the needs of their particular classes. Nevertheless, all need to be able to respond positively to the question 'Am I in the long term being fair in my teaching, or am I by neglect or trivialization marginalizing in the eyes of my pupils an important part of the religious heritage of humankind?'

Third, we need to be sure that the study of religions does not in itself reinforce the antipathies of the past. As John Hull has recently emphasized, traditional sources can, for polemic reasons, exhibit antagonism and bias towards alternative points of view (Hull, 1992). Sometimes our perceptions of this owe more to what is read back into the writings rather than to the intentions of their original authors. The most terrible example of this has been the use over the centuries of the Christian New Testament to support the most gross forms of anti-semitism, even though most of the authors of such documents were Jewish in their origins. But often it is due to misrepresentations contained in the sources themselves. Teachers have to beware especially, when using traditional stories retold for modern pupils, that they do not choose authors who reinforce or repeat such errors.[3] When appealing to the traditional sources themselves teachers owe it to their pupils to make them aware of the nature of such distortions.

Fourth, we need to distinguish clearly between affirmations of faith appropriate to the believer and matters of public knowledge acceptable to all. Given that the evidence is strong enough pupils can be asked to accept the latter, but it is not part of the school's educational task to try to ensure that they join in the former. Pupils may study documents expressing faith. Indeed, it is often necessary to do so in order to grasp something of a religion's most powerful convictions. But the objective has to be understanding not belief.

Fortunately, it is now rare for school books to ask for straightforward declarations of faith, but there is a more subtle problem. Books may imply that the reader shares the particular faith stance of the author, or, even more problematically, portrays its belief presuppositions as matters of fact not faith. On the other side of the coin lie books that contain attacks on a religion which are the outcome of ideological differences concealed as matters of fact. Islam in particular has suffered from this kind of distortion, but similar things have happened to most other religions.

Fifth, the sheer diversity of the religious phenomena being studied has to be acknowledged. Often in the past individual religions have been presented in school books as monolithic unities. Yet most living religions involve in practice an incredible variety of beliefs and practices. Even the most regulated faiths are not in reality monochrome uniformities. In order to counteract this there has been an increasing trend in recent text books and other materials to encourage pupils to study the lives of actual believers and their families.[4] When well done, this can add to the authenticity and liveliness of the material and enable pupils to identify more easily with the people being studied. It can also help them to grasp something of the very different ways members of the same religion can live out their faith and thus act as a very salutary corrective to those stereotypes which so easily distort the study of religion.

Sixth, the links between religions need to be acknowledged. Religious diversity is not the whole story. Good teaching has long recognized this, and it is partly for this reason that thematic teaching has been so popular in religious education. The connections between the different religions can be explored through such shared phenomena as rites of passage, festivals, sacred places and people, and there are innumerable books on the market that help the teacher of pupils of all ages to do this.[5] Obviously, if this is done in an unthinking way, confusion can result. It is important in such study to do justice to the distinctive characteristics and the integrity of the different religions being studied. Nevertheless, many teachers have found this to be a valuable way to approach the study of religions. In the recent debate on religious education in the House of Lords this approach was vigorously attacked by various speakers on the grounds that it does not suffi-ciently respect the coherence of each faith (Hansard, 1992, col. 252–256). But this would only follow if no space were to be offered to pupils for the study of the separate faiths with their differences as well as similarities.

Finally, the affective element in religion needs a proper recognition. There has been a tendency in the past to reduce the study of religion to the investiga-tion of sets of particular beliefs or distinctive rituals and rules of conduct. The unintentional consequence has been that too often the religions of the faith minor-ities in this country have been seen by many pupils as bizarre and alien, ex-pressed in languages not their own and involving unintelligible modes of behaviour.

What has frequently been underestimated is the strong emotional element present in all the major world religions. Recent research into the British population as a whole has shown how widespread are such religious experiences even in our own apparently secular country. The picture of religion conveyed to pupils would be seriously distorted if such phenomena are ignored. For facts can be learned and rituals observed, but if the living heart of religion is passed over, its study will inevitably become a very sterile exercise. In response to this challenge teaching materials are now becoming available which encourage teachers to explore with their classes this aspect of religion.[6]

What *is* required is not merely factual information about such experiences but an entrance into them. This is very difficult to achieve. The personal integrity of the individual pupil has to be respected, the possibility of rational reflection preserved and access provided to at least some of the very diverse experiences embodied in the major world faiths. Nevertheless, teachers who have tried this approach have found that not only has the range of the materials they use been extended and enriched, but their teaching methods have also been transformed. Poetry, music, drama, dance and the expressive arts can all contribute to such work. It is in this area that the contributions of the different religions can meet with the pupils' expressions of their own experiences of life.

Conclusion

It cannot be claimed that the 1988 Education Reform Act has intentionally helped forward the kind of pluralist religious education advocated here. Yet it has not made it impossible. A framework has been created in which it could be energetically pursued. Although recent pronouncements from the government show a strong desire that 'Christianity should lie at the heart of religious education' (Hansard, 1992, col. 275) and that 'Proper regard should continue to be paid to the nation's Christian heritage and traditions' (DEF, 1992, p. 37), this is coupled to a belief that pupils should also develop a proper understanding and appreciation of those other faiths present in this country. What is now required is a far greater commitment of resources and time than the subject has so far enjoyed. Given this commitment, it could make an irreplaceable contribution to the education of all our pupils who inevitably will have to live in a multicultural, multifaith world.

Notes

1 Some LEA Agreed Syllabus Conferences are already adopting or are on the way to adopting a similar format to that employed in National Curriculum subjects, with attainment targets, programmes of study and teaching levels. See, for example, Suffolk County Council's Report *RE in the Basic Curriculum* (1991) and Bedfordshire County Council's *Attainment and Assessment in RE, Draft Guidelines* (1991). Both of these documents draw on the whole range of religions. See also *RE, Attainment and National Curriculum* (1991), London, Religious Education Council.

2 There is now available a considerable body of excellent teaching materials for use in both primary and secondary schools. Only a very little can be referred to here and in the notes below. *RE Today* (CEM), *Look Hear!* (AVA Magazine Ltd) and *Resource* (Professional Council for Religious Education) are very readable magazines which offer reviews of the whole range of such materials; a more scholarly publication is the *British Journal of Religious Education* (CEM). There are also numerous resource centres where such material can be seen and sometimes borrowed. Two most noteworthy collections are to be found in the BFSS RE centre at the West London Institute of Higher Education and the Westhill RE Resources Centre, Westhill College, Birmingham.

For the earlier years of the primary school there is *A Gift for the Child*, Grimmit, M. *et al.* (1992), Hemel Hempstead, Simon & Schuster Education: a religious education teaching pack aimed at pupils from three to nine and emanating from the work of the University of Birmingham's 'Religion in the early years' Research Project. This represents a remarkable advance on earlier productions for this age group. It shows how material from the major world religions can be used with younger children in an authentic yet imaginative way. Even more significantly, it suggests ways in which even at a young age pupils can gain access to elements of the world faiths in a way that 'encourages intimacy and appreciation without requiring or implying adherence'.

For older primary pupils two recent teachers' books offer practical advice on religious education from a world religions perspective; *The Junior RE Handbook,* edited by Robert Jackson and Dennis Starkings, Cheltenham, Stanley Thornes, and *Religious Education in the Primary Curriculum* (1991) by Owen Cole and Evans-Lowndes, Norwich, RMEP.

Spanning both the primary and the secondary age range is the *Westhill Project RE 5–16*, eds. J. Rudge *et al.* (1987–), Cheltenham, Stanley Thornes. This provides sets of graduated pupils books and teacher guides on individual religions seen as world faiths; each religion is illustrated by some exceptionally well produced large scale photographs. Published so far are Christianity, Islam and Judaism.

Nor need the teacher be limited to written materials. There is available a large amount of other audio and visual materials, including slides, tapes, records, videos and religious artifacts. Central Television's series *Believe it or Not* is amongst the best known of schools TV programmes that explore world religions for secondary pupils.

3 Examples of stories told in a positive way include *The Stories from. . .*series (1987) London, Macdonald. These are intended mainly for primary pupils and cover the Christian, Hindu, Jewish and Muslim Worlds.

4 A good example of this is the Cambridge Project (1990) edited by Jean Holm, Harlow, Longman, which consists of a series of text books intended for primary pupils. Titles include *Growing up in Judaism* by Jean Holm, *Growing up in Hinduism* by Jacqueline Hirst with Geeta Pandey and *Growing up in Islam* by Janet Ardvan. Even more specific is the work beginning to emanate from the 'Religious Education and Community' Project at the University of Warwick directed by Robert Jackson, with books such as *Listening to Hindus* (1990) by Robert Jackson and Eleanor Nesbitt, London, Unwin Hyman. Hodder and Stoughton, London, have recently published, *Christians in Britain Today* (1991), a book based on interviews with present day individuals. Intended for older pupils, it reflects the wide diversity within British Christianity.

5 The *Religion In Life* series (1984) of five text books by John Bailey, Huddersfield, Schofield & Sims, provides a good illustration of this approach at the secondary level. *Religious Education Topics for the Primary School* (1989) by John Rankin, Alan Brown and Mary Hayward, Harlow, Longman, offers something similar for primary children. A text book exploring one theme, creation, in a pluralist way, is *Worlds of Difference* (1985) by Martin Palmer and Esther Bisset, Glasgow, Blackie. This is supported by two series of posters, entitled *Creation Stories I and II* from Pictorial Charts Educational Trust, London. This same organization provides many other well produced posters on world religion themes.

6 *New Methods in RE, An Experiential Approach* (1990) by John Hammond and others, Harlow, Oliver & Boyd, is the authoritative teachers' book which expounds this approach, and provides practical advice for its implementation. A critical assessment of such work can be found in Thatcher, A., 'A critique of inwardness in religious education' in the *British Journal of Religious Education*, **14**(1), pp. 22ff.

References

ALVES, C. (1991) 'Just a matter of words? The religious education debate in the House of Lords', *British Journal of Religious Education*, **13**(3), pp. 168ff.

DEPARTMENT OF EDUCATION AND SCIENCE (1985) *Education for All: Report of the Committee of Enquiry into the Education of Children from Ethnic Minority Groups* (The Swann Report), Cmnd 9543, London, HMSO.

DEPARTMENT OF EDUCATION AND SCIENCE (1989) *Circular No 3/89, The Education Reform Act 1988: Religious Education and Collective Worship*, London, HMSO.

DEPARTMENT OF EDUCATION AND SCIENCE (1991) Letter to Chief Education Officers, 18 March 1991, London, DES.

DEPARTMENT FOR EDUCATION (1992) *Choice and Diversity — A New Framework for Schools, A White Paper on Education*, London, HMSO.

HANSARD (1992) *House of Lords Debate on Religious Education in Schools*, 17 June 1992, London, HMSO, col. 250–282.

HARTE, J.D.C. (1991) 'Worship and religious education under the Education Reform Act 1988 — a lawyer's view', *British Journal of Religious Education*, **13**(3), pp. 152ff.

HOWARTH, R. (1991) 'The impact of the Education Reform Act on new agreed syllabuses of religious education', *British Journal of Religious Education*, **13**(3), pp. 162ff.

HULL, J. (1991a) Editorial, *British Journal of Religious Education*, **14**, p. 1.

HULL, J. (1991b) 'Agreed syllabuses and the law', *Resource*, **14**(1), Autumn 1991, pp. 1ff.

HULL, J. (1992) 'The transmission of religious prejudice', *British Journal of Religious Education*, **14**(2), pp. 69ff.

ISLAMIC ACADEMY (1986) *Resources for the Teaching of Islam in British Schools*, Cambridge, The Islamic Academy.

ISLAMIC ACADEMY (1991) *Faith as the Basis of Education in a Multi-faith Multi-cultural Country*, Cambridge, The Islamic Academy.

MABUD, S.A. (1992) 'A Muslim response to the Education Reform Act 1988', *British Journal of Religious Education*, **14**(2), pp. 88ff.

NATIONAL CURRICULUM COUNCIL (1991) *Religious Education, A Local Curriculum Framework*, York, National Curriculum Council.

ORCHARD, S. (1991) 'What was wrong with religious education? An analysis of HMI Reports 1985–1988', *British Journal of Religious Education*, **14**(1), pp. 15ff.

SARWAR, G. (1991) *British Muslims and Schools*, London, The Muslim Educational Trust.

TAYLOR, M. (1991) *SACREs — Their Role and Function: A Study of Their First Year*, Slough, The National Foundation for Educational Research.

Part Three

The School

Chapter 15

Whole School Issues

Daphne Gould

Context

Many families from the ethnic minorities have made their homes in the large cities and urban areas of Britain, but this is gradually changing as they move farther afield, to the small towns and the country communities, as generations of immigrants have done before them. In London, many Asian families who have settled in the East End are beginning to trace the same paths as those followed by the Jews some sixty years earlier.

The presence of these different cultures brings a richness to this country which enhances the experiences of its population. Schools which are fortunate in having a number of children from other cultures will be exposed to the influence which they bring to all areas of the curriculum. It is perhaps most apparent in the arts. Music, fine arts, dance and drama all benefit, not only from the individual work of the pupils, but also from displays around the school and from that added dimension which is brought to all discussion both in and outside the classroom.

Whilst many ethnic groups live, side by side, in understanding and harmony, there is also tension and misunderstanding, ignorance and aggression. Racism is frequently not even thinly disguised. Schools, therefore, have a great responsibility through their leaders to educate young people to take their place in a society freed from bigotry and prejudice. Teachers and senior administrators in our schools have a particular obligation, because it is they who have to prepare young people for adult life. That preparation must include education for racial harmony as well as world citizenship. If young people are given knowledge and made aware of other cultures and the needs of other people, then there is the strong expectation that they will develop understanding and trust.

The Role of the School

It must not be thought that a child's experience is free from bias or racism until the age of eleven or even five. Stereotypical views can begin to be formed in the home and during preschool experiences. Teachers of all young people from the nursery to university have, therefore, a heavy responsibility for this part of their pupils' education. All schools which are educating young people effectively need to ensure that multicultural education permeates the entire curriculum and that the total staff (teaching and non-teaching) perceive the implementation of a multicultural policy as part of their duty. In schools outside the main cities the statement is still too frequently made that, 'We have no black pupils. We do not need a multicultural policy. There is no problem here'.

The Whole School Policy

The school structure and the curriculum must reinforce the ethos of the school, but this is not the starting point. Every school needs a whole school policy on multicultural education and equal opportunities which has total staff ownership. It must be remembered that the process through which the whole school passes to form that policy is itself of vital importance. Such a process needs to be established by the senior management team in consultation with the entire staff. Once the policy becomes accepted, it must be rigorously implemented. There is strength in unity, and total commitment is achieved when full consultation has taken place.

What is significant about this process? It is important that all are involved: teachers, governors, parents and all the support staff, including the kitchen staff, school keepers, cleaners, office staff, librarian, technicians and, in addition, representatives from the senior pupils. This broad representation from all sectors of the school and from parents and members of the local community will result in the assurance that the policy will be implemented. All staff, teaching and non-teaching, should contribute, not only to the formulation, but to the development and review of policy.

The introduction of compulsory competitive tendering (CCT) into all levels of local Government, including schools, is having a major impact on the task of the head and senior management. Schools no longer control an essential part of the work force. The staff concerned are employed directly by an outside contractor. As a result those members of the non-teaching staff do not necessarily have the same loyalty to the school and neither are they part of the process for developing whole school policies. Heads will need to spend considerably more time and energy if they wish to influence effectively the non-teaching staff and to ensure that they accept the school's policies for equal opportunities, to include race, gender and class.

The school which is about to establish a multicultural education policy needs to be clear concerning the breadth of the content. It must certainly refer to the equal entitlement of pupils and how it can be ensured. It will also address such practical issues as (not in order of priority) assemblies, uniform, school meals, religious holidays, extra-curricular activities, school displays and the language policy. In addition, there needs to be a clear statement concerning the role of the school in the community, and policy documentation of the action which the school will take in the event of racial harassment.

Communication

Communication is a word which is frequently tossed around but which all consider to be important. Effective communication does not occur by osmosis. It relies upon a properly established framework. There must be an identifiable and accepted path for all consultation to follow, and a process through which innovation and change can advance.

Most innovation stems from a single person, or a group of people, sharing a concern about a particular issue or incident and forming a working party. It is essential, as far as multicultural education is concerned that such a body is given proper authority. The group should nominate a member to keep the minutes or notes which, within a few days, can be circulated to all the other members of the school; good communication at all levels is essential.

The remit of the working party needs to be clear, and its parameters and function understood by all. It is a 'think tank' which reports to those who are responsible in the school for the delivery of all facets of the curriculum — usually the heads of faculties or departments. The senior management team has to accept ultimate responsibility until the governing body has had an opportunity to become involved formally and is able to ratify the policy. The quality of the Head's leadership is an essential factor throughout.

It is important that the school policy on multicultural education should be publicized and made widely available and that senior management should develop an effective framework to make the policy work. They will need to sustain commitment, check the process of implementation and evaluate and review progress. Such 'action plans' need careful consideration. They should set out the targets to be aimed at, the detailed tasks needed to achieve them, who is responsible for doing what, and how success is to be judged (Hargreaves and Hopkins, 1991). To complement this, INSET work is vital and teachers should be encouraged to attend courses, seminars and conferences concerned with multi-ethnic education.

The School Development Plan

It is essential that the multicultural policy of the school should be fully integrated into the School Development Plan. This major school document will itself have to pass through a process of full consultation. The purpose of such a plan is to focus the attention of all members of staff on the school's strategies for managing development and change. It will include a formal statement of the aims and objectives of the school and offer a clear plan for innovation. It will provide a comprehensive approach to all aspects of planning, curriculum and assessment, teaching, management and organization, finance and resources. It will also refer to inservice and staff development. By incorporating multicultural policies into such an instrument of change, the school can ensure that issues of equality and cultural diversity become part of the progressive development of the whole life of the school.

The Role of the LEA

Schools are not operating in isolation; at the present time most function within a Local Authority which has responsibility for resources and which is required by the 1986 Education Act to issue a formal statement on the curriculum referring to equal opportunities. The individual school must ensure that it functions within these parameters, because it is important that the school's policy is viewed as part of a unified response which is shared by other schools in the Local Education Authority. (Grant Maintained and Independent Schools have their Governing Bodies to whom they are answerable.)

This may well become harder to achieve. The recommendations of the White Paper on education, *Choice and Diversity*, of July 1992 anticipate that the power of the local education authority will decline still further. It will therefore be difficult to introduce any common structure or strategy which will ensure that all schools address multicultural issues and prepare their students for the plural society in which they will live.

Whilst recent legislation has left schools in competition with each other, multicultural education is one area where there should be total unity. Parents must be left in no doubt that there is a common purpose, shared by all educators, that all children must be educated to take their place in a plural society. All Headteachers should work together with a common policy so that whichever school is selected by the parents, the child will receive a multicultural education.

The Governing Body

There are many ways in which Governors can encourage the formulation and implementation of multicultural policies. They can ensure that they themselves receive training in equal employment practices. They can try to reflect in their own membership the community which the school serves. They can monitor all data on the school's performance in relation to ethnicity and gender. For example, analysis of the results of key stage testing, of GCSE and A levels will show how far real equality of entitlement is being ensured. Similarly the breakdown of data on setting, banding and streaming, rates of truancy, exclusions and suspensions, and the destinations of school leavers will give important information on how far multicultural policies are being implemented in practice. Governors can also require inspectors to consider issues of equality in their reports on the school organization and curriculum. Adequate funding should be targetted for multicultural education and money set aside for staff training and development, school and family liaison, parental involvement and the use of support staff. Governors are now also responsible for all staff selection. This is a further reason for them to be fully involved in the policy-making of the school. Only then will they have a clear perception of the needs of the school — an essential factor when appointing staff.

Staffing

Inevitably, therefore, this school policy will include recommendations for staff selection and the staffing structure. A gender and ethnic balance which mirrors that of the school community should be a school aim. A school which has a number of ethnic minority pupils will certainly benefit by having this reflected in the staffing of the school.

The status of all who work in the school is important. If teachers from the ethnic minorities are associated exclusively with mother tongue teaching or with language support within the classroom, negative messages may be given to the pupils and other staff. In no way is this statement intended to detract from the quality and the essential nature of that work, rather it is to ensure that teachers from the ethnic minorities are viewed as candidates for any posts, including those in senior and middle management.

It must be emphasized that all role models should be positive. The philosophy of equality of opportunity relates to the pupils as well as the members of staff. The pupil is entitled to the best teacher available, and a high level of teaching. It is, therefore, unhelpful and illegal for an appointment to be made solely on the grounds of gender or ethnicity. All role models need to be a positive reinforcement of all that is intellectually stimulating. The appointment must not be made because it is expedient.

Staff selection begins with the identification of a vacant post, coupled with the needs of that post. Advertisements and job specifications should include a positive reference to equal opportunities and multicultural education. The information and selection criteria sent to candidates should expand fully on this dimension, and leave applicants in no doubt as to the priorities of the school. It is important to note in detail the response from the candidates. It is their responsibility to convince these selectors that they are committed to and will implement the policy. The written response should demonstrate the manner in which the candidate has taken account of equal opportunities in her own teaching, and in the learning materials and resources which she has herself developed. The candidate who merely states that she or he believes in equal opportunities is wasting time; if unsupported, this is a meaningless statement and totally inadequate. 'Why?' and 'How?' are the questions which the questioner will undoubtedly wish to ask in order to probe the true commitment and knowledge of the candidate.

In recent years staff selection has become increasingly more sophisticated. The formal, short interview has been enhanced by, and extended to include, a presentation prepared on arrival and possibly an informal day spent in the school, meeting members of staff who have been well briefed and who contribute to the decision-making process. Depending upon the subject area of the vacancy, the candidates may be asked to bring a selection of their own work, or that of their pupils. This will certainly reveal their commitment to the school's policies.

It could be anticipated that if the staff selection is sound, the curriculum will look after itself. Unfortunately all schools have to function with the staff who are *in situ*. Management is about succeeding with those members of staff who have been inherited, not all of whom will be supportive. Awareness raising among the staff and professional training are, therefore, important issues.

Visitors

People who work in or visit schools for short periods can come from a wide variety of backgrounds. Some may be students completing their teaching practice, others may be temporary teachers. Many will work within a department. Therefore, departmental handbooks must be available with guidelines to ensure that visitors comply with the policies and the ethos of the school.

Student teachers in particular need to be prepared for their professional duties in all aspects of multicultural education, an area which in the past has been neglected in some teacher training establishments. Few students will have the opportunity

to experience working in a multiethnic school, but all need the k
which fits them to educate all young people to take their place in
society.

The attitude of all visitors who come to the premises shou
monitored. Local Management of Schools has given Heads very
powers. As consumers, they can now place their custom wherever t
Racist or sexist comments from the window cleaner or the tank driver who is
delivering the oil can be most effectively dealt with by terminating the contract,
and stating the reason — a considerable embarassment to the firm concerned.
There is at least one driver, in the East London area, who has reason to regret his
racist comments.

Attention to detail is essential if the policy is to be implemented successfully.
Because there is a precise policy and structure *in situ* however, it does not mean
that it is inhuman and formal. The manner in which policy becomes practice
gives the opportunity for creating warmth and humanity. In this respect the position
of the senior management team and the Head must never be underestimated.

The Role of the Head

In old Czechoslovakia there is a saying that 'The fish starts to stink from the head':
not a pleasant thought, but one which is accurate. Everyone in the establishment,
staff, pupils, parents, governors and visitors, must know and understand the Head's
philosophy. The Head sets the tone of the school, and there is still much to
recommend leading by example. She or he can demonstrate an understanding of
the complexities and subtleties of providing for equality of opportunity, and show
awareness of the needs of pupils both as individuals and as members of different
ethnic, religious and cultural groups.

The innovative Head will create opportunities to ensure that his or her beliefs
are known by all. They will be apparent in the detail of everyday routine as much
as large policy decisions. They will be clear in the way in which all visitors are
treated. Waiting in that cold busy corridor is not particularly hospitable, and
although few schools can boast a luxurious reception room, even the most cramped
conditions can, with a little ingenuity, be made attractive. Plants, an easy chair,
a bit of carpet and a few magazines can make a significant difference. The first
necessity is to view a welcoming atmosphere as important.

The pupils will be aware of the Head's philosophy from the substance of the
materials chosen for assemblies and collective acts of worship. The manner in
which pupils are treated around the school, the informal conversations which all
staff have with pupils and the methods used to share information also give very
strong messages.

Discipline

The ultimate aim of school discipline must be effective self-control, achieved
when pupils understand, accept and practise what is expected of them, because
they wish to do so. When disagreements are debated, differences discussed and

ysical force is considered to be totally unacceptable, a positive and progressive atmosphere will permeate the school. Trust in one another is built up from the moment the children enter the school. The pastoral curriculum, well planned, monitored and regularly evaluated, is a vital instrument for the support of the formal curriculum in reinforcing multicultural education.

Racist incidents and sexual harassment will occur, and for that reason, a strategy for dealing with them is essential. All staff should be aware of the formal procedures for dealing with racist incidents, and all pupils should be aware of the school rules prohibiting racial harassment, abuse and name-calling. Any incident must involve not only the victim, but also the perpetrator and the families. A positive outcome will be time-consuming, but progressive senior staff will view it as time well spent, since it affects the quality of the atmosphere within the school.

Of course, punishment is sometimes necessary, but difficult to administer. It can, however, be very effective when the punishment is determined by the perpetrator of the offence. Resentment tends to be lessened, and negotiation provides the opportunity for further discussion. The time thus given can have a civilizing effect upon young people, many of whom lack the opportunity for conversation with peers from a different cultural background outside the school.

A comprehensive equal opportunities document will not only address the issue of discipline, but will also identify the need to monitor the number, frequency and characteristics of the incidents which occur. Not every incident which involves a member of an ethnic minority is a racist incident. In the urban situation, events in the community are often reflected by the behaviour of the pupils in school. Sensitivity in the manner in which the situation is resolved is a most important factor.

The Education Reform Act

The 1988 Education Reform Act states that the curriculum should promote the spiritual, cultural, mental and physical development of pupils at the school and of society and prepare them for the responsibilities and experiences of adult life. It is important, therefore, that the school's multicultural policy document addresses issues of the curriculum. The curriculum must broaden the horizons of all pupils, raise their levels of achievement and prepare them for active citizenship. Teachers will wish to view ethnic diversity as a strength, which is reflected in what and how they teach. It will influence the resources used, the methodology and the classroom displays.

The content of the basic curriculum will not only need to reflect the multicultural society in which we live, but must also have regard to the specific needs of a particular school. All departments need to examine the syllabuses being studied, in order to ensure that they are appropriate and meet the requirements of their particular pupils. The necessity for local modification in the Religious Education courses is obvious, but it is also the case that the study of a wide variety of cultures throughout the curriculum enables all pupils to raise their expectations. Moreover, it encourages them to challenge what they read, see and hear. The curriculum should cover issues of personal racism and make the school's policies clear to all pupils.

Language

Those institutions which have a very large majority of a particular ethnic group will experience a tension between the necessity to encourage all pupils to develop their English language skills (in order that they are truly bilingual and able to follow higher education or vocational courses), and giving status to, and valuing, the pupils' own first language. It is an issue which requires sensitivity and a common approach from all staff. Pupils are only too aware that their examinations will be taken in their second language, and that their level of competency in English is therefore of great importance.

Information on the home and community languages of pupils should be readily available to all staff. The perception which the adults in the school have of a pupil's own language and the manner in which that perception is conveyed to the pupil are vital factors. Those few staff who have become at all competent in the pupils' own languages know how powerfully this can enhance good staff/student relationships and raise pupils' own self images. To value a child's language and to give it status is to acknowledge the importance of all language skills and the power which a high level of competency gives to the person, both as a student and later as an adult.

The Modern and Community languages studied will generally be determined by the ethnic backgrounds of the children. The recent modifications to the ERA allow schools to offer pupils the opportunity to study their mother tongue in Year 7 and to sit for the GCSE examination in Year 9. This will have the added advantage of allowing pupils to study another language in Key Stage four, and thus add breadth and balance to their educational experience.

The Informal Curriculum

As this chapter has unfolded it has become abundantly clear that multicultural education should incorporate the entire life of the school. School policy should therefore be concerned not only with the formal but the informal curriculum. There have been many terms to describe the informal curriculum — the 'hidden' curriculum being one. However, the word hidden seems to be a singularly inappropriate choice, as the visitor to the school is only too well aware of the value which the school places on the informal curriculum. It is the distinctive ethos of the school which greets the visitor as soon as she or he enters the building. A school with an effective and positive ethos is a place where no person is unimportant and where everyone is respected and cared for. Overt signs of abuse, graffiti on the building or objectionable badges worn by pupils, give undesirable messages. Greeting signs in many different languages reinforce a positive environment, and the visitor feels respected and welcomed. They help to create the impression of a cultured and civilized environment in which it is a pleasure to spend six hours every day.

In schools graffiti is an important issue. The multicultural policy, therefore, will outline a code of practice for all to follow. As soon as graffiti appears, all have a responsibility to ensure that it is reported and removed, possibly by the Head or a senior member of staff. This gives the message that it will not be tolerated. To buy cans of 'graffiti gobbler' and expect the school-keeping staff to do the rest is insufficient. Graffiti is a form of vandalism and should be perceived as such. Young people must know that the senior management views graffiti anywhere as totally unacceptable. A similar attitude should be displayed towards any external symbol which could cause anxiety or embarrassment to anyone in the institution. This includes undesirable pamphlets, badges and unacceptable spoken and body language.

The environment is an important display area, both inside and outside the classroom. It should reflect the variety of cultures and languages found in the school so that all individuals in the community can feel valued. Regardless of the ethnic composition of the school, images in halls, corridors and classrooms should reflect the cultural diversity of the wider British society and of the world. The languages department is in an enviable position in this respect. Their domain can become a centre for the different cultures and a place where discussion and debate are encouraged.

Schools are often disadvantaged by a dual use of the premises, frequently with those who share neither the same values nor expect the same code of behaviour. Recent legislation now makes it possible for Heads to expect and insist upon a similar code of behaviour to that of the school.

The informal curriculum deserves to be examined with seriousness by the school because a written policy which ignores this area would be meaningless. Failure to acknowledge it will be detrimental to the culture of the school.

Parents and Community

The school should try to ensure that it serves the local community and that parents, community groups and outside specialists are welcomed and encouraged to contribute to the life of the school. Parents of ethnic minority children should be as proportionately involved as other parents in school activities — on the governing body, in the classroom and on visits out of school. Information sent home should be easily understood and available (where appropriate) in languages other than English, and the school should develop means for liaising and collaborating with parents over the education of their children. It is important that the views of parents should be listened to seriously and sensitively so that, despite all the difficulties, a real partnership can develop between parents and teachers within the community.

Conclusion

As the reader has worked through this chapter, the words of the 1985 Swann Report will have become even more powerful. The Report states: 'The fundamental change needed is a recognition that the problem facing the education system is not just how to educate the children of the ethnic minorities, but how to educate all children' (DES, 1985). It is hoped that this chapter has served to reinforce the strength of that statement.

Finally, the school which has taken ownership of, and is implementing, its multicultural education policy as an integral part of its whole curriculum, is providing a rich educational experience which will prepare young people to contribute effectively to the pluralist society in which we live, and to the wider community of nations.

It is the responsibility of all those in any way involved in education to ensure that their policy becomes practice. The policy creates a rationale to which all are committed, and because everyone has been involved in its development, there is ownership.

References

DEPARTMENT OF EDUCATION AND SCIENCE (1985) *Education for All, The Report of the Committee of Enquiry into the Education of Children from Ethnic Minority Groups*, London, (The Swann Report) Cmnd. 9543, HMSO.

HARGREAVES, D.H. and HOPKINS, D. (1991) *The Empowered School: The Management and Practice of Development Planning*, London, Cassell.

DEPARTMENT FOR EDUCATION (1992) *Choice and Diversity, A New Framework for Schools*, London, HMSO.

Chapter 16

A Primary School Case Study

Marie-France Faulkner and Rachel Willans

St Luke's is a Church of England primary school in Cambridge with pupils from a variety of cultural backgrounds. Over a third of our pupils are bilingual and twenty languages are spoken by the children within the school. Apart from English, Bengali and Cantonese predominate. We also have the children of visiting scholars from all over the world, but unfortunately they are with us for only a short period of time. There is no doubt that these children help us to introduce a 'multicultural perspective into the curriculum. . .[thus]. . .enriching the education of all our pupils' (NCC, 1990a, p. 3).

The whole school policy of Equal Opportunities is the keystone of our school curriculum. This policy was the result of a year-long series of discussions by the staff, governing body and local community associations. At the end of that year a consensus was reached, and we produced the policy which is now the basis of the school philosophy and which permeates all our planning. A year later, we were delighted to discover that the policy, accepted and implemented by all within the school community, was developing in a more creative way than we had anticipated. It was at this point that the National Curriculum was introduced. After initial concern, we realized that its aims and requirements expressed our own. For instance, in the Proposals for Science, we found this statement, 'Pupils should come to realize that the international currency of Science is an important force for overcoming racial prejudice' (DES, 1988a, p. 92).

The aim of our policy is to equip the children with the essential skills of numeracy, literacy, science, basic technology, aesthetic and religious education so that they can become fully participating members of our multicultural society. We are determined to ensure that all children have equal access to the whole school curriculum and to encourage in all members of our community an understanding of, and respect for, their own and other cultures and religions. Our experience has shown that in the primary sector, the most effective way of working is cross-curricular. Unfortunately, the demands of the National Curriculum could challenge this methodology. Now that the history and geography curricula have been introduced, many teachers (particularly of Years 5 and 6), are feeling pressured into compartmentalizing subjects. We agree with NCC Guidance *The Whole Curriculum* which stresses that cross-curricular elements are the ingredients 'which tie together the broad education of the individual and augment what comes from the basic curriculum' (NCC, 1990a, p. 2).

In order to encompass all the National Curriculum requirements, we have found it necessary to follow a two-year planning cycle, which we have based on the science document, as this was one of the first to be produced. We have incorporated the geography and history core study units into this cycle. Careful planning is essential to ascertain that the cross-curricular approach, central to our aims, is preserved.

The school is divided into four units. Unit 1 consists of the two Reception classes. Each of the other three units contains children belonging to two or three different years. Thus Unit 2 contains Year 1 and Year 2 children, Unit 3 is composed of pupils from Years 3 and 4, and Unit 4 has classes of pupils from Years 4, 5 and 6. Each Unit meets regularly to plan its topics, making certain that each term has a different curriculum emphasis and that there is scope for a variety of mathematical and language approaches.

This necessitates a thoughtful choice of topic. When selecting a theme, we look for a subject that is both broad and global in perspective so that it can encompass all the National Curriculum areas and give us the opportunity to show the invaluable contributions that different cultures have made to our growing body of knowledge and to our values. Recently, topics within the school have included Books, All Around, Journeys, Change, Energy, Together and To Market to Market (figure 16.1). It is important that we not only constantly raise the children's awareness of their immediate environment but also that we broaden their knowledge of the wider world. We aim also to challenge their preconceptions and encourage them to discuss their views. To this end we involve the children in collaborative learning. This approach is extremely well illustrated in two excellent books, *Theme Work* from the Birmingham Development Education Centre, 1991, and *World Studies 8–13* by Fisher and Hicks (1985). Further material suitable for use in collaborative work can be obtained from Oxfam at 274 Banbury Road, Oxford OX2 7DZ; Christian Aid, P.O. Box 100, London SE1 7RT and Judith Aston, The Resources Centre, Cambridge University Department of Education 17, Brookside, Cambridge, CB2 1JG.

We also believe that children's learning about different cultures can be enriched and reinforced by visits to museums, workshops, and art galleries. A particularly successful visit was made to the Fitzwilliam Museum in Cambridge, where, under the guidance of Frances Sword, the Education Officer, we studied and compared exhibits from Christian, Islamic and Buddhist cultures. We also arrange for pupils to visit local places of worship, including a mosque, a synagogue and a combined United Reformed and Church of England church.

These are extracts from the follow-up writing of two children after a visit to the mosque which were later published in the School Magazine:

The man at the mosque was very nice. He talked about the Koran, which is the Muslim book. The man said that if he went to someone's house and the Koran had a worn look, he would think that people had been using it well. Better than putting it on a shelf. He also told us about the Five Pillars of Islam. We went up stairs, the ladies and children go up there. I felt warm and safe and welcome. *Toby Lazarus.*

We went to the Mosque. I felt comfortable. I saw the books. It was interesting. I learned about the mosque and about the Muslim faith. I saw the Muslim writing. Muslim people take their shoes off and go into the Mosque. I am a Hindu, we pray in a different way. *Piran.*

Figure 16.1 To market to market (Designed by the authors for their school, St. Luke's)

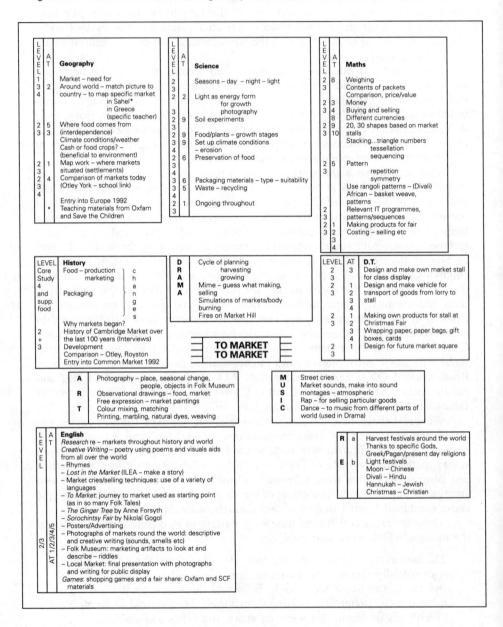

In our policy document we state

> Our overall aim is to provide all children, irrespective of race, colour, creed or language with the English language skills necessary for effective communication and learning. We are very proud of our linguistic diversity and aim to promote an interest in, and respect for, all the languages and the varieties of language that the children bring to school.

We are also very aware of the importance of the images and attitudes we present to the pupils. We hope to develop mutual respect between children of different racial, cultural, and gender groups by using materials and resources which positively reflect and support our pluralist society. We are also aware of the danger of stereotypes and the need for constant and critical reassessment of our resources. Indeed, in this process, we have been concerned to find that a number of recently published 'multicultural' materials are in fact guilty of subtle racism and of reinforcing false assumptions, such as that all African and Asian countries are economically and culturally deficient.

At St Luke's we are committed to introducing the children to literature from around the world through stories and poems. We feel that

> In this active involvement with literature pupils gain more lives than their own. They will encounter and come to understand a wide range of feelings and relationships by vicariously entering the world of others, and in consequence they are likely to understand more of themselves. (DES, 1988b, p. 27)

Teachers often find it hard to read in unfamiliar dialects and therefore we have found tapes by the authors themselves of great value because they convey the rhythm and flow of the language. At St Luke's we are fortunate that various writers have come to the school to read their writing and to work with the children; we have welcomed John Agard, James Berry, Ruth Craft, Nicholas Fisk, Mick Gowar, Sally Robey and Diane Wilmer. Such workshops are invaluable and enhance the children's awareness of all aspects of the language. As a result of the workshop with John Agard, the children wrote collaborative poems which were subsequently published by Eastern Arts. Three are below:

Happy Birthday Trees

Caterpillars
Stop nibbling the leaves
Woodcutters
stop chopping the trunks.
Beetles
stop chewing the bark
Wind
stop your shaking
Acid rain
stop your killing.

Let
the birds nest
in their branches.
Let the people rest
in their shade
Let
the children bite
their tasty fruit.
Let them be
Happy Birthday trees!

Happy Birthday Birds

No more cages
to trap you in
Free to escape
into the sky to sing
No more starving
when winter comes.
Kind hands scattering
tasty breadcrumbs
No more shivering
in the cold air

Strong winds
guiding you safely
in a hot country
and come next spring
bringing you home
to a new family
Happy Birthday

Happy Birthday Sky

No thick black clouds
No rain allowed
No clapping of thunder
No roaring of helicopter
No nasty smoke
To make you choke
A bright sun
will keep you warm
The birds will hum
for today
you mustn't cry
It's your birthday
Sky!

Birthday

Workshop group and poems by:

John Agard	Lily
Adam	Madalena
Anna	Mercy
Geoffrey	Mimi
Gordon	Mustafa
James	Sam
Jila	Shelly
Johnston	Susie
Kelly	Tina
Kobir	Tom
Kong	
Le Oanh	

When John Agard returned to Cambridge this year, thirty five children clamoured to go to a reading of his work on a Saturday afternoon!

Within the classrooms, we aim to provide bilingual texts (fiction and reference) and during quiet or shared reading time we encourage the children to read to other children in their mother tongue. We are concerned, however, about the paucity and quality of bilingual materials available. It was for this reason that, with the assistance of Eastern Arts, a project was undertaken with our neighbouring Community College, Chesterton, to write bilingual books for children with a reading age of between 5 and 8 years. Anawara Jahan, a Bangladeshi writer, came to Cambridge and worked with six groups of eight children from a variety of cultural backgrounds. She told the children six traditional Bengali stories speaking in both Bengali and English; these were then retold by the children. The children first decided that they would have to draft the stories in English as so few of them could write in Bengali! The project promoted not only respect for the Bengali speakers and writers but also developed an understanding of the different structure of languages. The children were fascinated by the fact that in the Bengali script there is no full stop, a line is used instead, and that in certain instances the English text had to be revised so that the Bengali could be an exact transcription. These books (see figures 16.2 and 16.3) are now in use in both St Luke's and Chesterton and interest has been shown by other schools.

The wren waited till Bushy came. When Bushy came he said: "Hello little wren." Rainbird answered: "Go away!" Rainbird kicked Bushy in the face and flew off.

Source: St. Luke's School 1990

217

Haru had some food. Hura had the same food. The people said "What a clever goat !" BUT the manager said "Take your goat out of my cafe."

Figure 16.3 Haru and his Goat

Source: St. Luke's School, 1990

218

Within the school we have always aimed to promote other languages. For two years we have held a Writing Week when all the children have been introduced to a wide variety of scripts by their peers, bilingual students from Chesterton and members of the community. They have thus become aware of different forms of writing and have begun to appreciate and respect the bilingual and multilingual abilities of their friends (see figures 16.4 and 16.5). We fully support the views expressed in the English non-statutory guidance that 'Home language support can facilitate bilingual pupils' access to the curriculum and thereby enhance their learning of English' (NCC, 1990b, p. C2 2.9).

We would very much like bilingual support within our school as there is now a considerable body of research to verify the importance of such help (Frederickson and Cline, 1990). Unfortunately, there is at present no funding for this. We have however just acquired a folio in Bengali which we hope to make accessible to pupils.

'There are rich opportunities. . .to demonstrate that no one culture has a monopoly of achievements. . . .' (DES, 1989, paras 1.44–1.46). This applies equally to all subjects. In maths and science, for example, we point out to children that number patterns have fascinated generations throughout the world and that different cultures have developed particular scientific strengths all of which have contributed to our present knowledge. We also follow the advice of the Science Proposals by choosing 'Science books and other learning materials which. . .include examples of people from ethnic minority groups working alongside others and achieving success in scientific work' (DES, 1988a, p. 92, 7–16).

Whilst we applaud the aims of the National Curriculum, we feel very critical of the present mode of assessment. The standard assessment tasks at Key Stage 1 show little awareness of the needs and development of the bilingual child. The Science National Curriculum document rightly says that 'The language of science can be complex and the science teacher will naturally seek to be sensitive to the children's understanding of language and especially terminology when introducing scientific ideas and concepts' (DES, 1988a, p. 92, 7–13). Yet the science standard assessment tasks themselves have relied heavily on specific scientific language and not on the grasp of the concept. For example, one bilingual child called 'a heavy stone', 'a strong stone' and referred to it 'waving' instead of 'floating'. This caused the teacher problems in assessing that child. The standard assessment tasks also seem to ignore the weight of recent research evidence, which states that it may take up to two years for the bilingual child to acquire skills to be fluent in face-to-face oral communication and that they may take five to seven years to acquire the full range of literacy skills. This was particularly evident in the writing task, where the children experienced difficulties in sustaining a sequenced story. Again, the science document affirms that it is important that 'pupils' own experience should be used as a basis for learning so that they can genuinely be agents of that learning' (DES, 1988a, p. 92, 7–15). In a national science test, however, the children were asked to show awareness of the change of seasons of the Northern hemisphere — a task possible only for those children who had been in the country for at least two years. Equally, in maths, the children were asked to design a board game with rules, a task which made heavy language demands and which was culturally divisive since many children have little experience of such games outside the school environment.

Depressingly, our experience so far has shown that the national tests seem to

Marie-France Faulkner and Rachel Willans

Figure 16.4   Bilingual Sheet — Japanese/English

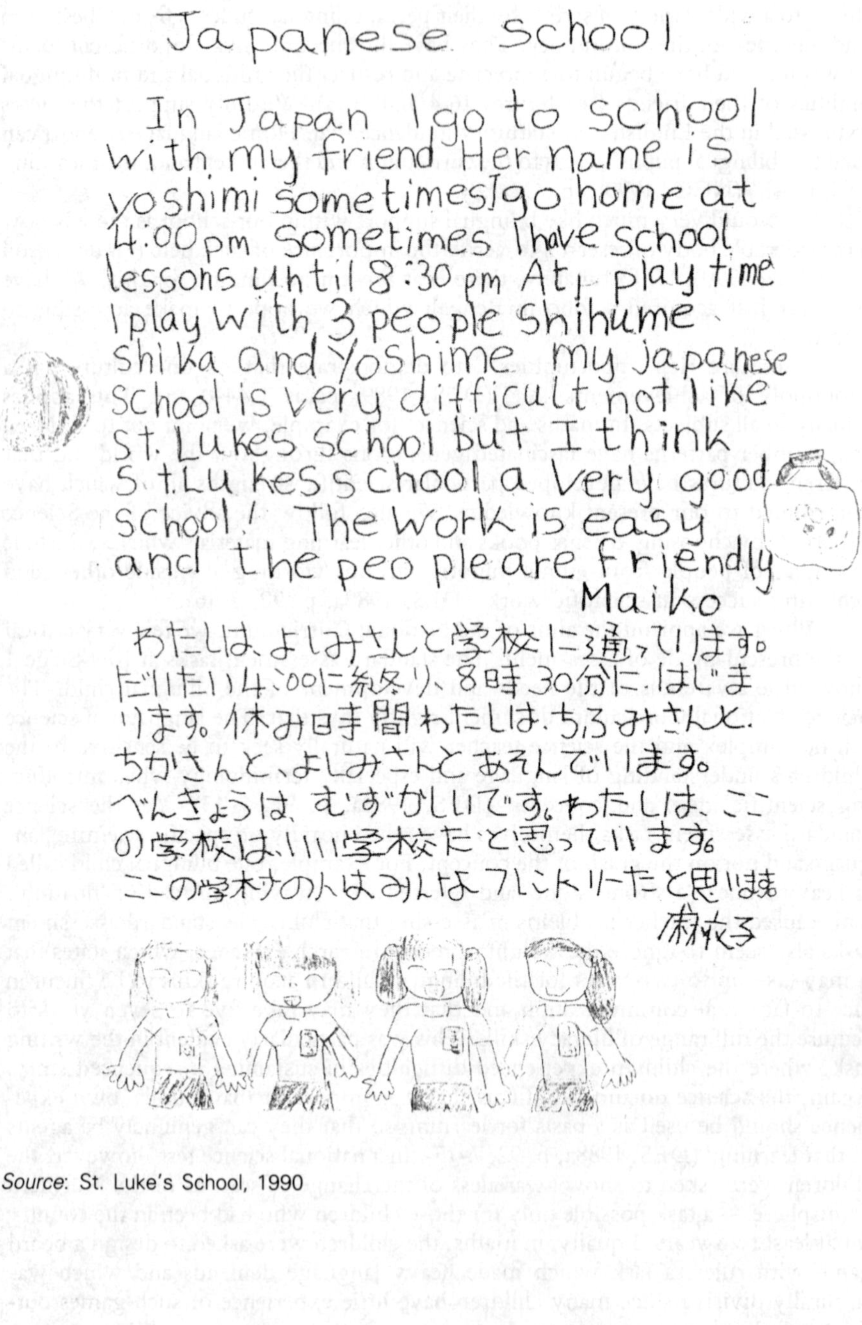

Japanese school

In Japan I go to school with my friend Her name is yoshimi sometimes I go home at 4:00 pm Sometimes I have school lessons until 8:30 pm At play time I play with 3 people Shihume shika and Yoshime my japanese school is very difficult not like St. Lukes school but I think S.t.Lukes school a very good school! The work is easy and the people are friendly

Maiko

わたしは、よしみさんと学校に通っています。
だいたい4:00に終り、8時30分に、はじまります。休み時間わたしは、ちろみさんと、ちかさんと、よしみさんとあそんでいます。
べんきょうは、むずかしいです。わたしは、この学校は、いい学校だと思っています。
ここの学校の人はみんなフレンドリーだと思いま

麻衣子

Source: St. Luke's School, 1990

220

Figure 16.5 Bilingual Sheet — Bengali/English

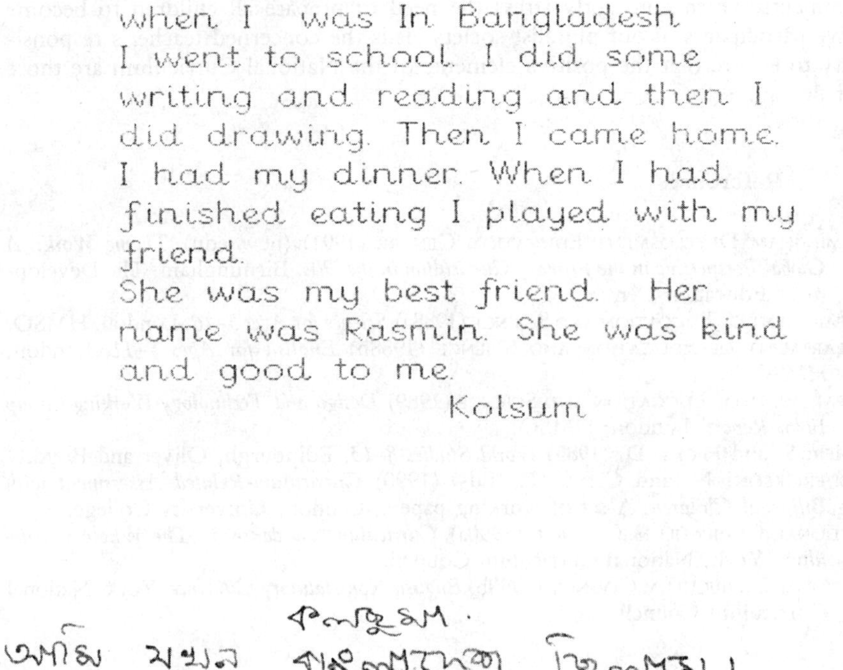

when I was In Bangladesh
I went to school I did some
writing and reading and then I
did drawing. Then I came home.
I had my dinner. When I had
finished eating I played with my
friend.
She was my best friend. Her
name was Rasmin. She was kind
and good to me.

                   Kolsum

কলসুম ।

আমি যখন বাংলাদেশে ছিলাম ।
আমি স্কুলে গিয়ে ছিলাম।
আর আমি সামান্য লেখা পড়া করেছি।
তারপর আমি ছবি এঁকেছিলাম ।
শেষে আমি ঘরে এলাম ।
ঘরে এসে আমি খাবার খেতে শুরু করলাম।
যখন আমি খাওয়া শেষ করলাম ।
আমি আমার বন্ধুর সাথে খেলাছিলাম ।
সে আমার খুব ভাল বন্ধু ছিল ।
রাসমিন ছিল আমার ভাল বন্ধু ছিল ।

Source: St. Luke's School, 1990.

have been set to fail the majority of our bilingual children. This is especially sad when one considers the sensitivity and awareness of most of the curriculum documents which constantly stress the need to prepare all children to become active participants in our pluralist society. It is the concerned teacher's responsibility to ensure that the positive elements of the National Curriculum are those that prevail.

References

BIRMINGHAM DEVELOPMENT EDUCATION CENTRE (1991) (new edn) *Theme Work: A Global Perspective in the Primary Curriculum in the '90s*, Birmingham, The Development Education Centre.

DEPARTMENT OF EDUCATION AND SCIENCE (1988a) *Science for Ages 5–16*, London, HMSO.

DEPARTMENT OF EDUCATION AND SCIENCE (1988b) *English for Ages 5–11*, London, HMSO.

DEPARTMENT OF EDUCATION AND SCIENCE (1989) *Design and Technology Working Group Final Report*, London, HMSO.

FISHER, S. and HICKS, D. (1985) *World Studies 8–13*, Edinburgh, Oliver and Boyd.

FREDERICKSON, N. and CLINE, T. (Eds) (1990) *Curriculum-Related Assessment with Bilingual Children*, A set of working papers, London, University College.

NATIONAL CURRICULUM COUNCIL (1990a) *Curriculum Guidance 3: The Whole Curriculum*, York, National Curriculum Council.

NATIONAL CURRICULUM COUNCIL (1990b) *English Non-statutory Guidance*, York, National Curriculum Council.

Chapter 17

A Secondary School Case Study

Carlton Duncan

The important advances rightly and properly made by the black communities in the 1960s and throughout the following two decades, compelling both official and academic notice of their educational struggles, are seriously threatened, some would argue, by the provisions of the 1988 Education Reform Act. In particular, the anti-racist and multicultural curriculum is at risk. In this chapter these two terms are used as interchangeable for the reasons that follow.

The history behind multicultural education has left a lingering tendency to define multiculturalism in terms of such peripheral issues as what some call the 'three Ss'. . .learning to tie a sari, to cook samosas and play steel drums'. Presumably, if we learn other peoples' culture, we become more sympathetic to, and more tolerant of, their needs. The problem with this rather simplistic approach is that, in many schools, it quite frequently leads to the once-a-year event, best described as the annual multicultural sheep dip, which is then taken to mean that they have done their bit for multicultural education. It also concentrates all efforts in multiracial or predominantly black schools. White schools can take the view that they need to do nothing as 'we haven't any problems here'.

This conception of multicultural education has been forcefully rejected by pure anti-racist strategists. In its place they would argue, we need a systematic redistribution of the power arrangements in schools and other social institutions as well as in society generally. Black people need to have direct access to these avenues of power so that they can institute the necessary changes upon which equality and justice depend.

Whilst there can be no denying that there is validity in this kind of argument, it has to be readily admitted that anti-racism in its purest form takes the whole issue of equality out of the educational arena and places it squarely in the political camp. This is a pity, because such an action, together with the outright rejection of multiculturalism, is tantamount to 'throwing away the baby with the bath water'.

There is much that educationalists can achieve by merging the insights of both schools of thought. Learning to understand all the peoples who constitute our schools, society and the wider world helps us to be more imaginative and caring in the ways by which we staff our schools, dispense the curriculum and organize and manage all our arrangements. It becomes easier to identify where inequitable blockages and barriers occur and to find ways of eradicating them, thus giving all our children greater access to knowledge which is, in itself, access to power. In short, anti-racism and multiculturalism go together nicely from the education practitioner point of view.

It is for this reason that we at George Dixon School prefer to see things in an anti-racist multicultural sense. In this context multiculturalism is not limited to an understanding and an enabling of ethnic minority cultures. Essentially, it is about the identification and removal of racist values from the school curriculum.

Why a National Curriculum?

The National Curriculum will:

give a clear incentive for weaker schools to catch up with the best and the best will be challenged to do even better;

provide teachers with detailed and precise objectives;

provide parents with clear accurate information;

ensure continuity and progression from one year to another, from one school to another;

help teachers concentrate on the task of getting the best possible results from each individual child. (Adapted from the Secretary of State for Education's Speech to the North of England Education Conference — 6 January, 1989).

Sold like this, the Tory Government had little difficulty in getting the ERA onto the statute book. Even the teachers' unions made no significant fight. Yet, as we shall see, the teaching profession, parents, particularly black parents, and all with an interest in education, have a great deal to worry about as far as these reforms go. For example, the subject matter and attainment targets of the core and foundation subjects are determined by subject working parties whose membership was determined by the Secretary of State for Education. Is it significant that black involvement with these working parties was either minimal or marginalized? Does this explain the attitude to multicultural education, and the absence of references to anti-racism in the working parties' reports?

Even where, as in the English Working Party Report, there is a clear recognition of the need for a multicultural approach to the teaching of the National Curriculum, obstacles were presented in the person of the then Secretary of State for Education (John McGregor) who ruled that books and other literature written by non-white and non-European authors should not be considered when setting the attainment targets in English Literature. It follows that testing in relation to such literature is ruled out. The effect of this ruling is to marginalize the importance of reading third world literature. An account of how we at George Dixon School seek to counteract this difficulty is outlined below.

The requirement of testing at ages seven, eleven, fourteen and sixteen presents yet other problems. Given that there is as yet no announcement as to how we will avoid culturally biased testing, the injustices described by Bernard Coard's *How the West Indian Child is made Educationally Subnormal in the British School System* (Coard, 1971) seem certain to repeat themselves in respect of today's black children.

Even if we were to accept the view that testing is solely to determine good schools from bad ones and not to segregate children into successes and failures, the problem for black children remains very pronounced. This is so because the schools which are bound to fail this kind of test are largely those which are least well resourced and are in a very poor state of repairs and run down. These, of course, are the inner city schools where black children predominate. How can they escape the stigma of failure?

At our school, teachers are expected to have regard for much more than raw data in the whole area of assessment of our pupils. We reflect the position advocated by the then Department of Education and Science in its draft policy statement *Records of Achievement at 16* (DES, 1983). This showed that it was the intention of the Government that every pupil should leave school with a record which detailed all his/her positive achievements throughout his/her school experiences. It is hoped that by 1993 this policy will be in full operation in every school. At George Dixon this is already very much a reality.

The record has three main elements. These are: the details of all public examination results; other evidence of academic achievements; and information about the pupil's personal characteristics and achievements. The second element enables the school to complete a profile of the pupil's total positive academic experiences throughout his/her school days, whilst the third provides the opportunities to record the pupil's achievements beyond the classroom or school. We can thus benefit from the judgment of the pupil made by others not normally associated with the school authority. Such others might legitimately include parents, religious leaders, community leaders and, indeed, the pupils themselves. Additionally, and most importantly, our arrangements ensure a number of one-to-one contacts between teachers and pupils to discuss and authenticate the Records of Achievement and Profiles. This way, we are able to make a much more meaningful assessment of our pupils than could be obtained solely from raw test data.

Without examination certificates the black potential employee is at a considerable disadvantage. Profiling and Records of Achievement may well provide us with a means of countering some of the difficulties the black child faces in school. They have the effect of getting pupils more involved in their work and increasing motivation. They also give more positive information to potential employers who may be helped to overcome some, at least, of their unfounded prejudices against black candidates.

Some caution, however, must be advised. We must not allow the non-realization of our low expectations to prejudice in any way what we record about black children. For example, remarks such as '*Baljit has done surprisingly well in. . .*' are unhelpful and likely to negate the purpose of the Record of Achievement. Further, activities and their valuation can be culture loaded. At George Dixon we remain very alert to this possibility. Excellence in Urdu, Creole, Punjabi and so on is rated as highly as excellence in English. It will not do to reject or omit an activity simply because it does not accord with the teacher's own value system. It is for this reason that it is extremely valuable to draw upon the judgment, skills and expertise of the different communities.

There is also the tendency of the National Curriculum to set numerous attainment targets per subject with little scope for a multicultural and anti-racist approach. History, in particular, is guilty of this shortcoming with mathematics and science not far behind. This presents a time constraint which is seriously threatening to the advancement of multiculturalism and/or anti-racism; for uncommitted teachers are quick to argue their pupils' risk of failure as a reason for pursuing strictly the attainment targets as prescribed.

The advances already made in the areas of anti-racism/multiculturalism within the curriculum and schools generally are thus clearly endangered. But there is a further threat. The governors of schools now have a greater say in curriculum matters. They must resist any white parental pressures to turn the clock backwards in schools where movements towards education justice for all has begun. Equally, they must take the lead in prompting change in schools where this process has not yet started. A consideration of how the National Curriculum is taught at George Dixon is set out below and will demonstrate how some of these problems might be overcome for the good of all.

Another area where the Government's claim to be just to all pupils is open to suspicion is that of Religious Education (RE) and Collective Worship. There is a requirement that these must reflect 'a broadly Christian' bias. In schools where this is unsuitable, parents can 'opt out' their children, get nothing or arrange, possibly at their own additional expense, what they would deem suitable. Schools have a further option. They can go 'cap in hand' to the local Standing Advisory Council on Religious Education (SACRE) for a determination — that is, permission to do something more suitable for the needs of the school. At George Dixon Secondary School in Birmingham, we have successfully chosen this last option, for it is only too obvious to us that, despite the greater work and organization involved, pupils' needs should come first. However, it does seem somewhat bizarre as a principle of justice and equity for all that some pupils should have their rights provided by law whilst the rights of others have to be sought as a concession. Local SACREs ought to grant these permissions without question.

Schools should remind parents that RE now has a special status as part of the basic curriculum of the school and should make available to them, as we have done, the locally agreed syllabus or a summary of it. Similarly, schools and their governors ought to include details of the arrangements for collective worship and RE in the school's prospectus or brochure. Parents will then be able to use the LEA's or school's complaints procedure (which must be in place by law) to ensure that their RE and collective worship needs are being met.

Although many of the National Curriculum Working Party Reports have advocated a multicultural approach to the subject matter of the curriculum, none has indicated the need for more black teachers to advance this process. Yet, this is a vital necessity, particularly in the absence of compulsory relevant training for all other teachers. Role models are a must if our black pupils are to feel inspired and suitably motivated and thus given an equal chance in the educational race.

As a school, we have always managed to attract a fair number of black teachers. This is so largely because our Anti-racist Policy recognizes that good teachers are not to be found exclusively amongst the ranks of white European males. We, therefore, endeavour not to close off the possibility of blacks and women being appointed at the shortlisting stage. Furthermore, the selection panels are chosen for their sensitivity to, and training in, equal opportunities issues. This way, the likelihood is that candidates of every kind will be appointed to the school through time. Prior to this, much thought will have gone into the drafting of the advertisements and their placements. We need to send a message to potential candidates that we mean business in this important area of equal opportunities.

Once appointed, black teachers, like everyone else in the school, are enabled to participate fully in the decision-making machinery of the school. This not only gives real professional experience to these teachers, but helps to transmit the kind of messages the school wishes all pupils, black and white, to hear and see. For this reason, black teachers at George Dixon can hold their own in competition for promotion within and without the school — as is evidenced by the number of such black and white teachers who move on to very senior posts elsewhere and the number who remain at the school in senior positions.

We find many of the National Curriculum Council's Subject Working Party Reports helpful. They encourage teachers to build a multicultural dimension into the curriculum — even if they are reluctant to use the term 'anti-racism'. This must be an important lead for practitioners even if in some subjects, such as mathematics, this guidance is only grudgingly given, and, as in the case of history, totally absent from others.

However, multiculturalism has gone too far, is too deeply rooted in our present ideals of justice for even the most conservative of schools, governments or laws to justify turning back. In any case, the committed practitioner can find much in the Act and its guidelines as well as in the resulting curriculum working parties' reports to justify continuing to adopt an anti-racist/multicultural stance. Both Section 2(a) of the ERA and para. 3.8 of the DES document — *National Curriculum, from Policy to Practice* (DES, 1989c), tell us that the National Curriculum arrangements, planning and realization should embody both moral and cultural considerations. These statements provide both legal and ethical reasons for the committed and informed practitioner to embark upon the road to anti-racism and multiculturalism.

Similarly, the need to have regard for the cultural composition of the school and of society generally in our National Curriculum arrangements, points us in the direction of a multicultural curriculum. Quite clearly anti-racist/multicultural issues should permeate all curricular thinking henceforth.

Of course, such official statements could have been far more explicit, but practitioners with a commitment to equality and justice in education will require no further lead. However, the legislators' failure to be explicit provides the opportunity for the unwilling, the sceptical and the uncommitted either to ignore the law or to plead ignorance of its intention.

The National Curriculum at George Dixon Secondary School

We have a clearly worked out anti-racist/multicultural policy which deals with all identifiable and important aspects of the school and which indicates the particular ways by which racism might reveal itself. The policy goes on to say how such instances of racism should be dealt with and by whom. Of critical importance is the curriculum in all its forms. An examination of some of the main subjects of the National Curriculum in operation at our school will reveal the kind of anti-racist/multicultural considerations built into our policy and practice.

History

The National Curriculum Council's Working Party Report — *History in the National Curriculum* (NCC, 1990) states that pupils must:

> . . .be taught about the cultural and ethnic diversity of past societies. Through history, pupils acquire understanding and respect for other cultures and values. They should develop. . .the quality of open-mindedness which questions assumptions and demands evidence for points of view. The study of history has sometimes concentrated on political at the expense of social, economic and cultural aspects. This has meant the neglect of important groups in past societies. . .

> The attainment targets require pupils to think about the limitations of evidence. Pupils might consider why evidence is sometimes unavailable for the history of particular groups. For example, pupils might explore why text books contain few references to the role of black troops in World War 1.

> [Pupils] will be able to explore conflicting viewpoints. This will help them identify and thus challenge racial and other forms of prejudice and stereotyping.

> Pupils should understand that history books reflect the age and culture in which they were written. Many text books and other resources carry hidden messages. Pupils should learn how to identify these.

To the committed equal opportunity practitioner, these are some very useful statements. They provide definite ways of avoiding Eurocentric curricular roads and they open up routes of greater balance and equity. Yet, it might well be contested that because the National Curriculum dictates (DES, 1991a) that at Key Stage 3 as many as seven of the eight study units must be about British or European history, little regard is being shown for the other peoples of our schools and society. Cultural, political, economic and other historical achievements in other parts of the world and by other peoples appear to be of almost no importance, and it is clear that similar emphasis is being placed on British history at Key Stage 4.

But at our school, ways are intentionally sought to enable all pupils to identify positively with the curriculum, whilst having due regard for the attainment targets in history to avoid jeopardizing the eventual public examination chances of the pupils. The history Department endeavours to give full recognition to other cultures as each unit of the National Curriculum is introduced. Although the content of each unit is largely prescribed, the Department is determined to build in, and give recognition to, the parts played by particular groups, thus affirming the importance of these groups in the minds and eyes of all pupils. Moreover, a careful selection of contents, materials, examples and illustrations serves to avoid negative images and the reinforcement of stereotypes of non-white groups.

The Department in question is determined to avoid the misrepresentation of the social and economic history of societies. They wish to reflect the fact that the United Kingdom is a multicultural society. In this way, they expect pupils to respond more positively to their studies and to one another — because all pupils are given genuine and positive recognition in terms of their background and culture via the curriculum.

English

Some extracts from the National Curriculum Programmes of Study in English:

> It is important that pupils working towards Level 7 and beyond have increasing opportunities to use spoken standard English, and in particular that those who do not speak it as a native dialect should be helped to extend their language competence so that they can use standard English with confidence. (DES, 1989b, p. 27)

For Key Stages 3 and 4

> Teachers should encourage pupils to read a variety of genres, e.g. auto-biographies, letters, diaries or travel books, as well as short stories, novels, poetry and plays. These should include literature from different countries written in English. (DES, 1989b, p. 31)

At George Dixon, the English Department regards it of paramount importance that children can express themselves well. To do this, pupils must have something to say. The stimuli provided to this end are drawn from the world around them, and pre-eminently from our multicultural society with all its richness and variety. Opportunities are thus created for all pupils of whatever background to make significant contributions in which they can feel immense pride. Care, however, must be taken to be positive and encouraging in our selection of stimuli for such purposes.

The National Curriculum in English is largely based upon the 1989 Cox Report which states:

> All pupils need to be aware of the richness of experience offered by writings in English from different countries, so that they may be introduced to the ideas and feelings of countries different from their own, and so we shall help the cause of racial tolerance. In Britain today, our multicultural society must be taken into account by anyone establishing texts for a national curriculum. (DES, 1989a)

Our English Department has, of course, identified within the National Curriculum, hindrances to a multicultural approach. One such hindrance is the emphasis on the pre-twentieth century literature and some of the works which are said to have been most influential in shaping and refining the English language. Such writings clearly may present some of our pupils with linguistic difficulties — particularly where English is not the preferred language of the home.

In spite of these difficulties, the Department is determined to find means of enabling all pupils to identify positively with their learning experiences in English.

Staff realize, for example, that a low attainment mark in English for some pupils is not necessarily a reflection on the pupils' abilities, but could be an indication that those pupils need special help in English language. Additionally, every effort is made to present a diversity of world views in order to encourage a positive attitude towards literature of all cultures and to develop an understanding of all humanity. The Department also seeks to open up avenues of critical awareness in pupils by encouraging them to analyze the attitudes of authors, their values and their use of language. Thus pupils are well equipped to detect corruptible, manipulative and racist use of language. The Department also exercises care in its choice of syllabuses so as to give pupils the maximum chance of success. It facilitates visits from Asian and Afro-Caribbean writers and poets, and promotes pupils' work for publication.

Science

Although science teachers and their mathematics colleagues are often prone to tell you that their disciplines are value-free and as such do not lend themselves to multiculturalism, it must be admitted that the Working Party's (National Curriculum Science) statement in the area of multiculturalism is one of the most useful of all such working parties' statements.

> Teachers must take account of ethnic and cultural diversity within their school population and within society at large. Different ethnic groups will have different interpretations of the view of science presented in the Science Order and the sections on non-statutory guidance. . . . The language of science can be complex and the science teacher will naturally seek to be sensitive to the pupil's understanding of language and terminology. . .

> It is well established that the choice of learning context has a strong effect on the pupil's performance and this applies particularly to ethnic minority pupils. . . . In setting up learning and assessment tasks, it is vital that ethnic or cultural bias is excluded from any activity. . . . Cultural diversity can be a positive influence on the richness of the curriculum, provided the teacher does not take a narrow view of 'correctness' for example, in a discussion on diet or alternative energy.

> People from all cultures are involved in scientific enterprise. The curriculum should reflect the contributions from different cultures, for example, the origins and growth of chemistry from ancient Egypt, Greece and Arabia to the later Byzantine and European cultures, and parallel developments in China and India. It is important that science books and other learning material should include examples of people from ethnic minority groups working alongside others and achieving success in scientific work. Pupils should come to realize the international nature of science and the potential it has for helping to overcome racial prejudice. (NCC, 1989, 7.6 to 7.8, p. A10)

Scientific studies prepare young people for adult life in which they have to work with other people, make decisions which could impact on others, make choices and form reliable opinions for themselves. The discipline of science can be useful to train and prepare young minds to reject unfounded rumours or suggestions. As an educational vehicle, science is ideal for alerting young people to the dangers of stereotypes and preconceptions.

Our school's science Department believes that the statements of attainment in National Curriculum science are so prescriptive that they place a considerable time restraint on practice and make it difficult to widen approaches and methods. Nevertheless, means are found to circumvent some of these difficulties. Every opportunity is taken to illustrate topics, for example, diet, nutrition, health, energy sources and the ecosystem, by reference to different cultures. Key Stage 4 provides other examples such as water desalination and purification in Arabia and the energy needs of Third World Countries. Pupils are also encouraged to learn about nations' mutual interdependence. For example, the study of the production of aluminium involves tracing its route from the extraction of ore in Jamaica, the purification of the ore in Eire and its refining in Anglesey. Staff carefully select materials which portray pupils from all ethnic backgrounds taking part in scientific investigations (a good example of this is the Oxford Science Course).

The Department is convinced that multicultural science largely depends upon the staff's knowledge and the resources at their disposal. Therefore careful selection of materials, books and other resources is always paramount, and teachers' own self-study materials which provide relevant contextual and factual knowledge are much in evidence.

The Department sees its approach to the teaching of science as leading to the enhancement of knowledge for both teachers and students, thus engendering mutual respect and promoting empathy between pupil and teacher and between pupil and pupil. Above all, this kind of approach stimulates a desire for learning which in turn leads to greater and more equitable opportunities for all pupils.

Mathematics

At our school the mathematics Department refreshingly rejects the general proposition to which most other mathematics departments have so willingly subscribed: that mathematics is a value-free subject and as such does not influence the minds, attitudes, and values of our children.

On the contrary, they argue:

> mathematics has a particular role to play in promoting the creation of a society in which proper respect is shown to all cultures, and in which people from all backgrounds are given equality of opportunity. (Coles, 1991)

The Department believes that whilst there might be some truth in the view that mathematics is culturally neutral at the abstract or higher levels of mathematics, at school levels the subject must be based on the concrete experiences of the pupils in order to give validity and reality to the subject.

Great care is therefore taken by the Department to discharge their responsibility to all pupils. To ensure that they are receiving a worthy education much emphasis is placed on:

1 The examination of both the content of lessons and the methods employed to deliver that content;
2 The inclusion of contributions of different cultures;
3 The enabling of all pupils to have an equal chance of deriving benefit.

In carrying out these tasks the Department is not helped by the National Curriculum Council's Working Party's first report. It recognized that children whose mother tongue is not English are likely to be at a disadvantage, and that cultural conflict in addition to covert racial prejudice in the form of lower expectations of black pupils may be an obstacle to academic progress. However, it gave no clear lead as to how mathematics might make a contribution in overcoming these difficulties.

Not only did the Working Party miss the opportunity to give a lead, but it denied that there is a relationship between multi-ethnic mathematics and black pupils' self-esteem. It also refused to acknowledge the positive effect that multi-ethnic mathematics can have on race relations.

Many of those who argue for a multiracial approach to the mathematics curriculum do so on the basis that such an approach is necessary to raise the self-esteem of ethnic minority cultures and to improve understanding and respect between races. We believe that this attitude is misconceived and patronising. (NCC, 1988, 10.22, p. 87)

Nevertheless, the Working Party had some useful points to make. For example, they were concerned that assessment should have regard for the linguistic and cultural differences of our pupils.

. . .there will need to be provision for adapting SATs so that they are set in contexts with which pupils are familiar. Pupils with a poor command of English may need to be tested in their mother tongue if their mathematical attainment is to be fairly assessed. (NCC, 1988, 10.23, p. 87)

Further, the Working Party accepted that all children should learn that mathematics is not solely a white European invention. '. . .it is right to make clear to children that mathematics is the product of a diversity of cultures. . .' (NCC, 1988, 10.20, p. 87).

Whilst the latest provisions regarding National Curriculum Mathematics are silent on these issues and therefore do not improve the situation, mathematics teachers can find ample room for multiculturalizing the subject on examination of the attainment targets at the various Key Stages.

Pupils should make use of knowledge, skills and understanding outlined in the programmes of study in practical tasks, in real life problems and to investigate within mathematics itself. At all levels pupils should be expected to use with confidence the appropriate mathematical content specified in the programmes of study relation to the other attainment targets. (DES, 1991b, Attainment Target 1: Using and applying mathematics)

At George Dixon, the mathematics Department has been quick to identify these possibilities and grasp them for the benefit of all pupils. In the first term at the school, the initial project undertaken by Year 7 pupils is related to the study of number systems. Pupils learn that the familiar number system is based upon the work of Indian and Arab mathematicians. They also look at the ways in which other number systems, such as the Babylonian and Chinese, have developed. Children are also encouraged to demonstrate any other number system with which they or their families are familiar. In this way it is made clear to them that all pupils, their background and culture are valued equally.

At the point where algebra is introduced, further opportunities are provided to reflect different cultural contributions to mathematics. For example, in teaching the derivation of the word algebra, pupils will learn of the Arabic contribution. Again, those patterns of numbers which are referred to as Pascal's Triangle were really produced and brought into use by the Chinese, at least 500 years before Pascal was born in France. All children are given that knowledge at our school. This clearly reinforces the fact that the school and the mathematics Department greatly value the contributions made by non-European cultures and demonstrates the power of mathematics as a universal means of communication.

The Department encourages different calculation methods in order to provide opportunities for all pupils to contribute ideas drawn from other cultures. Where language might be an obstacle, pupils are encouraged to perform calculations in those languages in which they feel most comfortable, as long as the methods and results are clearly set out.

The Department has proudly pioneered the use of course work assessment which helps to encourage pupils to relate mathematics to their real world. It is necessary to introduce a caution at this point. The real world which we portray must be full of positive images and not negative preconceptions or stereotypes. Materials produced by this Department use names and images which reflect the multiracial nature of our society. The same type of care is taken when selecting externally produced texts and other supporting resources.

In the study of statistics, the Department makes great use of the opportunity to challenge some common myths and falsehood. For example, many people assume that all the problems of African and Asian countries are a result of the overcrowding in these countries. The Department challenges this view by getting pupils to calculate and compare the density of population in countries in different parts of the world which in many instances turn out to be more sparsely populated than the UK and many other European countries.

Finally, the Department is conscious of the self-fulfilling character of low expectation. All teachers within the Department are therefore constantly steered away from such pessimistic preconceptions. Teachers actively and openly 'talk up' pupils' chances, expect them to achieve, and so they do.

We could go on illustrating the practice of every Department within our school, because no subject area is exempt from striving for equality and justice for all pupils. But space will not allow.

Cross-Curricular Issues and Other Subjects

The foundation subjects are certainly not a complete curriculum. . . . The whole curriculum for all pupils will certainly need to include at appropriate (and in some cases all) stages:

- careers education and guidance;
- health education;
- other aspects of personal and social education; and
- coverage across the curriculum of gender and multicultural issues.

. . .they are clearly required in the curriculum which all pupils are entitled to by virtue of section 1 of the Act. (DES, 1989c, para. 3, 8)

At our school a special working party has been established to advise on how best we can fulfil our duty to our pupils in these areas of the curriculum in spite of the time constraints imposed upon us by the National Curriculum core and foundation subjects. This working party is shortly to report to the school's curriculum committee. However, we believe that some very good practices remain in force during this interim phase under the school's Personal and Social Education (PSE) arrangements.

Sex Education

The present climate is one in which there is considerable interest in how schools impart knowledge regarding issues to do with sex, so much so that Parliament has turned its attention to such affairs. The local education authority, the governing body and head teacher are now required to ensure that '. . .where sex education is given to any registered pupils at the school it is given in such a manner as to encourage those pupils to have due regard to moral considerations and the value of family life'. (Education Act (No 2) 1986, 5.46).

Irrespective of such parliamentary intervention, we at George Dixon feel that the assumption should never be made that it is safe to teach about sexual activities to black children without more consultation and advice. Such issues are important for all children but in the case of some communities religious and cultural considerations weigh very heavily. The practitioner needs to be on guard. It would have been most helpful if Parliament had seen fit to insert 'culture' within the section as a consideration too. It is not enough to rely on guidelines whether given nationally, locally or by school governors and head teachers. The only safe and proper thing to do is to seek substantial and meaningful consultation with relevant parents and communities. Not to follow this advice is to risk major conflicts of a cultural and/or religious nature.

Some of the issues upon which we seek agreement with parents in this area of education include questions about both content and delivery. How much should pupils be taught at what ages? Should classes be single sex in composition? Is it acceptable that male teachers should teach sex education to girls? Parents' and community guidance on all these issues is vital.

The multicultural school should not assume uniformity of parental views. Meeting all tastes and wishes under these circumstances presents enormous challenges; but it is wiser to respond to these challenges than to follow easier but discriminatory routes.

Careers Choice, Practice and Development

Careers guidance is seen

> . . .as comprising planned sequences of experiences designed to facilitate the development respectively of (a) opportunity-awareness, (b) self-awareness, (c) decision-making and (d) transition learning. (Watts and Fawcett, 1984)

This is an excellent definition of careers education. Whilst it is recognized that not all schools deliver this entire package, it has to be admitted that such a model, at least, offers the best chance of complete development towards career choice for pupils. Whatever the context, all schools will need to have regard to the different cultural needs and experiences of all its pupils if they are to benefit from the model equitably. Careers teachers/personnel and institutions are also affected by racist thinking and practices. Here too, as elsewhere in education, the black child is negatively stereotyped and consequently often discouraged from making ambitious strides.

In particular, black Afro-Caribbean parents and youths have for many years articulated concern and disgust at the system, procedures and people in educational institutions which have failed them in both the academic and pastoral aspects of school. Vocational guidance is but one aspect of education which black Afro-Caribbean communities feel have contributed to black children's failure. But what of the successful. black child? They are so few, and at what cost to our children and our communities are they successful? (See DES, 1985, chapter 3, annex 'A').

The main equal opportunity messages from a recent survey of the destinations of 16-year-old-pupils pupils from Birmingham Schools were as follows:

> A significant shift in the ethnic make-up of the population of school leavers is taking place and will continue into the next century. Black school leavers continue to be significantly under-represented in quality jobs and on employer led YTS schemes leading to jobs with training and prospects. This may result in the creation of a pool of unskilled and untrained black labour force for the coming decade with social and economic consequences which the city cannot afford. The minority ethnic school leavers, and girls especially, are entering a narrow band of occupations more likely to be lower level in terms of training, skills and, ultimately, pay and prospects.
>
> Providers of opportunities in employment, training and education need to adopt positive policies and practices to open up access to all — this will increasingly become an economic and commercial necessity as falling rolls have their impact. (Birmingham City Council, 1988)

The answer to many of these difficulties lies in measures designed to alter attitudes and expectations held by teachers about black pupils. The observations of many black Afro-Caribbean parents and pupils about their experiences at the hands of careers teachers and officers strongly indicate a need for adequate training — both at initial and in service levels.

Black role-models in positions of authority would help considerably. Schools need to re-think their staffing and promotion policies with alarming speed if we are to make inroads upon this problem before we lose yet another generation of black youngsters.

Further, the advice given to young people must never be demotivating, must never be of a stereotypical nature. Young people need to be guided in making sensible career choices, but in doing so, their own aspirations and enthusiasm must be encouraged and supported. Careers teachers and advisers must be aware of the debilitating dangers of low expectations, negative preconceptions and stereo-types as and when they advise black children. These are the kinds of influences which underpin the organization thinking, staffing and practices at our school.

Race and Cultural Issues

Personal and Social Education (PSE) must take on part of the responsibility for eradicating the ignorance and preconceived stereotypes held by white children about other races and cultures. Although there is room for spontaneous educational discussions around matters of this kind, PSE syllabuses must include these issues quite purposefully. We at George Dixon School believe that no responsible teacher can allow racist views to go unchallenged — not if we subscribe to the principles of fairness and justice.

References

BIRMINGHAM CITY COUNCIL (1988) *Survey of the Destinations of 5th Year Pupils from Birmingham Schools*, Birmingham, Birmingham Careers Service.

COARD, B. (1971) *How the West Indian Child is made Educationally Subnormal in the British School System*, London, New Beacon Books.

COLES, A. (1991) Unpublished report of the Head of the Mathematics Department of George Dixon Comprehensive School, Birmingham.

DEPARTMENT OF EDUCATION AND SCIENCE (1983) *Records of Achievement at 16*. London, HMSO.

DEPARTMENT OF EDUCATION AND SCIENCE (1985) *Education for All, The Report of the Committee of Enquiry into the Education of Children from Ethnic Minority Groups* (The Swann Report), London, HMSO.

DEPARTMENT OF EDUCATION AND SCIENCE (1989a) *English for Ages 5 to 16* (The Cox Report), London, HMSO.

DEPARTMENT OF EDUCATION AND SCIENCE (1989b) *English Statutory Order*, London, HMSO.

DEPARTMENT OF EDUCATION AND SCIENCE (1989c) *National Curriculum, from Policy to Practice*, London, HMSO.

DEPARTMENT OF EDUCATION AND SCIENCE (1991a) *History Statutory Order*, London, HMSO.

DEPARTMENT OF EDUCATION AND SCIENCE (1991b) *Mathematics in the National Curriculum*, London, HMSO.

Education Act (No 2) (1986), London, HMSO.

NATIONAL CURRICULUM COUNCIL (1988) *Mathematics Working Party Report*, York, National Curriculum Council.

NATIONAL CURRICULUM COUNCIL (1989) *Science Working Party Report*, York, National Curriculum Council.

NATIONAL CURRICULUM COUNCIL (1990) *History in the National Curriculum: Working Party Report*, York, National Curriculum Council.

WATTS, A.G. and FAWCETT, B. (1984) 'Pastoral care and careers education', in BEST, R., JARVIS, C. and RIBBINS, P. (Eds) *Perspectives on Pastoral Care*, Oxford, Heinemann Educational Books.

Part Four

Policy and Practice

The European Dimension and the National Curriculum

Witold Tulasiewicz

Preamble

This chapter attempts to define the nature and scope of the European Dimension — the cross-curricular element still to be explicitly integrated into the National Curriculum — and to examine its implications for multicultural education. The term European Dimension can also be used to refer to a package of more global educational and related measures recommended by the relevant Task Force of the European Community.

General Considerations

In school curriculum terms, multiculturalism is understood as more than teaching about other cultures — art, folklore, language, religion, or indeed cuisine. Often it is an introduction to the whole way of life of the community. How this is achieved, in the British context at any rate, varies from school to school. But multiculturalism is more than school knowledge alone (who are our neighbours?). It includes attitudinal elements (overcoming prejudice) and skills (how to get on with others). The ability to live and work together happily and productively requires multicultural education to teach that societies are enriched mixtures of different cultures rather than to emphasize the differences between them.

   Much of what pupils actually learn about Europe in school is domestic, capable of everyday use, such as a smattering of a foreign language and the ability to function in another country's daily culture. Yet often this is not perceived by pupils, because of the academic character of the European facts with which they are presented in history, geography or literature. In practice, everyday culture is more likely to be picked up with national subjects such as French or Spanish (for example, posting a letter in Spain), whereas European is more often associated with the 'high' culture of academic disciplines (such as Charlemagne or Monnet with politics and history, or the influence of the climate in the Loire valley with human geography).

   In different countries multiculturalism is linked with the presence of different influences; Asian and Afro-Caribbean in Britain, Japanese and Vietnamese in

Western Canada, or East German in the Federal Republic. At first glance the last example may appear less distant than the first two, but it can be just as alien and present as much challenge in school and in society at large (Tulasiewicz, 1991). Furthermore, typical British pupils are likely to have more difficulty with the European Dimension than with the American or Canadian because they are more aware of its diversity. Pupils learning about Europe are confronted by a plurality of countries and the reality of a variety of cultures and languages. The European dimension as a whole may not at first be visible (Slater, 1990). Research has also shown that British children often do not see themselves as European unless they are personally involved (Bell, 1990). Even so, the average school pupil is more likely to associate the European dimension with a way of life than with what is offered by way of 'high' European culture (Williams, 1981).

In British curriculum usage, the phrase European Dimension — European Awareness can also be introduced at this stage — refers to all or most of Europe and those parts of the world associated with Europe. Confining the European Dimension to the European Community (EC) may help to present a more compact whole, but it is also open to the accusation that it ignores the rest of the world. Indeed the Dimension must extend beyond the established territorial Europeans, to include not only the Welsh as well as the English, the Bretons as well as the French, but also all those recent Europeans who live in Europe but whose roots are in Morocco, Bangladesh or Turkey.

A Curriculum Dimension

The National Curriculum Council and the Department of Education and Science (now the Department for Education) use the term theme for cross-curricular components like Education for Citizenship and Economic Awareness. The topic Life in Multicultural Europe is mentioned under dimensions in *Curriculum Guidance 3 The Whole Curriculum* (NCC, 1990a). The European Dimension is referred to in Education for Citizenship in the March 1990 document, but not in the *Education for Citizenship* booklet of November 1990 (NCC, 1990b). With no firmly fixed place in the curriculum, the term European Dimension is appropriate.

Thus the challenge presented by this curriculum component is considerable. It is more than a single subject which can be tackled as a discrete element in teaching (Craft and Bardell, 1984). Moreover, British pupils, whatever their ethnic culture, are used to learning their national curriculum subjects to equip them to live British lives. The European Dimension in contrast, according to the NCC definition (Appendix One), is seen as part of an education specifically intended for interaction, for cooperation with others, including non-British, to facilitate living and working in the United Kingdom as a part of Europe, and in other European countries. Conversely, it also prepares Britons to receive non-British Europeans into Britain.

This life skills approach explains the close link between the European Dimension and Education for Citizenship (NCC, 1990b). Educating the European citizen, which is a part of the European Dimension, involves the future citizen's attitudes and views. Community resolutions show a concern with the 'safeguarding of the principles of democracy, social justice and respect for human rights' in the European Dimension (Council, 1988). NCC guidance allocates these issues to other parts of the National Curriculum. Both reflect the need for pupils' personal commitment.

The implications for the syllabus of a European Dimension/European Awareness course are clear. Multicultural education taught through European Awareness must adopt the pedagogical approach of cooperative education. Nevertheless, the distinction made at a British Council Seminar in July 1990 between preparing a European Citizen and teaching about Europe is not helpful, since a citizen must be knowledgeable about things European to acquire the right attitudes and dispositions.

A European Dimension

Since the collapse of the religious and educational unity of Europe, the aim of schooling has been to serve the nation state. The tradition of medieval scholars travelling all over Europe from Cracow to Oxford and from Uppsala to Sevilla was replaced by a national if not nationalistic education, particularly so at elementary and secondary levels. The emergence — but not until World War One — of common international interests in education led to the introduction of extra-curricular elements in some schools. These are best described as international or comparative studies and are a part of a national education. They are not a call for international involvement through action. European experience, as an early curriculum component marked by school visits and twinning programmes for those who could afford them, had a similar function. Community-inspired European Dimension and multicultural school programmes offer a totally different educational experience.

This is because although the European ingredient may be politically national, serving the interests of the union of states of the European Community, it is delivered in the context of the plurality of European cultures. Just as multicultural education aims to promote better intercultural relations, so the European Community's policy is to facilitate positive relations among Europe's various constituent elements by taking account of its human and institutional diversity. But its political power gives European Community, and thus by definition pluricultural resolutions and directives, a legal status and protection throughout Europe. This protection of the cultural variety of Europe, bigger and more heterogeneous than that of a single nation, provides a clearer acknowledgment of pluralism and a firmer protection of multicultural interests and education than that given by individual member states. As a consequence, many of the smaller nations of Europe, like the Celts or Catalans, are seeking the shelter of the European umbrella.

If the European Dimension helps prepare the future citizens of the multicultural society of Europe, will that society promote equally strongly all the cultural elements existing within it? In other words, does multicultural education mean education for the coexistence of cultures, or does it have an explicit brief for protecting and preserving individual cultures, including non-territorial ones? The Council of Europe passed a multicultural society declaration in support of the Convention on Minority and Regional Languages, which includes ethnic community languages. The Council of the European Communities has spoken out in similar terms. The aim of living and working comfortably has to be understood in the context of educating European citizens capable of speaking other languages, but who have the right to expect to have their own languages recognized and spoken by others. The proclaimed principle of unity in diversity goes together with 'acquiring a view of Europe as a multicultural. . .community', in which the different cultures are regarded as an asset. Such statements indicate that the European Dimension includes many of the concerns of multicultural education.

The Status of the European Dimension — Education or Training?

In the European Community the role of education is understood to be strictly economic; education is therefore subordinated to vocational training. Mobility too, is dictated by vocational and professional priorities. Unlike the National Curriculum, the introduction of the European Dimension in schools did not originate with a British or DES initiative. The decision was taken at European Community level. Since the Treaty of Rome does not have an education clause — its Article 128 speaks of 'common vocational preparation' — the introduction of the European Dimension could be seen as having implications for vocational/ professional training only. Indeed, the right of migrant workers' children to receive mother tongue instruction and to learn their culture of origin (25 July 1977), arises from the right to free movement of labour, enshrined in Article 48 (see also Council of Europe, 1983). However, as early as 1973 the Janne Report postulated a common cultural/educational policy for member states. Higher and further education soon fell into the category of professional preparation. The resolutions of the Council of 9 February and 13 December 1976 which brought in the Action Programme, and the directive of 16 June 1976 which introduced the first mutual recognition of diplomas and gave a boost to professional exchanges, can be said to have confirmed the European Principle of cooperation to develop a Europe of quality and equal opportunity through educational measures.

Because member states are autonomous in matters of education, the wording of a definition for an open dimension such as the European Dimension was difficult to agree, as was the kind of pedagogical direction it should have. However, the final 24 May 1988 Resolution (Council, 1988, 88/c 177/02) which is binding, requires member states to set out their policies for incorporating the Dimension in education, specifying school curricula, and to propose initiatives to strengthen it. The Committee of Ministers of the Council of Europe had promoted a similar initiative in 1983 (R(8)4).

The DES did not formulate its response until February/March 1991. The NCC produced its definition in 1990 (Appendix One). A 23 September 1991 Community report (SEK(91)1753) on progress made reveals similar findings in all member states. To protect national traditions standardization across the sovereign member states was deemed undesirable. So although 'unnecessary divergencies were to be avoided' (Council, 1989), German *Laender* could allow a different status to their Turkish minority's language education from that given to minorities in the Netherlands (Tulasiewicz, 1991; Shennan, 1991). Still, the multicultural and multilingual character of Europe made necessary the 'harmonization of vocational preparation' to enable different nationalities working together to take part in the economic and social development of the Community (Council 1988). In this scenario Europe becomes one focus, the common elements being the education of European citizens and consumers, the European identity being delivered in national variants, with European aspects promoted by exchanges and links. Classroom practice, however, continues to vary between different countries.

The Single European Act and Future Developments

The Single European Act was signed in February 1986, and comes into effect on 1 January 1993. Its advent, with its free movement of people, goods, capital, services and ideas, is bound to accelerate developments in education. The Act does not refer to education, but the prospective removal of economic barriers with its expected consequences in terms of economic, financial, social, political and technological change has led to an increased interest in training and education. Education fosters economic mobility among Europeans by developing a European consciousness as well as imparting the knowledge and skills required for the liberated traffic. In the medium term (1989–1992) existing educational and training measures were reinforced: mutual recognition of qualifications (including teacher education) and the rights to mobility, distance learning, links and exchanges were extended (Council, 1989). The longer term 1992–1995 plans are more specifically educational, taking in secondary education. Guides to European education systems (for parents) and pedagogical subject guides (for ethnic teachers) are being produced. After Maastricht 1991, education is expected to be included (article 126) in the proposed revised version of the Treaty of Rome, although member states' autonomy and diversity will be protected. The conclusion must be that there will be an increase in Community decisions which will further affect school curricula.

The difference between educating in and for the multicultural Community and multicultural education in an individual country like Britain, is one of scale. The distance between the existing cultures, the type of local legislation provided and its status affects the interdependence of non-territorials, and the degree of commitment. Significantly, with the exception of the definitions referred to above and a newsletter published by the NCC in February 1991 (NCC, 1991), no official guidance on multicultural or European education has been published to date. However, in readiness for 1993, a DES study of multicultural education was set up in February 1992. In March 1992 the DES also published Policy Models for Implementing the European Dimension (DES, 1992). These are general policy suggestions which, for example, emphasize the obvious link with TVE (Technical and Vocational Education), education and industry. This document which sums up much of the earlier debate is too recent to have had much impact to date.

Defining the Scope of the European Dimension

A definition of European Studies for any level of education is difficult enough, but studies at least implies a corpus of subject matter. Dimension, on the other hand, is no excerpt from a larger whole, but affects the whole itself, whatever that is meant to be. It includes disparate elements, such as knowledge, skills, attitudes and commitments taught at different times and under different headings. For example, the topic 'rebuilding of Europe after World War II' in a GCSE history syllabus constitutes part of an attainment target (AT3 level 9) in history. Knowledge of the 'economic and social aspects of Europe' (from the NCC definition of the European Dimension) is part of a syllabus which could be found within a GCSE history study unit but is not. While language skills levels in GCSE syllabuses have been determined, Citizenship Education implying a European identity or the 'acquisition of a view of . . .a multicultural, multilingual community' or an 'understanding of common European ideals', is more difficult to quantify (NCC, 1990a).

This situation is further complicated, since a number of elements — promoting positive attitudes to the environment and commitment to human rights for example — are not only aspects of the European Dimension as formulated by the European Community but have also been included among the themes of the National Curriculum. Pluralism appears in the Education for Citizenship theme; multicultural education is itself a dimension. Knowledge and skills, as well as attitudes and commitments, are included in the various Community definitions of the European Dimension, making it both a transmission instrument of knowledge of the European Community and a transforming one: 'enabling pupils. . .to live and work. . .in other European countries' (see Appendix One).

The aims attached to the European Dimension were stated more emphatically than is normally the case with school subjects in the definition produced by the NCC Citizenship Task Group (Appendix One). This became the departure point for teaching about the European Dimension in schools and colleges and led to initiatives, funded by the DES, from agencies such as the Central Bureau for Visits and Exchanges, the UK Centre for European Education, LEAs and professional associations. These include teacher exchanges, language assistants programmes, European Schools competitions, European Awareness projects which would identify LEA commitment and practice, and rolling programmes for the dissemination of information to schools.

The Dimension has been linked to attainment targets and programmes of study of the National Curriculum and to other cross-curricular themes such as environmental education and economic and industrial awareness. However, the presence of Europe in these is only marginally more than had previously been the case with examination syllabuses in subjects like history, art and music. Geography has a complete attainment target on the Community (AT3: The UK within the European Community). Modern foreign languages give it a rather vague mention in the programmes of study of foreign cultures (DES, 1990, 6.12 and 10.18). General anti-racism and equal opportunities awareness appear to be given more prominence, a multicultural education criterion. Additional new material is introduced in the study of non-English texts in English, AT2 Reading, levels 7 to 10 (DES, 1989). Examining organizations like SEAC (School Examinations and Assessment Council) insist on account being taken of the European Dimension in GCSE and A and AS examination syllabuses (see also Goodson and McGivney, 1985).

Action by the DES — The Impact of the European Dimension

The four objectives of the 1988 EC Resolution are 1) Sense of European identity and the foundations on which the European peoples intend to base their development, 2) Economic and social development, progress towards European Union, 3) Awareness of the advantages which the Community represents, and 4) Improving knowledge of the Community.

These objectives are replicated in the seven objectives published in the DES February/March 1991 statement (DES, 1991 — Appendix Two). The DES has more emphasis on explicit items of knowledge (of 'European histories, geographies and cultures. . .'), on preparation for work, and on skills ('interest in and improving competence in other European languages'). Languages are not in the NCC definition, but are a part of the European Lingua Programme (1989), a separate European education initiative. Responsibility for action is shared by the usual authorities, with central Government adopting policies supporting language teaching and learning, links and exchanges, and financing the work of some non-Governmental organizations. This activity, actively sponsored by the European Commission's Task force, has implications beyond school curriculum concerns in the narrow sense of the word.

The European Dimension in schools and teacher training, the promotion of teacher mobility, and links and exchanges are included in the proposals of Action A1. Action A2 (strengthening the European Dimension in Education) is well advanced, consisting of the dissemination of information by and in LEAs and other institutions (for example, Eurodesk in Scotland), and participation in EC vocational programmes of exchanges (EVE). The task of action programme A3 (inclusion of the European Dimension in school curricula) is claimed to have been advanced by the arrival of the National Curriculum. Most progress has been made in modern languages, contact between schools across Europe using modern technology and European work experience, promoted by the European Community. Action A4 (teaching material) is difficult to implement in the United Kingdom, since to date the DFE has no brief to vet materials. The ability of new teachers to deliver the European Dimension (Action A5) is safeguarded by clause 6.2 in the new Council for the Accreditation of Teacher Education (CATE) document ('teachers must be able to incorporate in teaching the European Dimension. . .'). Contacts between pupils and teachers (Action A6) and complementary action (Action A7), which has resulted in British participation and initiatives in international gatherings on matters of concern connected with the European dimension, have had the support of the DES, and of other statutory and voluntary organizations (DES, 1991).

The content given in the DES outline response to the Brussels Resolution (DES, 1991) shows the full extent of the European Dimension as distinct from its character as a school curriculum element, though the two cannot be kept entirely separate. It is possible to reduce language work if to tolerate fellow Europeans you need only a few words of their language, and if your lack of skill is compensated for by other factors — a desire to get to know and understand them. On the other hand, the possession of skills is indispensable for the economic success of co-operation. Financial support has been inadequate, so that specific curriculum guidance and advice on exactly what form and content the European Dimension should assume has not matched official British concern with other parts of the National Curriculum. Britain devotes most of her energy, in the words of a junior minister in 1990, to 'improving the quality of her own education', presumably in national rather than Community terms, emphasizing competitiveness rather than partnership in dealing with the Community.

To date NCC has not realized its promise of comments on the nature of the European dimension and detailed guidance. Fortunately, a good deal of this work is produced by the professionals involved (Appendix Three). Meanwhile in

Vienna a conference in 1991 looked at the extracurricular content of the European Dimension, and a 1992 Council of Europe project is examining the European Dimension in secondary education. The Council of Europe has been promoting the European Dimension by advocating and supporting European networks in tertiary education and by promoting centres and clubs.

Finding a Syllabus

In these circumstances a European Dimension syllabus may assume a multiplicity of shapes. It may be based on definitions and information in resolutions and programmes extolling the benefits of cooperation in the European Community, or it may be apparent in accounts of actual teaching practice in an increasing number of schools (Appendix Three). Since approaches to the European Dimension are less constrained by examination syllabus prescriptions, or, as in Britain, not examined as such, there are noticeable differences from the traditional parts of the curriculum. It consists of much out-of-school activity (exchanges, visits, with or without pupil assignments, projects and competitions, links of all sorts), involving contacts with personnel other than teachers, and especially allowing pupils to 'do' things.

Syllabus Components

It was suggested earlier that a European Dimension syllabus consists of four parts:

a) *Knowledge.* When appended to other subjects this is in danger of losing much of its specific European core (SEAC, 1991). There is room for the introduction of themes and topics of particular interest to European youth in addition to the internationally acknowledged political, socio-economic and ecological concerns which could be made to focus more on interdependence in the European Community.

b) *Skills.* These include language acquisition which, in any case, is becoming more identified with Europe — although Greek, Danish and even Portuguese are hardly available outside their countries of origin, and there is no agreement on the provision of teaching ethnic community languages. Travel skills have also been recognized as a new concern in schools.

c) *Attitudes.* These necessarily include commitment to the Community, with the choice between British and European citizenship present in pupils' consciousness, and with European loyalties contending with national factors like mother tongue, religion and the rest of everyday culture. Here the teacher's role is particularly delicate since he or she is transmitting values, such as democracy or equality, which are first seen and perceived as British rather than European. But European Citizenship emphasizes the obligation to help develop a Europe of quality and equality, to demonstrate the benefits of pooled experience, to respect diversity and to promote shared democratic values.

d) *Exchanges and Links*. These may constitute a separate group. They are the most common of European initiatives and available at every level. The names Erasmus, Comett and Arion have become household words throughout the Europe of training and education.

It is important not to look at these four activities in isolation. Indeed, some pursuits, like properly organized exchanges, combine them all. Electronic Mail contacts can lead to personal meetings and joint projects.

Bilateral or European Dimension

The bilateral nature of much European activity can itself be problematic. An Anglo-French exchange may have to stand for all of Europe. The danger is that preparation to work with partners in member states may involve an exclusive concern with one foreign culture and one foreign language. Such bicultural experience is only a partial European one. Although much more complex and costly, European sponsored initiatives involving several countries are therefore encouraged (examples can be found in *Europa*, *Edit* and *Euroednews*). But teaching multicultural knowledge, skills and attitude formation need not be confined to the wider Community. It can start at home. Experience with non-territorial cultures is easily acquired in the home country.

In addition, new developments in the National Curriculum, like teaching language awareness and knowledge about language (Cox, 1991; Mittins, 1991) hold out the promise of the involvement of more than two language components in an educational interchange. At present much of this material is firmly anchored in English mother tongue lessons.

New Areas of the European Dimension

The European Dimension has not simply introduced established material into the curriculum. Pupils have been enabled to learn about hitherto neglected areas of knowledge: schools, health or politics in other countries. Much new content has also been negotiated democratically with teachers or school governors and introduced by the pupils themselves. Furthermore, the National Curriculum's advocacy of current themes rather than the vertical, cumulative approach of adding material over a number of school years, has been useful. Such themes can be adjusted to become topical. For example, the information collected on a trip abroad can be used to advantage as resource material.

The definitions of the European Dimension mention living and working in Europe 'comfortably but not uncritically' (see Appendix One). A socio-political awareness extending to all of Europe must therefore be part of the school curriculum. It should include a recognition of the administrative and procedural problems encountered in working for Europe. Citizenship presupposes knowledge and the attitudinal disposition to use it constructively in actions calling on citizenship skills (Citizenship, 1990).

Technical and Vocational Education and the European Dimension

There appears to have been much success in delivering the European Dimension at the level of work preparation and work experience among youth looking for employment. One way of exploring the Dimension is through work and work-shadowing contacts, starting before the statutory leaving age. Accounts of this practice show that the link between the educational and vocational sectors can provide mutual reinforcement and support of knowledge and skills (Blackledge, 1982 and Central Bureau, 1989). At this level as well as language and other vocational skills, attitudinal qualities — democratic behaviour, respect for the environment and good work attitudes — can be acquired. Edward Heath expresses similar views in his Foreword to *Education in a Single Europe* (Brock and Tulasiewicz, 1993). TVE also offers an opportunity to engage and foster attitudinal and personal skills. Additionally, collaboration in work/work and work/school situations encourages the development of work counselling and guidance and fosters enterprise.

The European Dimension Abroad

In other European Community countries similar curriculum development is underway. Germany is involved in exchange and partnership schemes, 3,500 with French schools alone. A Europe in the Classroom programme has been in existence since 1978. In two *Laender* foreign languages are taught in primary schools. The recent educational reform in Spain gave priority to strengthening the European component, with more European languages and culture to be taught, and all teaching materials to have their own specific European profile. The Ministry of Education produced 70,000 copies of European games for use in primary schools. Three primary teacher training centres have been established, each employing a European Dimension specialist. The importance attached to an early start with the European Dimension is much in evidence throughout Europe. Ireland, in collaboration with Britain including Northern Ireland, Belgium, Germany and the Netherlands, has initiated with partner schools, a six-year programme of curriculum development, producing and exchanging videos on health and drugs, dealt with as European problems. In the European Studies Project (1991), experts as well as young people are examining issues such as: What stops youngsters from gaining a wider view of Europe? What is it like to be a European? Why is a citizen of Northern Ireland a citizen of Ireland and Europe?

Delivering the European Dimension — Classroom Implications

The NCC Citizen Task Group envisaged delivery of the cuckoo element of the European Dimension in the National Curriculum through cross-curricular themes as well as the attainment targets and programmes of study of core and foundation subjects. Multicultural education likewise is a cross-curricular element. The question of whether some subjects are perceived to be more multicultural than others was addressed by a team of multicultural curriculum researchers in Cambridge (King, 1992). The answer depends at least as much on the emphasis given to elements within each individual subject and the pedagogy used, as on the subject content itself. Shared European experiences have ranged from kite-making and flying to real work contracts with wine growers.

Successful teaching of the European Dimension can be measured by criteria evaluating the sophistication and nature of European knowledge and skills included or by the complexity of the multicultural concepts expected of the pupils. A history lesson in an English school will usually have a British starting point, (such as patterns of migration in history AT1 level 9). However, a topic such as an investigation into acid rain can be given a European context, and so create some attitudinal involvement, even though the main objectives will be scientific. Other initiatives can produce more personal identification with Europe. For example, in a Sheffield geography project, classes of multicultural European pupils interviewed and measured fellow Europeans' own perceptions of being European. Knowledge can be assessed in formal examinations, like those mounted for the European studies Project by the Associated Examining Board, while visits and exchanges can be evaluated by the volume of enthusiasm generated. Joint work experience can demonstrate the overall quality of the skills gained, as well as revealing the attitudes shared with partners.

It is however extremely difficult for schools to ascertain if the prejudices of pupils have been successfully overcome. There is evidence of more commitment to Europe among school pupils and students and a greater tolerance than among adults, including teachers. This attitude seems to cross the borders of European nation states rather more easily than the ethnic barriers within member states themselves. Indeed, local community elements tend to be underrepresented in lessons about Europe, which identify the French to the virtual exclusion of the Algerians in France. On the other hand, Asians tend to feel more comfortable in their own Europe of extended families, and seem to be more knowledgeable about Europe than their English or German peers (Tulasiewicz, 1991).

Clearly teachers must be open-minded themselves and knowledgeable about the Community, and in possession of language or other skills if they are to successfully deliver the Dimension. They must be able to function off school premises, possess the talents of tour operators and competition organizers and even demonstrate the catering skills of a resourceful chef!

Young children show more curiosity and usually have fewer inhibitions, so that a start with the European Dimension should be made in the primary school where the interdisciplinary teaching style seems to be tailor made. Delivering the European dimension through subject Attainment Targets can start in Key Stage One. For example, Mathematics AT1 (using and applying mathematics), taking in a topic like European food, can be taught by weighing and measuring an aubergine in grams. The vegetable itself may reappear in a biology lesson and its provenance discussed. Jean Gibson (Gibson, 1991), develops other ideas for use with younger pupils. It is advisable to start with one region or country and to move to wider European themes and issues as the pupils grow older (Peacock, 1985).

Senior pupils can start with one school subject taught in an interdisciplinary fashion or with an interdisciplinary topic like transport in Europe. Concentration on what is held in common with the part of Europe being studied aids successful teaching, as does direct experience. Both help overcome the problem of distance (though there is no firm evidence to show whether pupils respond more easily to distant or less distant cultures). Links and exchanges can also foster an understanding of distance. However, educational autonomy can make large-scale exchanges very difficult to arrange. For example, Dutch colleagues' proposals at a sub-network 13 (Erasmus exchange plans) meeting to coordinate the exchanges between a number of teacher training institutions were frustrated because of clashes of holiday dates fixed independently by each state. Visits are best when they require the completion of specific tasks, which may have been set by the pupils themselves. General curriculum skills can be developed when practised in unfamiliar surroundings, or through a different medium. A common European Dimension certificate, including language and travel skills, could be used as a qualification for Europe-wide employment.

Delivering the Multicultural Dimension

Unlike the European Dimension, multicultural education teaches a new setting which to most people is less familiar, and which does not enjoy the same political support. It teaches facts, skills and attitudes while at the same time seeks to banish the evils of prejudice and racism, by teaching about their origins, the reasons for their appearance and the societal support they receive. Multicultural education in the ethnic communities is surrounded by caveats. The European Dimension, on the other hand, unfolds an ideal world, where economic cooperation and growth values predominate. However, common European ideals together with an awareness of European development past and present should include knowledge of racial or cultural persecution and exploitation. The holocaust was a European phenomenon. Indeed, much persecution world-wide has European origins. Significantly the 1988 Resolution does not mention racism.

Is the European Dimension Multicultural Education?

A difference between the European Dimension and multicultural education is that as a rule multiculturalism is taken mainly to refer to the situation of non-territorial minorities (NCC, 1991). It promotes identified cultural diversity without the support of the perceived advantages of an economic union or a grand concept like that of a shared European heritage with values and ideals held in common. 'Unity in diversity' is a phrase often heard in the Community and the Council of Europe. In the case of ethnic multicultural education, as it were on the defensive, all these are more difficult to perceive. A socio-politically united Europe will continue to be a diversity entrenched and protected on a scale unique in any geographical area. Since minority community groups form part of the multicultural reality of a member state, they are entitled to similar consideration.

Cultural Interdependence

The fear that the European Community of interests will inhibit individual ethnic groups from playing an independent and significant part in it, may be groundless (Anderson *et al.*, 1979), especially if Europe is seen as a community of interdependences in which individuals and groups can move freely. The sovereignty of the member states of the European Community safeguards the existence of their own national culture(s), and this sovereignty can only be curtailed by members' voluntary decision. In Britain non-territorial minority rights are protected by British law and usage, in which context certain European Community laws also apply. Although these are not laws formulated by the ethnic groups themselves, they do guarantee the recognition of cultural diversity in the European Community. This multicultural character of Europe is reaffirmed by the increasingly closer friendly intra-Community links which involve a two-way free traffic of people and goods requiring everyday encounters and the ability to cope with diversity. Such free two-way traffic demonstrates the interdependence and equal standing of those who are culturally different. It differs from the one-way traffic pattern of immigration which effectively reduces the status of one of the cultures involved. The European solution is to extend the two-way pattern and protection to all ethnic cultures in Europe. Many multicultural interests therefore look to Europe and its 'unity in diversity' measures for a new approach to multicultural education.

The emphasis on interdependence can transform multicultural education initiatives regarded as concessions by the dominant majority into information seeking and rights obtained by equals. This is the fundamental difference between multicultural concerns acknowledged as European and multicultural education as practised with non-territorial immigrant cultures. Although attitudes towards different groups in individual member states may still vary (for example, the needs of Urdu or Turkish speakers may be treated differently from those of Greek speakers), nevertheless, the differences between European and individual state practices are becoming blurred as a result of European legislation for cultural maintenance and protection, and the spread of European Dimension education. Greater equity is more likely to be achieved when the fulfilment of needs related to cultural difference is seen as an entitlement of equals and not dependent on tolerance alone. The proposal to grant voting rights to a number of long settled Turks in Germany is an example. By linking the European Dimension with Education for Citizenship, such an extension of human rights to all parties can become a commitment to action and not just a theoretical construct. In addition, the European Community's commitment to non-European problems (for example, North and South world inequalities) can provide a platform for demonstrating united European action, to which all groups in Europe, including the minorities as part of the whole, can make a contribution.

The European commitment ought to entail that provision for the European Dimension in education should be similar in all the member states. In fact national interests and feelings may limit this. However the socio-political tradition of the European Community is moving towards according to cross-national human rights and other democratic values an equal priority and respect with that given to the knowledge and skills required for economic success. The former values are more readily acknowledged when they are recognized as being, not a well-intentioned, altruistic gesture, but as vital for the frictionless and economically productive running of the Community.

This two-way traffic in turn requires that all cultures, including the ethnic community ones which are the concern of much multicultural education, are not preserved as museum pieces but are prepared to engage in a living dialogue with other cultures, passing the test of not being closed to them. Teaching and teaching materials must reflect both common European ideals and ethnic differences. Encountering such problems of dynamic change helps learners who are studying the European Dimension to analyze the world around them and to avoid bias in doing so.

Outlook

Ideally the principle of mutual interdependence ought be seen as extending to all the cultures of Europe. To achieve this the concept of territoriality would need to be modified and extended to areas where most workers practise a non-territorial, but compact common culture. New workers who wished to live in those areas would be expected to accept this interdependence. Though this is an unlikely prospect at present given the still prevailing ghetto-syndrome, it may yet come about. It would avoid the often bloody striving for power in unequal ethnic situations (Banks and Lynch, 1986). European Community laws, like those of 25 July 1979 or 27 May 1989 which provide for the statutory education of groups such as travellers, or the right to education in the mother tongue, could be used as a precedent for the statutory recognition of all the identities and rights of non-territorial cultures for interdependence and education in Europe.

Extending cultural rights to all who live in Europe is made more complicated by the process of European Community expansion, since the type and amount of attention must be decided by the votes of the entire community, including the minorities. The education task required to achieve the economic, socio-political and attitudinal objectives of living together is a call for openness to and readiness for change.

The Role and Preparation of Teachers

The full mobility of teachers throughout the European Community will eventually enable them to teach, not only their own mother tongues as a foreign language, but also other school subjects in the multicultural Europe, including the European Dimension (Tulasiewicz, 1990). This will make teacher training and employment the shared concern of member states, so that significant differences between them will become problematic.

Organizations like UKCEE are active in disseminating the European Dimension for teachers and have provided them with information about society, school systems, curricula, teaching methods and conditions of employment in Europe (Convey, 1990, 1992). Other agencies, like the Central Bureau and the Centre for Information on Language Teaching, have done the same for efficient language teaching skills.

The European Community is already involved in teacher preparation. Summer Universities and the establishment of Erasmus Networks have been two of the initiatives taken. The third Summer University, at Nantes in 1991, analyzed language policies, including what can be called multilingual respect, cognitive and affective knowledge about Europe, and the norms, behaviour and socio-cultural values found in Europe which include readiness to adjust and to learn from each other.

Multiculturally and politically skilled teachers, unprejudiced, flexible and mobile, must be able to communicate in the new Europe, which means coping with differences. Language awareness facilitates not only ranging through different cultures, but developing an empathy for them. The 'Anthropology of European Society' has emerged as a discrete academic discipline, with 'open multicultural awareness' as a stance to be adopted by teachers. Appropriate pedagogic expertise, like work with topics, supervision of course work, and organization of out of school activities, must be added to the list. Distilling the multicultural European component requires an awareness of and a commitment to the principle of interdependence of cultures. Despite some moves for the ghettoization of education, future teachers must expect to teach diverse groups and be professionally prepared for this.

Supporting European Dimension Initiatives

Government commitment to the European Dimension consists of responses and undertakings given in compliance with Community directives and resolutions, the detailed implementation of which is left to individual member states. The British Government is fully committed to general European initiatives which help raise the level of education, like combating illiteracy and furthering IT/ET. Concern with the living worlds of work and the environment are objectives which a British Government, committed to the raising of standards and a preparation for work, can readily accept. On the other hand, the relative neglect of specific European values and ideals as curriculum elements reflects the primarily economic commitment to European integration of the Government. This neglect, compounded by a reduction of HMI involvement, is bound to reduce the full potential of the intercultural dimension via Europe.

Conclusion

A European Dimension, open to individual interpretations, is a sign of vitality, but at times lacks a focus of aims and methods. The National Curriculum as such does not explicitly restrict, but in the circumstances it is unlikely that the present generation of youngsters will experience a European Dimension beyond some extras in knowledge and exchanges, although no doubt modern foreign languages will thrive. What is urgently needed is good dissemination in schools of the intercultural skills of multicultural education combined with a European Dimension which looks towards interdependence and equality of differences. Continental unification is happening through cooperation, which allows differences and options to flourish freely (Carneiro, 1991). This development is bound to affect multicultural education in an integrated curriculum for all.

References

ANDERSON, L. and BECKER, J. (Eds) (1979) *Schooling for a Global Age*, New York, McGraw Hill.
BANKS, J.A. and LYNCH, J. (Eds) (1986) *Multicultural Education in Western Societies*, London, Holt, Rinehart & Winston.

BELL, G. (1990) 'European curriculum in the primary school', paper from British Council seminar on Teacher education in Europe, London, British Council.

BELL, G. (1992) *Developing a European Dimension in Primary Schools*, London, Fulton.

BLACKLEDGE, R.C.R. (1982) 'Reflections and observations on the CDCC Project No. 1', *Preparation for Life*, Strasbourg, Council of Europe.

BROCK, C. and TULASIEWICZ, W. (Eds) (1992) *Education in a Single Europe*, London, Routledge.

CARNEIRO, R. (1991) 'Revista do Centro de Educacao Europeia', *Europa*, 1/2 avril 1991, Lisboa.

CENTRAL BUREAU FOR EDUCATIONAL VISITS AND EXCHANGES (1989) 'Work experience and work shadowing', in *Schools Unit News*, London.

CITIZENSHIP (1990) *Report of the Commission on Citizenship*, The Speaker's Commission on Citizenship, London, HMSO.

CONVEY, A. (Ed.) (1990) *Teacher Training and 1992*, A Report of the UK Centre for European Education 1989 Conference, London.

CONVEY, A. (Ed.) (1992) *Approaches to the European Dimension in Teacher Education*, London, UKCEE and CBEVE.

COUNCIL (1988) 'Resolution of the Council and the ministers of education meeting within the Council on the European dimension in Education', paper from Council of the European Communities, General Secretariat 24 May, 88/c 177/02, Brussels, European Educational Policy Statements.

COUNCIL (1989) 'Education and training in the European Community, guidelines for the medium term 1989–1992', paper from Council of the European Communities COM (89) 236, Brussels.

COUNCIL OF EUROPE (1983) *Compendium of Information on Intercultural Schemes in Europe, Education of Migrants' Children*, Strasbourg, Council for Cultural Co-operation, School Education Division.

COX, B. (1991) *Cox on Cox, An English Curriculum for the 1990s*, London, Hodder & Stoughton.

CRAFT, A. and BARDELL, G. (Eds) (1984) *Curriculum Opportunities in a Multicultural Society*, London, Harper Education Series.

DEPARTMENT OF EDUCATION AND SCIENCE (1989) *English for Ages 5 to 16*, London, HMSO.

DEPARTMENT OF EDUCATION AND SCIENCE (1990) *Modern Foreign Languages for Ages 11 to 16*, London, HMSO.

DEPARTMENT OF EDUCATION AND SCIENCE (1991) *The European Dimension in Education*, A Statement of the UK Government's Policy and Report of Activities Undertaken to Implement the EC Resolution of May 24, 1988 on the European Dimension in Education, London.

DEPARTMENT OF EDUCATION AND SCIENCE (1992) *Policy Models: A Guide to developing and implementing European Dimension policies in LEAs, schools and colleges*, London, HMSO.

EDIT AND EUROEDNEWS, see Appendix Three.

EUROPA (1991) see Carneiro above.

EUROPEAN STUDIES PROJECT (1991) This project, which started in 1986, is directed by R. Anderson and is situated in the Ulster Folk and Transport Museum, Cultra, County Down, Northern Ireland and is being disseminated in 1992.

GIBSON, J. (1991) 'Europe's place in the world' in UK Centre for European Education, *Edit*, no. 1, London.

GOODSON, I.F. and McGIVNEY, V. (1985) *European Dimensions and the Secondary School Curriculum*, London, The Falmer Press.

KING, A.S. (1992) 'The Multicultural Dimension of the National Curriculum: an INSET project' *Cambridge Journal of Education*, **22**(1), pp. 17–23.

Witold Tulasiewicz

MITTINS, B. (1991) *Language Awareness for Teachers*, Milton Keynes, Open University Press.
NATIONAL CURRICULUM COUNCIL (1990a) *Curriculum Guidance 8, Education for Citizenship*, York, National Curriculum Council.
NATIONAL CURRICULUM COUNCIL (1990b) *Curriculum Guidance 3, The Whole Curriculum*, York, National Curriculum Council.
NATIONAL CURRICULUM COUNCIL (1991) *News Issue*, No. 5, February 1991, York, National Curriculum Council.
PEACOCK, D. (1985) 'Europe in the school curriculum. Raising the issues' *Euroednews*, **17**, London, UK Centre for European Education.
SCHOOL EXAMINATIONS AND ASSESSMENT COUNCIL (1991) *Exploring European Harmonisation Post-16*, European Colloquium Report, London, HMSO.
SHENNAN, M. (1991) 'Preparation for Life in European Society' in id., *Teaching About Europe*, London, Council of Europe and Cassell.
SLATER, J. (1990) *European Awareness Pilot Project* sponsored by the DES in collaboration with the Central Bureau for Educational Visits and Exchanges, the UK Centre of European Education and the Society of Education Officers, Central Bureau, London.
TULASIEWICZ, W. (1990) in TULASIEWICZ, W. and ADAMS, A. Eds (1990) *Teachers' Expectations and Teaching Reality*, London, Routledge.
TULASIEWICZ, W. (1991) co-directed an EC-funded pilot research project, *Comparative studies of multicultural classrooms in the EEC*. Fifteen researchers from three Community countries took part. The first phase was completed in October 1991. A research publication by ADAMS, A., CONVEY, A., TAVERNER, D., TULASIEWICZ, W. and TURNER, K. (1992) *The Changing European Classroom: Multicultural Schooling and the New Europe*, is published by the Department of Education, University of Cambridge, Cambridge.
WILLIAMS, R. (1981) *Culture*, London, Fontana.

Appendix One

From the NCC Citizenship Task Group (1990).

EUROPEAN DIMENSION: NCC DEFINITION

The major purpose of the European Dimension Resolution is to strengthen pupils' sense of European identity; to prepare them to take part in the economic and social development of the Community following the European Single Act; to improve their knowledge of the European Community and of its member states; and to inform them of the significance of the cooperation between those states and the other countries of Europe and of the world.

The European dimension in education should enable pupils to live and work with a degree of competence in other European countries, to reflect critically on experiences in them so as to give an informed understanding of the predicaments and aspirations of other Europeans in order to reflect critically on or challenge existing perceptions.

EUROPEAN DIMENSION: AIMS

The aims of promoting the European dimension for pupils would be to:

- inform the whole curriculum and act as a focus point for pupils' acquisition of knowledge and skills acquired in various curriculum areas;

- promote a sense of European identity, including the provision of first hand experience where appropriate;
- help pupils to acquire a view of Europe as a multicultural, multilingual community which includes the UK;
- enable pupils to acquire knowledge, skills and experiences which enable them to live and work in Europe comfortably but not uncritically;
- prepare young people to take part in the economic and social development of the community and make them aware of opportunities and challenges;
- develop knowledge of economic and social aspects;
- encourage awareness of the variety of histories, geographies and circumstances;
- further an awareness of European development past and present with 1992 only a stage;
- promote an understanding of common European ideals while developing an awareness of Europe's interdependence with the rest of the world.

Appendix Two

From The Statement of the UK Government's Policy and Report of Activities undertaken to implement the EC Resolution of May 24, 1988, on the European Dimension in Education (DES, 1991).

The Objectives of the European Dimension in Education

The Government has been and will continue to be active in promoting the objectives of the EC Resolution on the European Dimension in education. The Government's policies are aimed at:

- helping pupils and students to acquire a view of Europe as a multi-cultural, multi-lingual community which includes the UK;
- encouraging awareness of the variety of European histories, geographies and cultures;
- preparing young people to take part in the economic and social development of Europe and making them aware of the opportunities and challenges that arise;
- encouraging interest in and improving competence in other European languages;
- imparting knowledge of political, economic and social developments, past, present and future, including knowledge about the origins, workings and role of the EC;
- promoting a sense of European identity, through first hand experience of other countries where appropriate;
- promoting an understanding of the EC's interdependence with the rest of Europe, and with the rest of the world.

Appendix Three

There are a number of UK organizations, some with sister branches in other Community countries, concerned with the European Dimension. One is *The Central Bureau for Educational Visits and Exchanges (CBEVE)* which regularly publishes *Schools Unit News*. It has also published (1991) *European Awareness Developmental Projects Report No. 1*. Another is *The UK Centre for European Education (UKCEE)* which regularly publishes the news sheet *Euroednews* and the magazine *Edit* (European Dimension in

Teaching) which gives more detailed accounts of European Dimension schemes. The CBEVE is concerned with exchanges, the UKCEE with dissemination of information and resources. They administer European Schools and Colleges awards and other activities. *Scottish Modern Studies*, the *European Journal of Teacher Education* and especially *Teaching About Europe* must also be mentioned.

The concept of the European Dimension has spawned several research projects. Among those not listed above is G. Antonouris' work which has resulted in a useful pack for teachers from The Nottingham Trent University (Nottingham Polytechnic). The joint University of Central England (Birmingham Polytechnic) and Roehampton Institute of HE project attempts an institutional model for the preparation of European teachers.

Chapter 19

Black and Anti-racist Perspectives on the National Curriculum and Government Educational Policy

Maud Blair and Madeleine Arnot

The National Curriculum represents a particular selection and organization of knowledge. It compromises, like any other curriculum, between political and educational understandings about what should constitute legitimate school knowledge and how it should be transmitted. In other words, it establishes the priorities of the educational system in a particular political and economic context.

Taken from the perspective of those concerned about the education of black children within British society, this context is as important as the content of each subject defined by the legislation and its working group. The political climate makes sense of recent reforms of the school system and reveals the intended purposes and likely advantages and disadvantages for particular groups of pupils and for different types of schools. The range of strategies needed to tackle this complex area is more likely to be revealed if we take account of the range of educational policies in which the National Curriculum is situated.

The last thirty years have witnessed many attempts by central and local government and schools to tackle the problems associated with differences in educational achievement between white, black and ethnic minority pupils in Britain.[1] Accounts such as those by Kirp (1979), Mullard (1982) and Tomlinson (1980, 1983) and more recently Troyna and Williams (1986) demonstrate the shifting paradigms of government thinking — from concern about immigrant education, racial disadvantage and 'underachievement' to later, multicultural education. Official responses to such problems have been variously described as those of assimilation, integration and cultural pluralism, although the boundaries between such political approaches have never been clear (Mullard, 1982).

A number of themes can be drawn from the various academic and political commentaries on government policy in this area. Agreement can be reached that there has been no consistent or nationally coordinated policy on racial differentiation in education in the post-war period. Nor has there been a clear allocation of responsibilities for initiating new strategies to tackle the difficulties faced by black pupils in the educational system. On the whole, central government strategy has been to stress the autonomy given to local education authorities and schools by the 1944 Education Act and therefore to delegate responsibilities for any particular social inequality to schools and, in the last instance, to teachers as agents of change (Arnot, 1986, 1989).

The National Curriculum, in this regard, is no different. Teachers are being asked to put flesh on the bones of the curriculum skeleton, to design for themselves the cross-curricular dimensions and to find ways to raise the performance of all children within their own schools. For those committed to concepts of multi-culturalism, the encouragement to promote cultural diversity will be welcomed, particularly if feasible within the programmes of study now provided for each subject. For others, the search for spaces in which to work will be more frustrating, particularly if they are committed to challenging racism through their professional practice. The possibilities available to teachers, we want to argue, are conditional, not merely upon their good will or extended knowledge of a particular subject, but upon receiving support at the institutional level for their practice.

Black communities and those committed to anti-racist education have long believed that improving the educational performance of black children depends upon the political and financial relationship between central and local government. This relationship will affect more than the amount of resources available to train teachers to become aware of the issues and to develop appropriate curriculum materials. It will also affect the extent to which the necessary political climate is created in which racism in education can be seriously challenged in British society.

In the last few years the relationship between the DES/DFE, LEAs and schools has changed considerably, not just with the introduction of the National Curriculum and national assessment but with, amongst other things, the introduction of local management of schools, the reduction of local authority funds and responsibilities and the setting up of new types of schools (for example, city technology colleges and grant maintained schools). Most commentators notice particularly the enhanced role of the DFE in developing and implementing the National Curriculum. However for those involved in the development of multicultural or anti-racist education, the shifting priorities of the Home Office funding policies are equally, if not more, important. Paradoxically, while it has cut back the funds available for this type of educational initiative under Section 11 of the Local Government Act 1966, the Home Office, at the same time, has published a report that draws attention to the existence of racial harassment in schools and society generally (Home Office, 1989).

These developments are particularly significant for teachers working in multicultural schools, but they also affect those teachers who are committed to developing multicultural/anti-racist education in predominantly white schools. There are new restrictions now operating on school-based race equality initiatives which are likely to prevent the implementation of a multicultural dimension within the National Curriculum. At the same time, the need is just as great for that work to go ahead.

The response of the Conservative Party and what has been called the New Right in the last decade to issues of 'race' is therefore not an insignificant context for the National Curriculum, even if it can be shown to be contradictory and ill thought out (Rich, 1986; Jones, 1989). It is important in our view that schools and teachers are aware of the hidden politics of race behind such educational reforms. At the same time it is essential not to be defeated by those political influences and to develop coherent responses.

In this chapter, therefore, we intend to analyse the likelihood of institutional support in the context of the reality facing schools today. The first part briefly discusses the responses of black communities and the anti-racist educational movement to the Education Reform Act and their perception of the possibilities of improving the educational performance of black children and of tackling racism within schools in the new educational structure. The second part of the chapter outlines the shifting priorities of central government, especially in relation to targeted funding for black pupils' education and the official encouragement being given to institutions to tackle racial incidents and harassment. In the conclusion we suggest a range of national and institutional strategies which, we believe are needed, if the multicultural dimension of the National Curriculum is to be successfully implemented.

Anti-racism and the National Curriculum

The voices of black communities and educational practitioners are rarely heard in educational debates and have had apparently very little impact on the structuring of the new curriculum (Arnot, 1989; Burton and Weiner, 1990; Davies, Holland and Minhas, 1990) not least because such communities are positioned at the margins of government policy-making and are poorly represented in the teaching profession itself. Black communities historically share many of the concerns of those committed to anti-racist education, even if the latter have not often actively sought out the views of black parents and students (Gurnah, 1992).

The experience of powerlessness was quickly felt by black groups as the Education Reform Bill proceeded onto the statute books. Conferences held, for example, by the National Convention of Black Teachers, by the Centre for Urban and Educational Studies, the Afro-Caribbean Resource Centre (ACER) and the London Strategic Policy Unit revealed the anger and frustration in black communities at not being consulted directly over the proposals (ACER, 1987; Tomlinson, 1987). The experience of the CRE was no different, the only victory being a commitment by the DES to support the development of a code of practice for educational institutions (later published as CRE, 1989), rather than having such codes made part of the new legislation.

Since 1988, a number of concerns have been expressed about the provisions of the Education Reform Act — especially the possibility of increasing racial segregation of schools being encouraged through grant maintained schools and open enrolment (Hardy and Vieler-Porter, 1990; Glare, 1990). The National Curriculum similarly attracted a considerable amount of attention. Anxiety was expressed that the multicultural nature of British society would not be incorporated into the design of particular subjects, especially since there did not appear to be any black representation on the subject working groups and the majority of subject groups failed to take seriously their terms of reference (Arnot, 1989; Burton and Weiner, 1990; Davies, et al., 1990). Indeed, the Mathematics subject working group's report was even openly hostile to the concept of multicultural education.

Increasingly the response of black and anti-racist groups has been to identify a range of potential problems. For example, little official concern has been expressed publicly about the likelihood of cultural bias in national tests (except in an appendix to the Task Group on Assessment and Testing (TGAT) Report).[2] With no official programme for the in-service training of teachers, it is unlikely that low or inaccurate assessment of black pupils' abilities will be challenged. As the National Curriculum statutory guidance was published, it became clear that the home languages of ethnic minority pupils were not to be put on a par with modern foreign (European) languages and the multilingual diversity in schools and the needs of bilingual pupils were not being adequately recognized (Murshid, 1990). The provisions for a collective act of worship and religious education that is 'broadly Christian' also appears to fly in the face of current developments in multifaith education in schools.

In light of these concerns, it is not surprising, therefore, that the National Curriculum has received a somewhat hostile reception from those committed to anti-racism (*Multicultural Teaching*, 1988, 1989). More recently, however, some commentators have identified the possibility of using the National Curriculum to improve black children's performance (for example Anderson, 1989; Eggleston, 1990). They have focused particularly on the possibilities of raising teachers' expectations of black pupils' achievement through national assessment and the publication of results and of reducing racial differentiation of pupils by teaching a common curriculum. They also pointed to the fact that teachers would still have a certain autonomy because the prescriptions for the content of each subject do not determine either the pedagogy or the exact syllabus. They argued, therefore, that theoretically anti-racist education could still be sustained within the National Curriculum. Further, even though forced into competition for pupils, schools could develop performance indicators which incorporate equal opportunities as part of their development plan and encourage black pupils' achievement (Gill, 1989 and Chapter 20 in this volume). Others see the reform of school governing bodies as a chance to work closely with black communities and parents (Gurnah, 1989).

However such expectations are always likely to be problematic given the ideological underpinnings of the new curriculum framework. Articles in *Multicultural Teaching* and speeches at the NAME conferences and a range of academic authors have repeatedly pointed to the assimilationist approach adopted by the New Right and the ethnocentrism revealed in the content of particular subjects as defined by the subject working groups.[3]

It is difficult for anti-racist campaigners to respond to the new school reforms as it is still unclear whether black students will be any better off with the new curriculum and school structure. Although they will be entitled to receive the same education as other children in the school system, will they in reality be given the same chances to succeed? Will the new legislation make any difference to the known high proportion of black students amongst the categories of those suspended from school or might it lead to the worsening of the situation (Gillborn, 1988; Cooper, Upton and Smith, 1991)?

As committed teachers attempt to regenerate anti-racist work in schools, more attention is likely to be paid to the level of resources available to meet the needs of black children, on the one hand, and to implement race equality initiatives through in-service provision or curriculum development, on the other. Funding arrangements signify the government's underlying intentions and can shape teachers' work just as effectively as curriculum policy. In the next section, we shall investigate the tensions within government policy between supporting a multicultural dimension of the National Curriculum and targeting funding to help the performance of black pupils while at the same time cutting back resources for the maintained education sector.

Funding Multicultural Anti-racist Initiatives

Ouseley (1990) argues that one of the main reasons for the lack of significant progress in race equality has been the absence of a national strategy to tackle not only 'race' but other forms of social inequality. Instead there are a range of different funding strategies that have no obvious overall rationale but which directly affect the opportunities schools have to improve the educational experiences and the performance of black children and to reduce racial conflict through curricular reform. They also have a bearing on the extent to which the teaching profession as a whole can educate itself in the principles and practices of multicultural and anti-racist education.

Of particular importance to the promotion of race equality through education are the so-called formula funding and Section 11 funding; the first derives from the Education Reform Act 1988, the latter from the much older Local Government Act 1966. However, while formula funding concerns mainstream educational provision, Section 11 funding is premised upon a concept of positive discrimination designed to cater for the perceived special needs of children whose origins were in the New Commonwealth and Pakistan (Guy and Menter, 1992). Both sources of funding currently affect the staffing and resources of a school. In-service provision for teachers is controlled by a third important source of funds — so called GEST funding (Grants for Education and Training). Below, we shall briefly consider the concerns of black communities and those involved in promoting race equality about these current funding arrangements.

At present, formula funding affects the distribution of finance to schools. No longer will local education authorities manage school budgets, since under local management of schools the funds are allocated directly to them. The formula is based largely on the number and age of pupils on the roll. The policy signifies a deliberate reversal of the earlier approach to the funding of local education authorities. The concept of positive discrimination meant that extra funds could be allocated to those authorities who could demonstrate particular needs. The Grant Related Expenditure, now abolished, using a range of indicators resulted in more help being offered to inner city and 'poorer' schools. Formula funding, in contrast, is likely to reward popular schools and remove funding from those with falling rolls (a worrying possibility if there is 'white flight' from schools with high proportions of black pupils). Not surprisingly, therefore, there is concern by and for black communities about the potential for the new financial arrangements to be disproportionately damaging to the education of black children, most of whom attend inner city schools (Troyna, 1990; Hardy and Vieler-Porter, 1990; Guy and Menter, 1992). A key question for local education authorities is whether they can use the formula funding to improve the quality of schools which are in difficulties or to support schools who are unable to supplement their incomes with financial assistance from parents and the community.[4]

In 1984, local authority control over educational finance was reduced when the DES took on powers to allocate sums of money to LEAs for matters that it thought important. This support took the form of Education Support Grants (ESGs) of up to 75 per cent of the cost of each project which was a considerable incentive to schools starved of resources. A number of ESG projects on Educational Needs in a Multiethnic Society were set up between 1986 to 1988, following the publication of the Swann Report (DES, 1985). In 1986, 'teaching and planning of the curriculum in a multi-ethnic society' was a national priority area for in-service teacher education.

The onset of the 1990s however, brought significant changes in the government's criteria for allocating such funds to local authorities and saw a decided shift in priorities to the management and curriculum issues implicated in the 1988 Education Reform Act. ESG funds were combined with local authority training grants (LEATGS) into one central budget known as GEST (Grants for Education Support and Training), but whilst ESG funding had been used by some authorities to pay the salaries of specialist staff in multicultural education, GEST funds are strictly for training. It is again up to local authorities to decide how much of this local budget should be used to train teachers on race related issues.

As one of the cross-curricular dimensions of the National Curriculum, multicultural education would appear to have been placed more centrally in curriculum development, with local authorities given responsibility to ensure its implementation as part of their mainstream budget planning. The practical application of this theory, however, leaves less room for optimism. In the first place, it assumes a commitment by local authorities to race equality issues, which up until now has either been largely absent or often based on misguided, if not questionable, theoretical principles (Troyna, 1992). Second, local management of schools effectively places the responsibility for employing specialist staff and for training teachers in cross-curricular dimensions on the schools themselves. The extent to which schools will be prepared to use their limited budgets in this way is now being tested.

Some of these problems of resourcing multicultural/anti-racist initiatives had (particularly after the publication of the Swann Report) been partially obviated by the availability of Section 11 funding. Increasingly these grants were used for multicultural education, even in predominantly white schools. Centres for multicultural education were set up in various parts of the country and curriculum advisers and support teachers were employed to assist schools in understanding and implementing the principles of *Education for All*, as well as continuing the task of providing language support for children whose first language was not English.

Section 11 funding has a history which has been described as similar to a television soap opera — tragedy, farce, melodrama and pathos (Dorn and Hibbert, 1987). These government grants were introduced in the context of the 1960s, when harsh racially biased immigration policies were to be softened by strategies to assimilate those immigrants already in residence in the UK (Arnot, 1986). Section 11 funds identified ethnic minority children as having special needs which differentiated them from other British children. Cultural diversity of itself was interpreted as disadvantaging, especially if children were not English speakers.

These funds were initially distributed to schools which had a substantial proportion (more than 2 per cent) of children from Commonwealth origin who had been resident in Britain for less than ten years and whose language and customs differed from those of the community. The finances, although considerable, were not monitored (Dorn and Hibbert estimated that in 1985/8 Section 11 expenditure came to £110 million). The funds were being distributed more, it seems, to compensate schools for the presence of black children than to cater for the real needs of those children and their communities, (Hibbert, 1983; Dorn and Hibbert, 1987). Such communities, although supposedly the beneficiaries, were not being consulted about the use of these resources. This was particularly worrying if schools and local authorities were using the funds to support much reduced mainstream educational budgets.

By 1982 new criteria were published for Section 11 funding which tried to address some of the many criticisms made of it (see Dorn and Hibbert, 1987, for a full account). Not only were the criteria for application changed, but post holders were to be identified, consultation with the communities was necessary, and monitoring of the use of funds was introduced. Increasingly projects funded by Section 11 were to focus attention on the needs of black pupils rather than on general educational purposes.

This revision of Section 11 funding had the potential, on the one hand, to benefit black communities. On the other hand, it was also seen as an attempt to challenge the multicultural and anti-racist initiatives being developed by Section 11 teachers (often black) as well as to isolate black pupils' needs from mainstream educational concerns. However, some critics went further and pointed to the underlying ideological assumptions behind Section 11 criteria which originated in the 1960s. Dorn and Hibbert (1987) describe the legacy of Section 11 funding as one which,

> prefers voluntarism to compulsion, inexplicitness to explicitness, assimilation to antiracism, marginal rather than mainstream spending and is pre-occupied with racial disadvantage rather than racial discrimination (p. 60)

In 1990 after the National Curriculum had been established, the Home Office published new policy objectives for Section 11 funds for education, housing and employment, training, etc. The aims and objectives for schools are discussed in the following way:

> The Government's aim for Section 11 funding in education is that it should be used to remove barriers to true equality of educational opportunity for ethnic minority groups, where mainstream programmes alone are not sufficient to remove those barriers. The education service needs to equip ethnic minority groups with the knowledge, skills and understanding they require to participate fully and on equal terms in all aspects of British life while maintaining their own cultural identity.

Specific objectives for Section 11 funding are now as follows:

- to enable ethnic minority pupils aged under 5, particularly those whose mother tongue is not English, to gain the language competence and learning skills necessary for the early years of primary education;
- to give school-aged children whose mother tongue is not English a command of English which, as far as possible, is equal to that of their peers;
- to help school-age children from ethnic minorities to achieve at the same level as their peers in all areas of the curriculum;
- to strengthen ties between schools and the parents of ethnic minority pupils, where those ties are hard to establish because of parents' lack of English or because of cultural or social factors, so as to enable parents to become more fully involved in the education of their children and in the work of the schools;

• to offer ethnic minority pupils pastoral support in school which meets their needs (Home Office, 1990, p. 5).

The new criteria for applying for such funds (which are now to be limited to £100 million) are stringent indeed and clearly linked to the educational perform-ance of ethnic minority pupils. All projects must indicate the number of pupils they are intended to help, the particular needs being tackled through the project, the methods to be used, the techniques for monitoring the use of funds, the likely and actual effectiveness of the strategies in terms of improving performance. All projects are to be located within mainstream classrooms except, for example, those promoting better links between parents and schools. Even here the work with parents is to be assessed in terms of its effect on the performance of the ethnic minority child.

So how are black communities likely to respond to these new criteria? The aims and objectives are appealing, especially as the Home Office seems to recognize the contribution of ethnic minority groups to British society. The possibility also exists that the differences in academic performance of pupils from a range of ethnic origins, revealed by the Swann Committee and by ILEA Research and Statistics Branch (1990), are more likely to be recognized; the specific needs of these groups are therefore more likely to be catered for. Section 11 funding clearly is intended to be used particularly to remove the language barrier, an objective that will be supported by many black and ethnic minority communities especially in the context of national assessment.

However, the reliance of government on such a cultural and linguistic deficit model of ethnic minority communities is just as likely to generate feelings of anxiety and distrust, especially if it leads to the stigmatization of black children as 'failures' or the withdrawal of these children from mainstream education to special English classes to improve their language skills (a pattern that has already been shown to be discriminatory by a CRE Report (1986)). There is also still an as-sumption in the new criteria that black children and the black communities need to change themselves in order to overcome their disadvantages in what is already a 'fair and just society'. The thinking which lies behind the policy is revealed in the following comments: 'Good community relations cannot be achieved by gov-ernment action alone'. They 'must evolve from mutual understanding and respect among people of all races, which in turn requires a freedom from fear of racial violence, hatred or harassment and the removal of other barriers to equality of opportunity' (Home Office, 1990, para. 2). The reliance on self-help rather than government intervention is clearly expressed in the following passage of the re-port:

The government welcomes the contribution to national life already being made by members of ethnic minorities, and positively encourages mem-bers of ethnic minorities to become active citizens, participating in and contributing to mainstream economic and social development. It supports programmes designed to develop confidence, competence and self help among members of the ethnic minorities, to ensure fair access to services and training for employment and to encourage enterprise. (Home Office, 1990; para. 4)

Multicultural education is now clearly defined as outside the realm of Section 11 funds. Paragraph 11 reads, 'The Government will not fund programmes aimed at raising achievement generally through multicultural approaches' even though it accepts that, 'members of ethnic minorities, a growing proportion of whom were born in the United Kingdom, are an integral part of British society' (Home Office, 1990, para. 1). The main objectives of the new criteria are to focus specifically on English language teaching for children whose mother tongue is not English, rather than promoting the more challenging educational aims of extending the traditional 'British' curriculum, or of challenging racial prejudice in the school setting.

Black parents have been insisting since the late 1960s that, in order for their children to achieve academically, something needs to be done about racism. Targeted funding has been an important source of support for efforts to challenge racism in education. Yet there is no acknowledgment in the new policy criteria of the need to tackle racism as a national priority, despite the evidence of the relatively powerless position of black communities in Britain and the corrosive effects of racism on so called good community relations (Braham, Rattansi and Skellington, 1992). Pressure is not therefore being brought to bear on schools to tackle racial harassment and violence, even though they are being asked to find ways of improving black children's educational performance.

The message implicit in these new funding arrangements ties in, therefore, with what many black and anti-racist organizations see as the new version of assimilationist philosophy and ethnocentrism underlying the National Curriculum and central government policy (e.g. Davies, Holland and Minhas, 1990; Burton and Wiener, 1990). The suspicion is that government interest lies less in the direction of promoting 'racial harmony' and more in the direction of reducing the overall spending on Section 11 by setting up exceptionally inhibiting criteria. The reduced amount of monies now available suggests a determination to reduce this source of support for schools at a time ironically when not only is multicultural education meant to be a responsibility of all schools as part of the whole curriculum, but also when the incidents of racial harassment and violence in schools are reportedly on the increase.

Racial Attacks and Harassment

A year before the Home Office issued its new criteria for Section 11 funds, the Inter-Departmental Racial Attacks Group published its report on 'The Response to Racial Attacks and Harassment: guidance for statutory agencies'. The foreword which was signed by representatives from six ministries (including the DES) stated that:

> Racial attacks and racial harassment are still a serious problem for people from the ethnic minorities in some areas of Britain. Such incidents are very distressing and frightening for the victims. But more than that, they can do damage to community relations generally: where one community lives in fear of abuse or attack by members of another, a wedge is driven between them, and the ethnic minorities can begin to lose confidence in the institutions of British society.

267

The Report urged that especially for local statutory agencies, 'it is vital that visible and vigorous action is taken to combat racial attacks and harassment', which they defined broadly 'to refer to the whole range of incidents from murder to graffiti' (Home Office, 1989, para. 9). The reason for this broad definition is that

> Some incidents. . .will be recognized immediately as serious offences by the police and other agencies that encounter them. There may, however, be a tendency to view some minor incidents as unpleasant but essentially trivial anti-social behaviour that does not warrant any special attention. We should like to make it clear from the outset that we do not share this view. . . . It is important to recognize that when repeated over time, apparently trivial incidents of this kind create an insidious atmosphere of racial harassment and intimidation. . . . We are in no doubt that these apparently 'trivial' racial incidents are seriously damaging the quality of life for members of the minority communities in some areas of the country. (Home Office, 1989, para. 11)

Although the actual incidence of racial attacks is hard to assess, the statistics of reported incidents suggest that there is an increasing and 'worryingly large' problem particularly in metropolitan areas with high concentrations of ethnic minority communities.[5] The Report urged all local authorities to recognize the existence of the problem, consult with local communities and draw up an explicit policy for dealing with racial harassment. In the context of education the Report recognizes that:

> Racial harassment in educational establishments can only undermine the confidence of pupils and students. A pupil will find it hard to pay attention in class if he [she] is worrying about what will happen to him [her] in break or after school. Racial harassment therefore presents a serious obstacle to equality of opportunities and it is Government policy that LEAs should attach priority to dealing with it. (Home Office 1989, para. 125, [our additions])

LEAs are likely to be effective in tackling racial harassment if they 'require schools and colleges to draw up their own individual policies for responding to racial incidents' (Home Office, 1989, para. 128). Interestingly, courses on personal and social development were highlighted as providing 'an opportunity for direct teaching and discussion of race relations'. The Report recommended that racial harassment should feature in discussions between teachers and students, be put on the agenda of governors' meetings, and be brought up in discussions with parents so that there is a 'shared recognition of the problem'.

The Report also reaffirms the principles outlined by the Swann Committee when it urged schools and colleges in predominantly white areas to tackle racial prejudice and intolerance through in-service training courses, staff development and curriculum development.

However, as many teachers already know to their cost, racism is not an easy matter to take up in a school, nor is it an easy matter for parents to discuss. Further, without adequate finance, it is not clear that schools will be able to adopt many of the excellent suggestions contained in this report. It is ironic that, as we have already indicated, the sources of funding previously used to promote precisely the examples of good practice praised by the Home Office report have either been removed, or they now preclude anti-racist work, or the funds are so low that attempts to tackle racial harassment will not receive anything like the importance this Report recognizes that it requires.

There is a danger that by raising the issue of racism without adequate input, schools can turn inwards, and racial stereotypes can be confirmed rather than challenged. Teachers may rely on black children or their parents being experts on their own culture and customs or may consult black pupils (even at a very young age) about what the school should do about racism in, for example, the playground. Predominantly white schools may find no reason to develop policies in this area (Blair and Woods, 1992).

Some teachers may be of the opinion that whatever positive anti-racist measures are introduced into the school, they will be undermined by the children's home environment, especially if they come from a white working class family. Or teachers may take the view that it is better not 'to make an issue' of racial harassment because it might encourage a white backlash. Another view is that teaching children about racism is and should be the responsibility of the family (Bagley, 1992).

However, as Tony Jeffs (1988, p. 34) points out:

To leave political education to the family is to consign it to the realms of chance, especially for those who emanate from homes in which 'politics' plays no overt part, as it helps to ensure that they are denied the opportunity to gain, during their formative years, an informed understanding of the discourse of politics.

Clearly, the approach taken by school governing bodies is a critical factor in determining how policies on racial harassment are developed. Governing bodies need to place the question of equality of opportunity firmly on their agendas so that it permeates all aspects of the decisions they make for their schools. But as Deem, Brehony and Hemmings (1992) observe, governors are being faced by a dilemma because the free market philosophy of recent legislation conflicts with notions of social justice. It is unclear at the moment what the driving principles for schools will be, what with the increasing competition between schools. According to their findings, Deem, Brehony and Hemmings conclude that governing bodies are so constituted that those with most power are least conscious of issues of social justice. Middle-class parents and other representatives (for example, party political representatives) have greatest access to the dominant culture of the education system. They, therefore, have 'the cultural capital' to ensure that decisions are made in their favour. It goes without saying that those with least power are least able to influence what goes on in governors' meetings and to influence decisions which take into account disenfranchised groups. How much influence are black parents and anti-racist governors really likely to have in this political environment? It is not surprising that the new composition of governing bodies has already been perceived as 'yet another example of how the State seeks to undermine the anti-racist approach to education' (Rice, 1989).

Suggestions have been made that, with proper organization, it is possible to mobilize black parents to exert some influence on school governors' decisions even in predominantly white schools. Those black parents, who work collectively through local pressure groups sharing and communicating their concerns to the school governing body, are not as easy to marginalize. Whilst they may not have sufficient influence on school policy, black parents can at least ensure that they are not rendered invisible. This might be a more effective way to make parental power meaningful to the black community than trying to change school policy by being in a minority on the governing body (Forbes, 1989).

For school policies on racial harassment to be successful, top-down and bottom-up cooperation is necessary. Bagley (1992) illustrates the extent to which anti-racist INSET is fraught with problems and difficulties unless supported by a committed LEA and conducted by a carefully selected team of individuals. The team has to work in a united way within agreed parameters and definitions and be highly skilled in facilitating group work between teachers. If the team is not coordinated centrally and is not professional in their approach, teachers can be left feeling resentful and resistant. The report of the MacDonald Inquiry into the murder of Ahmed Iqbal Ullah at Burnage High School in Manchester argued that any in-service education of teachers that focuses on racism should not be developed by schools in isolation, but should take account of the social and political context of local communities (MacDonald, Bhavnani, Khan and John, 1989).

There is, unfortunately, no agreement on the sorts of strategies teachers can use to tackle racial discrimination and racial harassment effectively. The CRE (1989), for example, published their own recommendations on what should constitute a school's code of practice to avoid racial discrimination in, amongst other areas, admissions, assessment, exclusions, allocation to teaching groups and work experience. Recently Troyna and Hatcher (1991) have recommended that teachers adopt a child-centred approach to tackle racial incidents. Every child's circumstances, they argue, need to be analysed and taken into account when deciding what practical steps to take in cases of racial harassment or violence. This strategy, however, does not take into account the possibility that teachers or playground supervisors may unwittingly instigate a violent incident themselves through their handling of disputes between children, through comments or through their routine interactions with black children. There is also the problem that a child-centred approach might potentially encourage complacency on the issue of racism in those schools where there is no obvious racial conflict between children.

Such an individualized approach would have to take account of the fact that teachers may hold social stereotypes of children and find themselves grading the same offences differently when the perpetrators are of different sexes, social class or ethnic origin. We already know, for example, that Afro-Caribbean boys in secondary schools are disproportionally represented in suspensions from school, and that this may be a result of teachers interpreting their behaviour in particular ways (CRE, 1985; Gillborn, 1990; Cooper, Upton and Smith, 1991). Sometimes the immediate cause of the pupil's suspension might be rudeness (in one form or another) towards teachers. However, teachers often underestimate the depth of feeling and the sense of injustice that is generated by racist abuse and therefore only deal with its aftermath. How are violent reactions to racist abuse to be graded for both educative and punitive purposes?

Gordon makes an important criticism of the Report on Racial Attacks when he points out its tendency 'to treat racial violence and harassment as though they were unconnected to racism, sometimes even as if racism did not exist' (Gordon, 1990, p. 48). He recommends instead that:

Racial violence and harassment must be treated as crimes when that is what they involve but they must, at the same time, be understood and treated as aspects of racism. This is not an academic point but one which has immense practical implications. If racial attacks are simply crimes, then the answers, if not easy, may at least in some respects be clear: better police responses, better physical security arrangements, better support for victims and so on. But if racial attacks are aspects of racism, then the answers are wider than this. What is needed above all is preventive action and that must be action to challenge and undermine the racism, the racist culture, which gives rise to it. (Gordon, 1990, p. 49)

The Home Office report suggests that less time be spent on measuring the size of the problem and that teachers concentrate more of their energies on 'looking for practical ways of improving the response to the problem' (Home Office, 1989, para. 26). All local authorities should have a copy of this report which, although by no means perfect, provides useful guidelines for dealing with racist harassment in different types of institutions. Certainly the document could be used to trigger the sorts of school policy development that it recommends.

Conclusion

The success of anti-racist initiatives has depended to a large extent on the importance given to them by local authorities and the availability of funds from central government. Some local authorities succeeded in introducing reforms which were potentially far reaching in their pursuit of 'race' equality. In some cases, these initiatives were undermined by a range of issues, such as lack of commitment, abuse of resources, general inefficiency at a local level or the controversies and contradictory assumptions underlying the allocation of resources.

However, even if not totally successful, at least such initiatives in anti-racist education were able to develop as a result of the belief in teacher autonomy and the opportunities for local educational planning (Arnot, 1991).

As a result of the National Curriculum, teachers today have far less autonomy, local education authorities are being undermined and the political climate is more hostile to anti-racist education. Schools cannot now depend on having the resources to fund multicultural and anti-racist curriculum development, nor upon the existence of a team of multicultural advisors working through local education authorities. The curriculum materials teachers have developed thus far now need to be adapted to the new requirements of the National Curriculum and its attainment targets.

Targeted funding through Section 11 is more tightly controlled and its use is more prescriptive. Far more is now dependent on an individual school's commitment to tackling racism and improving the performance of black children. While the latter could be encouraged because of the publication of results and the competition between schools for pupils, on the face of it many schools may well consider that the issue of racism is of low priority. Yet, as we have argued, the two issues are intimately linked and without effective strategies for dealing with racial incidents and teaching about racism, the educational performance of black children is unlikely to be raised.

The multicultural dimension of the National Curriculum is being asked to carry considerable responsibility for improving the education of black children and teaching about 'race'. Teachers, without any guidance from central government and its agencies and without the help of in-service training, are being encouraged to develop an especially difficult cross-curricular dimension. The multicultural approach should theoretically be integrated into all school subjects *and* should encourage all children to think critically about racial issues in society.

In the event, schools will have to rethink and redesign the strategies they have been using to promote equal opportunities. If they are to be effective in providing all children with the entitlement they have been given under the Education Reform Act, schools will have to find new ways of working with communities to become more effective in teaching about racism in society, dealing with racial incidents and harassment and improving black pupils' performance.

The new criteria for Section 11 funding may yet generate interesting projects which raise teachers' expectations and encourage teachers to assess the effectiveness of their strategies. If disseminated, such strategies may benefit all children. Further, ethnic monitoring offers schools the possibility of identifying the obstacles faced by black pupils and the opportunity to plan their own strategies to improve academic performance.

It is unlikely that black communities will gain much from the addition of a multicultural dimension to the National Curriculum, unless more political commitment is shown to dealing with racism in society, and more efforts are made to provide for in-service education and school support in developing new strategies. Far more than classroom curriculum reform is needed to ensure the promotion of equal opportunities for all pupils.

Notes

1 We are using the term 'black' to refer to all children of Afro-Caribbean and Asian origin and the term ethnic minority to refer to children whose families have cultural origins in countries other than Britain.
2 It is unclear what impact the appendix written by Harvey Goldstein had on the main report (see DES, 1988).
3 *Multicultural Teaching* (1988, 1989, 1990); Davies, Holland and Minhas (1990); Burton and Weiner (1990); Troyna and Carrington (1990).
4 It seems that whatever funds are available for inner city schools in the future (for example, through GEST), they are likely to be demarcated for specific purposes such as truancy.
5 The CRE's report *Learning in Terror* (CRE, 1988) does not provide quantitative data, but shows different kinds of incidents which children experience.

References

AFRO-CARIBBEAN EDUCATION RESOURCE CENTRE (ACER) (1987) *Response to the National Curriculum 5–16*, London, ACER.

ANDERSON, B. (1989) 'Anti-racism and education-strategies for the 1990's; *Multicultural Teaching*, 7(3), pp. 5–8.

ARNOT, M. (1986) *Race, Gender and Education Policy Making*, Module 4, Open University Course E333, Milton Keynes, Open University Press.

ARNOT, M. (1989) 'Consultation or legitimation? Race and gender politics and the making of the National Curriculum', *Critical Social Policy*, **27**, pp. 20–38.

ARNOT, M. (1991) 'Equality and Democracy: A decade of struggle over education', *British Journal of Sociology of Education*, **12**(3), pp. 447–66.

BAGLEY, C. (1992) 'In-service provision and teacher resistance to whole-school change' in GILL, D., MAYOR, B. and BLAIR, M. (Eds) *Race and Education: Structures and Strategies*, London, Sage Publications.

BLAIR, M. and WOODS, P. (1992) *Race and Education: Structures and Strategies*, Block 1, Open University Course ED356, Milton Keynes, Open University Press.

BRAHAM, P., RATTANSI, A. and SKELLINGTON, D. (Eds) (1992) *Racism and Anti-Racism: Inequalities, Opportunities and Polices*, London, Sage Publications.

BURTON, L. and WEINER, G. (1990) 'Social justice and the National Curriculum', *Research Papers in Education*, **5**(3), pp. 203–27.

COMMISSION FOR RACIAL EQUALITY (1985) *Birmingham LEA and Schools: Referral and Suspension of Pupils*, London, CRE.

COMMISSION FOR RACIAL EQUALITY (1986) *Teaching English as a Second Language*, Report of a formal investigation in Calderdale, Local Education Authority, London, CRE.

COMMISSION FOR RACIAL EQUALITY (1988) *Learning in Terror: A Survey of Racial Harassment in Schools*, London, CRE.

COMMISSION FOR RACIAL EQUALITY (1989) *Code of Practice for the Elimination of Racism in Education*, London, CRE.

COOPER, P., UPTON, G. and SMITH, C. (1991) 'Ethnic minority and gender distribution among staff and pupils with emotional and behavioural difficulties in England and Wales', *British Journal of Sociology of Education*, **12**, pp. 77–94.

DAVIES, A.M., HOLLAND, J. and MINHAS, R. (1990) *Equal Opportunities in the New Era*, Paper 2, London, Hillcole Group.

DEEM, R., BREHONY, K. and HEMMINGS, S. (1992) 'Social justice, social divisions and the governing of schools', in GILL, D., MAYOR, B. and BLAIR, M. (Eds) *Racism and Education: Structures and Strategies*, London, Sage Publications.

DEPARTMENT OF EDUCATION AND SCIENCE (1985) *Education for All: Report of the Committee of Enquiry into the Education of Children from Ethnic Minority Groups* (The Swann Report), Cmnd 9543, London, HMSO.

DEPARTMENT OF EDUCATION AND SCIENCE (1988) *National Curriculum Task Group on Assessment and Testing, A Report*, London, HMSO.

DORN, A. and HIBBERT, P. (1987) 'A comedy of errors: Section 11 funding and education', in TROYNA, B. (Ed.) *Racial Inequality in Education*, London, Tavistock.

EGGLESTON, J. (1990) 'Can anti-racist education survive the 1988 Education Act?', *Multicultural Teaching*, **8**(3), pp. 9–11.

FORBES, A. (1989) Parental Power and Black Governors, NAME Conference, Workshop report back.

GILL, B. (1980) 'Indicators and institutional evaluation', *Multicultural Teaching*, **8**(1), pp. 8–12.

GILLBORN, D. (1988) 'Ethnicity and educational opportunity: case studies of West Indian male-white teacher relationships', *British Journal of Sociology of Education*, **9**(4), pp. 371–86,

GILLBORN, D. (1990) *'Race', Ethnicity and Education*, London, Unwin Hyman.

GORDON, P. (1990) *Racial Violence and Harassment*, London, Runnymede Trust.

GREATER LONDON ACTION FOR RACIAL EQUALITY (GLARE) (1990) *Race, Equality and the Education Reform Act*, London, GLARE.

GURNAH, A. (1989) 'Translating race equality policies into practice', *Critical Social Policy*, **27**(3), pp. 110–24.

GURNAH, A. (1992) 'On the specificity of racism', in ARNOT, M. and BARTON, L. (Eds) *Voicing Concerns: Sociological Perspectives on Contemporary Educational Reforms*, Oxford, Triangle Books.

GUY, W. and MENTER, I. (Eds) (1992) Local Management of Resources, in GILL, D., MAYOR, B. and BLAIR, M. (Eds) *Racism and Education: Structures and Strategies*, London, Sage Publications.

HARDY, J. and VIELER-PORTER, C. (1990) 'Race, schooling and the 1988 Education Reform Act' in FLUDE, M. and HAMMER, M. (Eds) *The Education Reform Act 1988*, London, Falmer Press.

HIBBERT, P. (1983) 'Funding inexplicitness: a look at Section 11', *Multiracial Education*, 11(1), pp. 11–16.

HOME OFFICE (1989) *The Response to Racial Attacks and Harassment: Guidance for Statutory Agencies*, Report of the Inter-Departmental Racial Attacks Group, London, HMSO.

HOME OFFICE (1990) *Grant Administration Criteria: Section 11 of the Local Government Act 1966*, October, London, HMSO.

ILEA RESEARCH AND STATISTICS BRANCH (1990) *Differences in Examination Performance*, London, ILEA.

JEFFS, T. (1988) 'Preparing young people for participatory democracy', in CARRINGTON, B. and TROYNA, B. (Eds) *Children and Controversial Issues*, London, Falmer Press.

JONES, K. (1989) *Right Turn: The Conservative Revolution in Education*, London, Radius.

KIRP, D.L. (1979) *Doing Good by Doing Little: Race and Schooling in Britain*, California, University of California Press.

MACDONALD, I., BHAVNANI, T., KHAN, L. and JOHN, G. (1989) *Murder in the Playground: The Report of the MacDonald Inquiry into Racism and Racial Violence in Manchester Schools*, London, Longsight Press.

MULLARD, C. (1982) 'Multicultural education in Britain: from assimilation to cultural pluralism' in TIERNEY, J. (Ed.) *Race, Migration and Schooling*, London, Holt, Reinhart and Winston.

MULTICULTURAL TEACHING (1988) *Gerbil Issue*, 6(2).

MULTICULTURAL TEACHING (1989) *Anti-racism: Towards the 1990s*, 7(3).

MULTICULTURAL TEACHING (1990) *Achievement: Race and the National Curriculum*, 8(3).

MURSHID, T.M. (1990) 'Needs, perceptions and provisions: the problem of achievement among Bengali (Sylhetti) pupils', *Multicultural Teaching*, 8(3), pp. 12–15.

OUSELEY, H. (1990) 'Resisting institutional change' in BALL, W. and SOLOMOS, J. (Eds) *Race in Local Politics*, London, MacMillan.

RICE, A. (1989) 'The politics of anti-racist education', *Multicultural Teaching*, 7(3), pp. 13–14.

RICH, P.B. (19867) 'Conservative ideology and race in modern British politics' in LAYTON-HENRY, Z. and RICH, P.B. (Eds) *Race, Government and Politics in Britain*, London, MacMillan.

TOMLINSON, S. (1980) 'The educational performance of ethnic minority children', *New Community*, 8(3), pp. 213–30.

TOMLINSON, S. (1983) *Ethnic Minorities in British Schools*, London, Heinemann.

TOMLINSON, S. (1987) 'Reports', *New Community*, 15(1), pp. 103–9.

TROYNA, B. and WILLIAMS, J. (1986) *Racism, Education and the State: The Racialization of Education Policy*, London, Croom Helm.

TROYNA, B. (1990) 'Reform or deform? The 1988 Education Reform Act and racial equality in Britain', *New Community*, 16(3), pp. 403–16.

TROYNA, B. and CARRINGTON, B. (1990) *Education, Racism and Reform*, London, Routledge.

TROYNA, B. and HATCHER, R. (1991) 'Racist incidents in schools: a framework for analysis', *Journal of Education Policy*, 6(1), pp. 17–31.

Chapter 20

Pedagogy and Assessment: School Processes

Bruce A.G. Gill

Values and the Curriculum

It has long been recognized that the school curriculum has served as a legitimator of knowledge. Those elements not selected for inclusion in the school curriculum have tended to be perceived, at best, as being not quite up to standard and, at worst, as being unworthy of any serious study. The questions of what it is that the curriculum values in this way, why it is valued, by whom and how this sense of value is communicated to learners hold important implications for pedagogy as they lead to a consideration of the objectives that teachers set out to secure and the methods teachers employ in achieving them. These aspects of curriculum planning and delivery are not new, but gain an added significance in the context of a National Curriculum which claims to form some kind of common agenda for the nation. Similarly, school processes such as those relating to pupil assessment, pupil grouping and record keeping should be examined to discover the values that underpin policy and practice. Again the existence of the National Curriculum charges the enterprise with special significance.

The political context in which the Education Reform Act, 1988, (ERA) came into being makes it difficult to separate completely the reforms from, among other considerations, national policy in respect of race relations. Consequently, education policy at local level with regard to multicultural education, anti-racism and race equality is thrown into sharper focus by the presence or absence of related requirements within the National Curriculum itself.

A particular feature of the political context within which the National Curriculum arose was the prominence given to the themes of heritage and tradition. These themes provoked issues of identity and 'belonging' which were echoed in the various debates about the content of the National Curriculum as the different subject Working Group reports were prepared, discussed and finalized. The amendment to the ERA proposed by Baroness Cox would have had the effect of giving second class status to all religious faiths other than Christianity, while the debate about language, grammar and reading revealed a preoccupation (on the part of some lobbyists) with preserving tradition, an opposition to increased cultural diversity and fears of lowered standards. Furthermore, some commentators, like Donald Naismith, have argued that the National Curriculum should be a syllabus for patriotism,

...specifying among all the other necessary things, in a balanced way, the contribution Britain has made to history and the world. (Naismith, 1988)

The debates about modern languages and the community languages, religious education and collective worship, and teaching English and history show themselves to be also debates about people, about belonging and about views of what it means to belong to the nation. It is a sad reflection on the state of the nation that these debates have tended to communicate to linguistic, faith and ethnic minorities that they are second class citizens, if indeed they are seen as 'belonging' at all. An education for racial equality has to address the impact of such values on the individual learners themselves, the effects upon pupil achievement and institutional practices as well as upon race relations across the nation as a whole.

The multicultural dimension of the National Curriculum is articulated in the advice given in Curriculum Guidance 8, *Education for Citizenship* (NCC, 1990a) and issue Number 5 of *NCC News* (NCC, 1990b). Many educational professionals working for greater race equality feel that, compared to the National Curriculum, a number of the LEA policy positions on race equality have tended to express a greater commitment to multicultural, anti-racist principles and their implementation. The concern is that despite the rhetoric surrounding the notion of citizenship and the 'multicultural dimension', a central purpose of the National Curriculum is in fact to impede developments in this area.

It should be noted that the National Curriculum is not the whole curriculum and that the National Curriculum has to be mediated through pedagogy. Teachers, therefore, have significant opportunities to intervene in the processes of delivering the specified curriculum, the content of which might well relate to ideological and educational positions reflecting views of race and education typified by those of the 1950s and 1960s. Pedagogy, then, is critical to the process and this leads to the speculation as to whether an important intended purpose for assessment is that it function, not so much as a measure of pupil performance, but more as a mechanism to temper teacher intervention.

Speaking more generally on the matter of assessment, Nicholas Beattie puts it like this:

> To state the dilemma baldly: if you trust teachers as professionals, you will be able to take a correspondingly relaxed view of testing and thus mitigate some of the more interventionist or authoritarian aspects of a defined central curriculum. If you do not so trust them, then correspondingly elaborate testing procedures are required to monitor their impact and effectiveness. (Beattie, 1990, p. 33)

This analysis seems to attest to the framework of values within which the National Curriculum and National Assessment are being implemented. A central feature of this framework would appear to be the belief that, generally, curriculum content should be specified; that this would be a means of preserving national heritage and tradition; that standards would be raised; and, that teachers are likely to subvert the process.

Phases in National and Educational Policy Making

The 1985 Swann Report pointed out that educational policy in the 1950s and 1960s initially responded to the presence of immigrant children in schools by seeking strategies to absorb these pupils into the majority population as quickly as possible. The rationale was not peculiar to education and merely reflected the rationale underpinning national policy on race relations at that time. In education this assimilationist approach argued that if elements such as differences of language, culture and religion were removed or remedied and the children's lack of English addressed, immigrant children could more easily be merged into mainstream society. The immigrant children were very much seen as 'the problem' and solutions in terms of remediation and dispersal strategies were employed to address 'the problem'. Shifts in thinking toward the late 1960s and mid-1970s contributed to the development of an integrationist position which sought to give some recognition for the languages, customs and religions of children from a minority ethnic background.

It was felt important for teachers to acquire a greater awareness of the children's backgrounds and to apply this knowledge to teaching. The main aim however was still to absorb the pupils into mainstream society with the minimum disruption to the majority population. During this entire period black pupils were being placed in reception and language centres or were being assessed as educationally subnormal, as policies and procedures (in the main predicated on the assumption that the norms of the majority population were appropriate for assessing their needs) were applied to them uncritically. Small wonder then that large numbers of children of minority ethnic background were denied their curriculum entitlement and that great disquiet was aroused within the black communities which were quick to perceive the failures of the education service. Black communities responded with self-help initiatives as evidenced in the supplementary school movement, mosque and other community-based schools.

The evident failure of the assimilationist and integrationist approaches contributed to the emergence within education of multicultural approaches which reflected the cultural pluralist position that marked the direction in which national policy appeared to be heading. During the late 1970s and early 1980s the first local education authority guidance notes on multicultural education appeared, and these were followed by the first policy documents. Multicultural education, a professional rather than community response to the issue, was much criticized, particularly on the grounds that it failed adequately to address the issue of racism, and so it was that at this time that positions on anti-racist education began to be reflected in educational policy but with no evident counterpart at national policy level.

Although the successive phases can be clearly identified, the analysis is deceptive in its simplicity. The phases do not mark neat transitions in thinking across the whole population, rather they refer to stages in thinking in the area of race policy. Consequently, policy responses emerging in the late 1980s or early 1990s should not be assumed to reflect the more recent thinking in race policy, neither should it be assumed that policies originating from earlier positions have been superseded by later thought and so have been altered or discontinued. In fact, the emergence of an anti-racist education policy position in the absence of an equivalent position at national level would suggest that at best a tension might lie between Government education policy and the newer race equality policies being developed within

277

the education service. The serious consequences of applying policies predicated on the assumed needs of 'immigrant' children to children born in Britain, but who might be black or of minority ethnic background, should not be underestimated.

To the tension between central and local education policy with regard to race can be added the tensions existing within the ERA itself. Beattie argues that it exhibits:

> ...a basic confusion between centralism and localism. The National Curriculum sections of the ERA, essentially centralising and directive in character, sit uneasily with a variety of other arrangements which undermine the Local Education Authority as intermediary between centre (DES) and periphery (school): 'opting out', City Technology Colleges (CTCs), open enrolment, local management of schools (LMS). Built into the very heart of the new system is a tension between on the one hand a central requirement (which is also a local or individual entitlement), and on the other a fragmented delivery system supposedly made dynamic by competition for pupils, parental support, finance and staff. (Beattie, 1990, pp. 36–7)

The ERA as a package should also be seen alongside other national policies for health, employment and housing and the broad thrust of these in terms of reducing the powers of local authorities, increasing centralized control of services and making them subject to the discipline of the market. As the education service moves toward the possibility of becoming a nationalized enterprise, the question has to be raised of the feasibility of ensuring the delivery of pupil entitlement in such a context.

Some Concerns

Once it was clear that there was to be a national arrangement for assessing pupil performance a major issue arose around the means by which assessments would be made. The debate about whether this would be through standard assessment tasks or tests, and whether the range of purposes of the assessment (diagnostic, formative, summative, evaluative) could all be served by the same arrangement were important considerations. Fears that 7-year-old children would be required to sit paper and pencil tests were initially allayed when the report of the Task Group for Assessment and Testing (TGAT) (DES, 1988) was published, and it became apparent that its recommendations were broadly in line with current educational thinking. However, it should be remembered that this relief was probably matched by consternation on the part of the Government as the 'leaked' letter of the then Prime Minister, Margaret Thatcher, to the Secretary of State for Education made clear her wish that the tests be cheap, easy to administer and free from teacher judgement. This combined with rumours of DES officials' preoccupation with whether or not schools had safes in which to keep the brown envelopes (presumably containing the test papers) led many to suspect that, whatever happened, eventually the system would be one of simple pencil and paper tests.

The standard assessment tasks (then known as SATs) that were developed and first used with 7-year-olds in 1991 failed all three criteria specified in the letter. Furthermore, during the implementation of National Assessment in the academic year 1990/91, it became clear to anyone to whom it had not previously occurred that the most important aspect of the assessment arrangements was in fact the on-going teacher assessment. This actually reflected the TGAT proposals that the assessment system be formative and criterion referenced. The arrangements, in actuality, emphasized pupil progression and the role of moderation. However, as Christie points out,

> The essential problem is that in a decentralized decision-making structure where teachers make direct judgements about standards, there could be as many interpretations as there are teachers, but these differences in interpretation will be attributed to differences in pupils' performance between classrooms. . . .teacher assessment is coloured by the teacher's as well as the pupil's interpretation of the task. (Christie, 1990, p. 201)

The Government decision to publish the 1991 Key Stage 1 results surprised many teachers and education officers who had believed the rubric stating that the results would be unreported in the first year. The league table of LEA results received great press attention with those LEAs identified as being at the bottom of the league subjected to much uninformed criticism. The credibility accorded to the figures represented in the tables was out of all proportion to their validity. Despite inconsistent return rates from LEAs, lack of moderation of the assessments themselves and the fact that they were being tried for the first time, headlines appeared in the press proclaiming one LEA *Bottom of the Class* or more sensationally, *Dunce of Britain* (Conway, 1992). Unsurprisingly perhaps, in this LEA over 25 per cent of the Year 2 pupils had a home language other than English.

Two LEAs were not included in the tables because they had not sent in returns. One of these LEAs had a large pupil population of bilingual pupils of Bangladeshi background and felt the returns to be inappropriate. Headteachers in the other LEA had decided not to make returns to their LEA. The Secretary of State exerted pressure to ensure that both LEAs provided the required data, and the league table was updated. The latter of these LEAs, however, published its own table showing its actual place in the table based on a 92 per cent return. In addition, this LEA presented three other possible placings it might have achieved based on random samples of 50 per cent of its own returns (50 per cent being the average rate of return from all LEAs). The enormous variations in these placements showed the league table to have little validity.

The impact of the published league tables was nonetheless great and, as feared, the prospect of published results is driving LEAs and schools to compete with each other. The nature of the competition is, however, not likely to lead to improved education for the pupils who most need it. Rather, schools and LEAs are being driven towards arrangements that will most quickly present the best public image. Greater momentum has thus been given to attempts by increasing numbers of schools to move toward pupil selection. Concomitantly, pupils with special learning needs are increasingly being seen as a liability as these schools seek to improve their results.

The same issue is replicated within schools as discussions focus on classroom organization and the kinds of arrangements needed to meet the demands of the National Curriculum. These discussions quickly lead to consideration of the arrangements that might ensure that the assessments made of pupils are assessments which place the school in the most favourable light. In the secondary phase, more schools are reviewing their position on mixed ability teaching. In the primary phase, the practicalities of implementing Key Stage 2, with its increased subject specialist teaching demands, is leading to recommendations for a reduction in topic work. This may well signal the advent of a trend toward streaming or setting within vertically grouped classes.

It perhaps does not need to be stated that these trends run counter to the kind of practice that has been associated with good pedagogy as far as multicultural and anti-racist education has been concerned. The point here is that it is not merely anti-racism that is targeted by the changes, but even more so a view of education derogatively perceived as being 'progressive'. So, as 1991 drew to a close, the Plowden Report of 1967 came under fire and a high profile review of primary education was initiated. Whatever the reasons for this particular attack on primary education, it is reasonably clear that assessment arrangements are likely to feature in any solution to the perceived problem.

The test or task question strikes at the heart of the relationship between pedagogy and assessment. Arguments for 'tasks' included the fact that tasks are closer to the normal work of the classroom, are practical and relevant and relate to the detail of the programmes of study that are being followed. Pupils would be able to work in conditions with which they were familiar and as a consequence the assessments made would be more meaningful and appropriate as measures of performance. Teacher assessment was preferred because it reflected progression, and it was recognized that the records kept and the reports of the assessments that were made could be submitted for moderation. In short, the TGAT emphasis on formative and diagnostic approaches to assessment, while in keeping with educational practice, appeared to be at odds with the intended summative and evaluative outcomes that Government sought for the purposes of its wider strategic and policy aspirations. It was therefore significant to many educationists that by the middle of 1992 education practitioners were being required by the Department for Education to refer to the national assessments explicitly as 'tests'.

The tasks as recommended by TGAT are not free from teacher interpretation, however, and the tasks themselves have a moderating effect on those teacher assessments made as part of the ongoing routine classroom work. Concerns still abound around the question of the extent to which notions of race affect teacher judgements, and assurances are required about the safeguards that can be built into the arrangements to address this. Research evidence from Cecile Wright's study (1985) shows this still to be very much a live issue in respect of children of Caribbean background. This study which looked at pupil performance in internal school examinations, their placement in CSE or O level GCE groups and teacher judgements expressed in school reports or comments made to the researcher, found apparent misplacement of pupils upon ethnic grounds.

Previous research had identified difficulty on the part of white teachers in making discriminating judgements between the abilities and the behaviour of pupils of West Indian origin and had attributed this more to difficulties in perception across ethnic boundaries than to overt racial discrimination. Cecile Wright's study, however, while permitting this as a partial explanation, brought forward data which made it very difficult to accept this as a sufficient cause for the misallocation of pupils in bands and sets. In one case, the school possessed an internal report indicating that in all subjects a particular pupil's grades were A or B, yet the pupil was allocated to the bottom of three bands. Wright concluded that relationships between teachers and pupils of West Indian origin in the schools concerned were often antagonistic and,

> The pupil-teacher relationship influenced the teachers' professional judge-ment of the pupils' ability and some West Indian pupils may have been placed in inappropriate ability groups and examinations sets, so restricting their educational opportunities. (Wright, 1985, p. 22)

Findings of CRE reports on the numbers of black pupils suspended or expelled from schools suggest that such antagonism is not restricted merely to those schools observed by Cecile Wright and raise the prospect that across the phases of edu-cation and across the country increased teacher judgement in pupil assessment might well lead to further disadvantaging of black pupils, unless school processes are altered significantly. If this does not happen, the paradox remains of the as-sessment arrangements for the National Curriculum offering the best hope of 'fair' assessment for pupils of West Indian background to the extent that those arrangements are free from teacher judgement. The crucial question of why such antagonism might exist quickly returns this discussion to considerations of iden-tity, belonging and value. Yet here the National Curriculum seems set to under-mine or halt those strategies which are intended to bring improvement through fostering in all pupils a sense of respect and value for the cultural diversity within the nation.

Among a cluster of race equality concerns that can be identified around the assessment issue, that of linguistic disadvantage is one of the most prominent. Apart from the matter of modes of assessment discussed above, this entails issues both of assessing pupils' progress in English (when English might be their second or third language) and using English as the medium of assessment in relation to other subjects of the curriculum. Clearly, schools which do not have language development policies designed to support bilingual pupils and widen the know-ledge and understanding of all pupils are not well placed to respond positively to these implications for bilingual pupils. Neither are such schools likely to have a curricular framework to assist them in placing the National Curriculum in a broader multicultural and anti-racist perspective. As a result, such schools will be more likely to find themselves in the circular pattern of making inadequate provision and then judging the children themselves as inadequate.

Other concerns include those about the effectiveness of the constraints on headteachers who might seek to modify or disapply the National Curriculum on racial grounds and the effect of modification and disapplication in reinforcing negative labelling of black children. The history of children being referred to schools for the educationally subnormal, the disproportionately high numbers of black children referred to special schools in some LEAs and the CRE findings of high numbers of black pupils being suspended or expelled from schools in different LEAs strongly suggest that these concerns must be taken very seriously.

The construction of the tests or tasks raises issues of gender and race with regard to cultural and linguistic biases and also with regard to the types of activities singled out for assessment purposes. Concerns exist over the status of subjects that are assessed and the relationship between core and non-core subjects. The possibility that there might not be formal national assessment of art, physical education, music and religious education suggests further marginalization of some children of minority ethnic background, as it is in these subject areas that some pupils from certain minority ethnic groups are currently registering their only academic successes in schools. A central concern must be that of the ultimate purpose of the National Curriculum. Is it really to raise standards, as the rhetoric states, or is it to effect standardization of what is taught? These two aims are not at all necessarily interdependent, and it may well prove ill-advised to assume that the latter is a necessary precondition of the former.

Interventions

Recognizing the diminishing role of the LEA and the increasing autonomy of educational institutions, the various networks and organizations within the anti-racist education movement will need to develop new strategies to address the changing circumstances. Interventions will continue to be needed in education policy-making at institutional, local and national level, but it will become more difficult to determine who should intervene and on what basis. Certain processes, target audiences and aims can, however, be identified as a starting point in respect of pedagogy and assessment.

First, the curriculum planning process needs to reflect anti-racist commitment through both content and methodology. The target audience are the various curriculum managers based in schools, senior managers themselves and the increasing army of consultants who are now supplementing and complementing advice given by LEA inspection and advisory services.

Second, the processes of teacher assessment demand that teachers are enabled to counter bias in their assessments and are alerted to the positive value of spontaneous advice highlighted by Cecile Wright. A particular focus here might be to target the work of moderators, not only in respect of National Assessment, but also in terms of requiring moderation of assessments as a general principle. Within this approach could be the requirement that arrangements be made for the systematic moderation of work of pupils from minority ethnic backgrounds.

Third, LEAs are required to produce curriculum policy statements, and these should be reviewed periodically. The policy writers and the policy generation process itself offer scope for intervention with the aim of including appropriate references to gender and race equality in all statements.

Finally, central Government agencies such as the Department for Education (where officers and HMI need to be encouraged to move to a more explicit equal opportunities commitment and agenda) merit a range of responses appropriate to the changing working relationships of officers and inspectors.

While such objectives can be specified with reasonable clarity, within the anti-racist movement itself a further important area of work urgently needs attention so that these objectives may be addressed coherently. This work relates to specifying and promoting the nature of anti-racist pedagogy.

What Pedagogy?

Some of the recent attacks on multicultural and anti-racist pedagogy have advanced arguments along the lines that any approach calling itself multicultural or anti-racist is inimical to good education. This line was adopted by Margaret Thatcher in the Conservative conference in 1987 when she stated,

> Children who need to count and multiply are learning anti-racist mathematics — whatever that may be.

As Troyna and Carrington (1990) explain, others who have made similar observations have gone on to conclude that perhaps the National Curriculum, with its structure of core subject areas and assessment arrangements, might well provide a 'window of opportunity' for pupils of minority ethnic background in situations where alleged anti-racist approaches might be depriving them of those opportunities open to their white middle-class peers.

However, as Leicester (1989) has observed, these positions acquire some force from the thinking on the New Right which argues that British culture, because it embodies culture-transcendent principles by which all cultures are evaluated, is naturally superior. This leads one of their proponents to assert,

> In the light of those considerations, it seems to me that there can be no real argument for a 'multi-cultural' curriculum. To adopt such a curriculum is to fail to transmit either the common culture of Britain or the high culture that has grown from it. (Scruton, 1986, p. 134)

The view could be taken that such attacks on 'multicultural' pedagogy were inevitable because ethnocentric perspectives are part and parcel of the politics of the Right. This on its own should not constitute a reason to dismiss the arguments, rather than refute them. However, attacks on multicultural pedogogy directed at apparent deficiencies with regard to pupil achievement should be taken even more seriously by educational professionals who claim to be anti-racists.

Indeed, in the last years of the ILEA the controversy surrounding Highbury Quadrant School (where a teacher claimed to have been victimized for not attending an assembly on Nelson Mandela) centred on this issue. The school was criticized for neglecting the basics of good education and good school management, yet it was acknowledged that the school had a strong commitment to multicultural and anti-racist education. If the situation at the school has been reported at all accurately, it must raise questions of pedagogy that should greatly concern all who are working for racial equality in education. A pedagogy without a commitment to raising pupil achievement is worthless. If directed in large measure toward black pupils of minority ethnic background, such a pedagogy can only be construed as a mechanism to disempower those who are already disadvantaged, and consequently has to be seen as a major collusion with institutional racism. Chatwin (1989) is correct in observing that the black communities will ultimately hold the anti-racists to account for the failure of so called anti-racist strategies to deliver. What is needed is a sound and coherent anti-racist perspective within which increased pupil achievement is seen as a significant indicator of effectiveness. The focus of such a framework needs to be the school processes themselves and, as

Cecile Wright has put it, the recognition by schools of their responsibility in the achievement and underachievement of all their pupils.

> . . .pupils subjected to negative teacher attitudes and the resultant processes are unlikely to attain examination results which match their ability and potential. (Wright, 1985, p. 22)

It is possible that some schools, motivated by self interest as they compete for pupils in the market place, might take the view that every step should be taken to maximize pupil potential so as to improve school effectiveness and remain attractive to clients and customers. This economic imperative should not, however, be relied upon to bring wholesale benefit to pupils who are black and of minority ethnic background. These pupils are more likely to find that they have a restricted choice of effective schools. Instead, emphasis needs to be placed on the moral imperative which demands that the education service responds to the challenge of ensuring an effective education for all pupils. This challenge is one of developing appropriate pedagogy and assessment within the framework of the National Curriculum, which is itself a shifting and evolving construct. Tensions will inevitably exist between the objectives of raising achievement as a means to increase empowerment and the extent to which the National Curriculum framework exists as a means of control.

References

BEATTIE, NICHOLAS (1990) 'The wider context: Are curricula manageable?', in BRIGHOUSE, T. and MOON, B. (Eds) *Managing the National Curriculum*, London, Longman.

CENTRAL ADVISORY COUNCIL FOR EDUCATION (1967) *Children and their Primary Schools: A Report of the Central Advisory Council for Education* (The Plowden Report), London, HMSO.

CHATWIN, RAY (1989) 'Are anti-racists underachieving?', *Multicultural Education Review*, October, 1989.

CHRISTIE, TOM (1990) 'Monitoring the effectiveness of the National Curriculum: receiving and interpreting feedback', in BRIGHOUSE, T. and MOON, B. (Eds) *Managing the National Curriculum*, London, Longman.

CONWAY, SARI (1992) 'Week by Week' in *Education*, 179.11, March, 1992, p. 207.

DEPARTMENT OF EDUCATION AND SCIENCE (1985) *Education for All, The Report of the Committee of Enquiry into the Education of Children from Ethnic Minority Groups*, London, HMSO.

DEPARTMENT OF EDUCATION AND SCIENCE (1988) *A Report, of the Task Group for Assessment and Testing* (TGAT), London, HMSO.

LEICESTER, MAL (1989) 'Deconstructing anti anti-racist cognition', *Multicultural Teaching*, 7(1), Spring 1989, p. 11.

NAISMITH, DONALD (1988) 'My country right or wrong', *Telegraph*, February, 1988.

NATIONAL CURRICULUM COUNCIL (1990a) *Curriculum Guidance 8: Education for Citizenship*, York, National Curriculum Council.

NATIONAL CURRICULUM COUNCIL (1990b) *NCC News, Issue 5* York, National Curriculum Council.

SCRUTON, ROGER (1986) 'The myth of cultural relativism', in PALMER, F. (Ed.) *Anti-Racism: An Assault on Education and Value*, London, Sherwood Press, pp. 127–35.

Troyna, B. and Carrinbgton, B. (1990) *Education, Racism and Reform*, London, Routledge.

Wright, Cecile (1985) 'The influence of school processes on the educational opportunities of children of West Indian origin', I: Learning environment or battleground? II: Who succeeds at school — and who decides?', *Multicultural Teaching*, 4(1), Autumn 1985, p. 12.

Notes on Contributors

Anthony Adams is a lecturer in English education at the University of Cambridge Department of Education. His main interests are in the area of language education, particularly with regard to language awareness, and information technology and English education. He is author of many books on English teaching including *New Directions in English Teaching* (Falmer Press). He also edits a series for the Open University Press entitled, 'English, Language, and Education'. In 1989–90 he chaired the steering committee of a UFC INSET programme based in the University of Cambridge on multicultural education.

Madeleine Arnot is a lecturer in the sociology of education in the Department of Education, University of Cambridge. Previously she taught in the School of Education at the Open University. She has published widely on feminist theories of education and on state responses to gender and race equality issues. Relevant publications include *Race and Education Policy Making* (Open University Course Unit E333), editor of *Race and Gender: Equal Opportunity Policies in Education* (Pergamon) and (co-edited with L. Barton) *Voicing Concerns: Sociological Perspectives on Contemporary Education Reforms* (Triangle Books).

Alan Bishop is Professor of Education at Monash University, Australia. Previously he was a lecturer at the Department of Education in the University of Cambridge, England, specialising in mathematics education. His educational background includes three years as a graduate student at Harvard University, USA, and he has worked in several other countries as a visiting lecturer or professor since then. He has a strong interest in social and cultural aspects of mathematics education, and is the author of *Mathematical Enculturation: A Cultural Perspective on Mathematics Education*, Kluwer.

Maud Blair is a lecturer in the School of Education in the Open University. Before that she worked as an Advisory Teacher for multicultural education in Cambridgeshire. She taught in schools in Zimbabwe and in England and also worked as a Youth Development Officer and a Community Researcher in Cambridge.

Martin Booth is lecturer in education with particular responsibility for history in the University of Cambridge Department of Education. He has taught in grammar and comprehensive schools and has written and researched on the teaching and learning of history. He is a member of the School Examinations and Assessment Council's History Committee, an ordinary vice-president of the Historical Association and co-editor of the GCSE Modern World History Review *Hindsight*.

Michael Byram is Reader in Education at the University of Durham, responsible for initial and in-service education for foreign language teachers. He was Head of Languages in a comprehensive school in Kent before moving to Durham in 1980. Since then he has published on education for linguistic minorities and foreign language teaching. Since 1985 he has directed several research projects concerned with language teaching and cultural studies. Two main publications are *Minority Education and Ethnic Survival* and *Cultural Studies in Foreign Language Education*, Multilingual Matters.

Sudha Daniel is currently employed as an advisory teacher for multicultural education in the London borough of Sutton. Before that he worked as an education officer at Leicestershire Museums and the Commonwealth Institute. He was employed as a secondary art teacher in Malaysia and is a practising fine artist.

Carlton Duncan was born in Kingston, Jamaica, West Indies, and came to the UK in January 1961. He is currently Headteacher of one of Birmingham's largest schools (George Dixon Comprehensive) and was for four years headteacher of Wyke Manor Upper School in Bradford. Between 1976 and 1982 he was Deputy Headteacher and Director of Personal Development at Sidney Stringer School and Community College in Coventry. He was also a member of the Rampton and Swann National Inquiries which produced the Reports, *West Indian Children in Our Schools* and *Education for All*. Carlton Duncan is the author of many articles and several books in the general field of education, including *Pastoral Care: An Antiracist/ Multicultural Perspective*.

John Eggleston is Professor of Education at the University of Warwick. He is editor of *Design and Technology Teaching*, Chair of the Editorial Board of *International Journal of Technology and Design Education*, and a member of the Design and Technology Association. He is consultant for the development of Key Stage Three Standard Attainment Tasks in Technology for the School Examinations and Assessment Council and a former member of the Assessment of Performance Unit of the DES. He chairs the Judges of the annual Young Electronic Designer competition. He has written a range of books and articles on Design and Technology including *Teaching Design and Technology* (Open University Press, 1992) and has lectured on the subject in many countries.

Marie-France Faulkner is currently a Section 11 teacher at St Luke's Church of England Primary School in Cambridge, a multicultural city school. Previously, she taught adults and secondary age children in a variety of educational establishments in France, Northern Ireland, Sussex and Cambridgeshire.

Bruce Gill taught in an inner London comprehensive school for eight years and in a range of Birmingham schools after he moved there in 1983 to work as an advisory teacher in the Afro-Caribbean Teaching Unit (ACTU). He has worked as General Inspector with responsibility for Multicultural Education in Birmingham and as Inspector for Equal Opportunities in the ILEA Inspectors Based in Schools (IBIS) Team. He is currently Head of the Inspection and Advisory Service in Lambeth.

Marjorie Glynne-Jones is senior inspector in the London Borough of Tower Hamlets. She began her career as a teacher, undertaking a longterm study of children's musical development, 5–14, which was published in 1974. A period as a teacher trainer and course developer followed at Middlesex Polytechnic where she was principal lecturer and Music Chairperson. She joined the ILEA music inspectorate in 1981, later taking responsibility as a district secondary inspector. She is involved nationally and internationally in writing, lecturing and consultancy in music education.

Daphne Gould has 38 years of teaching experience in secondary modern, grammar and comprehensive schools, all in the London area. She spent 23 years in Mulberry School in the London Borough of Tower Hamlets; a school for some 1,300 girls of whom 90 per cent come from Bangladesh. She was Deputy Head for six years and for the remainder Head. She was appointed to what was to become the National Curriculum Council in 1988 and remained as a member of the Council until August 1991. During this period she chaired the task group for Multicultural Education. She is at present a governor of Stratford School. In 1988 she received the OBE for services to education.

David Hargreaves is Head of the Department of Education, University of Cambridge.

Anna King is senior lecturer at King Alfred's College in the Department of Religious Studies and Philosophy. Previously she taught in Cambridge University Department of Education and was Course Director of their UFC INSET Project: *Multicultural Education in a Pluralist Society*. She is also a tutor for the Open University and a member of the Runnymede Trust's working group on *Equality Assurance*. Before teaching in local schools and colleges, she did research in social anthropology at Oxford University and carried out several periods of fieldwork in North India.

Rachel Mason is Head of the Centre for Postgraduate Teacher Education at De Montfort University. She has worked in art teacher training in England, America and Australia and is President of the National Society of Education in Art and Design.

Peter Mitchell is a lecturer in Cambridge University Department of Education responsible for the teaching of religious studies. Previously he was a member of the staff of a College of Education and taught for some years in secondary schools in the East End of London. He has published articles in philosophy and ethics and in religious education. He is currently director of a research project examining Muslim attitudes to education in this country.

Michael Reiss read Natural Sciences at Cambridge University and then did a PhD and postdoctoral work in evolutionary biology. After completing a PGCE he taught in schools for five years before moving to the Department of Education in Cambridge as a lecturer in science education. He is also an ordained minister in the Church of England. He is the author of several books and health education packs and has published widely in the fields of evolutionary biology, science education, health education and theology.

Brent Robinson is lecturer in Information Technology in education at Cambridge University. He was a teacher of English and is currently researching the use of electronic communications in English-related activities within the curriculum.

Maggie Semple is currently Head of Education at the Arts Council of Great Britain. She was formerly Director of the Arts Education for a Multicultural Society Project (AEMS) and a teacher of dance. In August 1990 Maggie Semple was invited to be a member of the DES National Curriculum Physical Education Working Group.

Sally Tomlinson is Goldsmiths Professor of Policy and Management in Education, Goldsmiths College, University of London. Before she was appointed Professor of Education at University College, Swansea, she worked at Lancaster University for thirteen years, teaching and researching in the areas of race, ethnicity and education, and special education. She has published numerous books and articles in these fields.

Witold Tulasiewicz is a Fellow of Wolfson College, Cambridge, and currently visiting professor at the University of Calgary. He is actively involved with British/European Community relations, and is an advisory committee member and consultant for the Central Bureau for Educational Visits and Exchanges (CBEVE) and for the Teacher Training Committee of the UK Centre for European Education (UKCEE). He has written and lectured widely on Europe in the Curriculum. He co-directed (with Anthony Adams) the Brussels-funded research project *The Changing European Classroom after 1992*.

Rex Walford was both a schoolteacher and a lecturer in a teacher-education college before becoming lecturer in Geography and Education at the University of Cambridge. When the Council of British Geography was formed in 1988, he was elected its first Chairperson. He is also Chair of the Education Committee of the Royal Geographical Association and a Trustee and Past President of The Geographical Association. He has written many books and articles about geography teaching, and the use of games and simulations as a classroom technique. He chaired the GA Working Party which produced the Report *Geographical Education for a Multi-cultural Society* and was also a member of the Working Group appointed by the Secretary of State to shape the National Curriculum in Geography.

Rachel Willans entered the teaching profession as a mature student having previously worked in the theatre and in youth employment. She began teaching in a reception class and has since taught all age groups in the primary sector and also children with special needs in a middle school. She applied for a post at St Luke's Primary School in Cambridge, where she now teaches, because of the cultural diversity of the school and community.

Index

A.S.E. Multicultural Working Party 63
access 6, 10, 15, 52, 114, 125, 129–44,
    133, 135, 146, 163–4, 168, 176,
    196, 212, 223–4
achievement 4, 14, 16, 33, 88–9,
    112–13, 116, 126, 129–31, 133, 138,
    149, 208, 219, 228, 233, 262, 265,
    267, 276, 283–4
Adams, Anthony 8, 49–61, 56
Adzido Pan African Ensemble 166–7
Agard, John 216
Allison, Brian 145, 147, 156
Alves, C. 188
Anderson, Beverley 6, 262
Anderson, L. *et al.* 251
Anketell, R. 120
antiracist education 22, 25–6, 33, 44,
    55, 64, 68–9, 73–4, 80–1, 84–5,
    98, 101–2, 114, 153, 223–4,
    226–7, 245, 259–72, 275–7, 280,
    282–3
Aplin, R. 178, 181
Araeen, R. 155
Archer, A.B. 92
Archer, Margaret S. 21, 27
Areas of Experience in foreign language
    180–2
Arnot, Madeleine 11, 14, 16, 259–72
art 9, 17, 111, 116, 126, 128, 131,
    145–59, 202, 245, 282
Ascher, M. 37–8
Ascher, R. 38
assessment 3, 6–8, 11, 15–16, 35–6, 78,
    82, 89, 94, 97, 105, 130–1, 136,
    156, 182, 191–2, 219, 224–5,
    232–3, 261–2, 266
    and pedagogy 275–84

Association for Curriculum
    Development in Geography
    (ACDG) 97, 105
attainment, levels of 49, 99, 128
Attainment Targets 5, 249–50
    art 146, 149, 152–3, 155
    design and technology 109–11,
    115–16
    English 49, 54, 56–9, 224, 230
    foreign language 178–9, 181–2
    geography 99–100, 102–4, 245
    history 79–86, 88–9, 226, 228, 244
    Information Technology 118, 122,
    125–6
    mathematics 34–5, 38, 42–3, 226,
    232–3, 250
    music 128, 131, 133–4, 136–7, 140–2
    RE 187, 191
    science 69, 226
attitudes 242, 244–5, 247–51
awareness 182–3, 248

Bagley, C. 269–70
Bailey, Peter 44
Bailey, T. 155
Baker, Kenneth 6, 101
Banks, J.A. 253
Bannerman, Helen 55
Barbour, I.G. 68
Bardell, Geoff 94, 241
Barrett, Frank 52
Barth, F. 175
Bazalgette, C. 126
Beattie, Nicholas 276, 278
Becker, H. 153
Bedini, S.A. 71
Bell, R. 38

belonging 4, 14, 275–6, 281
Bernal, Martin 164
Bhavnani, T. 270
bias 5, 11, 16, 70, 93–4, 122–3, 147,
    187, 195, 202, 225, 230, 253, 261,
    282
bilingualism 181, 215–21, 262, 279, 281
Bishop, Alan J. 16–17, 32–47, 73
black artists and performers 153–6, 162,
    165–6, 171
black perspective on National
    Curriculum 259–72
black settlers in Britain 82–3
Blacking, J. 144
Blackledge, R.C.R. 249
Blair, Maud 11, 14, 16, 259–72
Boardman, D. 105
Booth, Martin B. 8, 15, 78–89
Bourdieu, P. 147, 148
Boyd-Barratt, O. 124
Braham, P. 267
Brandt, Godfrey 79–80, 84–5
Brehony, K. 269
Brett, G. 155
Brinkley, P. 85
British history 78–9, 81, 228
Brook, C. 249
Brooke, J.H. 68
Brophy, M. 73
Brown, C. 114
Bullivant, B.M. 14
Bunge, William 92
Burns, C.J. 71
Burton, L. 261, 267
Byram, Michael S. 15, 173–85

Carneiro, R. 254
carnival, Afro-Caribbean 154–5
Carrington, Bruce 7, 283
Carter, Ronald 57
case study
    primary school 212–22
    secondary school 223–36
centralization 7, 175, 187, 189, 278
Chambers, E. 155
Chapman, L. 157
Chatwin, Ray 283
Christianity 187–92, 197, 262, 275
Christie, Tom 279
citizenship 4, 11–13, 17, 36, 202, 208,
    241–2, 245, 247–8, 252, 276
Clarke, Kenneth 101, 189
class, socio-economic 14, 18, 51, 56, 81,
    155, 159, 178, 269

Cline, T. 219
Coard, Bernard 225
Coles, A. 231
Collins, H.M. 66
commitment 85, 88, 129, 131, 242, 247,
    250
communication 59, 114–15, 123, 125,
    141, 155, 157, 177, 179, 182,
    203–4, 233, 254
    electronic 119–22, 248
composing music 130–8, 142
computers 32, 59–60, 107, 118–19,
    123–5
confidence 16, 60, 136–7, 164, 184, 233,
    268
Congdon, K. 159
content of curriculum 11, 78, 81–4,
    100, 102, 122, 126, 169, 180, 182,
    208, 224, 228, 232–3, 248, 250,
    259, 262, 276, 282
context 40, 44–5, 60–1, 66, 69, 70, 81,
    110, 124, 134, 142–3, 146, 149–50,
    156, 158, 170, 177–8, 230
Convey, A. 254
Conway, Sari 279
Cook, Ian 94
Coolidge, J.L. 40
Cooper, P. 262, 270
core curriculum 4, 7–8, 11, 22, 49, 99,
    101, 128–9, 187, 192, 224, 234,
    249, 282–3
Cornelius, M. 38
counting 37–8
Cox, Brian 25, 49, 53, 55, 57, 248
Cox Report (1989) 49–51, 53–5, 58,
    176, 229
Craft, A. 241
Critchlow, K. 40
Crump, T. 38
crusades 86
Crystal, D. 58
Culpin, C. 86–7
culturalization of teaching mathematics
    32–47

Dabydeen, D. 55
dance 162–71, 202
Daniel, Sudha 9, 17, 145–59
databases 118–19, 122, 124–5
Davies, A.M. 261, 267
Deem, R. 269
Degge, R. 149, 154
Deshpande, P. 24
design and technology 109–16, 126

designing in mathematics 37–8
dialect 50, 57–9, 176, 215, 229
Dilke, O.A.W. 40
disadvantage 3, 5–6, 13–14, 35, 51, 56,
   113, 115, 124, 133, 225, 232, 259,
   264, 266, 281, 283
Ditchfield, C. 63
Dodd, P. 39
Domesday Survey (1086) 85–6
Dorn, A. 264–5
Doye, P. 177
Driver, R. 64
Duncan, Carlton 14, 223–36
Dust, K. 158
Dyson, T. 64

Education Reform Act (1988) 2, 4–7,
   26, 99, 128, 208, 223, 227, 261,
   263–4, 272, 275, 278
   RE 187–93, 197
Eggleston, John 9, 14, 109–16, 262
Eliner, Sid 167
empowerment 4, 12, 223–4, 269, 284
English as subject 8–9, 29–30, 49–61,
   119, 126, 229–30, 245
   Knowledge About English 53, 56–9,
   248
entitlement 3, 5–6, 12, 15–16, 22, 124,
   128, 187, 203, 205–6, 234, 252,
   262, 272, 277–8
equality 2–4, 6, 11, 13, 15, 17, 43–4,
   63, 116, 203–5, 223, 226–8, 233,
   247, 252, 254, 262–3, 264–5, 271,
   275–7, 282–3
   in- 7, 12, 73, 260
Esarte-Sarries, V. 177, 183
ethnocentrism 91, 93, 154, 168, 228,
   262, 267, 283
Eurocentrism 94, 145, 148, 165, 171
European Dimension and National
   Curriculum 240–54
evaluation 11, 109, 125
Evans, Emrys 56
exchanges and links, European 242,
   244, 246, 248, 250–1, 254
expectation
   differential 113, 116
   pupil 208
   social 43
   teacher 6, 16, 34, 64, 125–6, 135,
   232, 236, 262
experience
   art 159
   background 10, 45, 69, 219

cultural 119, 156
educational 4, 60, 113, 116, 118,
   129–30, 164, 209, 225, 236, 263
   European 242, 250
   life 5, 54, 148, 154, 176, 180, 183,
   185, 193, 196, 202, 208
   musical 128, 130, 133–6, 140, 142–4
   technological 123, 126
explaining in mathematics 38
Eysenck, H.J. 66

Faulkener, Marie-France 212–22
Fauvel, John 40–1
Fawcett, B. 235
Feldman, E. 149, 157
feminist science 64–5
Fensham, P. 66
File, Nigel 82
Fisher, S. 58, 105, 213
Flegg, G. 38
Flood, M. 105
Forbes, A. 270
Frederickson, N. 219
Freyberg, P. 64
funding, section 11 and formula 263–7,
   269, 271–2

Gans, H. 147
Garson, S. *et al.* 59
Gater, S. 64
GCSE 129, 131–2, 156, 178–80, 205,
   209, 244–5
Geertz, C. 148
Geographical Association 97–8
geography 9, 91–107, 212–13, 245
Geography Report of Schools Council
   94–9
Geography for the Young School
   Leaver Project (GYSL) 94, 96–7
Gerdes, P. 39
German, Gerry 94
Gibson, Jean 250
Gibson, Rex 55
Gill, Bruce A.G. 16, 262, 275–84
Gill, Dawn 73, 94–9
Gillbourn, D. 113, 262, 270
Glynne-Jones, Marjorie 9, 17, 128–44
Goodenough, W.H. 174
Goodson, I.F. 124–5, 245
Gordon, P. 270–1
Gould, Daphne 202–11
Gould, S.J. 66
governors 205, 226, 262
Graburn, N. 151

graffiti 209–10
Graham, D. 24
Gray, J. 41
Griffiths, P. 54
Grigsby, J. Eugene, Jr 151
Grinter, Robin 6, 73
group projects 42–4, 60, 85, 125
Guesne, E. 64
guidance 2, 8, 10–15, 21–5, 27, 50, 70,
    78, 89, 99–100, 111, 122, 128, 130,
    132, 134–6, 141, 143, 182–3, 190,
    212, 219, 241, 246, 262, 272
  career 235–6, 249
Gundara, J. 147
Gunner, E. 55
Gurnah, A. 261–2
Guy, W. 263
gypsy wagon painting 153

Halliday, M.A.K. 174
Halstead, J.M. 14
Hamilton, J. 64
Haque, Shaheen 148, 165
Harding, S. 66
Hardy, Jan 6, 261, 263
Hargreaves, D.H. 204
Harris, J. 51–2, 58
Harte, J.D.C. 188
Harvey, William 67
Hatcher, R. 270
Hayes, J.R. 71
Heater, D. 12–13
Hemmings, S. 269
Hempel, S. 25
heritage 8–9, 17, 26, 79, 81, 116, 118,
    130, 134–5, 139–41, 143, 149, 151,
    156–7, 171, 175, 195, 197, 243,
    251, 275–6
Hiatt, L.R. 67
Hibbert, P. 264–5
Hicks, David 58, 93, 98, 105–6, 213
history 8, 15, 78–89, 212–13, 227–9,
    244–5, 250
  and other subjects 35, 40, 58, 70–1,
    147, 149, 164–6, 175
Hoess, Rudolf 87–8
Holland, J. 261, 267
Holocaust 87, 251
Honeyford, Roy 26
Hopkins, D. 204
Howarth, R. 192
Huckle, John 96
Hudson, Nick 87
Hughes, Langston 162

Hughill, B. 26
Hull, John 189, 195
humanization of mathematics 35, 40–3

identification 109
identity 275, 281
  cultural 4, 17, 50, 52, 140, 150–1,
    154, 169, 174, 253, 265
  ethnic 175
  European 244–5
  national 8, 15, 18, 125, 174, 176
  personal 12, 15, 18, 194
  racial 26
  social 177, 180
Indian art 149–52
information handling 122, 125
Information Technology (IT) 9, 61,
    118–27
Ingle, R.B. 67
interdependence 251–3, 254
interdisciplinary curriculum 2–4, 7,
    10–12, 15, 24, 40, 99, 102, 116,
    151, 155–7, 159, 162, 164, 171,
    212–13, 234, 245, 249–50, 260,
    264, 272
involvement, pupil 85, 105, 215, 225

Jahan, Anawara 216
James, Herbert 54
Jeffs, Tony 269
Jenkins, K. 85
Jessup, B. 149
Jeyasingh, Shobana 170
John, G. 270
Jones, C. 176
Jones, K. 260
Jones, L. 71
Jones, R. 67
Joseph, G.G. 38, 40
Joseph, T. 155
justice 4, 17–18, 73
  social 2–4, 7, 12–13, 15–16, 112, 193,
    223, 226–7, 233, 241, 266, 269–70

Kamin, L. 66
Keep, R. 120
Kennedy, E. 162
Kent, G. 72
Khan, L. 270
Kimberley, K. 176
King, Anna S. 2–19, 249
Kingman Report (1988) 49, 56–8, 176
Kirp, D.L. 259
Klein, G. 111

knowledge 17, 35, 43, 65–8, 82, 100–2, 106–7, 111, 131, 133, 145, 151–2, 156, 159, 213, 223, 242, 244–52, 254

language
  awareness 177–8, 180, 248, 254
  community 115, 122, 242–3, 247
  English as second 51, 70, 114, 123, 169, 209, 229, 232, 262, 264–7, 277, 279, 281
  minority 3, 5–6, 8, 10, 22, 33–4, 45, 51, 58, 181, 205–6, 216, 219
  modern foreign 8, 15, 59, 119, 173–85, 245–6
  Welsh 51–2, 176
Latour, B. 66
Lawlor, R. 38
Lawton, Denis 21
Leach, S. 55
Leicester, Mal 283
Levidow, L. 73
Lewis, R. 22
Lindsay, L. 73
Linsell, D. 86–7
listening to music 130–2, 135, 139–43
literature 50, 53–5, 215, 224, 229–30
Local Education Authority (LEA) 3, 7, 22, 59, 187–9, 191–3, 204–5, 259–60, 263–4, 268, 271, 276, 278–9, 282
locating in mathematics 37–8
London Borough of Newham 83
Longino, H.E. 66
Lynch, J. 253

Mabud, S.A. 187
MacDonald, I. 270
McFee, J. 149, 154
McGivney, V. 245
McGregor, John 82, 101, 224
McLean, B. 73
Maitland, S. 73
making and investigating 146, 152
Maroon Wars 84
Mason, Rachel 9, 17, 145–59
mathematics 8, 16–17, 49, 111, 116, 219, 227, 231–3
  as cultural knowledge 37–40
  National Mathematics Curriculum (NMC) 32, 35–6, 43, 46, 232
measuring 37–8, 69, 71–2
Menter, I. 263
Miller, A. 178, 181

Mills, D. 105
Minhas, R. 261, 267
Mitchell, M. 40
Mitchell, Peter 187–97
Mittins, B. 248
modelling 122, 125
modern foreign language 8, 15, 59, 119, 173–85, 245–6
Modood, Tariq 17
Morgan, G.J.D. 71
Mullard, C. 259
Multicultural Task Group 11, 21–7
Murray, Karl 165
Murshid, T.M. 262
music 9, 17–18, 128–44, 202, 245, 282
Music Curriculum Association 139–41
Mutasa, N. 71

Naismith, Donald 275–6
Nasr, S.H. 67–8, 71
National Curriculum Council (NCC) 2–3, 5, 8–14, 21–5, 27, 69–70, 80, 89, 99–101, 115, 132, 136, 140, 162, 164, 190–1, 241, 243–4, 246
National Curriculum Working Group 224, 227
  for art 156
  for English 49–50, 56, 224
  for foreign languages 58, 178–83
  for geography 99–102
  for history, final report 78–83, 228
  for mathematics 32–5, 45, 232, 261
  for music 128–32, 136, 140–1
    final report 146–7
  for physical education 163–4
  for science 68–9, 230
  for technology 111
Nettleford, Rex 167–8
New Right 8, 13, 25, 260, 262, 283
Noades, Ron 166
Noakes, J. 87
Ntuli, Pitika 171

opportunity 5, 8, 45–6, 69, 111–12, 115–16, 119–20, 125–6, 129, 133, 147, 151, 157, 159, 166, 170, 176, 179–81, 183, 208, 229, 233, 263, 265, 281, 283
  equality 3, 5–7, 9–10, 13, 16, 18, 21, 24, 46, 51, 100, 113, 122, 163–4, 168, 179–80, 203–4, 206–8, 212, 226–8, 231–2, 235, 243, 245, 262, 266, 268–9, 272, 282

Orchard, S. 192
organisation
classroom 32–5, 134–7, 280
school 15, 22
Osborne, R. 64
Ouseley, H. 263
overloading of teachers 7, 15, 36, 105
Owusu, K. 154–5

Palmer, F. 22
Parekh, B. 14
Peacock, D. 250
Peacocke, A.R. 67
Pearce, S. 26
performance 15, 51, 145, 230, 260,
262–3, 266, 271–2, 276, 278, 280
performing music 130–2, 134, 136–9,
142
Perl, T. 40
physical education 9, 17, 128, 131,
162–71, 282
Pickles, Anne 166
Pike, G. 105–6
Pilgrim Fathers 86–7
planning and making 109–10
playing 37–8
pluralism, cultural 43–7, 79–81, 146,
187–8, 192–4, 211, 215, 222, 242,
245, 259, 277
Polkinghorne, J. 68
Poole, M.W. 68
Porter, A. 12
Power, Chris 82
prejudice 3–4, 10, 34, 60, 69, 73, 79,
91, 103, 105, 153, 157, 159, 169,
180, 193, 202, 212, 225, 228, 230,
232, 250–1, 267–8
Pridham, G. 87
programmes of study 50, 54, 69–71, 81,
83, 99, 105, 111, 118, 122, 128,
136–7, 139, 141–3, 146, 163, 179,
181, 187, 191–2, 233, 245, 249,
280

Qadir, C.A. 71

racism 3–4, 10, 12–13, 15–16, 18, 35,
44, 55–6, 60, 80, 83, 87–8, 92,
94–6, 98, 100, 113–14, 145, 151,
154, 159, 169, 173, 193, 202–3,
207–8, 215, 227, 230, 235–6, 251,
260, 263, 266–72, 277, 280–1, 283
Rader, M. 149
Raleigh, M. 59

Rattansi, A. 267
Reiss, Michael J. 9, 63–74
relevance of curriculum 3, 45, 63, 93
religion
art 150, 152
Information Technology 124
minority 3, 8, 14, 16, 18, 234, 277
national 247
physical education 168–9
science 67
religious education 8, 116, 126, 187–97,
208, 226, 282
resources 16, 27, 40, 42, 46, 119, 122,
131, 155, 157–9, 171, 192, 195–7,
204, 206, 208, 215, 225, 228,
230–1, 233, 248, 253, 260, 262–4,
271
Rice, A. 269
Rich, P.B. 260
Richardson, Robin 105–6
rights 12, 18, 154–5, 241, 245, 252–3
Robinson, Brent 9, 118–27, 120
role model, teacher as 206, 226, 236
role play 85–6, 88, 106, 120–2
Roman Empire 83
Ronan, C.A. 71
Ross, A. 40
Ross, J. 154–5
Russell, N. 67, 71
Ruthven, K. 44
Rutter, M. 89

Sacks, Jonathan 12
Sadler, E. 114
Sarland, C. 54
Sarup, M. 13
Sarwar, G. 190
Savva, H. 51
Sawyer, W. 56
Scholes, Robert 55
School Examination and Assessment
Council (SEAC) 5, 70, 89, 101,
245
school, whole 202–11
science 9, 49, 63–74, 111, 126, 212–13,
219, 230–1
Scott, I. 155
Scott, P. 64
Scruton, Roger 283
Seely, J. 59
Selby, D. 105–6
Semple, Maggie 9, 17, 162–71
Shan, Sharan-Jeet 44
Shange, Ntozake 171

Sharp, S. 158
Shennan, M. 243
Shirts, Gary 106
simulation 44, 106, 120–2
Skellington, D. 267
skill 244–52
Slater, J. 241
Smith, C. 262, 270
Smith, D. 153
Smith, D.J. 89
Smithers, A. 112
socialization 174–7
Solomon, J. 65, 71
staffing 205–6, 226–7, 236, 263
stamps, Royal Mail 64–5
standard assessment tasks (SATs) 5–7,
    51, 70, 88–9, 139, 219, 232–3,
    278–9
Standard English 50, 52–3, 59, 175,
    229
Standing Advisory Councils for
    Religious Education (SACRE) 187,
    191–2, 226
Starkey, H. 178, 181
Start, K. 56
Statement of Attainment 8, 16, 49–50,
    69–70, 80–3, 85, 88–9, 101, 104,
    136, 142, 179, 231
Statutory Order
  foreign language 179–83
  geography 102
  history 78, 80–5
  Information Technology 122, 125
  music 128, 132, 136, 139, 141–3, 146,
    149
  technology 110–11
Steiner, M. 105
Stenhouse, L. *et al.* 89
stereotyping 14, 16, 60, 73, 79, 92, 98,
    107, 112, 118, 153–4, 156–8, 166,
    169, 178–80, 196, 202, 215, 228,
    231, 233, 235–6, 269–70
Sternberg, Robert J. 66
Storm, Michael 96, 98
Styles, M. 54
success 113–14, 175, 225–6, 230, 235,
    262, 282
superiority, cultural 153–6
Supple, Carrie 87
Swann Report (1985), 4, 17, 25–6,
    51–2, 89, 145, 176, 194, 210,
    263–4, 266, 268, 277
Swetz, F.J. 40
syllabus, European 247–8

Taber, Anne 145
Tacky's Rebellion in Jamaica 84
Taylor, Monica 191
Taylor, R. 158
Taylor, S. 177
technology 9, 110, 115, 131
  design and 109–16, 126
  see also Information Technology
Temple, R. 63, 67, 71
Tharani, Nadir 165
Thatcher, Margaret 26, 33, 44, 53,
    56–7, 278, 283
Thomas, A.G. 92
Thorpe, Edward 167
Tiberghien, A. 64
tokenism 46, 71, 79, 81, 170
tolerance 13–14, 78–9, 89, 121, 125,
    163, 175–6, 190, 223, 229, 246,
    250, 252, 268
Tomlinson, Sally 11, 21–7, 89, 259,
    261
training, teacher 8, 147, 157–8, 171,
    206–7, 246, 254, 260–1, 263–4,
    268, 270, 272
Troyna, Barry 6, 73, 259, 263–4, 270,
    283
Trudgill, P. 123
Tulasiewicz, Witold 240–54
Turner, A.D. 67
Turner, F. 24
Turner, S. and T. 70

understanding art 146
Upton, G. 262, 270

values 8, 12–14, 16–18, 26–7, 33, 35,
    42–3, 60, 66–7, 96, 111, 124–5,
    130, 134, 138, 143, 149, 154, 157,
    159, 163, 174–7, 194, 210, 213,
    225, 230–1, 233, 251, 254, 275–6,
    281
van Sertina, I. 71
Vieler-Porter, Chris 6, 261, 263
Vikings 83
visitors to schools 206–7, 209
vocationalism 7, 129, 243, 246, 249
Vygotsky, L.S. 174

Wagner, D.L. 67
Wales, Statutory Order for music in
    128–9, 132, 137, 139, 141–4
Walford, Rex 9, 91–107
Walters, S. 155
Ward, A. 65

Watson, K. 56
Watts, A.G. 235
Weiner, Gaby 83, 261, 267
Wellington, J. 66
Wells, S. 56
Wilkinson, D.A. 68
Wilkinson, J. 51–2, 58
Willans, Rachel 212–22
Williams, I.W. 70
Williams, J. 259
Williams, R. 241
Woods, P. 269

Woolgar, S. 66
world awareness 3–4, 10–11, 13, 17–18, 22, 45, 61, 193, 213, 230
world music 139–44
Wright, Cecile 280–2, 283–4
Wright, David R. 105
Wyvill, B. 65

Young, J. 73

Zaslavsky, C. 38
Zientek, P. 112